From Asparagus to Zucchini
A Guide to Cooking Farm-Fresh Seasonal Produce

From Asparagus to Zucchini

A GUIDE TO
Cooking Farm-Fresh
Seasonal Produce

JONES
BOOKS
Madison, Wisconsin

This book is brought to you by

Madison Area Community Supported Agriculture Coalition (MACSAC)

PO Box 7814
Madison, WI 53707-7814
608/226-0300
info@macsac.org • www.macsac.org

MACSAC is a nonprofit organization whose mission is to create a sustainable, just, and locally based food system by: 1) educating the public about sustainable food production and the benefits such a food system has for our health, environment, local economies, and small farms, and 2) working to strengthen community supported farms in the southern Wisconsin region by facilitating ongoing education and support among the farms.

Individual copies and discounted wholesale orders of this book are available through MACSAC. Contact us at the address above or visit our website at www.macsac.org for more information.

Jones Books
309 N. Hillside Terrace
Madison, Wisconsin 53705
www.jonesbooks.com

Third edition, first printing

Library of Congress Cataloging-in-Publication Data
    From asparagus to zucchini : a guide to cooking farm-fresh seasonal produce / Madison Area Community
    Supported Agriculture Coalition.—3rd ed.
        p. cm.
    Includes bibliographical references and index.
    ISBN 0-9721217-8-1 (alk. paper)
    1. Cookery (Vegetables)   I. Madison Area Community Supported Agriculture Coalition (Madison, Wis.)
    TX801.F76 2004
    641.6'5—dc22

                                                                                        2004015684

Printed in the United States of America on recycled paper

Acknowledgments

This book was made possible by the hard work, dedication, and community spirit of a large number of people associated with the Madison Area Community Supported Agriculture Coalition (MACSAC). MACSAC is an organization comprised of community supported agriculture (CSA) farms, farm members, and community activists who work to spread the word of CSA in Madison, throughout southern Wisconsin, and beyond.

We wholeheartedly thank the following people for their contributions to the original *From Asparagus to Zucchini:* Sara Tedeschi, who suggested the idea of a MACSAC "food book" and spent the winter of 1995-96 researching and writing the text that accompanies each vegetable section; Bill Redinger, creator of the original artwork found throughout the book; Doug Romig, who graciously volunteered to do the layout of the book and later admitted that he had no idea what he was getting himself into; Terese Allen, who carefully edited all the recipes and provided professional consultation; and Laurie McKean, the "Food Book Queen," who wrote several pieces for the book and served as *A to Z's* fund-raising, production and distribution coordinator, guiding the project through its early years with great skill, enthusiasm, and endurance.

Additional help came from: Angele Theriaul; Ted Sickley; Sharon Lezberg; Jenny Pardee; Mary Eberle; John Hendrickson; Laurie Lambert; Lydia Oberholzer; Linda Poehlman; Kristen Iwanaga; Trish Bross; Claire Strader; Sandy Eldredge; Linda Halley; Marcy Ostrom; Nancy Lee Bentley; Barb, Dave, and Rebecca Perkins; David Bruce; Connie Firosz; Pat Thomas; Rhonda Krantz; Mark McEahern; Karen Foley-Strauss; Bill Wenzel; Steve Stevenson; Kathy Martin-Taylor; Margaret Krome; Odessa Piper; Deb Boehm; and Becky Steinhoff. Special thanks go to Elizabeth Henderson and David Stern of Rose Valley Farm in Rose, New York, for producing their own cookbook in 1994, which provided us with a model and inspiration. Thanks, also, to all the wonderful people who contributed original recipes.

MACSAC is indebted to the following for their financial support of the first edition of this book (subsequent editions have been funded by book sales): the Center for Integrated Agricultural Systems, University of Wisconsin-Madison, which administered the grant from the USDA Federal-State Marketing Improvement Program; Common Ground Co-op, Champaign, Illinois; Magic Mill Natural Foods Market, Madison, Wisconsin; Mifflin Street Co-op, Madison, Wisconsin; Whole Foods, Madison, Wisconsin; and the Williamson Street Grocery Co-op, Madison, Wisconsin, to whom we offer a special "gracias" for the significant contribution made to this project through its Community Reinvestment Fund.

The following people put together the book's second edition, published in 2003: Terese Allen, Chris Rietz, Michael Nash, Doug Wubben, Susan Streich-Boldt, Melissa Mauer, Carl Swanson, Gina Schumacher, Mary A. Schumacher, John Hendrickson, Bill Redinger, Kay Jensen, Jodi Pahs, Julie Kreunen, and Shirley Young. A special salute goes to Michael Nash for his original cover art and production work for that edition.

For this, the third edition of *A to Z,* three key players deserve recognition: MACSAC staffer Doug Wubben, for his fearless management of yet another round of improvements; cookbook author Terese Allen, who edited the book, coordinated the collection, testing, and editing of recipes, and served as project consultant; and personal chef Pat Mulvey, who tested and contributed many recipes. Kudos, also, to Sara Tedeschi, who penned introductions to the new recipe sections, and to Bill Redinger and Cris Carusi, for additional help with this edition. We also send out a grateful salute to publisher Joan Strasbaugh, who, by overseeing the production and distribution of this edition, is helping us further spread the good word about good food, and to graphic designer Janet Trembley for the book's beautiful new look. And a big thanks to Harriet Brown for her careful editing.

Finally, one more big thank-you and a thunderous round of applause for everyone who has ever served on MACSAC's Food Book Committee. You did it.

Recipe Contributors

From Asparagus to Zucchini's recipes were created by growers, farm members, home cooks, and chefs passionate about fresh food and seasonal cooking. Cookbook author and MACSAC member Terese Allen edited the hundreds of new recipes in this edition with assistance from personal chef Pat Mulvey. Many of the dishes—indicated by "MACSAC"—also came from their personal collections.

Table of Contents

Resources

Food for Thought

Introduction to Third Edition

Doug Wubben, MACSAC Program Coordinator, on behalf of the MACSAC Food Book Committee

We didn't know. When members of the Madison Area Community Supported Agriculture Coalition (MACSAC) first came together around a kitchen table in 1995 to begin work on a recipe-resource book, we knew that by helping community supported agriculture (CSA) farm members utilize the variety of produce they received, we would be helping local farms by creating happier farm members. We didn't realize there would be such a tremendous response from farms and their members all over the Midwest. When orders began coming in from California, New York, Washington State, and Tennessee, we quickly realized our "Food Book" was filling a need felt by farms across the country, too.

While this book was conceptualized with subscription farm members as the primary audience, we also hoped to reach fresh food lovers everywhere. Much to our delight, that soon began to happen. Libraries, universities, and numerous state Departments of Agriculture made the book available to their constituents, students, and staff. Food co-ops, other natural food stores, farmers' markets, roadside stands, and restaurants have all found it to be a useful resource to offer their staff and customers.

After numerous printings and an expanded second edition, and with increasing numbers of individual home cooks from all over telling us it had become an indispensable addition to their kitchens, we decided to take our "great little regional cookbook" and go national.

From the members of the CSA community in southern Wisconsin, welcome to this third edition of *From Asparagus to Zucchini,* intended for cooks everywhere who want to "buy local, cook seasonal, and eat fresh."

We're excited about this edition for several reasons. In the past, whenever MACSAC had considered releasing the book through the traditional, trade-published route, it always created the uncomfortable fear of loss of control. Then we met publisher Joan Strasbaugh of Jones Books, who was so enthusiastic about the book that we sat down with her and worked out an agreement that would work for us both. This is still MACSAC's book; that is, a group effort of, by, and for the CSA community. But, as its distributor, Jones Books is helping us take the message of sustainably produced foods to an ever-growing number of people who want to eat well, to eat "right."

While the second edition added such improvements as a recipe index and expanded resource sections, the vegetable chapters, which contained mostly recipes from other cookbooks, proved too big a project to take on at the time. We are proud to announce that the third edition not only has new recipes, but each and every "non-original" recipe has been replaced with original creations—from farmers, CSA supporters, chefs, food writers, and just plain good cooks.

Another exhilarating change is the book's new cover and page design, the work of graphic designer Janet Trembley. We think the new look reflects a sense of fun, flavor, and adventure—just what cooking with farm-fresh seasonal produce is all about.

The book has become a little more polished, but it retains its roots in the sustainable farming community from which it sprang. The "Food for Thought" section introduces readers to the concept of community supported agriculture, takes a critical look at our current food system, and describes what it means to eat a more local and seasonal diet.

The main section of the book, "The Vegetables"—which contains the recipes—has received a complete overhaul. Most of the "original originals" are still here, but there are also more than 325 brand-new recipes. We've added entire new chapters, too—one on sweet potatoes and one on wild foods—and expanded the bean chapter to include shell beans and dried beans.

We were blown away by the response we received to our call for recipes. Many came from within our own farming community. Others came from "Food Book" fans across the country. The book boasts creations from season-conscious celebrity chefs like Lucia Watson, Deborah Madison, and Odessa Piper. Many recipes were contributed by cookbook author and longtime CSA supporter Terese Allen, who also coordinated, tested, and edited submissions. Personal chef Pat Mulvey, who assisted with this heroic effort, contributed many of her own recipes. The result is a recipe collection that has been kicked up a notch, with hundreds of lively, approachable dishes that deliver not just flavor and nutrition but a fair shake for farmers and earth-friendly dining.

The vegetable and herb sections are arranged alphabetically, and each includes historical and nutritional information, plus general cooking and storage tips. We've tried to include more recipes for less common foods, such as rutabaga, fennel, greens,

celeriac, bok choy, and parsnips. Because the idea is to eat local, and because most of the book's contributors live in the Midwest, root vegetables and other crops that thrive in northern climes are part of our focus. But the range of vegetables we cover is extensive, and there's truly something for everyone.

Our Seasonal Combinations chapter offers dozens of recipes that combine vegetables in season at the same time, and the Kids' Recipes chapter has many ideas about how to include young people in the process of preparing and eating good food. The final article in this section focuses on home food preservation techniques.

We greatly revised the last section of the book, Recommended Resources, during the last edit, expanding the focus beyond the Midwest to provide resources suitable to our growing national audience. This edition still includes information about MACSAC and a tribute to the farms in our area. The remaining resource sections—covering farmers' markets, organizations, cookbooks, websites, and much more—will be useful to people regardless of which part of the U.S. they live in. Some resources cross national boundaries as well.

Please enjoy this book—it's a tribute to MACSAC's commitment to education, cooperation, and community, and a celebration of the glorious goodness of fresh food.

Thinking Outside the Shopping Cart

Compiled by John Hendrickson

- In the conventional food system, food travels 1,500 or more miles on average from farm to table. Food travels 45 miles on average for CSA farms serving Madison, Wisconsin.

- Only about 10 percent of the fossil fuel energy used in the world's food system is used for producing the food; the other 90 percent goes into packaging, transporting, and marketing. Locally produced food is more energy-efficient, with the majority of energy use going toward food production.

- On any given day more than half the U.S. population eats no fruit or vegetables. By joining a CSA farm, you and your family are ensured a weekly supply of fresh, delicious, and nutritious vegetables.

- Only 1 of 10 children ages 6 to 11 eats the recommended 5 daily servings of fruit and vegetables. Surveys of CSA members reveal that by becoming CSA members, households significantly increased their consumption of vegetables and fruit.

- Since the turn of the 20th century, 97 percent of fruit and vegetable varieties have become unavailable commercially, replaced by only a few uniform varieties.

- CSA farms are extremely diverse, growing 30 to 50 different types of crops and hundreds of different varieties. Many CSA farms grow heirloom varieties known for their taste rather than their ability to withstand shipment across the country and the globe.

- Only one quarter of all Americans know their next-door neighbors. CSA farms re-create and build community by bringing people together around farms and food. CSA pickup sites promote interaction among neighbors and neighborhoods.

- In a typical year, more than 10,000 new food items are introduced in grocery stores—mostly highly processed, packaged convenience foods. Many CSA farms introduce people to lesser-known crops such as sunchokes, fennel, and celeriac as well as unique varieties of common vegetables such as purple potatoes, yellow watermelon, and beauty heart radishes.

- Conventional farmers receive less than 25 cents of your consumer food dollar on average. CSA farmers receive 100 percent of your consumer dollar, and this helps keep small family farms in business.

- The average U.S. citizen spends less than 12 percent of his or her disposable income on food. A CSA membership is both a great value and a great way to support the local economy with your food dollars.

Top 10 items purchased at grocery stores

Marlboro cigarettes
Coca-Cola Classic
Pepsi-Cola
Kraft processed cheese
Diet Coke
Campbell's Soup
Budweiser beer
Tide detergent
Folger's coffee
Winston cigarettes

Top 10 items delivered by a typical CSA farm

Tomatoes
Lettuce
Carrots
Beans
Potatoes
Peppers
Squash
Onions
Peas
Broccoli

Community Supported Agriculture

John Hendrickson and Marcy Ostrum

Community Supported Agriculture (CSA) is part of a growing social movement that engages urban and rural citizens in taking responsibility for the land on which their food is grown.

In its simplest terms, CSA consists of a partnership between agricultural producers and consumers. Consumers, known as shareholders or members, provide enough money in early spring to meet a farm's operating expenses for the upcoming season. In exchange, the members receive a portion of the farm's produce each week throughout the season.

Members receive only what is grown on the farm and in season. If a farmer has a crop failure, or if heavy rains or a cold spring delay the onset of planting, members may not receive particular crops, or may find that they are eating cool weather crops for longer than usual. If a farmer has an abundant harvest, members reap their share of the bounty. As a result, farmers and consumers share in the risks and benefits of farming.

Origins and Growth of CSA

CSA first came into practice in the early 1960s in Germany, Switzerland, and Japan. As a response to concerns about food safety and the urbanization of agricultural land, groups of consumers and farmers in Europe organized themselves into cooperative partnerships in order to fund farming operations. These original CSA farms were founded on the basis of a strong consumer commitment to paying the full costs of ecologically sound and socially equitable agriculture.

In Japan, mothers troubled about the rise of imported food and the loss of arable land started the first projects in 1965. Community supported agriculture came to the United States in 1986, when two farms were started on

the east coast. Since that time, community supported farms have been organized throughout North America, most notably in the Northeast, the Pacific coast, the Upper Midwest, and Canada. There are now an estimated 1,400 community supported farms in North America.

In Wisconsin and Minnesota, the first CSA projects were established near Milwaukee and the Twin Cities in 1988. In 2003, more than 60 community supported farms grew food for an estimated 4,600 households throughout Wisconsin. Many of these farms have joined with each other to form associations or networks. Within these networks, CSA farms exchange information, coordinate public outreach, and develop support systems for new or struggling farms.

How It Works

Members of CSA farms pay a fee early in the year and in return receive a weekly portion of the farm's harvest throughout the growing season. As food is harvested, it is divided into shares and distributed through centrally located pickup sites, or picked up at the farm. The harvesting and distribution of farm produce are often cooperatively administered by farmers and members.

Each community supported farm organization consists of land, farmers, and members. Typically family-operated, the farms vary in size from 1/2 to 300 acres and may involve anywhere from 10 to 500 households. Most CSA farms use organic and/or biodynamic growing methods and provide their members with a wide range of fresh produce. Many of these farms grow more than 40 different vegetables, herbs, and fruits. Some farms also supply meat, eggs, honey, and other farm products.

CSA farmers utilize a number of farming methods, including succession planting of cool season and warm season vegetables, the use of season-extending greenhouses, and root cellars for storage, to provide produce for up to 10 months out of the year.

CSA farms rely to varying degrees on member volunteers to work on the farm and help with various administrative tasks. Many CSA farms could not survive without their "core group." A core group is made up of committed member volunteers who work with farmers to organize and manage distribution sites, plan what to grow, and find new members. By assuming these responsibilities, core groups enable farmers to focus on producing food and caring for the land.

Coloring the growing CSA movement is diversity in the nature and goals of individual projects. As each farm has evolved, it has developed its own distinctive organizational structure, which shapes the character of the relationship among shareholders, farmers, the land, and the larger community. In Santa Cruz, California, a 2.5-acre vacant lot was turned into a CSA project, offering homeless people an opportunity to work and provide important services to the community. On the other coast, the Food Bank Farm in Amherst, Massachusetts, provides fresh vegetables for local food pantries in addition to traditional CSA shares to those who can afford to be members.

Each CSA farm has its own emphasis and unique characteristics. Some CSA farms supply root vegetables to members well into the winter months. Others have a prairie restoration project and welcome members to help with prairie planting and burning. Yet others focus on member involvement and education, and provide numerous opportunities for members to help with planting and harvesting. The diversity of farms allows members to join the community supported farm that best fits their needs and interests.

The Social Goals of CSA

CSA is a response to the growing social and environmental problems of the modern food system.

For farmers, CSA is designed to provide a more equitable return for their labor and investment while relieving them of the burden, uncertainty, and impersonality of conventional marketing. Unlike conventional agriculture, where the farmer bears the risks of weather, pests, and the marketplace alone, the entire CSA community shares both bounty and scarcity. The costs of ecologically sound farming practices are factored in from the beginning and shared by the members. CSA also eliminates waste because the farm plans to meet only the needs of its members. By closely linking farms and consumers, CSA provides opportunities for increased understanding between rural and urban communities.

CSA farms can also become focal points for education and community building. In addition to receiving fresh produce, members usually have several opportunities to visit the farm. Many CSA farms host field days and workshops to educate members about sustainable farming and healthy food choices. Festivals and potlucks bring people together socially throughout the season. Consumers gain a new voice in how their food is grown, processed, and distributed, while choosing where their food dollars go.

John Hendrickson, a founding member of MACSAC, works for the UW-Madison Center for Integrated Agricultural Systems and grows and sells funky cherry tomatoes, edamame, and other produce at his farm, Stone Circle Farm.

Marcy Ostrum, now the Small Farms Program coordinator at Washington State University, is a longtime MACSAC supporter, CSA member, and researcher.

For more information about Community Supported Agriculture, or to find a CSA farm near you, see the Resources section at the back of this book.

Eaters Talk: Comments from CSA Members

Many people prefer the connection to a farmer and a specific farm found in CSA to the anonymity of conventionally grown and store-bought produce. The following are comments from CSA members about how they feel about being involved with a community supported farm.

I like knowing where my food is coming from and how it's been grown and how it's been handled. I think the distance from consumer to production of the food is alarming.

I loved the idea of seeing the people who grew our food.... I liked that connection with the land, food, and community.

It is real easy when you shop at [the supermarket] to start thinking about food as just another product. You can go to the store and buy a tomato or you can go to the store and buy a toaster and they feel kind of the same. Tomatoes aren't toasters. You can live without a toaster, but you can't live without food.

CSA also offers a chance for people to learn about food production in ways not offered by conventional food purchases.

I thought it was kind of neat having to shell [the dried beans]. You'd do all that [work] and you'd only end up with a small container. I said, "Wow... I never knew this."

It reminds you at a more basic level where your sustenance comes from, the idea that you eat different things during the course of the growing season because different things grow at different times. Otherwise, you go to the grocery store and the lettuce is always there...everything is always there so you end up eating a pretty restricted group of vegetables.

A Case of Apples and Oranges: What's So Special About Eating Locally?

Sharon Lezberg

I find that I can learn a great deal about the agriculture and food ("agro-food") industry by looking at the advertisements in industry trade journals. In reading *The Packer,* the trade journal for the produce industry, I came across an advertisement for a shipping company that proclaimed: "We have an environment for everything on earth." The corresponding picture shows planet Earth as viewed from space, partially veiled in glorious blue swirling clouds, and neatly contained within a refrigerated truck. Indeed, advancements in refrigeration technology and transportation networks, coupled with communication technologies for rapid product sourcing and purchasing, allow shippers to manipulate the "environment" to transport virtually any product from anywhere on earth, and at any time during the year, to load our supermarket shelves.

A second advertisement in *The Packer,* this one from a fruit production and distribution company, describes a specialty fruit as "the color of money." The advertisement implies that the fruit is not primarily a source of nutrients or sustenance but, rather, a money-maker for the food retailer. This advertisement promotes the notion that our food today is merely a commodity. Yet food is and always has been more than commodity; it is connected to personal well-being, to relationships with family and friends, to the vitality and persistence of community and culture, and to the care of and respect for the land.

The message that the agro-food industry tells us through these two advertisements is that production of food is about manipulating the environment for the greatest profit. Along the way, the food industry also manipulates our relationships with other people, both those who produce the food and members of our own communities. One characteristic of the conventional food production, distribution, and marketing system in the United States is an increasing distance between producers and eaters. In pulling the two apart, we have lost sight of relationships of obligation and responsibility for each other and for the land that sustains us.

Oranges: What's Behind the Labels?

The labels on packaged products may provide information about ingredients and price, but, beyond that, all else remains invisible. Every time I eat, I am reminded of how precious little I know about the food that I eat, how it was produced, and the people who produced it. I usually do not know who benefited from the production of the product, or who stood to lose. The environmental and social repercussions of my food choices are hidden behind product labels, advertisements, and brand names. And when I seek out more information about conventionally produced food, what I find can be highly problematic: that farmers receive disproportionately little for the food they grow, that the food industry is highly concentrated, and that the practices being used in food production, processing, and distribution are destructive to the land, the food itself, farmers, and communities.

One little-recognized aspect of our agro-food system is that farmers receive a very small percentage of the money that consumers spend for food. For every loaf of bread that I buy, 5 percent of the retail price goes to the farmer for wheat. An average 10 percent of the cost of frozen french fries is paid to the farmer for potatoes.

As shown in Figure 1, the farmer's share of our food dollar has continuously declined. In 1970, the farm value share of retail price was 37 percent, down to just 20 percent in 2000.

When the cost of production and labor is subtracted, farmers often realize very little, if any, profit. So where does all the money go? As Figure 2 shows, 80 cents of every retail food dollar is used to "add value" to our food; that is, to process, package, transport, and market the product to us. Taken together, these costs are referred to as the Marketing Bill. In 2000, the total marketing bill for domestically produced farm food reached $537.8 billion dollars, up 716 percent from 1970.

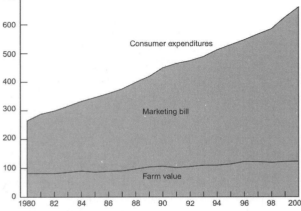

Figure 1
Consumer Food Spending Rose 47 Percent Between 1990 and 2000

Billion dollars

Consumer expenditures

Marketing bill

Farm value

Note: Data for foods of U.S. farm origin purchased by or for consumers for consumption both at home and away from home.
Source: USDA's Economic Research Service.

Another concern regarding the food industry is the unparalleled degree of concentration in all sectors of marketing (processing, distribution, retail, and food service). The 1980s were a time of corporate takeovers and mergers. Phillip Morris Company, for example, purchased General Foods, Kraft Foods (the corporate parent of Oscar Mayer, which was originally a locally owned and managed company), and Jacobs Suchard, a European chocolate and coffee manufacturer. Approximately 10 percent of the products on the shelves of our supermarkets are from Phillip Morris, including such popular brand names as Post, Velveeta, Tombstone Pizza, Stove Top, Kool-Aid, Philadelphia Cream Cheese, and Jello.[1]

Concentration is also apparent in the wholesale and retail industries. By 1990, 16 percent of wholesale food firms accounted for almost 90 percent of the industry's assets. Chain stores have gained control of the retail grocery store market, and as of 1990 accounted for 65.2 percent of all grocery store sales.[2]

Many production methods used in conventional agriculture degrade the land and our communities. Conventional agriculture is characterized by monocropping and mechanization practices that can lead to soil erosion, ground and surface water contamination, and high rates of pesticide and fertilizer use. Modern, mechanized agriculture also depends on the use of fossil fuels for all aspects of production, including fertilizer manufacturing and energy supply for tractor and farm implement use. The energy expended to get food from the farm gate to the grocery store, however, far exceeds the energy used on the farm. Food processing, packaging, transportation, and marketing eat up 75 to 85 percent of the energy used in the food system.[3]

With mechanization and modernization, farmers are often compelled to either expand the size of their operations in order to achieve economies of scale or leave farming altogether. In Wisconsin alone, an average of 1,500 farms were lost each year during the 1987 to 1992 census period. The number of dairy farms during that same time period dropped even more precipitously, at a rate of 19 percent each year.[4] Ironically, much of the competition for Wisconsin dairy farmers now comes from very large dairy operations in Texas, California, Arizona, and New Mexico. A critical issue in the loss of farm numbers is not so much whether larger farms are more economically efficient, but whether the intense economic competition forecloses self-employment opportunities for people who would prefer to operate small to medium-size farms. This, in turn, opens up the question of whether lost

Figure 2
Labor Took Biggest Chunk of Food Dollar in 2000

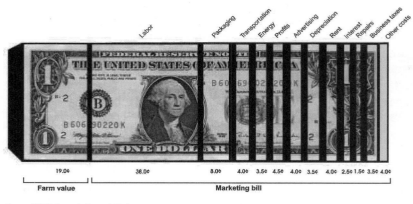

Source: USDA's Economic Research Service.

which Andean farmers alone cultivate more than 3,000 varieties.[9] In contrast, only four varieties of potatoes account for 75 percent of the crop grown in the United States.[10] The top ranking potato is the Russet Burbank, the potato favored by McDonald's for french fries. Potatoes are vulnerable to potato blight, and the Russet Burbank is especially susceptible, but McDonald's demands consistency and replicability in its french fry. As a consequence, farmers must apply more fungicide to ward off late blight rather than switch to cultivars that have higher resistance.

opportunities on the farm lead to increased unemployment, or toward less satisfying employment for those who are shut out of farming.

The production practices used on large corporate farms are not always and necessarily environmentally destructive and socially unjust. They are, however, invisible to us. Thus, it is disconcerting to learn that nearly 50 percent of all farm workers (excluding farmer owners/workers) live below the official U.S. poverty line. Of farm workers born outside the United States, 62 percent live below the poverty line.[5] The majority of farm workers are minorities, and many, due to language, class, and education barriers, have little recourse with which to demand fair pay and employment practices. While the EPA introduced worker protection standards (requiring employers to provide farm workers with protective clothing and adequate bathing and emergency facilities) and chemical use regulations for conventional farms in 1992, the United Farm Workers claims that these rules are not strong enough.[6] Despite regulations, farm workers still suffer more than 300,000 acute illnesses and injuries each year as a result of exposure to chemicals.[7]

As biological diversity is threatened by modern industrial systems, so, too the diversity of domesticated plants and animals is threatened by the modern agro-food system. The conventional agriculture system relies on only 20 major crops for 90 percent of the food grown and marketed.[8] As the number of species used for food crops declines, genetic diversity and future options for the development of plant and animal strains are reduced. Yet market farmers will only grow what they can sell. Potatoes provide an illustrative example. There are more than 5,000 varieties of potatoes known worldwide, of

Apples: Why Eat Locally?

As with many products we buy at the store, we rarely see the implications of our food purchases. But is "out of sight, out of mind" an adequate operating principle for our relationship with the very stuff that sustains us? Or should we take more responsibility for the way food is produced, processed, and brought to our tables?

Marti Crouch, a professor of biology at Indiana University in Bloomington, Indiana, illustrates these invisible relationships by contrasting imported bananas with locally grown wild pawpaws. Bananas, she writes, are "…available year round, so I come to expect everything all of the time. The chemical composition of the bananas I buy is likely to be uniform because of the genetics and production methods used in plantation agriculture. All of the processes of growth and transport that got them to me are invisible, hidden by time and distance, and I am thus shielded from both positive and negative aspects of banana production by being alienated from the whole."[11] Eating a locally grown fruit, on the other hand, provides knowledge about a particular place, and purchasing from local producers supports a regional economy.

Eating locally improves the visibility of production practices and decreases the distance between eaters and producers. As one local farmer put it: "That's the way modern farming is: 'Get out of here,' 'no trespassing.' I'm inviting people…[to] come out and see where your food is at."[12] By being in proximity to the source of our food, we can go out beyond the grocery store to see how our food is produced and to establish relationships with the people who produce our food. In this way, eating locally makes it easier for us to act on our responsibility for the health and vitality of a place and the people of that place.

Eating locally offers an alternative to "buying in" to the conventional agro-food system. There are numerous options available for consumers to support an alternative food system that is guided by adherence to the principles of environmental sustainability, social responsibility, equitable distribution of resources, and circulation of capital within our own community. Purchasing food directly from a farmer, either through community supported farms or farmers' markets, shortens the chain between farmer and consumer, assuring that the food dollar benefits the producer rather than marketers and advertisers.

Likewise, processed and prepared items are available that are produced directly by small and medium-size businesses within the region. Purchasing these items can bolster the local economy and provide us with more democratic control over production. At the retail end, consumer- and worker-owned and -managed grocery cooperatives adhere to specific cooperative principles that allow members oversight and responsibility for determining which items should be stocked and sold.

Switching, whenever and wherever possible, from oranges to apples—from eating food imported through the global food system to food grown in a local region— allows consumers to participate in determining production and distribution practices. Consumers can choose to support local farmers, socially and environmentally sustainable production practices, and community businesses. In this regard, eating locally is eating responsibly, allowing us, as well as the farmer, to assume relationships of obligation and care for the land and for each other.

1   Richard J. Barnet and John Cavanaugh. 1995. *Global Dreams: Imperial Corporations and the New World Order.* New York, NY: Simon & Schuster.

2   Economic Research Service (ERS). 1993. *Food Marketing Review, 1992-1993.* Commodity Economics Division, ERS-USDA. Agricultural Economic Report No. 678.

3   Geoff Tansey and Tony Worsley. 1995. *The Food System: A Guide.* London: Earthscan Publications Ltd.

4   Frederick H. Buttel. 1994. "Agricultural Change in Wisconsin: New Perspectives from the 1992 Census of Agriculture," in *As You Sow: Social Issues in Agriculture.* No. 33. Madison, WI: University of Wisconsin-Madison, Dept. of Rural Sociology.

5   Shea Cunningham. 1994. "Farm Workers in the 90s: Where Do We Stand?" Food First Action Alert. Oakland, CA: Institute for Food and Development Policy. Fall.

6   Dubey Siddhartha. 1994. "After Chavez: Still Seeking Safe Sprays out in the Fields," *Audubon.* July: p. 22.

7   Ivette Perfecto. 1992. "Pesticide Exposure of Farm Workers and the International Connection," pgs. 177-203 in *Race and the Incidence of Environmental Hazards: A Time for Discourse.* Boulder, CO: Westview Press.

8   Kenny Ausubel (ed.). 1993. Organic Seeds 1993 Catalog. Santa Fe, NM: Seeds of Change.

9   Cary Fowler and Pat Mooney. 1990. *Shattering: Food, Politics, and the Loss of Genetic Diversity.* Tucson, AZ: The University of Arizona Press.

10 Martin Teitel. 1992. *Rainforest in Your Kitchen.* Washington, D.C.: Island Press.

11 Marti Crouch. 1993. "Eating our Teachers: Local Food, Local Knowledge." *Raise the Stakes, Planet Drum Review.* Winter.

12 Lydia Oberholtzer. 1996. Interview with Farmer. *A Chicken in Every Pot: A Comparison of the Relationships in Conventional and Alternative Broiler Commodity Chains.* Unpublished Master's Thesis.

10 Easy Steps to Incorporate More Local and Seasonal Food into Your Diet

Lauri McKean

1. Start slowly. Eating local and seasonal food often requires that you make some changes in food preparation, meal planning, and shopping. You may find that your tastes, and those of family members, also change as you learn to eat locally available foods. Do not expect these changes to occur overnight. Set reachable goals by incorporating seasonal food slowly into your meals and shopping.

2. Be conscious of the source of your food. When at the grocery store, check food labels for their origin and then check to see if there are any alternative products that have been produced closer to home. If there are none, ask your grocer to start stocking local foods.

3. Develop a connection to your food. One of the most basic ways to do this is to plant a garden, even if it is only one potted tomato plant sitting on the porch. Another option is to become connected to the people from whom you buy food, be they vendors at a farmers' market or CSA farmers.

4. Make a commitment that your food buying practices reflect your principles. Purchasing locally grown and seasonal foods can benefit the economy, the environment, and personal nutrition in many ways. Buying locally grown food benefits the local economy since most of the profit ends up in the local community. It also benefits local farmers since more of the money goes directly to the farmers and not to the "middle people." The food is often more nutritious, fresh, and tasty than food shipped from other parts of the United States or other countries. Additionally, food that is produced without the use of synthetic pesticides and fertilizers is healthier for consumers and better for the environment.

5. Be creative and flexible in your cooking. Seasonal cooking presents a culinary adventure through a wide world of vegetable dishes. Some vegetables taste very different when they are fresh and well prepared. While you may have always hated beets that come from a can, you may find you love fresh beets prepared in a salad or borscht.

6. Plan for the winter—and do not despair when it arrives. With a little planning and some work in the summer, you can enjoy local foods all winter long. It is relatively easy to can your own tomatoes, pickles, and jams, and even easier to put some food away in a freezer or store squash and root crops in a basement. Some area stores and co-ops also carry locally grown crops, such as apples, beets, celeriac, sprouts, potatoes, onions, garlic, squash, turnips, and rutabagas, throughout much of the winter.

7. Learn how to substitute. This is a great way to incorporate unfamiliar foods into your diet while enjoying your favorite dishes. For example, substitute the long-storing celeriac root for celery in the winter. Try baking with local honey or maple syrup instead of cane sugar, which is grown in southern climates and uses large amounts of synthetic chemicals. Winter salads can have wonderful flavor and color with local sprouts and grated winter vegetables rather than lettuce shipped from California. Treat recipes as a starting point from which ideas can be generated, instead of something that must be followed exactly.

8. Buy fewer convenience foods. Convenience foods, in general, are more expensive, excessively packaged, and less fresh and nutritious than food you prepare at home. Additionally, the ingredients in these convenience foods are seldom locally grown or organic.

9. Encourage your favorite restaurants to consider purchasing produce from local farmers. Madison, Milwaukee, and Chicago restaurants have the option of working with "Home Grown Wisconsin," a farmer-restaurant cooperative that coordinates the supply and distribution of locally grown produce to restaurants. Look for (or develop) cooperatives like this in your region.

10. Enjoy it all. Enjoy the tastes, the challenge, the relationships you develop with producers, and the knowledge that you are doing something good for yourself and the earth.

Lauri McKean was an active member of MACSAC for many years and was the guiding spirit and driving energy behind From Asparagus to Zucchini *from its inception.*

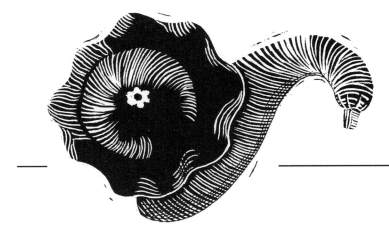

Eating Seasonally: A Personal Reflection

David Bruce

At one time, food production and preparation was a fundamental part of most people's lives. Across much of the Americas, corn, beans, and squash, known as the "three sisters," were the basis of the local diet and sound farming practices. These once sustainable and resilient systems, with their slight varietal and cultural differences, have been transformed into strip malls that feature the same fast food restaurants found in San Salvador, Jakarta, and Moscow. Somehow I think things should be different, though it is hard to imagine how to get away from the pervasive uniformity and extensive spread of those places. But there are ways to do things differently, as the 4,000 to 5,000 Wisconsin households involved with community supported agriculture are proving each harvest season.

Central to community supported agriculture is eating locally and seasonally. To be a CSA member is to take a revolutionary step and try changing one's eating, which often means changing one's lifestyle and daily practices. It means stepping out of the current food system, which is dependent on fossil fuels and the pervasive use of pesticides, herbicides, and chemical fertilizers. To eat seasonally requires a heightened awareness of the natural world—a recognition of what the earth is offering for our use during the different seasons.

Here on our farm we try, as much as possible, to eat seasonally. On this cool April day we are excited to steam up the first spring nettles, the freshness of which makes our frozen greens from last fall seem lifeless and boring. The wild and natural offerings of the earth reflect the eating practices of traditional people around the world. Our nettle dish reminds me of how the Tlingit ate hemlock shoots, rich in vitamin C, in the early spring. Natives of Turtle Island followed the buffalo, seasonally eating first fresh and then dried meat, until the spring and the return of the buffalo.

As the new millennium continues, I see that we are children flooded with toys, unable to control our frenzy or share logically. Whatever item we want is at our fingertips, and the gas to get there is artificially cheap and easily attainable. As a child during the first "Earth Day," I remember a newfound interest in environmentally sound living. Twenty-some years later, I find myself steadfastly advocating seasonal, local food in order to do better for my own kids and the world they live in.

Our modern American culture, operating in debt, is borrowing from the well-being—literally dipping from the source—of the future. Megafood and Safeway will not always be side by side, stocked to the gills. That plethora is deceiving, and ultimately dependent on want and deprivation in other countries. If you have ever visited a third world country, the return home to the modern grocery store, with Day-Glo displays and abundant foods, is shocking.

To do better, for ourselves, our kids, our parents, and our

neighbors, we can choose to eat locally grown, organic, seasonal food. It is a call to responsibility, and it takes work, tenacity, understanding, education, and daring resolve. It means shifting paradigms, and not eating what is easiest and most convenient. It means learning to be flexible, to try new things, to eat your greens, to lovingly wash, cut, cook, spice, and savor the things that can be grown at the time in the place where you are now. It is a simple concept, and one advocated by a popular bumper sticker: "Live simply so that others may simply live."

Seasonal eating is an extension of ideas that have been growing quietly for years. It is in concert with foodsheds—independent, self-reliant food economies. It is a conscientious objection to what we are doing to our home. It is civil disobedience against the bribe of apparent abundance and convenience as a statement and demonstration of local environmentalism, the daily practice of bioregional living and deep ecology. It is an attempt at harmony. I'm talking a purist walk, I know, and I'll be the first to say I don't yet live it totally. I'm a devoted coffee consumer, and I like to buy the little red organic bananas for my kids. Still, I hold a goal of eating primarily what is produced here, where I live, in the Driftless region of southwest Wisconsin. And what I can't grow here—like basmati rice or coffee beans—I'll try to buy from organizations that return a fair price to producers.

That's theory. In practice, I'm talking about generating new regional pride that is reflected in our foods. Different beer at every inn, changing to reflect the seasons: A bock, marzen, pale ale, bitter, oktoberfest, winterbrau, according to the appropriate grain and technique for the time of the year. Every culture has its indigenous bread, whether called a tortilla or a chapati. The different wines of the different regions of Europe reflect grapes adapted to specific areas. So many of these things are special because we cannot get them at the Stop-N-Go.

Let me put it another way. As a Wisconsin vegetable farmer, I know that by the time my melons are ripe, many people have already been eating melons grown and shipped from Mexico for a month and a half. As a result, a locally grown melon may not seem all that special, much less command a decent price. But think about how good that melon tastes to us on the farm, after having waited all summer for it.

Our food is reflective of the seasons. In the peak of the long light, our bodies are renewed with asparagus, salads, and steamed beet thinnings. In the heat of the summer, cucumbers, tomatoes, and peppers cool and nourish us, replacing lost fluids and minerals. In December and January, our bodies want the warmth and energy of the stored squash and potatoes. In February and March we have such a hankering for salad that we grow lots of sprouts and eat them alone with our favorite dressing!

Those who are stepping into seasonal eating by participating in a CSA deserve recognition for their extra efforts. It is revolutionary eating, refusing to be a part of the environmental degradation that characterizes the current food system. It is charitable eating, wanting those who produce your food to be earning a decent standard of living, and so loving others as yourself. It is Zen eating, requiring mindfulness, a simplifying of and a concentration on what we consume. It is environmental eating, for what better action than to provide an example to those around you on living more harmoniously in your world? With revolutionary spirit, charitable hearts, thoughtful practice, and sensitive action, we can learn to eat seasonally. As we do so, we learn about our region and, with creativity and caring responsibility to place, we can develop our own regional epicurean fare.

David Bruce has been a longtime student of sustainable agriculture as a university student, an employee for an organic certification agency and an organic produce cooperative, and as a full-time farmer at Dog Hollow Farm in southwestern Wisconsin.

Ode to Celeriac

Constance Firosz

Succulent ruby tomatoes, lush and heavy with the
    promise of pleasures to come,
Eggplants, peppers hot and sweet, milky ears of
    yellow corn,
A tender fan of lettuce leaf,
Peas packed neatly in translucent pods.
I bite a melon, sun trapped in a webbed rind and
Juice runs down my chin.
In the summer heat,
I do not so much eat as
Succumb.
Dinner is a seduction of
Color, passion and firm, moist flesh,
Each bite always the first,
Reckless and unthinking.

Too soon the earth leans away from the sun and
At the first rumor of frost,
My summer love shudders and is
Gone without a word.
Alone now, I am besieged by
Bulldozer blasts of Arctic air which
Pound the walls of the house and
Rattle the windows
Like a skeleton
Dancing in a tree.
I wrap my arms around my ribs and
Rock and rock and rock and
Weep for the summer lost.

It is then an unlovely knob, gnarled and lumpy
Surrounded by its aura of tiny roots, fine as any
    baby's hair,
Patiently remembers itself to me.
Simple in its Quaker gray and brown,
Unassuming, steady, and
Clear.
Promising only to be,
The twisted, leathery skin hides the
Sweetness locked within;
An enchanted toad,
Spellbound, waiting for release.

And so I light the fire, sharpen my knives, and, in the
    winter's gloom,
I work the kitchen magic.
Loneliness and dark are
Shut out and obscured by steamy windows as

I peel and boil and mash with potatoes and garlic—
Celeriac.

Heaped upon my plate, sprinkled with the bite of strong
    black pepper,
A little river of golden butter courses down
And puddles beneath my fork:
I am filled and sated,
Humbled by the grace and generosity of my
Steadfast Friend.

Summer will come again
And I will be foolish.
But when my fickle summer lovers abandon me
    once more,
Always, there will be the solace of the faithful, the true,
    the root—
Celeriac.

---

*Constance Firosz was a shareholder and active core group
member of Zephyr Community Farm, one of Madison's first
CSA farms.*

Reorganizing Your Time and Reorienting Your Talents for Regional and Seasonal Eating

Nancy Lee Bentley

Eating practices have changed dramatically in this country from what they were a mere 50 or so years ago. These days, food comes from faraway sources, whereas in the past, people ate what was grown, for the most part, within a local region. How can we get back in touch with our food and reconnect with the land on which food is grown? One place to start is to reduce the amount of packaged and processed food in our diets and to eat fresh, locally grown food instead. In northern regions, with their long, harsh winters, eating locally grown food implies developing a seasonal palate, where the food prepared changes with the seasons. But can one eat fresh, seasonal food—all year round—in the north? What about the winter?

Seasonal eating, particularly in northern climates, requires a slight adjustment in what and how you eat. In Wisconsin, for example, Vitamin C will probably come from tomatoes, cabbage, or rose hips instead of orange juice. You may eat lots of greens in spring, and a lot of squash in the fall. You may find yourself preserving food during the summer, instead of buying frozen vegetables at the grocery store in the winter.

There is no doubt that this way of eating requires more of you: more thought, commitment, time, and active participation. But it gives back more as well: more taste, vitality, heritage, well-being, and reconnection with source and self. The key to getting back more from your food is to make the decision to take responsibility for your food choices and eating habits.

Managing a Seasonal Diet

A key part of managing a seasonal diet is planning. Before you start cooking, devise a food plan. Whether you are in a CSA, gardening for yourself, or just taking advantage of buying direct from local farmers' markets, make a master plan as a guide to help you organize your food year. You will have to set aside time for processing excess produce from the spring, summer, and fall seasons, which means you have to know when certain foods are harvested (ask your farmer for

estimates). Decide whether you will be making and freezing pesto, canning tomatoes, or pickling cucumbers. Do you plan on making summertime strawberry jam and fall raspberry jam for holiday gifts? Do you want to have a freezer full of zucchini bread ready for unexpected visitors?

Creating a plan will provide you with a map that can even out the peaks and valleys of seasonal supply. For my plan, I construct a simple grid chart with months down the left column and food headings along the top. I insert the type and quantity of specific foods that I expect over the harvest season. The chart also includes my food processing and preserving plans. I also use this chart to make monthly and weekly plans for meals.

Another key step to managing a seasonal diet is procuring the tools and equipment needed to enjoy and stock a seasonal larder. A food processor with detachable blades is ideal for slicing and chopping vegetables. A work bowl and S-shaped knife are the best tools for making pestos and herb pastes, for grinding and pureeing herbs, vegetables, and fruits for sauces, and for preparing condiments such as chutneys, jams, butters, and salsas. Other indispensable items include canning jars and kettles, dehydrators, and barrels, crates, and baskets for root cellaring.

Once the equipment is in place, it is important to preserve the quality and integrity of your harvest by careful and timely handling and storage. Observe proper temperatures and make sure to cool produce quickly after harvest to maintain vitality and freshness. Plan ahead so that you can process (freeze, dry, store, or can) produce as soon as you get it, thereby preserving the flavor, vitality, quality, and nutrition of your finished products.

Once processed or readied for storage, dry food (for example, dry beans and dehydrated vegetables and grains) should be kept in dry, airtight containers. Moist foods, like lettuce and fresh herbs, should be washed and kept moist by misting and/or storing in containers. Some CSA growers provide cotton bags with drawstrings for leafy greens. These reusable bags can be misted. You can also make your own bags to store the harvest.

Get your produce into the refrigerator as soon as possible, since heat and light always reduce shelf life and freshness. To learn more about optimum temperature and storage conditions for various food items, consult standard recipe books or food processing manuals such as *Stocking Up, Managing Your Personal Food Supply,* or *Gardening for Maximum Nutrition.*

Prepare meals with a new perspective. Instead of thinking about meals as individual units or challenges, start working with a plan to prepare meals for larger blocks of time, such as a week. Organize your time and thinking so that you are prepared to do bulk cooking in advance of mealtimes. For example, plan blocks of time on the weekends or evenings when you can prepare components of several meals. If your family likes chicken on Sundays, roast several at once and use leftovers for salads, soups, stews, and casseroles. Freeze packets of chicken so that it can later be incorporated into quick tacos, enchiladas, or crepes. Make extra gravy or sauce, which can be frozen for future use. Make soup stock from the bones at the same time, throwing together a soup for early in the week that needs only to be reheated when you get home.

For vegetarian meals, cook big pots of beans and then season smaller portions for different meals. Soak beans overnight to reduce cooking time. Likewise, soak or cook grains like brown rice for several meals. Making chili while processing tomatoes isn't that much more work. Doing your cooking in batches like this will make day-to-day meal preparation easier and you a much more organized, efficient, and satisfied cook.

One other important thing to remember is to *un*cook in the summer. Pot meals like soups, stews, crockpot meals, and casseroles are easy and efficient cold-weather fare. In the summer, however, salads are readily available and easily prepared. Crisp, fresh, raw salads are cooling and quick to fix—just what a body can use when the temperature is sweltering. To prepare a satisfying meal, add some grains and nuts or dense protein as a condiment, and use lots of herbs and whatever-you-have-on-hand vegetables in the salad.

Some Seasonal Meal Plan Suggestions

Spring
- Spring greens stir-fried with tofu
- Pasta primavera with fresh herbs, pesto, greens, and mushrooms
- Vegetable crepes with cheese
- Fresh green vegetables and herb cream soup with breadsticks

Summer
- Fresh rainbow garden vegetable salad (a plate of fresh, just-picked garden vegetables)
- Cooked grain and vegetable salads like taboulleh made with bulgur, quinoa, barley, millet, or rice
- Fresh sliced tomatoes, cucumbers, basil, and fresh mozzarella cheese drizzled with extra virgin olive oil and balsamic vinegar and served with garlic bread or crackers
- Cold gazpacho soup with sour cream or yogurt, served with breadsticks

Fall
- Ratatouille
- Fresh tomato sauce with pasta
- Stuffed acorn squash with grains and raisins
- Fresh pizza made on focaccia

Winter:
- Soups and stews made with potatoes and other root vegetables
- Mashed potatoes and rutabagas with croutons and cheese
- Tempura vegetables (try sweet potatoes for a treat)
- Hot coleslaw
- Sauerkraut with roasted potatoes and dill seed with summer sausage or tofu dogs
- Grilled onion and roasted root vegetables with tempeh or turkey

The Vegetables

Asparagus

Asparagus officinalis

One of the very first spring messengers of the garden is the perennial asparagus spear, with its nose poking through the moist soil. Asparagus stands alone in its unique and simple gourmet qualities. Interestingly, asparagus is related to onions, garlic, and other members of the lily family.

Asparagus has been used since ancient times in many parts of the world. Its name is most likely derived from the Persian word *asparag,* meaning "sprout." However, the Greek word *aspharagos* means "long as one's throat," and in England during the 18th century this vegetable was known as "sparrow grass." Regardless, its popularity lives on.

Asparagus season is short, adding to its specialness. Enjoy it thoroughly while it's here!

Not only is asparagus a culinary delight, it is also a nutritional winner. Generally, raw asparagus ranks high in vitamins A, B-complex, and C, and is also rich in minerals from the soil, particularly potassium and zinc. Nibble on some tender asparagus raw for its full flavor and nutritional value. Like other vegetables, it will lose some, though not all, of its B-complex and vitamin C during the cooking process. Popular also with those who are counting calories, asparagus contains no fat and only 35 calories per one-cup serving.

Cooking Tips

- Snap off or remove with a knife the bottommost woody part of the spear.

- Try tender asparagus spears raw. Chop into a salad, or enjoy with a dip.

- Asparagus is best cooked simply. Here are two suggestions:

  Arrange spears loosely in a skillet with an inch of lightly salted boiling water. Simmer for 3-5 minutes or until bright green and tender, but not mushy. Remove from heat and run under cold water to stop the cooking process.

  Steam asparagus upright in a tall covered pot over approximately one inch of water until tender, about 10 minutes. This method cooks the tougher bottoms more thoroughly while gently steaming the tender tops.

- Try serving asparagus *warm* topped with butter, lemon, and a sprinkle of Parmesan cheese.

- Try serving *cold* with a simple vinaigrette, or try olive oil with fresh-squeezed lemon and a sprinkle of salt.

- Try it on your kids! It's mild in flavor and fun to chomp down, raw or cooked.

Storage Tips

- Wrap asparagus in a damp cloth and store in the hydrator drawer of the refrigerator. An alternate storage technique to retain vitality is to bundle spears with a rubber band and place upright in a container with an inch of water.

- Refrigerate immediately and use as soon as possible. Asparagus' sugars will turn rapidly to starches, reducing flavor quickly.

For additional recipes that feature asparagus, see the Seasonal Combinations chapter.

Asparagus Risotto Cakes   MACSAC

1 pound asparagus, tough ends removed
1 tablespoon olive oil
1 cup finely chopped onions
1 tablespoon minced garlic
1 1/2 cups arborio rice
1 pinch saffron threads, crushed
3/4 cup white wine

6-8 cups chicken stock, hot
2 tablespoons butter
1/2 cup freshly grated Parmesan cheese
1 teaspoon lemon juice
salt and pepper to taste
1/2 cup bread crumbs
oil or butter for pan-frying cakes

Steam asparagus over boiling water 4-5 minutes. Rinse in cold water and chop. Heat olive oil in saucepan over medium flame; add onions and cook until translucent. Add garlic; cook 1 minute longer. Add rice and stir 2 minutes. Add saffron and wine. Simmer hard, stirring, until liquid is reduced by half. Add 1/2 cup stock; stir until absorbed. Continue to add stock 1/2 cup at a time and stir constantly until absorbed, until rice is cooked through and begins to clump (this is more than you would cook it for normal risotto). Add butter, cheese, lemon juice, asparagus, salt, and pepper. Spread on baking sheet; cool. Form patties and dip into breadcrumbs. Heat oil or butter in skillet; sauté cakes until golden brown on both sides. Makes 4 large or 6-8 small servings.

Asparagus alla Milanese   Patrick O'Halloran, Lombardino's Restaurant

3-4 tablespoons extra-virgin olive oil, divided
1 1/2 pounds slender asparagus, trimmed and peeled
1 shallot, minced
1 clove garlic, thinly sliced 3-4 tablespoons

1 tablespoon white wine
salt and pepper to taste
6 organic eggs (as fresh as possible)
1/2 cup freshly grated Parmigiano-Reggiano

Heat 2 tablespoons olive oil in large skillet over medium-high heat, add asparagus, and sauté 1 minute. Add shallot and garlic; cook another minute. Add wine, stirring to release bits sticking to bottom of pan. Add salt and pepper. Keep heat low while you fry the eggs sunny-side up in more olive oil in a nonstick pan. Divide asparagus onto 6 warmed plates. Top each with one egg, a drizzle of olive oil, some Parmesan, and freshly ground black pepper. Makes 6 servings.

Simply Delicious Asparagus Soup   Matthew and Susan Smith, Blue Valley Gardens

8 tablespoons (1 stick) butter
3 1/2 - 4 cups chopped onions
8 cups chicken stock

2 pounds asparagus
1/2 cup cream
salt and pepper to taste
fresh lemon thyme or dill to taste

Heat butter in soup pot, add onions, and cook until tender. Add stock; bring to boil. Cut tips off asparagus; reserve. Chop stems and add to pot. Simmer gently until asparagus is very tender, 15-20 minutes. Puree in a food processor and return puree to pot. Add tips; cook gently 5-10 minutes. Stir in cream, salt, and pepper. Add lemon thyme or dill; if you use dried herbs, add them to the onions as they cook. Makes 8-10 servings.

Asparagus Guacamole   MACSAC

2 cups chopped, cooked asparagus
2 tablespoons plain yogurt or sour cream
2 tablespoons fresh lime juice
2 tablespoons minced green onion
2 tablespoons tomato salsa

1 tablespoon minced cilantro
1 teaspoon minced garlic, pressed
   to a paste with a fork
1/2 teaspoon cumin
salt and pepper to taste

Puree asparagus, yogurt, and lime juice in food processor or blender. Stir in remaining ingredients. Serve with tortilla chips or crackers, or as a sandwich spread. Makes 1 3/4 cups.

Basil

Ocimum basilicum

Basil, an annual herb in northern gardens, adds delicate flavor and aroma to many cultural dishes of Greece, Italy, and the Near East, as well as adapting itself well to varied dishes created in imaginative kitchens.

Basil is believed to have originated in India. There it was viewed as a holy plant and was grown around shrines and temples, infusing the air with its fragrance. A good Hindu was supposed to leave this life with a basil leaf on the chest to aid in passage to the next.

Basil is more commonly known for its primary role in tomato sauces, pesto, and salad dressings. Play around with these recipes and discover how flexible they are. Create your own tasty variations.

Basil, like tomatoes, thrives in the heat of the summer. The cool of spring and fall quickly weaken and damage the delicate herb. A spell of hot, humid weather will provide an abundance of basil—that's the perfect time to dry it or make tons of pesto to freeze for brightening up a bleak winter menu.

Cooking Tips

- Remove basil leaves from stems before using. Wash these gently to remove any garden grit.

- Chop basil with stems into soups and stews.

- Toss fresh whole basil leaves into green salads and chopped into pasta or rice salads.

- Top slices of tomato with chopped fresh basil leaves, olive oil, and a little salt and pepper.

- Layer basil leaves in a sandwich with slices of garlic and tomatoes, and cheese if you wish.

- Basil is famous in salad dressings (vinaigrettes), tomato sauces, and as the main ingredient in pesto, but don't forget to throw it into egg or cheese dishes, sautés, stir-fries, pureed vegetable soups, dips, and sauces. Experiment with its flavor and you'll find out where you like to use it.

Storage Tips

- Fresh basil deteriorates quickly. Use as soon as possible.

- For short-term storage, wrap in a lightly damp towel and refrigerate. Do not wash prior to refrigeration.

- Freeze fresh leaves in a plastic zip-lock bag. Remove air, seal, and freeze. Do not thaw before use.

- Pesto freezes very well in an airtight container. Some people freeze it in an ice cube tray. When well frozen, pop out pesto cubes. Bag them in a zip-lock bag and freeze. Take out only as many cubes as you need at a time.

- Basil can be dried easily. See chapter on home food preservation for information on drying herbs.

For additional recipes that feature basil, see the Tomato and Seasonal Combinations chapters.

Easy August Sandwiches   Linda Taylor, Good Earth Farm

1 loaf crusty French or Italian bread,
   sliced 3/4-1 inch thick
1/3-1/2 cup basil pesto
2-3 large tomatoes

1/2 red onion
1-2 tablespoons olive oil
1-2 tablespoons balsamic vinegar

Heat oven to 375 degrees. Spread bread slices on cookie sheet. Spread pesto on the slices and toast the bread. Meanwhile, thinly slice tomatoes and onions and marinate in equal amounts of olive oil and balsamic vinegar. When bread is toasted and pesto is warm, remove from oven. Top with drained tomato/onion mixture. Makes 4-6 servings.

Tomato Basil Dip   Ruth Chantry, Common Good Farm

3 cups diced fresh tomatoes
1 tablespoon or more minced garlic, mashed
   to a paste (use a garlic press or flat of a knife)
5 tablespoons chopped basil (chop it medium-fine)

1 tablespoon olive oil
dash of balsamic vinegar
salt and pepper to taste
thinly sliced, lightly toasted baguette slices

Lightly toss tomatoes, garlic, and basil. Drizzle with olive oil, splash with balsamic vinegar, and sprinkle with salt and pepper to taste. Give a quick stir and serve with baguette slices. This recipe, from cooking instructor Yana Beranek, easily doubles or triples. The quantities and flavors can be adjusted to one's own taste. It's beautiful when made with yellow and red tomatoes. Leftovers are good as a salad dressing. Makes about 8-12 servings.

Sunny-Side Ups with Pesto and Tomatoes   MACSAC

1 teaspoon olive oil
6 small tomatoes (about golf-ball size), quartered
1/2 small sweet onion, finely chopped

2 tablespoons pesto
4 eggs
salt and pepper

Heat oil in medium-size nonstick pan over medium-high flame. Add tomatoes and onion and cook them quickly, stirring often, until tomatoes give off juice and begin to thicken slightly, about 5 minutes. Reduce heat to medium and stir in pesto. Push mixture to sides of pan, creating a "ring" of sauce. Carefully break eggs into center of pan, cover, and cook until eggs are set, 4-6 minutes. Season with salt and pepper and serve immediately. Makes 2 servings.

Lemon Basil Shortbread Cookies   Jenny Bonde and Rink DaVee, Shooting Star Farm

3 cups flour
1 1/2 teaspoons baking powder
1/4 teaspoon salt
2/3 cup butter, softened
1 cup sugar
1 teaspoon vanilla extract

3 tablespoons chopped fresh lemon (or lime) basil
1 tablespoon finely grated or minced lemon or
   lime peel (use only the yellow or green portion
   of the peel)
1 cup finely chopped walnuts

Heat oven to 350 degrees. Mix flour, baking powder, and salt in a bowl. Mix butter, sugar, vanilla, basil, and lemon or lime peel in a separate bowl and beat with an electric mixer until well combined. With mixer set on low speed, slowly add the dry ingredients to the butter mixture. The mixture will be crumbly. Stir in the walnuts. Dump mixture into an ungreased 9-by-13-inch or similar-size pan. Press mixture to even thickness. Bake until edges begin to turn light brown, about 20 minutes—do not overbake. Using a sharp knife, slice shortbread into two-inch squares while hot. Let cool 10 minutes, then carefully transfer pieces to a plate or cooling rack. Adapted from a recipe on the Internet. Makes 24-30 cookies.

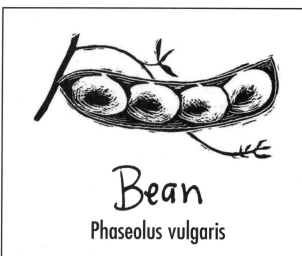

Bean

Phaseolus vulgaris

Beans are indigenous to Central America and the Andean regions of South America. Snap, string, and stringless snap beans are among the most widely used garden vegetables in the U.S. Green, yellow wax, and deep purple varieties are popular. These early season beans also offer a range of varieties, from the ultra-thin French filet to the meatier, wider wax and Italian-type beans. Nutritionally, this early, fresh phase of the bean is not as high in protein as its mature relative, the dried bean. However, its worthwhile amounts of vitamins A, B1, and B2, calcium, and potassium add to summer's wealth of health.

Less well known are fresh shell beans, the mature but still fresh stage of the bean. The bean seed is generally removed from the now fibrous and inedible pod and cooked fresh. Popular varieties include the lima (also called butterbean), fava, and soybean (also called edamame). The latter is a nutritional champ, containing all nine essential amino acids. It's also high in calcium, iron, zinc, several B vitamins, and the touted isoflavones, a set of sub-nutrients thought to reduce the risk of many forms of cancer, heart disease, and osteoporosis, and even to mitigate unpleasant symptoms of menopause. To avoid digestive difficulties, do not use shell beans raw.

Unlike fresh shell beans that require little additional flavoring to bring out their best, the vast variety of dried beans all benefit from added punch, so bring on your favorite combinations of herbs and spices and get ready for a savory cooking session. Their high protein content makes dried beans an excellent complement to most any meal and a staple for most vegetarians.

Cooking Tips

- Remove strings and stems of fresh beans before cooking. Beans retain more nutrients when cooked uncut.

- Steam or simmer fresh beans in boiling water for 5-10 minutes. Watch carefully for beans to brighten in color and become tender, but not soft or mushy.

- If intending to serve fresh beans chilled, cook less to retain more crispness.

- Boil shelled edamame in heavily salted water about 10 minutes. Eat them like peanuts—they're great with beer!

- Cooked soybeans may also be shelled and added to other dishes, such as salads, stir-fries, soups, and rice or seafood dishes.

- Most dry beans may be soaked in cold water 8-12 hours to help them cook faster, although some cooks feel the nutrient and flavor loss is not worth the time saved.

- If you do soak your beans, pour off the soaking water, add fresh water or stock, and simmer slowly for up to three hours with desired seasonings.

- Avoid rapid boiling of beans, which causes the skins to deteriorate and the beans to split.

- Add salt to dried beans after cooking or late in the cooking process to avoid toughness.

Storage Tips

- Refrigerate fresh in a plastic bag, and use beans as soon as possible, for they are perishable. Green beans will keep quite well for up to about a week.

- In general, shell beans are highly perishable and are best used within a few days. Store in a basket or paper bag and in the refrigerator.

- Fresh and shell beans are easily frozen for long-term storage. Blanch in boiling water 2-3 minutes, rinse in cold water, drain, dry well, and pack into airtight containers.

  Edamame may be frozen after blanching right in the pod.

- Dried beans have a shelf life of years. But don't keep them around that long—no more than six months with proper storage is recommended.

For additional recipes that feature beans, see the Seasonal Combinations chapter.

Prizewinner Green Beans with Tomatoes and Herbs   Mara Rosenbloom

2 tablespoons extra-virgin olive oil
1 clove garlic, minced
about 1/4 teaspoon red pepper flakes
1/2 cup sliced onions
2 teaspoons dried oregano
1/2 teaspoon dried ground thyme

1 pound green beans, ends clipped, beans cut in half
1 sprig rosemary, leaves torn off the stem
2 medium tomatoes, cut into wedges
   (peeling is optional)
salt to taste or 2 tablespoons salted butter

Heat olive oil in deep pan over medium heat. Add garlic and pepper flakes; sauté until fragrant. Add onions; sauté until translucent, 3-5 minutes. Add 1/4 cup water, the dried spices, and green beans. Stir, cover, and steam-cook beans until nearly done, 10-15 minutes. Stir in the rosemary and tomatoes. Cook very briefly, until tomatoes are warmed through and beans are done. Season with salt, or, if you prefer, melt salted butter over the beans before serving. This recipe won a prize in the 2002 Food for Thought Recipe Contest in Madison, Wisconsin. Makes 4 servings.

Green Bean Poriyal   Joan Peterson

2 pounds fresh or frozen French-cut green beans
2 tablespoons oil
1/2 teaspoon black mustard seeds
1 teaspoon urad dal (a small white lentil)
1 onion, finely chopped

2 hot green chiles, finely chopped
1/2 teaspoon salt, or to taste
1/4 fresh coconut, grated
1 tablespoon lemon juice
3-4 tablespoons sliced almonds

Cook beans in unsalted water until tender; drain. Heat oil in skillet over high flame until shimmering. Add mustard seeds, cover, and let sputter. When sputtering slows, reduce heat to medium and add urad dal. Fry until light brown—take care not to burn them. Stir in onion and chiles; sauté until limp. Stir in beans and salt. Turn off heat. Add coconut and lemon juice. Sprinkle with almonds. Makes 6-8 servings. This recipe, by Narasima Katari, is from *Eat Smart in India,* by Joan Peterson and Indu Menon.

Green Beans with Caramelized Onions   MACSAC

2 pounds green beans, stem ends snipped off
2 tablespoons butter
2 medium onions, sliced as thinly as possible
1 cup chicken stock

1 1/2 tablespoons sugar
1 tablespoon red wine vinegar
salt and pepper to taste

Cook beans in boiling salted water until crisp-tender, 2-4 minutes. Drain; immerse in ice water. Drain again and let stand to dry. Melt butter in skillet over medium flame. Stir in onions and cook them slowly until very wilted and deepened in color, about 15 minutes. Boil stock in a saucepan until reduced to 1/4 cup; stir in sugar and vinegar. Stir in onions. Simmer until slightly reduced. Combine onions and green beans; heat through. Season with salt and pepper. Makes 8 servings.

Zydeco Green Beans   Carrie Linder

6-12 sliced garlic cloves
6 teaspoons yellow mustard seeds
3 pounds green beans (thick or thin), trimmed
6-12 small hot peppers

6 dill heads or 6 teaspoons dill weed
3 1/2 cups white wine vinegar (no substitutes!)
2 tablespoons pickling salt
3 1/2 cups water

If you've never canned food before, read about it in a reputable cookbook before proceeding. Sterilize 6 pint jars. Divide garlic, mustard seeds, beans, peppers, and dill into jars. Bring vinegar, salt, and water to a boil; pour over beans, leaving 1/2 inch head space. Place lids on jars and process 5 minutes in a boiling water bath. Age the pickles at least one month before snacking on them. Adapted from *The Joy of Pickling,* by Linda Ziedrich. Makes 6 pints.

Roasted French Bean Salad with Pine Nuts and Parmesan   Angela Tedesco, Turtle Farm

1 pound *haricots vertes* (thin French green beans), washed and dried
4 tablespoons olive oil, divided
2 cloves garlic, minced

salt and pepper to taste
2 tablespoons wine vinegar
1/4 cup pine nuts
1/4 cup shredded Parmesan cheese

Heat oven to 425 degrees. Toss beans with 1 tablespoon olive oil. Spread in single layer on a baking sheet; roast on top shelf in oven about 15 minutes, stirring halfway through cooking time. Mash garlic with 1 teaspoon salt; add vinegar. Whisk in 3 tablespoons olive oil. When beans are done roasting, reduce oven to 350 degrees. Toss beans and dressing; season with salt (if necessary) and pepper. Spread pine nuts on baking sheet. Roast them, shaking pan occasionally, until lightly browned. Sprinkle pine nuts and Parmesan over tossed salad. Serve warm or at room temperature. Adapted from a dish tasted at Restaurant Rech in Paris. It may be made with regular green beans (roast them a little longer), and with sliced, sautéed portobello mushrooms instead of pine nuts. Makes 4-6 servings.

Shell Beans and Beyond   Jenny Bonde and Rink DaVee, Shooting Star Farm

1 pound in-the-pod shelling beans (cranberry, Tongue of Fire, etc.), shelled and rinsed
1 medium onion, quartered

4 sprigs fresh thyme
kosher salt
extra-virgin olive oil

Place beans, onion, and thyme in a medium saucepan with water to cover. Simmer gently until tender—this may take 15 minutes for really fresh beans, or up to 35 for older, drier beans. Drain; remove onion and thyme. Place beans in bowl, add a pinch of salt, and drizzle with olive oil. Eat warm or at room temperature. You also can further cook the beans in a skillet with oil, mash them up a bit, and serve on top of grilled bread. Cooked beans added to a skillet of freshly fried crumbled bacon is quite delicious, too. Makes 2-4 servings.

Fresh Fava Beans with Cilantro and Yogurt   Sarah Coyle, Vermont Valley Farm member

2 pounds in-the-pod fava or broad beans, shelled
1 tablespoon butter
3 cloves garlic, minced
1 small or 1/2 large bunch cilantro, chopped

1/2 teaspoon salt
1/4 teaspoon pepper
1/4 scant teaspoon cumin seeds, lightly crushed
1 cup plain yogurt, lightly beaten

Boil fava beans in just enough salted water to cover them until barely tender, 5-10 minutes. Drain. (If the shelled beans are larger than a small thumbnail, you should also slip the slightly bitter-tasting outer skin off the beans after they cool a bit. There's no need to do this if the beans are young, however.) Melt butter in a skillet over medium flame, add garlic and cilantro, and cook 1-2 minutes. Add beans and cook a few minutes longer, stirring often. Add salt, pepper, and cumin. Transfer to a serving dish; toss gently with yogurt. Serve with bread to scoop up the sauce, along with olives and other Middle Eastern foods. Adapted from *Food for the Vegetarian: Traditional Lebanese Recipes*, by Aida Karaoglan. Makes 4 servings.

Edamame Fried Rice   MACSAC

1 tablespoon sesame oil, divided
1 tablespoon each minced ginger and garlic
2 cups shelled edamame (fresh soybeans)
2 tablespoons bottled plum sauce

3 tablespoons soy sauce
1 cup raw white or brown rice, cooked and cooled
3 tablespoons tamari-roasted whole almonds
3 chopped green onions

Heat wok or large, heavy skillet over high flame until the air looks hazy over the pan, 2-4 minutes. Add 1 teaspoon sesame oil, swirl the pan, add ginger and garlic, and stir-fry 10-20 seconds. Add edamame; stir-fry 30 seconds. Add 1/3 cup water, bring to boil, and cook until edamame are tender and water has been absorbed, 3-5 minutes. Stir in 2 teaspoons sesame oil, plum sauce, soy sauce, rice, and almonds; stir-fry about 5 minutes. Sprinkle with green onions. Serve immediately. Makes 4 main-course or 8 side servings.

Finger Lickin' Edamame with Asian Sauce   Angela Tedesco, Turtle Farm

1 pound edamame (soy beans), in the shell
2 tablespoons soy sauce
1 tablespoon each sesame oil, canola oil,
   and rice vinegar

2 garlic cloves, minced
1 teaspoon brown sugar or honey
2 tablespoons sesame seeds

Boil edamame in salted water 5-8 minutes. Combine other ingredients in a saucepan and bring to simmer, stirring, to dissolve sugar or honey. Toss with hot edamame. Serve immediately, letting diners pop beans out of the pod. The glaze was inspired by a recipe in *The Roasted Vegetable,* by Andrea Chesman. The recipe works with shelled edamame, too. Makes 6-8 servings.

Calypso Beans and Pasta with Epazote   MACSAC

2 cups Calypso (or other) dried beans, soaked
1 tablespoon salt
1 tablespoon olive oil
2 teaspoons minced garlic
1 1/2 teaspoons chopped fresh epazote*
2/3 cup finely chopped carrot

1-2 finely chopped fresh chiles
2-3 chipotles (dried jalapeños), halved
6 ounces rotini pasta, cooked
6 cups chopped beet greens or chard leaves
salsa verde and grilled corn kernels

Combine beans, salt, olive oil, garlic, epazote, carrot, and chiles in medium saucepan. Cover by 2 inches with cold water. Bring to simmer, partially cover the pot, and cook gently until beans are tender, 1-2 hours. You should end up with a soupy mixture, so add hot water as needed during the cooking. While beans are simmering, pour 1 cup boiling water over the chipotles and soak until soft, 15-20 minutes. Strain liquid into beans. Scrape "meat" away from skin of soaked chiles and add it to the beans (discard the skin). When beans are done, stir in pasta and greens. Heat until greens are wilted. Season to taste with salt and pepper. Serve in big bowls topped with salsa verde and grilled corn kernels, if you like. Makes 6-8 servings.

*Epazote is a Mexican herb typically used in bean dishes. There's no substitute for its unusual flavor, but you can also use fresh oregano or cilantro, adding them toward the end of cooking.

Spunky Red Bean Chile Dip or Quesadilla Filling   MACSAC

1 1/2-2 cups cooked dried beans (use any red-type:
   cranberry, kidney beans, Jacob's Cattle, etc.)
1-2 teaspoons minced fresh garlic
1/2 teaspoon ground cumin
1/2-1 teaspoon bottled hot pepper sauce

3 tablespoons vegetable oil
2 tablespoons red wine vinegar
2 tablespoons chopped fresh cilantro
freshly ground black pepper to taste

Puree all ingredients in food processor until fairly smooth. Adapted long ago from a recipe in *Gourmet* magazine, this recipe can be used as a dip for corn chips or crackers, or to make quesadillas: spread dip on tortillas, add grated cheese, and grill on both sides in a hot skillet. Makes about 1 cup.

Armenian Bean Salad   MACSAC

1/2 cup thinly sliced green or Spanish onions
salt to taste
3-4 cups cooked white Northern or red
   kidney beans
1/2 cup finely chopped green pepper
1/2 cup minced parsley

1/3 cup fresh lemon juice
1/4 cup olive oil
pepper
Hungarian paprika (or allspice or cumin)
finely chopped tomatoes (optional)

Sprinkle onions with salt and work with your fingers until juicy. Toss with remaining ingredients except tomatoes. Cover and refrigerate. Toss again before serving and add tomatoes, if desired. Makes 3-4 cups.

Beet

Beta vulgaris

Ahhh, beets! The beetroot is perhaps the most controversial of the common garden vegetables. Many a palate has sworn off beet cookery, but the beet is making a comeback.

For starters, beets are very versatile, lending themselves well to basic usage, both cooked and raw, and incorporation into recipes. Beets are high in nutrients, such as vitamins A and C, and also the carotenes. If you are using your beet greens, you also get generous portions of vitamin C, calcium, and iron. The joy of beets does not end there. Beets are tremendously long-storing, sweet and delicious, and colorful. Discover a favorite beet recipe for yourself and rediscover beets.

If you grow to enjoy beets, you are in luck. They are available much of the year. In cooler climates, you may enjoy the first baby beets of the season mid- to late June. Beets are usually hearty in the garden throughout the season, finishing their growth with the first frosts. After harvest, beets will retain their integrity for three months or longer if stored under optimum conditions.

Cooking Tips

- No need to peel, only scrub clean; trace minerals lie just below the surface of the skin.

- Grate into most any salad, cooked or raw.

- Cube beets into veggie soups or stews.

- Serve sliced, steamed beets at room temperature tossed in olive oil with a dash of salt and pepper, or use a simple vinaigrette.

- To bake, cut off leaves and wash roots. Bake at 350 degrees for 1-2 hours or until easily pierced with a fork. Rub off skins and cut off roots. Serve whole or sliced.

- Young beet greens can be enjoyed tossed raw into a mixed green salad.

- Try beet greens steamed or sautéed, or in any dish calling for a mild, tender green such as spinach. See sections on Greens, Chard, or Spinach for more suggestions and recipes appropriate for beet greens.

Storage Tips

- Beet greens are best used fresh, as their integrity will diminish rapidly.

- Store greens wrapped in a damp cloth or in a plastic bag in a drawer of the refrigerator.

- To maintain firmness of beet roots, cut off leaves and stems 1-2 inches above the root crown. Store in a plastic bag and refrigerate in the hydrator drawer.

For more recipes that feature beets, see the Seasonal Combinations chapter.

Beet Soup   Dog Hollow Farm

4 large beets
1 large potato
other vegetables: celery, spinach, carrots, kale,
    chard, etc.

1 large onion
salt and pepper to taste
plain yogurt

Wash all vegetables and cut into chunks. Place in large steamer over boiling water; steam until very soft. Using the water from the steamer, and any other stock or water as needed, blend cooked vegetables until very smooth and thick. Return to pot; heat gently to avoid sticking. Add salt and pepper. Serve each bowl with a generous portion of yogurt in center of soup. Makes 4-6 servings.

Autumn Beet and Vegetable Salad with Blue Cheese and Hickory Nuts   MACSAC

Dressing:
1/3 cup minced shallots
5 tablespoons cider vinegar
3-4 tablespoons chopped fresh basil or parsley
1 1/2 tablespoons Dijon mustard
1/2 cup olive oil
salt and pepper to taste

Salad:
2 cups cooked, diced yellow or red beets
1 1/2 cups blanched, diced carrots
1 1/2 cups cooked, diced waxy-type potatoes
1 cup diced roasted red peppers
1 1/2 cups diced Jonathan apples
4-6 ounces blue cheese, crumbled
2/3 cup hickory nuts, toasted 6-8 minutes at 350 degrees

Make dressing: Combine shallots, vinegar, basil or parsley, and mustard. Whisk in olive oil in a thin stream. Season with salt and pepper. To assemble the salad, toss each type of vegetable and the apples, one type at a time, with enough dressing to barely coat them. Arrange in separate piles in a wide, shallow bowl. Serve at room temperature. Just before serving, sprinkle salad with blue cheese and hickory nuts, add more salt and pepper to taste, and toss gently. Makes 8-12 servings.

Beets, Oranges (or Peaches), and Raspberry Sauce   Angela Tedesco, Turtle Farm

1 pound beets, scrubbed
1-2 oranges or peaches
2 cloves garlic, minced
1/2 teaspoon salt

2 tablespoons raspberry vinegar
3 tablespoons olive oil
1 teaspoon grated gingerroot (optional)

Heat oven to 350 degrees. Place beets (in their skins) in a baking dish and cover with foil. Roast beets until tender, about 35-55 minutes, depending on their size. When cool, peel, slice thinly, and place them in a bowl. Peel the oranges (or peaches) and cut in half. Place flat sides down on cutting board and slice each into about 4 wedges. Remove seeds from orange slices. Add to beets. Make a vinaigrette out of the remaining ingredients: mash garlic with the salt, add vinegar, and whisk in olive oil. Stir in grated gingerroot, if using. Toss with beets and oranges. You can serve this immediately, but it's best if allowed to chill and mellow. This dish was inspired by recipes in Mollie Katzen's *Vegetable Heaven* and Renee Shepherd's *Recipes From a Kitchen Garden*. Makes 4-6 servings.

Yellow Beets with Orange Juice and Sherry Vinegar   MACSAC

1 pound yellow beets
2 tablespoons sherry vinegar

2 tablespoons orange juice concentrate (undiluted)
salt and pepper

Roast, steam, or boil beets until tender. Cool, peel, and slice them. Toss with sherry vinegar and orange juice concentrate. Season to taste with salt and pepper. Makes 4 servings.

Beets and Their Greens with a Sauce of Marjoram and Pine Nuts   Deborah Madison

Beets:
2 small red onions, sliced into thin rounds
white wine vinegar
8-12 small beets (golden and/or Chioggia),
   including the greens
olive oil
sea salt

Sauce:
1 small slice country bread, crusts trimmed off
2 tablespoons aged red wine vinegar
1 garlic clove, coarsely chopped
salt and pepper to taste
1/4 cup marjoram leaves
3 tablespoons capers
1/2 cup pine nuts, divided
1 cup finely chopped parsley
2 tablespoons pitted green or black olives
1/2 cup extra-virgin olive oil

Toss onions with enough vinegar to nearly cover them; refrigerate. Trim beets, leaving on an inch of stems and tails. Discard stems and any wilted leaves. Wash the good leaves; steam until tender, 3-5 minutes. Drain; chop coarsely. Toss with a little olive oil and sea salt. Steam beetroots until tender, about 25 minutes. Slip off skins, trim off tops and tails, quarter the beets, place in a bowl, and sprinkle with a little vinegar. To make sauce: Soak bread in vinegar on a plate. Pound garlic with 1/2 teaspoon salt in a mortar, then work in marjoram, capers, half the pine nuts, parsley, and olives, until coarsely pureed. Add soaked bread and olive oil; work it until sauce is thick. Add pepper and more vinegar, if desired. Toss beets with sauce, leaving streaks throughout. Place greens on small plates or large platter. Place beets on greens. Drain onions; strew them over beets. Garnish with remaining pine nuts. Deborah Madison contributed this from her book, *Local Flavors: Cooking and Eating from America's Farmers' Markets*. Makes 4 servings.

Beet and Horseradish Relish   Twinhawks Hollow Farm

horseradish root
1 cup sour cream

2 pounds beets, cooked and chopped
1 teaspoon sugar

Scrape and wash horseradish root. Grate desired amount into sour cream; let stand 2 hours. Blend beets, 2 tablespoons additional horseradish, and sugar until beets are coarsely chopped. Add sour cream mixture. Cover and chill several days to blend flavors. Makes 6-8 servings.

Beth's Grandmother's Pickled Beets   Beth Salerno, Good Earth Farm

2 pounds beets
1 medium white onion, sliced
1 cup sugar
1 1/4 cups white vinegar

1 teaspoon whole allspice
2 whole cloves
1 stick cinnamon

Boil or steam beets until tender. Reserve 1 cup of the cooking liquid, then drain beets and let them get cool enough to handle. Peel, slice, and pack beets and onions into 3 pint jars. Combine reserved liquid, sugar, vinegar, allspice, cloves, and cinnamon in a pot; bring to simmer and cook 5 minutes. Strain; pour over beets. Cool, cover, and refrigerate 24 hours. Makes 3 pints.

Fried Beets 'n' Carrots   Linda Derrickson, Sunporch Café

2 tablespoons olive oil
2 teaspoons cumin seeds
2 medium beets, quartered, sliced 1/4-inch thick

2 medium carrots, sliced 1/4-inch thick
tamari sauce
beet tops, fresh spinach, or Swiss chard

Heat olive oil in skillet. Add cumin; cook about 1 minute. Add beets and carrots; fry until tender. Remove from heat, sprinkle on a little tamari, and serve. Variation: If using young beets, save the tops. When the beets and carrots are tender, add chopped greens, cover, and cook until soft. Toss mixture, sprinkle with tamari, and serve. Makes 2-4 servings.

Two-Way Street Beets   MACSAC

2 bunches small beets
juice of 1 orange
1 tablespoon butter, softened
pepper

1 teaspoon peanut oil
1 teaspoon dark sesame oil
1 teaspoon hot chili oil
1-2 tablespoons soy sauce

Cut beets off stems. Gently scrub beets. Wash the greens. Cut stems into 3-inch pieces and coarsely chop the greens; set aside stems and greens in separate piles. Steam beets until tender, 20-30 minutes. Cool briefly, slip off skins, and cut into wedges. Toss with orange juice, butter, and pepper to taste; cover and keep warm. Meanwhile, heat heavy skillet over medium flame. Add oils. Add stems; sauté 2-3 minutes. Add greens; cook, tossing often, until limp. Toss in soy sauce and pepper to taste. Arrange beets over greens on platter. Makes 6 servings.

Roasted Beet Salad   Jenny Bonde and Rink DaVee, Shooting Star Farm

6-8 small beets, scrubbed, tops trimmed to 1 inch
olive oil
salt and pepper to taste
1/4 cup pecans
1 tablespoon Dijon mustard

4 tablespoons white wine vinegar
1/2 cup extra-virgin olive oil
4 cups baby salad greens
1/2 small bottle onion or sweet onion, thinly sliced
1/4 cup crumbled blue cheese

Heat outdoor or indoor grill. Place beets on heavy foil; drizzle with olive oil and sprinkle with salt and pepper. Wrap tightly; grill until beets can be easily pierced with a fork, about 30 minutes. Meanwhile, toast pecans in a dry pan on the grill, tossing frequently. Finely chop the nuts. When beets are cooled a bit, use a paper towel to remove the peel, stems, and tails. Cut beets into quarters. Combine mustard and vinegar in a bowl. Whisk in olive oil until thickened. Add salt and pepper. Toss salad greens in a bowl with a little dressing. Portion the greens onto 2-4 plates. Top with beets, onions, blue cheese, and pecans. Drizzle with as much more dressing as you like. Adapted from Michael Waupoose's winner in the 2001 Food for Thought Recipe Contest. Feta and walnuts may be substituted; dried cranberries may be added. Makes 2-4 servings.

And just in case anyone is still having problems getting down his or her beets…

Beet Chocolate Cake   Zephyr Community Farm

2 cups sugar
2 cups flour
1/2 teaspoon salt
2 teaspoons baking powder
1 teaspoon baking soda

3-4 ounces unsweetened chocolate
4 eggs
1/4 cup oil
3 cups shredded beets

Heat oven to 325 degrees. Grease two 9-inch cake pans. Whisk dry ingredients together. Melt chocolate very slowly over low heat or in double boiler. Cool chocolate; blend thoroughly with eggs and oil. Combine flour mixture with chocolate mixture, alternating with the beets. Pour into pans. Bake until fork can be removed from center cleanly, 40-50 minutes. Makes 10 servings.

Bok Choy

Brassica rapa var. chinensis

Bok choy, which may be written as bok choi, bak choy, or pac choi, is a traditional stir-fry vegetable from China. In eastern Asia, hundreds of plants in the brassica family are cultivated, many of them bok choy types. Only a few of these crops have transferred to use in the western world, and did not appear at all until the 1800s. As with many other Asian vegetables, bok choy is still a specialty crop in this country, but it is gaining popularity in the East-meets-West cooking style.

Bok choy's growing season is limited to the cooler weather of spring and fall. Spring crops, well loved by the tiny garden pest the flea beetle during its early spring feeding frenzy, must be covered well to survive. Like many brassicas, bok choy does especially well in the fall. Fall crops withstand light frost very well, actually increasing in sweetness.

Bok choy is a great nutritional gift and often touted as the garden vegetable highest in calcium. Whether this is the truth or not, you can be confident that bok choy is an excellent source of vitamins A, B-complex, C, and some minerals. All of this for only 24 calories per one-cup serving!

Cooking Tips

- For stir-fry, separate leaves from the thick white stem and chop both into 2-inch-wide diagonal chunks. The stem pieces should be added to the stir-fry several minutes before leaves, as they need more cooking time.

- Bok choy can complement a stir-fry with other vegetables, or can *be* the stir-fry. Try sautéing onions until they begin to soften. Then add bok choy stems, tofu chunks, soy sauce, and grated ginger root. Add the bok choy leaves last. Serve with rice or noodles.

- Bok choy, like other leafy greens, can be simply steamed. (Again, start stems cooking first.) Toss with a favorite marinade. Create an Asian flavor by tossing bok choy with a light coating of toasted sesame oil, soy sauce, and rice vinegar.

Storage Tips

- Wrap bok choy in a damp towel or put it in a plastic bag and place in the hydrator drawer of the refrigerator.

- Store for up to 1 week. Leaves will lose integrity and wilt if allowed to dry out.

For additional recipes that feature bok choy, see the Seasonal Combinations chapter.

Sesame Soy Braised Bok Choy   MACSAC

1 head bok choy
2 tablespoons peanut oil
1 tablespoon grated ginger
1 tablespoon minced garlic
1/2 cup chicken stock
1 tablespoon toasted sesame oil

2 tablespoons soy sauce
2 teaspoons rice vinegar
1 teaspoon sugar
salt and pepper
2 tablespoons sesame seeds

Trim the root end off the bok choy head. Slice the leafy portions of the plant from the stalks. Cut both the leaves and the stalks into large matchstick-size pieces ("julienne"), keeping the two piles separate. Heat very large, heavy skillet or wok until it looks hazy over the surface, 2-4 minutes. Add peanut oil and swirl it to coat the pan. Add bok choy stems; stir-fry about 5 minutes. Add ginger and garlic and stir-fry briefly. Add bok choy greens, chicken stock, sesame oil, soy sauce, rice vinegar, sugar, and salt and pepper to taste. Cover, reduce heat to medium-low, and cook until bok choy is tender and glazed with sauce, 5-8 minutes. Remove cover, sprinkle with sesame seeds, increase heat to medium-high, and cook until excess liquid evaporates, 2-3 minutes. Adjust seasonings to taste. Makes 4 servings.

Grilled Pork Chops and Bok Choy with Sesame Garlic Glaze   MACSAC

3 tablespoons soy sauce
1 1/2 tablespoons sesame oil
1 1/2-2 teaspoons bottled Vietnamese-style
  chili garlic sauce

4 pork chops (5/8-inch-thick)
8 large stalks boy choy (including greens),
  root ends trimmed

Combine soy sauce, sesame oil, and chili garlic sauce in a large, deep plate or dish. Place pork chops in the mixture, turning to coat all surfaces. Let stand at room temperature, turning the chops occasionally, while you prepare coals in an outdoor grill to medium-high heat. When coals are ready, remove chops from the marinade and grill them until just done, 3-4 minutes per side. Meanwhile, grill the bok choy stalks until tender, about the same amount of time as the chops, basting them with the remaining marinade while they cook. Serve with rice or an Asian noodle dish. Makes 4 servings.

Stir-Fried Bok Choy with Cashew Sauce   Jenny Bonde and Rink DaVee, Shooting Star Farm

1/2 cup raw cashews
1/4 cup white wine vinegar
1/4 cup sugar
1/4 cup soy sauce

1 tablespoon minced gingerroot
pinch of red pepper flakes
1 1/2 pounds bok choy
1/4 cup peanut oil

Toast cashews in a dry skillet, tossing frequently, until lightly brown and fragrant. Combine cashews, vinegar, sugar, soy sauce, ginger, red pepper flakes, and 2-4 tablespoons water in a blender or food processor; puree until smooth. Set aside. Wash bok choy stems and leaves well, making sure to rinse away dirt in the ribs. Separate the bok choy leaves from the stalks. Cut stalks into 1-inch pieces and roughly chop the leaves. Heat peanut oil in a large skillet over high heat until hot but not smoking. Add bok choy stems and cook, stirring often, until crisp-tender, 2-3 minutes. Add the leaves and cook until they wilt and turn bright green, another minute or so. Remove to a platter and cover with cashew sauce, or serve sauce on the side. This recipe is modified from one found on the Internet. You may substitute rice vinegar for the white wine vinegar (for a milder sauce) and toasted, salted cashews for the roasted nuts. Makes 4 servings.

Chicken with Bok Choy and Bitter Melon   MACSAC

1 small bitter melon (an Asian vegetable)
1 tablespoon salt
2 tablespoons vegetable oil, divided
1/2 pound skinless chicken breast meat, diced
1 teaspoon minced garlic

2 green onions, chopped
4-5 stalks bok choy or 2 heads baby bok choy, chopped
1 tablespoon soy sauce
1 tablespoon sugar
cooked rice

Cut bitter melon in half lengthwise; scoop out seeds and discard them. Chop the flesh, toss it with salt in colander, and let stand 20-30 minutes. Rinse well; squeeze out excess liquid. Heat 1 tablespoon of the oil over high heat in large, heavy skillet. Add chicken, garlic, and green onions; stir-fry until barely tender, 3-4 minutes. Remove to a bowl. Wipe out pan; heat again with remaining oil. Add bitter melon and bok choy; stir-fry until barely tender, 3-4 minutes. Stir in soy sauce and sugar. Stir in chicken and heat through. Serve with rice. Makes 2-4 servings.

Sake Braised Bok Choy   MACSAC

1 1/2 cups sake (rice wine)

6-8 heads green-stemmed baby bok choy

Heat sake in very large skillet over medium-high flame until it begins to simmer. Add baby bok choy heads, placing their stem ends toward the middle of the pan. Cover, reduce heat to medium, and cook until bok choy is barely tender, 3-5 minutes. Remove bok choy to a plate and keep warm. Raise heat to high and reduce sake until it reaches a glaze consistency. Drizzle glaze over bok choy and serve immediately. Makes 3-4 large or 6-8 small servings.

Bok Choy with Lemongrass and Red Peppers   MACSAC

3 very young, tender stalks fresh lemongrass
2 tablespoons vegetable oil
1 bunch bok choy, sliced on the diagonal
1 sweet red pepper, cut into thin strips
4 green onions, cut into 1-inch pieces

1 tablespoon minced garlic
minced red or green chiles to taste
2 tablespoons soy sauce
1/2 teaspoon sugar
4 tablespoons chopped fresh basil, mint, or cilantro

Thinly slice lemongrass on the diagonal. Heat oil over high heat in large, heavy skillet; add bok choy and stir-fry 3-4 minutes. Add red pepper; stir-fry 1-2 minutes. Add green onions, garlic, and chiles; stir-fry until bok choy is crisp-tender, 1-2 minutes. Toss in soy sauce, sugar, and herbs. Makes 4-6 servings.

Lunchtime Bok Choy Fried Rice   MACSAC

2 teaspoons peanut oil, divided
2 teaspoons sesame oil, divided
1/4 cup diced carrots
1 cup diced bok choy
1 1/2 cups leftover cooked rice
  (chilled or at room temperature)
1/2 cup leftover cooked diced lamb, beef, pork,
  or poultry

1/2 teaspoon minced ginger
3 tablespoons chopped green onion
1 egg
bottled chili garlic paste (optional)
1 1/2 tablespoons soy sauce

Heat a wok or cast-iron skillet over medium-high flame a few minutes. Add 1 teaspoon each of the peanut and sesame oils; swirl to coat bottom of pan. Add carrots; stir-fry 2 minutes. Add bok choy; stir-fry 2 minutes. Push vegetables to outer edges of pan, add remaining peanut oil, and swirl to coat exposed surface. Add rice, meat, and ginger; stir-fry 2-3 minutes. Stir in the green onion. Push the mixture to the outside edges of the pan, add the remaining sesame oil to the center of the pan, and swirl to coat exposed surface. Crack egg into the hot oil and scramble it. Cook until egg is set, then break up egg into pieces and toss it with the rest of the mixture in the pan. Add a little chili garlic paste, if desired, and stir in the soy sauce. Continue to stir-fry another moment or two, scraping all bits from the bottom of the pan. Serve hot. Makes 2 servings.

Flank Steak and Bok Choy in Oyster Sauce   MACSAC

12 ounces flank steak
4 tablespoons bottled oyster sauce
2 tablespoon rice wine or white wine, divided
1 teaspoon honey, divided
2 teaspoons cornstarch

1 pound bok choy
pinch salt
3 tablespoons peanut oil, divided
hot cooked rice or soba noodles

Slice flank steak across the grain into very thin slices (it's easier to do this if you partially freeze the meat first). Mix oyster sauce, 1 tablespoon of the rice wine, 1/2 teaspoon of the honey, and the cornstarch in a small bowl; set aside. Slice bok choy diagonally into 1-inch pieces. Heat a wok or large, heavy skillet over highest flame several minutes. Add 1 1/2 tablespoons of the peanut oil, swirl the pan, add bok choy, and stir-fry 2 minutes. Add a pinch of salt, remaining tablespoon of rice wine, remaining 1/2 teaspoon of honey, and 2 tablespoons water. Continue to cook, stirring constantly, until bok choy is tender, 1-2 minutes. Transfer bok choy to a serving platter; keep warm. Wipe pan clean and heat it again over highest flame. Add remaining 1 1/2 tablespoons peanut oil, swirl the pan, and add flank steak. Stir-fry until beef loses much of its redness, 2-3 minutes. Stir in reserved sauce mixture, bring to boil, and cook briefly until thickened. Pour flank steak over bok choy. Serve immediately with hot rice or noodles. Adapted from a recipe learned in a Chinese cooking class in the early 1980s. Makes 4 servings.

Spicy Bok Choy with Sesame Noodles   MACSAC

1 package (8-9 ounces) fresh sesame- or
   garlic-flavored linguine
1 tablespoon peanut oil
1 tablespoon sesame oil
1 tablespoon minced ginger
2 teaspoons minced garlic
1/2 teaspoon hot red pepper flakes

4 heads baby bok choy, bottoms trimmed,
   heads cut in half lengthwise
8-12 brown mushrooms, thick-sliced, or
   1 yellow sweet pepper, cut into chunks
1 cup sake (rice wine) or chicken stock
2 tablespoons soy sauce

Boil noodles in lots of salted water until barely tender. Drain and keep warm. Meanwhile, heat a wok or very large, heavy skillet over highest flame. Add oils, swirl the pan to coat its bottom, and add the ginger, garlic, and hot pepper flakes. (Keep your face away from the steam; it's spicy!) Stir-fry for 30 seconds or less, then add the bok choy and mushrooms (or sweet pepper) and continue to stir-fry another 2-3 minutes. Add the sake or stock and soy sauce, cover the wok, and let steam until everything is tender, 5-8 more minutes. Divide the noodles among 4 soup plates or deep bowls. Portion the bok choy mixture over the noodles. Serve immediately. Makes 4 servings.

Crunchy Bok Choy Ginger Salad   MACSAC

1 medium bunch bok choy
1 cup shredded daikon radish
1 tablespoon salt
1/2 cup slivered sweet orange, red, or yellow peppers
1/4 cup finely chopped green onions

1-inch knob of gingerroot, grated
2 tablespoons each chopped mint and cilantro
3 tablespoons rice vinegar
2 teaspoons honey
pepper to taste

Thin-slice the bok choy leaves. Thinly slice the stems on the diagonal. Toss bok choy leaves and stems, and the shredded radish, with salt in colander. Let stand to wilt vegetables, about 1/2 hour. Rinse, drain, and squeeze out excess liquid from mixture. Place in paper or cotton towels and squeeze again. Toss with remaining ingredients in bowl and chill before serving. Makes 6 servings.

Broccoli

Brassica oleracea

Broccoli has evolved from wild cabbage varieties growing along the coasts of Europe and was first cultivated by the ancient Romans.

The broccoli's recent rise to popularity is attributable to its fantastic nutritional makeup. When fresh and not overcooked, your broccoli will reach the table loaded with vitamin A, C, calcium, potassium, and iron. Broccoli is also touted as an "anti-cancer" vegetable due to a special enzyme called sulforaphane.

While certain varieties will stand up to some mid-summer heat or possibly even thrive during a cool spell, locally grown broccoli is generally available early summer and fall. As the broccoli's head is the plant's immature flower, prolonged heat will force the plant to flower too quickly, resulting in smaller, looser, and bolted heads.

Cooking Tips

- Soak head upside down in cold, salted water to remove any hidden field pests.

- Remove lowest part of the stem if woody or tough.

- Fresh broccoli can be eaten raw, chopped into green salads, or paired with a dip.

- Chop and separate florets, steam lightly for 5-7 minutes, and use as a dipping vegetable (chilled) or toss into a pasta salad. Light steaming increases digestibility, heightens color, and retains most of the nutrients.

- Toss broccoli florets into casseroles, quiches, stir-fry, on top of pizza, etc.

- Kids love "trees and cheese"—broccoli topped with cheese sauce.

- Top steamed broccoli with butter, a squeeze of lemon juice, and a sprinkle of your favorite grated cheese.

Storage Tips

- Broccoli is best used within a few days. Store in a plastic bag in the hydrator drawer of the refrigerator.

- For long-term storage, broccoli freezes well. Cut into florets and slice stems. Blanch for 3-4 minutes, rinse in cold water to stop the cooking process, drain, let dry, and place in an airtight container such as a zip-lock freezer bag. See chapter on home food preservation for more information on freezing vegetables.

For additional recipes that feature broccoli, see the Seasonal Combinations and Kids' Recipes chapters.

Pasta with Broccoli Florets   Lorene Ludy, Zephyr Community Farm member

florets cut from 1 head of broccoli
1/2 pound pasta
2 tablespoons olive oil
2 tablespoons butter

1 clove garlic, minced
1/2 pound mushrooms (whole, halved, or sliced)
1/4 cup grated Parmesan

Cook broccoli florets in boiling water 2-3 minutes. Remove with slotted spoon. Cook pasta in same water (or use fresh). Meanwhile, heat olive oil and butter in skillet. Sauté garlic and mushrooms 3-4 minutes. Stir in broccoli. Drain pasta. Toss with broccoli mixture and cheese. Makes 2-4 servings.

Tofu Broccoli Cashew Peanut Madness   Rob Summerbell, MACSAC member

1 tablespoon butter or oil
1 large onion, chopped
1 clove garlic, minced
1 pound herbed tofu, cubed
2 tablespoons tamari or soy sauce, divided
1/2-3/4 cup peanut butter, preferably crunchy

2-3 teaspoons lemon juice
1/4 teaspoon cumin or more to taste
cayenne to taste
1 medium head broccoli, peeled and chopped
hot, cooked brown rice
handful of roasted cashews, chopped

Heat butter or oil in skillet; add onion and garlic; sauté until soft. Add tofu and 1 tablespoon tamari; sauté until brown. Remove from pan. In same pan, mix peanut butter, lemon juice, remaining tablespoon tamari, cumin, and cayenne. Thin with up to 1 cup water to obtain gravylike texture. Stir in tofu mixture. Steam broccoli. Serve sauce over broccoli and brown rice, topped with cashews. Makes 4 servings.

Roasted Broccoli   MACSAC

1 head broccoli, large stem and medium stems
    removed and reserved for another use
1 1/2 tablespoons olive oil

1/2 teaspoon garlic salt
1 teaspoon balsamic vinegar
1/4 teaspoon ground black pepper

Heat oven to 400 degrees. Break broccoli head into medium florets and toss with remaining ingredients. Arrange in single layer on baking sheet. Bake 18-22 minutes, shaking the pan halfway through the cooking time. Remove from oven when broccoli is a deep green color with some darkened spots. Makes 4 servings.

Broccoli Basil Quiche   Julie Worzala

1 pie pan lined with pie dough
    (prepared from scratch or store-bought)
1 cup finely diced broccoli
2 green onions, chopped
1 cup shredded cheddar or Gruyere cheese
1 tablespoon flour

3 eggs, lightly beaten
1 cup half-and-half, heavy cream, or milk
2 tablespoons basil pesto
1/4 teaspoon salt
1/8 teaspoon pepper
1/8 teaspoon garlic powder

Heat oven to 425 degrees. Prick bottom and sides of crust and line with foil. Bake 8 minutes, remove foil, and bake another 8 minutes. Reduce oven to 325 degrees. Toss broccoli, green onions, cheese, and flour in a bowl. Spread mixture over the bottom of the crust. Whisk remaining ingredients in the bowl. Pour filling into crust. Bake until knife inserted near center comes out clean, about 35-40 minutes. Makes 6 servings.

Brussels Sprout

Brassica oleracea var. gemnifera

Brussels sprouts. You may love them or hate them. Perhaps as a child you were forced to face a pile of these funny little cabbages on your plate. You knew you were not going to like them…Well, it's true. Brussels sprouts, with their mildly pungent, mustard-like aroma and flavor are rarely a favorite in childhood. But do not give up on them. Fresh and well prepared, this vegetable will likely jump to the top of your list. You may be pleasantly surprised to find yourself among the growing ranks of Brussels sprout enthusiasts.

As their name suggests, Brussels sprouts were first cultivated in Brussels. Like broccoli, its ancestor grew wild in the low countries of Europe. The Belgians first selected the sprout for its enlarged auxiliary buds, resembling miniature cabbages.

Nutritionally speaking, Brussels sprouts contain high amounts of vegetable protein and carbohydrates. Brussels sprouts, along with some of the other cabbage family vegetables, are thought to be a digestive stimulant.

Brussels sprouts are best from cool climates. The sprout itself will improve in flavor, sweetness, and tenderness with exposure to a few frosts. The towering wide-leafed plant will be one of the last garden survivors when serious winter weather finally arrives.

Cooking Tips

- To clean and prepare for cooking, simply pare off the tough bottom part of the sprout stem and remove the two outermost leaves.

- Boil or steam sprouts approximately 5-8 minutes. Be careful not to overcook! They are best when tender but not mushy.

- Toss sprouts in olive oil, lemon juice, and a dash of salt and pepper, or top with a pat of butter.

- Marinate cooked sprouts overnight in your favorite dressing for use in salads.

- Toss sprouts into hearty soups and stews.

- Try a puree of Brussels sprout soup with snippets of fresh herbs and sautéed onion. Leave a few sprouts whole to float in the soup.

Storage Tips

- Refrigerate unwashed sprouts in a plastic bag.

- They're best if used fresh, but Brussels sprouts should retain integrity for up to 1 week. They will last longer but may sacrifice some nutrients and color, and will increase in odor.

- For long-term storage, Brussels sprouts may be frozen. Blanch sprouts for 3-5 minutes, rinse in cold water to stop the cooking process, drain, let dry, and pack into airtight containers, such as zip-lock freezer bags. See chapter on home food preservation for more information on freezing vegetables.

Brussels Sprouts with Bacon-Fried Green Onions   MACSAC

1 pound Brussels sprouts, trimmed and cut in
   half lengthwise
2 slices thick-cut bacon

12 slender green onions
2-3 tablespoons apple cider or beer
pepper

Bring a pot of salted water to boil; add Brussels sprouts and blanch 2-3 minutes. Drain. Meanwhile, cook bacon in skillet until crispy; remove bacon, drain on paper towels, chop it into pieces, and reserve. Discard all but 1-2 tablespoons fat in the pan. Cut off the top 3-4 inches from the green ends of the onions (reserve the ends for another use). Sauté the onions in the bacon fat until barely tender, 1-2 minutes. Stir in apple cider or beer and cook to heat through. Add the drained Brussels sprouts and reserved bacon to the pan, stir well, and heat through. Season with pepper to taste. Top each serving with three green onions crisscrossed atop them. Makes 4 servings.

Brussels Sprouts and Cherry Tomato Salad   MACSAC

4-5 cups small Brussels sprouts, trimmed
1 cup cherry tomatoes, halved
1 teaspoon minced garlic
1/3 cup julienned basil (that is, cut into thin strips)

3 tablespoons extra-virgin olive oil
1 tablespoon sherry vinegar
2 tablespoons grated Parmesan cheese
salt and pepper to taste

Add Brussels sprouts to boiling, salted water. Boil until crisp-tender, 3-5 minutes. Drain; immerse in ice water to cool. Drain well and let dry, or dry Brussels sprouts in kitchen towels. Toss with remaining ingredients. Serve at room temperature or chilled. Makes 4-6 servings.

Omelet with Brussels Sprouts Chiffonade, Seasoned Croutons, and Pecorino Cheese
Ben Hunter, Catacombs Coffeehouse

For each omelet:
6 Brussels sprouts
1 shallot
2 sprigs fresh thyme

1/4 of a skinny baguette, crusts trimmed off
about 1 tablespoon olive oil, or more as desired
salt and pepper
3 eggs
2 ounces grated pecorino cheese

Trim Brussels sprouts, cut them in half, and finely shave them with a sharp knife or on a mandolin so you end up with ribbons. Coarsely chop the shallot. Mash some salt and pepper with the thyme in a mortar and pestle. Rip the bread into 1/4- to 1/2-inch pieces. Combine Brussels sprouts, shallot, thyme mixture, bread, and olive oil in a bowl. Heat a 10-inch nonstick pan over high flame. Heat the broiler, too. Add Brussels sprouts mixture to the pan and cook, stirring often to prevent shallot from burning, until mixture crisps up, 6-8 minutes. Meanwhile, beat eggs in a bowl. Add eggs to pan, watch them sizzle, and when they begin to set at the edges, use a spatula to push cooked areas toward center of pan while tilting the pan to allow uncooked areas to cook. Do this until most of the omelet is cooked. Turn off pan and sprinkle cheese over the omelet. Place in broiler until eggs have risen and cheese is melted, 1-2 minutes. Begin to slide the omelet onto a plate, and when it is halfway there, tip the pan so the omelet folds in half. Makes 1 omelet.

Seared Brussels Sprouts Braised with Apple Cider   Ben Hunter, Catacombs Coffeehouse

12 large Brussels sprouts
salt

cooking oil
1/4 cup apple cider

Trim Brussels sprouts and cut in half. Heat a cast-iron pan over medium flame. Add some oil. Sprinkle salt evenly over bottom of pan. Lay Brussels sprouts cut side down in the pan. Cook until deep brown or almost black in some places, about 5 minutes. Add apple cider, cover pan, and turn off heat. Let them continue cooking off the heat another 5 minutes. Serve with grilled chicken or black-eyed peas. Makes 2 servings.

Brussels Sprouts with Bacon and Balsamic Vinegar   Lee Davenport, Harmony Valley Farm member

1 pound Brussels sprouts
1/4 pound bacon, chopped
1/2 cup finely chopped onion or shallots

1-2 tablespoons butter
3 tablespoons balsamic vinegar
salt and pepper to taste

Trim ends off Brussels sprouts and halve the large ones. Blanch in boiling water or steam over boiling water until just tender. Plunge into ice water to stop the cooking and preserve the bright green color, then drain well. Meanwhile, cook bacon until crisp and drain on paper towels. Remove all but 2 tablespoons of bacon grease from pan. Add onions; cook until brown. Add Brussels sprouts, butter, vinegar, salt, pepper, and bacon. Toss until hot. Makes 4 servings.

Roasted Brussels Sprouts with Crisped Pancetta   MACSAC

1 pound Brussels sprouts, trimmed
1 tablespoon olive oil
1/2 teaspoon garlic salt

1/4 pound pancetta (Italian bacon), cut into slivers
salt and pepper to taste

Heat oven to 425 degrees. Halve the large sprouts. Toss with olive oil and garlic salt; arrange in single layer on baking sheet. Bake, shaking pan halfway through roasting time, until tender (15-25 minutes, depending on size of sprouts). Brussels sprouts are done when they're deep green with several brown caramelized spots. Meanwhile, sauté pancetta over medium heat until crisp. Toss Brussels sprouts with pancetta. Season with salt and pepper. Makes 4 servings.

Sesame Garlic Brussels Sprouts   MACSAC

1/4 cup soy sauce
3 tablespoons toasted sesame oil
1/4 teaspoon crushed red pepper flakes

1 1/2 tablespoons minced garlic
1 1/2 pounds Brussels sprouts, trimmed and halved
4-5 tablespoons peanut or canola oil

Combine soy sauce, sesame oil, crushed pepper, garlic, and 3 tablespoons water in a large bowl. Blanch the Brussels sprouts in boiling water until partially tender, 3-4 minutes. Drain well. Heat wok or large, heavy skillet over high flame until the air looks hazy over the pan, 2-4 minutes. Add a small amount of the peanut oil, swirl the pan to coat the surface, and add about a third of the sprouts. Stir-fry until bright green and crisp-tender. Drain on paper towels. Stir-fry the remaining sprouts similarly, in batches. Add stir-fried Brussels sprouts to soy sauce mixture and toss well. Serve immediately or allow Brussels sprouts to marinate one or more hours before serving. Makes 6 servings.

Brussels Sprouts and Portobello Mushrooms   MACSAC

1 pound Brussels sprouts, trimmed
1 tablespoon olive oil
1 tablespoon minced garlic
1/2 red bell pepper, diced

4 ounces portobello mushrooms, diced (about 1 1/2 cups)
2 tablespoons balsamic vinegar
salt and pepper to taste

Add Brussels sprouts to a large pot of boiling, salted water and cook until crisp-tender, 4-6 minutes. Drain; immerse in ice water or run under cold water. Drain well; let stand to dry, or dry in a kitchen towel. (They may be held at this point until you're ready to finish the dish.) Heat olive oil in large, heavy skillet over high flame. Stir in garlic. Stir in red pepper and mushrooms. Sauté until mushrooms release juices and liquid evaporates, 10-12 minutes. Stir in vinegar; boil until dry. Toss in sprouts and heat through. Season with salt and pepper. Makes 4 servings.

Brussels Sprouts with Egg Crumbles   MACSAC

1 pound Brussels sprouts, trimmed
2 tablespoons butter, divided
3 tablespoons dried bread crumbs

1-2 hard-cooked eggs, chopped
salt and pepper to taste

Halve the sprouts lengthwise and blanch in salted, boiling water until barely tender, 4-6 minutes. Drain, immerse in ice water to cool, and drain again. Heat 1 tablespoon butter in skillet over medium flame. Stir in bread crumbs; cook, stirring, about 1 minute. Stir in chopped egg and transfer to a small bowl. Wipe out pan, add remaining butter, and melt over medium-high flame. Add Brussels sprouts and toss until hot. Season with salt and pepper. Place in shallow serving dish; sprinkle with topping. Makes 4 servings.

Lemon Marinated Brussels Sprouts   MACSAC

1 1/2 pounds Brussels sprouts
1/4 cup olive oil
1 tablespoon chopped fresh parsley
1 teaspoon minced garlic
1/2 teaspoon sugar
1/2 teaspoon dried oregano

salt and pepper to taste
1 teaspoon grated lemon zest (grate only the outer, yellow portion of the peel)
3 tablespoons lemon juice
1 tablespoon apple cider vinegar

Trim Brussels sprouts; cut larger ones in half. Cook in boiling water until barely tender, 5-6 minutes. Drain well. Combine remaining ingredients—except lemon juice and apple cider vinegar—in a medium bowl. Toss in the Brussels sprouts and let them marinate in this mixture 1-2 hours at room temperature (or longer in the refrigerator), tossing occasionally. Just before serving, mix in the lemon juice and apple cider vinegar. Adjust any of the seasonings to taste. Serve as an appetizer on toothpicks, as a side dish, or in salads. They're also great with a sprinkling of Parmesan cheese. Makes 6 servings.

Creamed Brussels Sprouts with Pearl Onions   MACSAC

1 pound pearl onions
1 pound Brussels sprouts
5 tablespoons unsalted butter, divided
1/2 teaspoon dried thyme
1 cup turkey or chicken stock
2 tablespoons flour
2 cups milk
1 cup heavy cream

1/2 teaspoon salt
1/2 teaspoon white pepper
1/2 teaspoon Dijon mustard
2 teaspoons lemon juice
1/4 teaspoon grated nutmeg
1/3 cup bread crumbs
1/3 cup Parmesan cheese

To make the onions easy to peel, boil them for 1 minute in water and drain. When they are cool enough to handle, cut an "X" in their stem ends and peel them. Cut an "X" into the stem ends of the Brussels sprouts and pull off any wilted leaves. Melt 2 tablespoons of the butter in a large skillet over medium-high flame. Add Brussels sprouts, onions, and thyme; sauté the mixture about 5 minutes. Add the stock, bring to a boil, cover, reduce heat, and simmer until vegetables are tender, 10-15 minutes. Meanwhile, melt another 2 tablespoons butter in a saucepan; whisk in flour and cook, stirring, about 2 minutes. Whisk in milk and cream; cook until thickened, stirring occasionally, about 5 minutes. Stir in salt, pepper, mustard, lemon juice, and nutmeg. Heat oven to 350 degrees. Toss vegetables and sauce in a 3-quart casserole dish. Mix bread crumbs and cheese; spread evenly over vegetables. Bake 30 minutes. Cut the last tablespoon of butter into bits; scatter over casserole and broil until browned, about 2 minutes. Makes 6-8 servings.

Burdock Root
(Gobo)

The burdock root is an unusual vegetable in this country. Also known by its Japanese name, gobo, the burdock root is native to northern China and Siberia.

Gobo has been an important vegetable in Japan, cultivated there since the tenth century. In recent years, burdock root has had a resurgence of popularity in Japan, particularly with the health-conscious in Tokyo and other urban areas.

The Japanese believe gobo to be a strong blood purifier, a support to healthy liver function, a tonic after sickness, and an aid to arthritis and skin diseases.

The burdock root belongs to the specialty market in this country, mostly found in Asian groceries. Most Americans are familiar with burdock as a common weed and the purveyor of the frustrating "burrs." They stick to anything, especially clothing and fur that transports their opportunistic seed pods to a new location. The tenacious burr supposedly inspired the inventor of Velcro.

Few of us, however, realize the excellent food value of the tremendously long root vegetable or its potential medicinal qualities. Nutritionally the burdock root offers a wealth of minerals, such as iron, chromium, magnesium, silicon, calcium, and potassium, in a very high-fiber package. Burdock roots are ready for harvest in the fall and, like many fall roots, make a fine storage crop.

Cooking Tips

- Scrub the burdock root well to remove mud and tiny root hairs. Do not peel. The skin contains flavor and nutrients. Cut away any damaged areas.

- Burdock roots must be cooked. Shred or thinly slice to insure tenderness. When cooking with other veggies, add burdock first and cook until almost tender before adding the others.

- Stir-fry burdock alone or with other vegetables. You can also deep-fry it in a tempura batter.

- Add burdock to soups, stews, or a seasoned broth.

- Steam and serve hot, dipped in soy sauce.

- Add shredded burdock to brown rice, along with shredded carrots and Asian mushrooms.

- Burdock goes well with other root veggies. See the sections on Rutabagas, Celeriac, Turnips, Carrots, etc.

Storage Tips

- Store burdock root in a plastic bag in the refrigerator for several days to a week.

- For long-term storage, burdock root may be packed in moist sand and kept in a cool location.

Kinpira Gobo (Spicy Burdock Root Sauté)   Harmony Valley Farm

3 medium burdock roots
1 carrot
1 teaspoon rice wine or apple cider vinegar
1 tablespoon tamari or soy sauce

1 1/2 teaspoons honey
1 tablespoon dark sesame oil
1/4 teaspoon hot pepper flakes
2 teaspoons toasted sesame seeds

Scrub burdock roots. Cut into 2-inch matchsticks; soak in cold water 1 hour, changing water once or twice. Peel and cut carrot into matchsticks. Mix vinegar, soy sauce, and honey in small cup. Heat oil in wok or heavy skillet. Stir-fry the vegetables 2-3 minutes (burdock should still be a bit crunchy). Sprinkle in pepper flakes; stir-fry 30 seconds. Add sauce; stir-fry 1 minute. Toast sesame seeds in dry skillet or hot oven several minutes, tossing often, and top dish. Makes 4 servings.

Burdock and Vegetables Soba Noodle Soup (or Salad)   Lucia Watson, Lucia's Restaurant

1 small package soba noodles
2 tablespoons toasted sesame oil
1 tablespoon soy or tamari sauce
a 1 1/2-inch knob of gingerroot, peeled
2 or more cloves garlic, minced and mashed to a paste
1 cup washed and stemmed cilantro, lightly chopped

a 6-inch piece burdock root, peeled and finely grated
6 cups chicken broth
4 cups mixed, chopped vegetables: carrots, cauliflower, broccoli, and scallions
sprigs of cilantro
additional soy sauce (optional)

Bring 2 quarts of water to a brisk boil. Add the soba noodles, stir, and cook *al dente,* about 5-7 minutes. Drain and toss with the sesame oil and soy sauce. Grate the ginger evenly into 4 serving bowls (squeeze the strings for their juice, too). Divide the pressed garlic, chopped cilantro, and grated burdock root into the bowls. Heat the chicken broth to a gentle boil, add all the vegetables and cook *al dente.* Add the cooked noodles and heat through. Ladle the noodle soup over the aromatics in each bowl, garnish with cilantro sprigs, and season to taste with additional soy sauce, if desired. You can vary this soup by adding tofu or cooked, sliced chicken breast, or by changing the vegetables with the season. In the summer, you can omit the stock and serve the dish cold, with roasted peanuts and chopped fresh mint on top. Makes 4 servings.

Lemony Burdock Sauté   Linda Halley, Harmony Valley Farm

burdock roots
2 teaspoons toasted sesame oil

1/2 teaspoon grated lemon peel (grate only the outer, yellow portion of the peel)
1 teaspoon white miso

Scrub the burdock but don't peel it. Shave the roots as thinly as possible with a sharp knife or on a mandolin, to make 2 cups. Heat the sesame oil in a pan over medium heat, add the burdock, and cook about 5 minutes, stirring frequently to remove the earthy taste. Add grated lemon peel and 1/2 cup water. Cover and cook until soft, 15-20 minutes. Stir in the white miso and simmer, uncovered, until excess water cooks off. Makes 4 servings.

Burdock Chips   Odessa Piper, L'Etoile Restaurant

burdock roots
vegetable oil

kosher salt to taste

Using a vegetable peeler, make slices from the burdock roots. Fry strips until crispy in oil heated to 325 degrees. Remove from oil and sprinkle with kosher salt. The crispy chips can be used for garnish on soups or as a fun side dish. Makes any number of servings.

Cabbage

Brassica oleracea var. capitata

Cabbage is perhaps the most globally cultivated of all the plants in the brassica family. It is eaten in almost every country around the world. With many different varieties available, cabbage adapts to many climes and altitudes. Fermented cabbage dishes like sauerkraut in northern Europe and kimchi in Korea were an early and widespread form of food preservation that has nourished humanity for centuries.

Here in the U.S., we see mostly the standard green, purple, and savoy cabbages. Most farms cultivate their cabbages in the early spring and fall, with harvests coming in the early summer and late fall, respectively. Fall varieties will grow into a tight, dense head, giving this vegetable remarkable storage capabilities with the appropriate root cellar conditions.

Cabbage weighs in at the bottom of the list, calorie-wise, with only 15 calories per one-cup serving, cooked. Though composed of 90 percent water, the cabbage still holds a significant quantity of vitamins and minerals, like vitamins A and C, calcium, potassium, and magnesium. Different varieties of cabbages have varying nutritional strengths. For example, the purple cabbage has more vitamin C, while the savoy has more vitamin A, calcium, iron, and potassium.

Cabbage, like other brassicas, has been used medicinally for centuries. Cabbage is still considered a beneficial digestive aid and intestinal cleanser.

Cooking Tips

- Cut cabbage head first into quarters, then diagonally across the wedge. Cut into thin slices for tossing raw into salads, or cut into thicker slices for steaming or boiling.

- Eat cabbage raw or lightly cooked. Overcooked cabbage may produce a strong odor and flavor.

- Steam wedges of chopped cabbage for 5-7 minutes. Top with butter and a pinch of salt and pepper or some grated cheese.

- Purple cabbage is very decorative and tasty chopped or sliced into green salads, pasta salads, fried rice, etc.

- Cabbage sautés and stir-fries very well with other vegetables. Experiment with a variety of combinations.

- Boil cabbage for five minutes with a chopped onion and add to mashed potatoes.

- Cabbage is well known in coleslaw. Chop cabbage to bite-size pieces, then toss with shredded raw carrots and green onion. Other diced or grated raw vegetables may be added. Add a mayonnaise/yogurt dill dressing or vinaigrette.

Storage Tips

- Refrigerate cabbage in a hydrator drawer. A plastic bag will help retain moisture but is not necessary. Do not remove outer leaves before storage.

- Properly stored, cabbage can last 3 weeks to 2 months in the refrigerator. It can last much longer in optimum root cellar conditions.

For more recipes that feature cabbage, see the Chinese Cabbage and Seasonal Combinations chapters.

Hot Cabbage Slaw   Madison Herb Society Cookbook, L. Poehlman

2 bacon strips or 1 tablespoon vegetable oil
1/4 cup chopped onion
6 cups shredded cabbage
chopped fresh dill to taste

pinch of sugar
salt and pepper to taste
1 tablespoon vinegar

Chop the bacon, fry in skillet, remove, and drain on paper towel. (Alternatively, heat oil.) Add onion and sauté until soft, about 5 minutes. Add 2 tablespoons water, the cabbage, dill, sugar, salt, and pepper; cover and simmer until wilted but still crunchy. Add bacon or oil and vinegar and toss. Makes 3-4 servings.

Spaetzle with Cabbage, Apple Wood-Smoked Bacon, and Cider Vinaigrette
Eric Rupert, Sub-Zero Freezer and Wolf Appliance Co.

4 slices apple wood–smoked bacon, chopped
3/4 cup whole milk
3 eggs
salt
2 cups flour
pinch of freshly grated whole nutmeg
3 cups apple cider

1 small red onion, finely diced
1 tart green apple, peeled, cored, and diced
1 tablespoon cider vinegar
pepper
2 or more tablespoons butter, divided
6 cups thinly sliced napa or savoy cabbage, divided
1/4-1/2 cup finely chopped flat leaf (Italian) parsley

Cook the bacon until fat is rendered and pieces are crispy. Drain on paper towels, reserving the fat. Bring a large pot of salted water to a rapid boil. Meanwhile, whisk milk, eggs, and 1 teaspoon salt in a bowl until smooth. Add flour and nutmeg, stirring just enough to make a slightly lumpy batter. Suspend a colander that has large holes over the boiling water. Pour the spaetzle batter into the colander and quickly press the batter through the holes, with your hand, into the water. Return water to a boil and boil the spaetzle 1 minute. Drain well through a clean colander. Toss with a small amount of reserved bacon fat. Set aside to air-dry.

Place apple cider in a saucepan, bring to a boil, and reduce it to 1/2 cup. Place the remaining bacon fat in another saucepan over medium-high heat. Add the onions and cook, stirring steadily, until translucent. Add the cider reduction, diced apple, vinegar, and salt and pepper to taste. Bring to a boil and let boil 1 minute. Set aside.

To finish the dish: Heat some of the butter in a very large nonstick sauté pan over highest heat. Add half the cabbage and season with a little salt and pepper. Allow the cabbage to wilt and brown a little, stirring occasionally. Remove to a bowl. Working in batches, cook and brown the rest of the cabbage and spaetzle. Combine all the cabbage and spaetzle in the pan and toss with the vinaigrette, reserved bacon, and parsley. Makes 4 servings.

Red Cabbage Slaw   Jill Watson, Taqueria Gila Monster Restaurant

1 head red cabbage
1 pound carrots
1 bunch cilantro
1/3 cup freshly squeezed lime juice

1/3 cup apple cider vinegar
2 tablespoons salt
1 tablespoon ancho chili powder

Quarter and core red cabbage. Slice thinly by hand or in food processor. Peel and grate carrots. Chop cilantro. Toss all ingredients. Let stand 1 hour. Toss again. Serve as a garnish for tacos, as a side dish for sandwiches, or as a picnic salad. Make 3-4 quarts.

Apple and Wine-Braised Red Cabbage   MACSAC

2 tablespoons canola oil
1/2 large head red cabbage, shredded or
   sliced as thinly as possible
1 onion, halved and cut as thinly as possible
salt and pepper

1/2 cup red wine
1/2 cup red wine vinegar
1/2 cup brown sugar
3 apples, cored and cut into eighths
1/2 cup raisins

Heat oil in large braiser or wok over medium-high flame. Add cabbage and onions; season with salt and pepper to taste, and stir well. Cover, reduce heat, and allow mixture to wilt slightly, about 5 minutes. Stir in wine, vinegar, and brown sugar. Cover and cook, stirring occasionally, about 45 minutes. Stir in apples and raisins; cook another 20-30 minutes. Add additional salt and pepper to taste. Makes 6 servings.

Red and Green Cabbage Salad with Thai-Style Fresh Herb Dressing   MACSAC

4-5 cups finely sliced or shredded red cabbage
4-5 cups finely sliced or shredded napa cabbage
1/2 cup slivered green onions

Dressing:
2 teaspoons minced garlic, pressed to a paste
1 hot chile (Thai, jalapeño, etc.), seeded and minced
3 tablespoons rice vinegar
1 tablespoon soy sauce
1 tablespoon tahini (sesame seed paste), peanut butter, or
   cashew butter
2 tablespoons olive oil
2 tablespoons dark sesame oil
2 tablespoons each chopped fresh mint, cilantro, and basil

Combine cabbages and green onions in a large bowl. Combine all dressing ingredients in a smaller bowl. Toss as much dressing as you like with cabbage. Serve immediately or chill for 1/2 hour. The dressing is adapted from one in *The Savory Way,* by Deborah Madison. Makes 4-6 servings.

German-Style Apples and Cabbage   MACSAC

4 packed cups thinly sliced red or green cabbage
   (3/4-1 pound)
3 cups peeled, sliced tart apples
1 cup sliced red onion
1/2 cup apple cider or beer

1/4 cup cider vinegar
1 teaspoon caraway seeds (optional)
1/2 teaspoon salt
coarsely ground black pepper to taste

Place cabbage, apples, red onion, and cider or beer in heavy saucepan or skillet. Cover and cook over medium heat until vegetables become slightly tender, about 8 minutes. Add remaining ingredients; cook another 7-8 minutes. Add more cider if necessary to keep vegetables from sticking. Serve with ring bologna, bratwurst, kielbasa, or sautéed mushrooms. Makes 6 servings.

Quick Meal Cabbage with Ham and Sesame Seeds   MACSAC

2 tablespoons vegetable oil or olive oil
2 teaspoons minced garlic
1/4-1/2 teaspoon hot red pepper flakes
1/2 cup thin strips of ham

6-8 cups shredded cabbage
1/2 cup chicken or vegetable stock or water
salt and pepper to taste
lemon juice
toasted sesame seeds

Heat oil, garlic, and pepper flakes in large skillet. Add ham; sauté 1 minute. Add cabbage. Stir in stock, cover, and simmer hard until most of the stock is absorbed and cabbage is wilted and tender, 5-10 minutes. Add salt, pepper, and lemon juice. Garnish with sesame seeds. Inspired by a recipe by Pam Anderson with Karen Tack in *Cook's Illustrated* (January 1995). Makes 4 servings.

Rosy Coleslaw with Apple and Green Onion   MACSAC

4 cups shredded red cabbage
1/2 cup shredded or chopped carrot
4 tablespoons finely chopped green onion
2 tablespoons fresh lemon juice

1 tablespoon sorghum syrup or maple syrup
1 tablespoon olive oil
1 large tart apple, peeled and finely chopped
salt and pepper

Toss all ingredients except salt and pepper. Chill 30 minutes, season to taste with salt and pepper, and serve. Makes 6 servings.

Portuguese Stone Soup   MACSAC

2 tablespoons olive oil, divided
3 linguica sausages (about 10 ounces) or other
   spicy smoked sausage, sliced
1 cup diced onion
1 cup diced carrot
1/2 cup diced celery
3 tablespoons minced garlic
8 cups chicken stock
1 bay leaf

1 teaspoon oregano
1/2 teaspoon thyme
4 cups (about 2/3 pound) very thinly sliced cabbage
2 cups diced potatoes
1 pound plum tomatoes (6-8), seeded and diced
1 can (14 ounces) cannelini beans, rinsed and drained
bottled hot pepper sauce
salt and pepper

Heat 1 tablespoon of the olive oil in a soup pot over medium-high flame. Add the sliced sausage and brown it well. Remove sausages from pot and add the remaining 1 tablespoon olive oil. When it is hot, add the onions, carrots, and celery; cook, stirring occasionally, about 8 minutes. Add the garlic and cook about 1 minute longer. Stir in chicken stock, bay leaf, oregano, thyme, and the sausage. Bring to a simmer and cook about 10 minutes. Add cabbage and potatoes; simmer 10 minutes longer. Add tomatoes and beans and simmer another 10 minutes. Season with hot pepper sauce, salt, and pepper to taste. Makes 8 or more servings.

Real Deal Homemade Sauerkraut   MACSAC

cleaned, shredded green cabbage

non-iodized canning salt

Weigh the shredded cabbage. For every pound of shredded cabbage you'll need 2 scant teaspoons salt. Place cabbage in large, clean bowl; add the salt and toss well with clean hands. Toss until the salt is very evenly distributed throughout the cabbage. Let mixture stand until limp, 15-20 minutes. Next, pack the cabbage into a clean ceramic crock or glass jug, pressing it down with each addition of cabbage. Fill the crock no higher than a couple of inches below its rim. Place a clean plate on top of the cabbage and weigh the plate down with a clean jar filled with water. Place this contraption in a cool place, like your basement (60 degrees or cooler is good, but not freezing). Over the next several hours, press on the jar to release liquid from the cabbage. The liquid has to cover the cabbage, so if it hasn't done so after several hours, remove some of the cabbage and replace the weights. Once it's covered with liquid, you can let alone to ferment. Fermentation will take around 14 days. (You'll notice some bubbles—and odors!—within a day or two.) A scum or mold may form; if so, just skim it off. Don't worry about the scum or the odor—that's just part of the deal with sauerkraut. For fun, taste the cabbage every day or two and notice the change in acidity and flavor as it ferments. When sauerkraut reaches desired flavor, can it (following the directions from a reputable canning resource), pack it into plastic bags or containers and freeze, or pack it into jars and refrigerate. The sauerkraut may be eaten as is, but the flavor improves when you simmer it with caraway seeds 20-60 minutes.

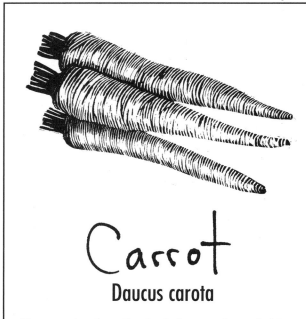

Carrot
Daucus carota

The carrot, a favorite staple in many households, belongs to the umbeliferae family. Among the other 2,500 members are parsley, celery, parsnip, cilantro, fennel, caraway, dill, and the lovely roadside weed, the flowering Queen Anne's lace. The carrot originated in middle Asia, first eaten by the hill dwellers of Afghanistan. The early cultivated varieties were purple and pale yellow. The first orange varieties did not appear until the 1600s in the Netherlands.

Though carrots are both popular and plentiful, it is difficult to grow a great carrot that is crisp and sweet. Carrots need the proper conditions to grow; soil type, pH balance, tilth, and a compatible seed variety are important factors in producing the ideal carrot. They may be planted in the cool of early spring. With successive plantings, carrots will remain in season through fall. With proper long-term storage, many varieties of carrots may be enjoyed throughout the winter.

Raw carrots are a favorite treat for many children. The crunchy sweetness will keep them asking for more. A child who pulls up his or her own carrot from the garden, brushing off the soil to take that first bite, will become a fan for life. Carrots are an excellent choice not only for taste but for nutritional value. They are very high in vitamin A and beta carotene, the substance responsible for their orange color. The carrot is also high in fiber, calcium, potassium, and other trace minerals.

Cooking Tips

- Scrub carrots with a vegetable brush under running water to remove dirt. Do not peel unless removing damaged areas. Carotene and trace minerals are close to the carrot's skin surface.

- Eat carrots raw to receive the most nutrients—whole, cut into sticks, or grated into salads.

- Light steaming will also retain most of the nutrients, about 5-10 minutes. Be careful not to overcook them.

- Fresh carrot greens can be chopped into a green salad or stir-fry.

- Greens can be dried and used as an herb like parsley.

- Fresh carrot juice, alone or with other vegetables, is a veggie lover's treat.

- Dice, slice, or cut in chunks and toss carrots into soups, stews, casseroles, and stir-fries.

- Blend into homemade tomato sauce to add sweetness.

- Try a simple puree of carrot soup with onions or leeks, freshly grated ginger, and a dash of salt or soy sauce.

- Sauté in butter with a little onion, salt, and fresh herbs of your choice.

Storage Tips

- Remove greens and refrigerate carrots in a plastic bag. Undamaged carrots will last 2-4 weeks when refrigerated properly.

- For long-term storage, pack carrots in a barrel with moist sand and keep in a cool location.

- For long-term storage, carrots can also be frozen. Blanch for 3 minutes, rinse in cold water to stop the cooking process, drain, let dry, and pack into an airtight container such as a zip-lock freezer bag. See chapter on home food preservation for more information on freezing vegetables.

For additional recipes that feature carrots, see the Seasonal Combinations, Kids' Recipes, and other chapters.

Carrots with Spiced Hickory Nuts or Pecans   MACSAC

1 cup hickory nut or pecan halves
4 teaspoons canola oil
2 tablespoons sugar
1/2 teaspoon salt
1/2 teaspoon ground cinnamon

1/4 teaspoon allspice
1/4 teaspoon powdered ginger
1/4 teaspoon dry mustard
1 1/2 pounds carrots, peeled and sliced

Heat oven to 325 degrees. Place nuts in single layer on baking sheet and roast 7 minutes. Meanwhile, mix oil, sugar, salt, and spices. Toss partially roasted nuts in spice mix and roast another 7 minutes. Steam carrots over boiling water until crisp-tender, about 7 minutes. Toss with spiced nuts and serve immediately. Makes 6 servings.

Honey Glazed Carrots with Fresh Mint   MACSAC

1 pound carrots
2 tablespoons butter
1 1/2 tablespoons honey

salt and pepper
1-2 tablespoons chopped fresh mint

Peel carrots and cut into evenly sized rounds or sticks. Combine carrots, butter, honey, and 1/2 cup water in large skillet over medium-high flame. Bring to simmer and cook until carrots are tender and most of the liquid has reduced to a glaze, 10-15 minutes. Season to taste with salt and pepper. Sprinkle mint on the carrots, toss well, and serve. Makes 4 servings.

Creamy Carrot Soup with Curried Beet Crème Fraîche
Tami Lax, Chef, formerly of L'Etoile Restaurant

12 sweet carrots
1 medium potato
2-3 cups half-and-half
salt and pepper to taste

1 large red beet
1 tablespoon curry powder
1 cup crème fraîche

Chop and peel carrots and potato. Place in 2-quart saucepan, cover with water, and cook until tender. Transfer into food processor; add half-and-half and blend until creamy. Season with salt and pepper. Peel and chop beet; roast in oven at 400 degrees until tender, about 45 minutes. Blend in blender with curry powder and crème fraîche. Use on soup for garnish. Makes 6-8 servings.

Carrot Almond Cake   Oak Ridge Farm

1 1/2 cups steamed, pureed carrots
6 eggs, separated
1/2 cup vegetable glycerine (or 2 cups honey
   or sugar)
2 tablespoons ground almonds or
   2 tablespoons flour

1 teaspoon grated orange zest
   (orange part of the rind)
1 teaspoon sea salt
1 tablespoon ground cardamom
cream cheese frosting (optional)

Heat oven to 350 degrees. Generously butter a 9-inch cake pan (round or square). Combine pureed carrots with egg yolks and glycerine. Mix in ground almonds, orange zest, salt, and cardamom. Beat egg whites in clean, separate bowl until stiff and fold into carrot mixture. Spread in pan. Bake until springy, about 45 minutes. Cool. Frost with cream cheese frosting, if desired. Makes 8-10 servings.

Cauliflower

Brassica oleracea var. botrytis

Cauliflower is another member of the versatile species brassica oleracea. Almost all parts of the plants within this species have been modified and emphasized genetically for consumption. For example, with cabbage we eat the large leaves tightly enveloping the terminal bud, whereas with Brussels sprouts we consume the enlarged auxiliary buds. For kale and other leafy varieties, we harvest the ever-regenerating and loosely growing heart leaves, while the most edible portion of the kohlrabi is an enlarged, bulblike stem. A fifth variation is the undeveloped flower buds of broccoli and cauliflower heads. If left to continue their maturation, they soon form sprays of small yellow flowers and go to seed.

Like most brassicas, cauliflower prefers cooler growing weather. It takes longer to mature than broccoli and most cabbages, averaging about 70-75 days in total.

Cauliflower is well worth the wait, however. When used simply but creatively, cauliflower proves very versatile, delicious, and nutritious. Cauliflower offers significant vegetable protein along with vitamins A, B-complex, C, and E, as well as a variety of minerals. Excessive cooking will destroy some B vitamins, much of the C, and all of the E.

Cooking Tips

- Soak head upside down in cold, salted water to remove any hidden field pests.

- Remove tough outer leaves, rinse the cauliflower head, trim off any blemishes, and core the head for even cooking. The head may be left intact or cut into florets.

- Steam 15-20 minutes for a whole head and 5-10 minutes for florets. Cook until tender but not thoroughly soft. Stop the cooking process by running under cold water. Overcooked cauliflower may have a stronger odor and flavor, and a tendency to go mushy quickly.

- Raw florets are popular with a favorite dip.

- Sauté or stir-fry cauliflower with other colorful vegetables for a decorative touch.

- Marinate steamed cauliflower in a favorite dressing, alone, or with other vegetables. Serve it chilled.

- Try cooked florets in your favorite pasta sauce, or pour sauce over entire cooked head.

- Top cauliflower with a lemon-butter sauce. Sprinkle with grated cheese.

- Use cauliflower puree for a creamy soup base or soup thickener.

Storage Tips

- Cauliflower does not keep well. Stored cauliflower may take on a strong odor and flavor over time.

- Refrigerate fresh cauliflower in a plastic bag. It should remain fresh for 1 week, and still be usable for up to 2 weeks.

- For long-term storage, cauliflower can be frozen. Blanch 2-4 minutes, rinse under cold water to stop cooking process, drain, let dry, and pack into airtight containers such as zip-lock freezer bags. Cauliflower will not be firm when thawed and is best used in soups and stews. See chapter on home food preservation for more information on freezing vegetables.

For additional recipes that feature cauliflower, see the Broccoli and Seasonal Combinations chapters.

Cauliflower Pie   Susan Hollingsworth, Harmony Valley Farm member

3 medium potatoes
2 tablespoons minced onion
salt and pepper to taste
1 head cauliflower, separated into florets
2 tablespoons butter

1 cup chopped onion
2-3 cloves garlic, minced
1 tablespoon chopped fresh basil
1 egg
4-6 ounces grated cheddar cheese

Boil potatoes 10 minutes; drain and cool. Shred (or mash) them; mix in minced onion plus salt and pepper. Press into buttered 9-inch pie pan; bake 30 minutes at 375 degrees. Steam cauliflower 10 minutes, then remove half the florets. Steam the rest 15-20 minutes longer and mash. Heat butter in skillet; add onions and garlic. Sauté until tender. Add basil, mashed cauliflower, salt, and pepper. Sauté 1 minute. Remove from heat; stir in egg. Spread into crust. Sprinkle on the cheese. Scatter partially steamed cauliflower florets on top. Bake 30-35 minutes. Makes 8 servings.

Cauliflower Blue Cheese Soup   MACSAC

2-3 tablespoons butter
1 cup chopped leeks
5-6 cups chopped cauliflower
3-3 1/2 cups chicken or vegetable stock

1/2 cup half-and-half
2-3 tablespoons chopped fresh tarragon, divided
5-6 ounces crumbled blue cheese, divided
salt and white pepper to taste

Slowly cook leeks in butter until tender. Add cauliflower and stock; simmer until very tender, 12-15 minutes. Puree. Add half-and-half, and half the tarragon. Simmer 3-4 minutes. Stir in half the cheese, salt, and pepper. Serve with more blue cheese and tarragon on top. Makes 6 servings.

Cauliflower Broccoli Salad with Apples and Raisins   Anne Dirks, Spiral Natural Foods

1 cup mayonnaise
1/4 cup sugar
2 tablespoons vinegar
3 cups chopped cauliflower
3 cups chopped broccoli

1/2 cup raisins
1/4 cup finely chopped red onion
1 apple (unpeeled), diced
2 tablespoons soy bacon bits
salt and pepper to taste

Mix first 3 ingredients. Stir in remaining ingredients. Serve chilled. Makes 6-8 servings.

Cauliflower Potato Curry   MACSAC

2 tablespoons peanut oil
1 teaspoon each: curry powder, turmeric, cumin,
  dried thyme
1/4 teaspoon cayenne pepper
2/3 cup chopped onion
1 teaspoon minced garlic
2 cups cubed waxy potatoes

1 cup vegetable (or chicken) stock or water
2 cups chopped cauliflower
1 medium carrot, chopped
2 slices fresh gingerroot
1/4 pound fresh beans, chopped
1 tablespoon fresh lemon juice
salt and freshly ground black pepper

Heat oil in deep skillet. Stir in dry spices. Add onion and garlic; cook over medium heat until tender. Add potatoes and stock, cover, and cook 10 minutes. Stir in cauliflower, carrot, and ginger. Cover and cook 5 minutes. Stir in beans. Cover and cook 5 minutes, stirring often. Remove cover; continue to simmer until most of the liquid has evaporated. Stir in lemon juice. Season to taste with salt and pepper. Serve over white rice and top with green onion. Makes 4 servings.

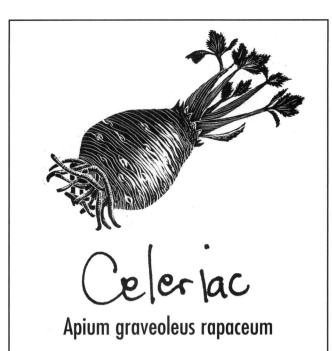

Celeriac

Apium graveoleus rapaceum

Celeriac, also known as celery root, has an obvious but unusual kinship to the common celery. Its stalks and foliage are similar to those of celery and are edible. However, the celeriac is cultivated for its edible bulbous root crown. Celeriac's growing season is very long, and it can be enjoyed all winter long with proper storage.

Celeriac is very popular in Europe, particularly in Germany and France where our commonly known stalk-type celery is rarely used. Actually, celeriac was not uncommon in American cooking back in the 1800s. An excellent storage crop, celeriac was a good choice for the home garden and root cellar. But as long-term storage became less important and eye appeal mattered more to the American consumer, celeriac fell out of favor and use. Though making a strong comeback, celeriac is still largely unknown here in the U.S.

Do not be put off by the celery root's rough exterior. Inside, a surprisingly delicious and versatile vegetable waits to be added to your culinary repertoire. Its excellent storage capability is coming back into style as many of us shift our diets to local and seasonal produce. Celeriac has an excellent crisp texture raw or cooked, and super-concentrated celery flavor, enhancing its usefulness as both vegetable and seasoning. Celeriac is high in carbohydrates, vitamin C, phosphorus, and potassium. It weighs in at 20 calories per one-cup serving.

Cooking Tips

- Slice off stalks at the root crown. Soak the root in warm water to loosen dirt in the crevices, then scrub thoroughly with a stiff vegetable brush. If exterior is too tough, peel with a sharp knife.

- Peeled celeriac will darken when exposed to air. To retard darkening, toss with lemon juice or keep in water. Lemon juice can also be added to cooking water.

- Parboil peeled celeriac whole for 20-30 minutes, half-inch to quarter-inch slices for 5-8 minutes.

- Bake celeriac in its skin at 350 degrees for 1 hour. Peel and prepare as needed.

- For extra celery flavor, use instead of common celery in soups, casseroles, stir-fries, etc. Use stalks and leaves for seasoning.

- Raw celeriac is excellent. Try celeriac sticks tossed in your favorite creamy dressing, or use for dipping. Grate it raw into a tossed green salad or a vegetable root salad.

- Try celeriac in hardy winter soups and stews, or puree for a flavorful, creamy soup base.

- Boil and mash celeriac with potatoes.

- Enjoy its full flavor simply topped with butter.

Storage Tips

- Do not wash celeriac before storing. Place it in a hydrator drawer or store it in a plastic bag and refrigerate for up to 1 month.

- Celeriac may be stored for 6-8 months under proper root cellar conditions.

- Celeriac may be dried and made into an excellent seasoning. See chapter on home food preservation for information on dehydrating.

Celeriac Potato Green Chili Soup Deb Boehm, Deb and Lola's Restaurant

1 large onion, sliced
2 tablespoons butter or vegetable oil
1 medium bulb celeriac, peeled and sliced
    1/4-inch thick
1 1/2 teaspoons chopped fresh thyme
3 large baking potatoes, peeled and sliced
    1/4-inch thick

4 1/2 cups whole milk
1/2 cup roasted, peeled, seeded, and chopped
    poblanos or Anaheim chiles
2 teaspoons salt
1/2 teaspoon black pepper
2 teaspoons sugar
1 tablespoon rice wine vinegar

Sweat onions in butter or oil over low heat until onion is completely cooked but not yet caramelized (15 minutes). Add celeriac and thyme; cook, stirring frequently, 5-10 minutes. Add potatoes, milk, and chiles; simmer until potatoes and celeriac are cooked through. Blend smooth in food processor. Season with salt, pepper, sugar, and rice wine vinegar. Makes 4 servings.

"Summer in Winter" Celeriac Carrot Slaw Jenny Bonde and Rink DaVee, Shooting Star Farm

1 large or 2 small celeriac bulbs
2 large carrots
2 cloves garlic or 1 medium shallot, minced
2 tablespoons sherry vinegar (red wine vinegar
    or lemon juice also work)

1/4 teaspoon salt
2 teaspoons Dijon mustard
1/3 cup olive oil
1 tablespoon sour cream
freshly ground black pepper

Peel celeriac with a sharp knife. Grate on large holes of box grater. Peel carrots and grate the same way. You'll have about 4 generous cups. Mix minced garlic or shallot, vinegar, salt, and mustard in small bowl. Whisk in olive oil until smooth and thickened. Stir in sour cream and fresh ground pepper to taste. Add more salt if necessary. Pour over grated vegetables and toss gently. Allow to marinate for 30 minutes. Makes 4 generous servings.

Celeriac au Gratin Harmony Valley Farm

2 large celeriac bulbs, peeled, sliced
    into 1/8-inch pieces
2 tablespoons butter
1 tablespoon flour

1 cup chicken or vegetable stock
salt and pepper to taste
1 cup grated Swiss or cheddar cheese

Simmer celeriac in water over medium heat until tender, 15-20 minutes. Drain. In medium saucepan, melt butter, add flour, and cook until golden. Slowly whisk in stock; cook until thickened. Add salt and pepper. Place drained celeriac in shallow baking dish; top with sauce, sprinkle with cheese, and bake at 375 degrees until golden, about 15 minutes. Makes 4-6 servings.

Curried Celeriac Carrot Puree MACSAC

1 pound celeriac, peeled and chopped
1 pound carrots, peeled and chopped
2 tablespoons butter
1 teaspoon grated ginger

1 tablespoon curry powder
2 tablespoons mango chutney
1/4 cup heavy cream
salt and pepper to taste

Boil celeriac and carrots until very tender, about 20 minutes. Drain. Meanwhile, melt butter in small frying pan, add ginger and curry powder, and sauté for about 30 seconds. Puree cooked vegetables, butter mixture, chutney, cream, salt, and pepper until smooth. Makes 4-6 servings.

Waldorf Salad with a Twist or Two   Linda Halley, Harmony Valley Farm

juice of 1 medium lemon
1/2 cup mayonnaise (regular or light)
1/4 teaspoon celery seed
1/4 teaspoon cardamom
pinch of salt
white pepper to taste
2-3 apples (unpeeled)
2 large pears

1/2 pound grapes, halved
1 pint ground cherries, husked, halved (optional)
1 cup sliced celery
1 cup shredded celeriac
about 1 tablespoon milk (optional)
2/3 cup crumbled blue or Gorgonzola cheese
2/3 cup chopped walnuts, black walnuts, or pecans
4 ounces arugula

Combine lemon juice, mayonnaise, celery seed, cardamom, salt, and white pepper in a large bowl. Cut apples and pears into 1-inch chunks; add to bowl. Add grapes, ground cherries (if using), celery, and celeriac. Add more mayonnaise or thin with milk as desired. Cover and refrigerate 1 hour. Stir in cheese and walnuts; spoon onto a bed of arugula. Makes 8 servings.

Corn Bread Celeriac Stuffing   MACSAC

6 cups cubed (1-inch cubes) corn bread
2 tablespoons canola oil, divided
1 teaspoon dried thyme
1 teaspoon dried sage
4 tablespoons butter
2 cups peeled, chopped celeriac

2 cups peeled, chopped red onion
1 cup peeled, chopped parsnips
2 cups cored, chopped apples
1 cup toasted, chopped pecans
1 egg, beaten
salt and pepper to taste

Heat oven to 350 degrees. Lightly oil a 9-by-13-inch baking dish. Toss cubed corn bread with 1 1/2 tablespoons oil, thyme, and sage. Spread on baking sheet; bake until toasted, about 15 minutes. Melt butter with remaining oil in large skillet over medium-high flame. Add celeriac, onions, and parsnips; sauté until tender, about 10 minutes. Season with salt and pepper. Stir in apples and sauté 2 minutes longer. Toss corn bread, nuts, and vegetables; mix with egg. Spread into prepared baking dish, cover with foil, and bake 45 minutes. Makes 8 servings.

Horseradish Mashed Potatoes and Celeriac   MACSAC

1 pound celeriac, peeled and cut into chunks
1 pound potatoes, peeled and cut into chunks
1 bay leaf
4 cloves garlic, peeled

1/2 cup heavy cream
4 tablespoons butter
2 teaspoons horseradish
salt and pepper to taste

Combine celeriac, potatoes, bay leaf, and garlic with water to cover; boil until just tender, about 20 minutes. Drain, remove bay leaf, and return vegetables to pot. Add cream, butter, and horseradish. Mash and season with salt and pepper. Makes 4-6 servings.

Potato Celeriac Salad with Blue Cheese Dressing   MACSAC

4 tablespoons lemon juice, divided
1/2 pound celeriac, peeled and cut into 1/2-inch dice
2 pounds red potatoes, cut into 1/2-inch dice
2 tablespoons minced parsley
4 sliced green onions

1/4 cup mayonnaise
1/4 cup sour cream
1/4 cup milk
1 cup crumbled blue cheese
salt and pepper to taste

Bring salted water to boil with 2 tablespoons lemon juice. Add celeriac and cook about 4 minutes. Add potatoes and cook until just tender, 4-6 minutes longer. Drain and let cool. Toss with parsley and green onions. Mix remaining ingredients and toss with vegetables. Makes 6 servings.

Wild Rice Celeriac Pilaf   MACSAC

1 tablespoon olive oil
3/4 cup finely diced celeriac
1/4 cup finely diced onion
1 cup wild rice, rinsed and drained
2 teaspoons dried thyme

1 cup chicken stock
1 cup beef stock
salt and pepper
2 tablespoons dried cranberries

Heat olive oil in a skillet. Add celeriac and onion; sauté until tender, about 5-7 minutes. Stir in wild rice, thyme, and stocks. Season with salt and pepper. Bring to boil, cover, and lower to a simmer. Cook until rice is nearly tender, 30-60 minutes (time depends on the kind and age of the rice). Stir in dried cranberries; cook until rice is tender, 5-15 minutes longer. Makes 4 servings.

Celeriac Potato Hash Browns with Jalapeño and Cheddar   MACSAC

1/4 pound bacon or 1 tablespoon canola oil
1 cup cubed (1/2-inch cubed) celeriac
3 cups cubed (1/2-inch cubed) russet potatoes
3 cups diced onions

3-6 tablespoons minced jalapeño
salt and pepper
1 tablespoon butter
1 cup grated cheddar cheese

Cook bacon in large skillet until crispy. Drain on paper towels and crumble it. Remove all but 1 tablespoon bacon drippings from pan. Bring a pot of salted water to a boil and parboil celeriac and potatoes about 6 minutes, then drain. Sauté onions in reserved bacon drippings (or in oil) until lightly browned, about 10 minutes. Stir in jalapeños and cook another 2 minutes. Mix all vegetables together in a bowl. Season generously with salt and pepper. Melt half the butter in a clean, 10-inch nonstick skillet over medium heat. Spread half the celeriac mixture in the pan, press it down with a spatula, and cook for 10 minutes. Carefully lay a plate over the pan and invert potatoes onto the plate, then slide them back into the pan. Sprinkle half the cheese over the top of the hash browns and cook 10 more minutes. Invert the hash browns onto a plate and keep warm, while you repeat the process with remaining butter, celeriac mixture, and cheese. Serve hot. Makes 6-8 servings.

Brussels Sprouts Celeriac Soup   MACSAC

2 tablespoons vegetable oil
2 cups chopped onions
1/2 pound Brussels sprouts, trimmed
1/2 pound celeriac, peeled and chopped
2 cups water

1/2 cup heavy cream
salt and pepper
1-3 tablespoons apple cider (optional)
6-8 ounces grated cheddar
4-6 slices French bread, toasted

Heat oil in soup pot over medium flame. Add onions and sauté until wilted. Stir in Brussels sprouts and celeriac. Add water, bring to boil, reduce to simmer, cover, and cook until vegetables are tender, about 15 minutes. Puree soup in batches in food processor or blender, then return soup to pot. Stir in cream and season to taste with salt and pepper. If soup tastes too bitter, stir in some apple cider until flavors are balanced. Heat broiler. Sprinkle cheese over toast slices and broil them until cheese is melted, 2-4 minutes. Serve each bowl of soup with a cheddar crouton on top. Adapted from a recipe in *Jane Grigson's Vegetable Book*. Makes 4-6 servings.

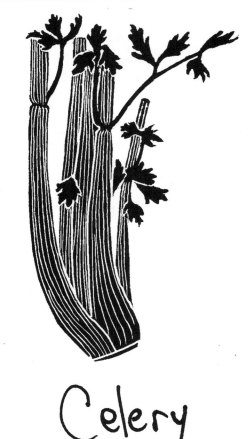

Celery

Apium graveoleus

Food historians tell us that celery was first developed and cultivated for the king of Persia around 2000 B.C. Revered in ancient times as rare and highly medicinal, celery now piles high in the supermarket and is a refrigerator staple.

Despite celery's common appearance, it is not easy to grow. Its special soil and water requirements can prove challenging. However, proper growing conditions and a fresh local source can yield celery superior in taste and texture to conventionally grown celery.

Celery is 94 percent water, but does contain vitamins A, C, B-complex, and E with a host of minerals. As might be expected from its texture, it is also high in fiber. Supposedly, chewing celery uses up more calories than the calories obtained from the vegetable itself!

Cooking Tips

- Celery is a standard addition to salads, casseroles, soups, stews, and stir-fries.

- Dice raw celery into tuna, chicken, egg, potato, and pasta salads.

- Try a lightly sautéed side dish with celery and vegetables of varying colors.

- Kids love celery "boats" filled with their favorite nut butter or soft cheese. They can make it themselves!

- Enjoy raw celery sticks with your favorite dip.

- Try a quick salad: half-inch celery pieces tossed with feta cheese, black olives, tuna chunks, and a lemon vinaigrette with fresh mint or basil.

Storage Tips

- Refrigerate as soon as possible or celery will go limp. Wrap in a damp towel or place in a plastic bag and store in the hydrator drawer of the refrigerator. It should keep for up to 2 weeks. Retain maximum crispness by storing stems upright in a container with an inch of water.

- For long-term storage, celery can be frozen. Slice, then spread out on a cookie sheet and place into the freezer. When all the chunks are frozen, pack them into an airtight container such as a zip-lock freezer bag and return to the freezer. Celery pieces will be soft when thawed and best used in soups and stews as opposed to salads.

- Celery leaves can also be dried. See chapter on home food preservation for more information about dehydrating or freezing vegetables.

Chow Mein James and Kathleen Mulvey

1/4 cup vegetable oil
3 cups thinly sliced celery
1/2 teaspoon salt
1/4 teaspoon ground black pepper
2 teaspoons sugar
2 cups chicken stock
1 1/2 tablespoons cornstarch

1/4 cup cold water
1/4 cup soy sauce
2 cups mung bean sprouts
2 cups slivered cooked chicken, turkey, or pork
chow mein noodles
cooked rice

Heat oil in a wok or deep skillet. Add celery, salt, pepper, and sugar; stir-fry 1 minute. Add chicken stock and bring to a boil. Simmer for about 8 minutes. Meanwhile, blend cornstarch, water, and soy sauce in a small bowl. Add to skillet and stir until mixture thickens. Stir in bean sprouts and meat. Cook until heated through, 2-3 minutes. Serve over hot rice with chow mein noodles. Makes 4 servings.

Blue Moon Salad MACSAC

2 cups finely diced celery
1/2 cup dried cherries
1/2 cup crumbled blue cheese
1-1 1/2 tablespoons lemon juice

1-2 tablespoons olive oil
salt and pepper
4 cups arugula, spinach, or sorrel leaves,
    cut into thin strips

Combine celery, dried cherries, and blue cheese in a bowl. Add lemon juice, olive oil, salt, and pepper to taste; toss gently. Serve on small mounds of arugula, spinach, or sorrel leaves. Makes 4-6 servings.

Braised Celery with Aromatic Cream Sauce MACSAC

8 large stalks celery
2 cups unsalted chicken stock
2 fresh allspice or bay leaves (or 1 dried)

1/2 teaspoon chopped fresh thyme (or 1/8 dried)
1/3 cup heavy cream
salt and pepper

Peel the rounded side of each celery stalk lengthwise with a potato peeler. Cut crosswise into 4-inch pieces. Place in a large skillet over medium flame, add chicken stock, allspice or bay leaf, and thyme. Bring to simmer, cover, and cook until celery is tender, 15-20 minutes. Uncover skillet, remove celery to a platter, and keep warm. Raise heat to high, add heavy cream, and cook, stirring occasionally, until liquid is reduced to a slightly thickened sauce. Season to taste with salt and pepper. Arrange celery pieces in a spiral, rounded side down, on the platter. Strain the sauce through a fine-meshed strainer and spoon over the middle of the celery pieces. Serve immediately. Makes 6 servings.

Fourteen Stuffing Ideas for Celery MACSAC

- soft goat cheese blended with chopped arugula
- soft goat cheese blended with chopped fresh dill
- finely chopped sorrel leaves mixed with a little mayonnaise
- egg salad
- tuna salad
- chicken salad
- caponata
- softened cream cheese mashed with smoked fish and lemon juice
- softened cream cheese mixed with crumbled blue cheese
- softened cream cheese mixed with chopped green olives and chopped walnuts
- softened cream cheese mixed with chutney
- pureed cottage cheese mixed with pesto
- pureed cottage cheese mixed with tapenade
- crunchy-style peanut butter, topped with dried cherries or cranberries

Chard
Beta vulgaris

For almost every dark leafy green lover, chard is a favorite. If you don't know chard, you are in for a treat. Chard is seasonal from spring through fall, ending finally with the onset of a heavy freeze. The two commonly cultivated varieties are the white stem and the ruby-red stem chard. Both have large, veined, semi-crinkly dark leaves.

Indigenous to the Mediterranean, chard is often referred to as Swiss chard due to its initial description by a Swiss botanist in the 16th century. Swiss chard has gone through eras of popularity and disdain over time. Currently it is gaining recognition in this country as a flavorful yet mild leafy green that is nutritious and versatile. Chard will soon rival spinach as a culinary staple in everyone's kitchen!

The common beetroot evolved from the leafy Swiss chard. Chard is high in vitamins A, E, and C, and minerals like iron and calcium. Minerals are more readily absorbed from chard than they are from spinach, chard also contains no oxalic acid, an element present in spinach that tends to bind minerals and render them unavailable during digestion.

Cooking Tips

- Wash the leaves by swishing in a water bath. Soil and particles will float away.

- If leaves are large and mature, remove stems to cook separately. Young tender leaves can be cooked whole.

- Chop leaves and stems diagonally across the leaf. Cut stems into 1-inch chunks and leaves into ribbonlike strips. Steam stem pieces 8-10 minutes and leaves 4-6 minutes.

- Raw baby chard leaves are wonderful in green salads. Many salad mixes include them.

- Sauté the leaves in garlic butter or with onion.

- Toss steamed chard leaves with olive oil, lemon juice, and salt and pepper. For an Asian flavor, toss with toasted sesame oil, rice vinegar, and soy sauce.

- Include chard in stir-fries with different colored and textured veggies. Serve over rice or noodles.

- For soups, add chard stem chunks 10 minutes and leaves 4-5 minutes before soup is done.

- Use Swiss chard in any recipe calling for fresh spinach, like quiches, lasagna, omelets, etc.

- Blend cooked chard (include cooking water) with a tart plain yogurt, herbs (like basil and thyme), and a dash of salt and pepper. This makes a healthy gourmet creamed soup that is easy, quick and delicious.

- See sections on Greens, Kale, and Spinach for more suggestions and recipes appropriate for chard.

Storage Tips

- Wrap chard in a damp towel or place in a plastic bag and keep in the hydrator drawer of the refrigerator.

- Chard is best used fresh, but will keep for 2-4 days if kept moist and refrigerated.

- Chard freezes well. Blanch chopped leaves for 3 minutes, rinse under cold water to stop cooking process, drain, squeeze lightly, and place in an airtight container such as a zip-lock freezer bag. See chapter on home food preservation for more information on freezing vegetables.

For additional recipes that feature (or substitute with) chard, see the Greens—Cooked, Spinach, Kale, and Seasonal Combinations chapters.

Swiss Chard Pie   Susanna Trucke, Dog Hollow Farm

1 onion, chopped
1 garlic clove, minced
2 tablespoons oil
1 bunch Swiss chard

6 eggs
1 cup shredded cheese
1 teaspoon salt
2 pie crusts

Heat oven to 400 degrees. Brown onion and garlic in oil. Trim and chop chard, add to pan, and cook down until wilted. Beat eggs in a bowl; mix in cheese, salt, and chard mixture. Pour into pie crusts; bake until knife inserted into center comes out clean, 30-40 minutes. Makes 2 pies.

Chard Soup with Cream Cheese "Croutons"   MACSAC

3 packed cups finely chopped chard leaves
4 cups chicken broth
salt (if necessary) and pepper

4 ounces (1/2 of an 8-ounce package) cream
    cheese, cubed and at room temperature

Combine chard and chicken broth in a pot. Bring to simmer and cook until chard is wilted and tender, about 6 minutes. You may leave it as is or puree it with an immersion blender or in a food processor or blender. Reheat if necessary. Season to taste with salt (if you've used canned stock, you may not need to add salt) and pepper. Divide the cubed cream cheese into 3 or 4 soup plates. Pour the hot soup over the cream cheese and serve immediately. Makes 3-4 servings.

Beans 'n' Greens   John Minnich, member of Zephyr Community Farm

3 cups black-eyed peas
butter or oil
1 large onion, chopped
a few garlic cloves, minced

1 teaspoon thyme
2-3 bay leaves
1 large bunch of Swiss chard, kale, or other greens
salt and pepper

Put peas on to cook in water. Heat a little butter or oil in a skillet. Add onions and garlic; sauté with thyme and bay leaves until tender. After cooking peas 1/2 hour, add the onion mixture and chopped greens. Cook 1/2 hour longer. Remove bay leaves. Season with salt and pepper to taste. Makes 8-12 servings.

Micah's Yummy Chard Pie   Ends Family, Scotch Hill Farm

2 tablespoons olive oil or canola oil
1 1/2 cups chopped onions
1 tablespoon minced garlic or several chopped
    garlic scapes
1 very large bunch or 2 medium bunches
    Swiss chard, spinach, or other greens, stems
    removed and leaves chopped
6-8 eggs

2 cups milk or half-and-half
1 teaspoon salt
2 8-inch deep-dish pie shells
2 cups grated cheddar or Swiss cheese
chopped ham, cooked bacon, diced tomatoes, chopped
    basil, blanched peas, or green beans (optional)
1-2 tablespoons chopped fresh dill

Heat oven to 400 degrees. Heat oil in a large skillet over medium flame. Add the onion and garlic; cook, stirring occasionally, until tender. Add chopped greens and cook, stirring often, until they wilt. Turn off heat. Beat eggs, milk, and salt in a bowl. Spread chard mixture in bottom of pie shells. Add cheese. Pour egg mixture over top. Add one or more of the optional ingredients, if desired. Sprinkle with the dill. Bake at 400 degrees until the pies are no longer jiggly in the center, 30-40 minutes. Makes 16 slices.

Rainbow Swiss Chard Appetizer   Mara Rosenbloom

3 tablespoons butter
2 tablespoons minced shallots
4 stems chives, chopped
1/4 teaspoon dried, ground thyme

1 bunch rainbow Swiss chard (about 10 stalks),
   finely chopped (use the greens for another recipe)
cream cheese, softened
toasted, sliced French bread or gourmet whole
   wheat cracker

Melt butter in pan over medium heat. Add shallots and sauté 2 minutes. Add chives, thyme, and chopped chard stalks; sauté until stalks are tender, tossing to coat with butter. Transfer to bowl and let cool, patting it with paper towels to soak up excess butter. Spread cream cheese on toasted bread or crackers. When chard is cool, spoon some onto each cracker. Makes about 4 servings.

Souffléed Twice-Baked Potatoes with Swiss Chard   MACSAC

6 large baking potatoes (about 3 pounds)
coarse salt
1 tablespoon butter, softened
1/2 cup hot milk

2 eggs, separated
3/4 cup cooked chard leaves (finely chopped)
2 tablespoons chopped fresh chives
salt and pepper to taste

Heat oven to 400 degrees. Scrub potatoes, prick with fork, and sprinkle with salt. Bake until tender, 1-1 1/4 hours. Reduce oven to 375 degrees. Cut a 1/2-inch slice lengthwise from each potato. Scoop out flesh from the slices. Scoop flesh from inside potatoes, to make shells with 1/4-inch-thick "walls." Mash all the potato flesh or pass through ricer. Fold in butter. Stir in hot milk. Beat egg yolks; stir yolks, chard, and chives into potatoes. Add salt and pepper. Whip egg whites in clean bowl until stiff but not dry. Fold a quarter of them into potatoes, then gently fold in the rest. Heap mixture into potato shells; place on baking pan. Bake 20-25 minutes. Inspired by a recipe in *Potatoes: From Pancakes to Pommes Frites,* by Annie Nichols. Makes 6 servings.

Swiss Chard and Chick-Pea Soup   MACSAC

3 carrots, diced
2 stalks celery, diced
1 cup diced red onion
1 sprig rosemary, leaves removed from stem
   and chopped
1 1/2 tablespoons crushed garlic
6 cups vegetable stock

2 cups chopped tomatoes
1 can (15 ounces) chick-peas, drained and rinsed
1 bunch Swiss chard, stems removed and greens
   roughly chopped (reserve the stems for another
   use or compost them)
salt and pepper

Combine carrots, celery, red onion, rosemary, garlic, and stock in a saucepan. Bring to a low boil and cook about 10 minutes. Add tomatoes, chick-peas, and chard greens. Simmer another 15 minutes. Season with salt and pepper to taste. Makes 6 servings.

Asian-Style Chard   MACSAC

1 bunch Swiss chard, cleaned
1 tablespoon peanut oil
1 tablespoon minced garlic

1 tablespoon soy sauce
2 tablespoons hoisin sauce
freshly ground black pepper

Cut off and discard thick stem ends of chard. Cut out ribs; chop ribs into 2-inch pieces; set aside in a pile. Stack the leaves in small piles; coarsely chop them. Heat oil in large skillet over medium-high flame. Add ribs; toss and cook 1-2 minutes. Add leaves and garlic; continue to cook, tossing often, until chard begins to wilt, 2-3 minutes. Stir in soy sauce and hoisin sauce; cook until chard is tender, 1-3 minutes longer. Add pepper to taste. Serve immediately. Makes 2-4 servings.

Swiss Chard Breakfast Burritos   Lisa Kivirist and John Ivanko, Inn Serendipity

approximately 3 cups cooked and seasoned
   Swiss chard*
6-8 flour tortillas
2-3 cups shredded cheese (like cheddar or Swiss),
   divided
4 eggs, beaten

2 cups milk
1 tablespoon flour
1 teaspoon mustard powder
salsa
sour cream

Oil a 9-by-13-inch baking pan. Divide cooked chard down center of tortillas. Sprinkle each pile of chard with 3 tablespoons cheese. Roll up tortillas and place seam side down in prepared pan. Mix eggs, milk, flour, and mustard powder. Pour over tortillas. Cover with foil and refrigerate overnight. The next day, let burritos come to room temperature. Heat oven to 350 degrees. Bake until eggs are set, about 45 minutes. Sprinkle remaining cheese on top and cover for last 5 minutes of baking. Serve with salsa and sour cream. This recipe can be adapted to use a variety of seasonal vegetables. Makes 4-6 servings.

*It's best to start by sautéing some onions and garlic; then add Swiss chard, cook it, and season it with salt, peppers, and fresh herbs (dill is delicious). A combination of spinach and zucchini works great, too.

Hot and Sour Soup with Swiss Chard   MACSAC

6 cups chicken broth
2 ounces dried mushrooms, soaked in water
   until plump and cut into strips (strain the liquid
   and use it for some of the broth)
1/4 pound chard leaves, cut into strips
3-4 tablespoons soy sauce
3 tablespoons rice wine vinegar
lots of freshly ground black pepper

2-3 teaspoons sesame oil
1/2 teaspoon hot chile oil
5-6 ounces baked tofu, cut into 1/2-inch cubes
4-5 tablespoons water mixed with
   2-3 tablespoons cornstarch
1 egg, beaten
1/4 cup chopped cilantro
3-4 slender green onions, chopped

Bring broth to boil in saucepan. Add mushrooms and simmer 5 minutes. Add chard; simmer 1 minute. Add soy, vinegar, pepper, sesame oil, chile oil, and tofu. Stir and heat through. Stir in cornstarch mixture. Add egg, stirring until cooked, 1 minute. Serve topped with cilantro and green onions. This recipe is adapted from *Great Greens* by Georgeanne Brennan. Make 6 servings.

Swiss Chard Omelet with Middle Eastern Savor   MACSAC

For each omelet:
1-2 teaspoons olive oil
3 eggs, beaten
1/2 cup chopped, cooked chard leaves and/or
   stems,* warm or at room temperature
1 tablespoon currants

1 tablespoon finely chopped kalamata olives
1 tablespoon toasted pine nuts
lemon juice
sea salt and freshly ground black pepper
herb sprig (rosemary, thyme, sage, etc.)

Heat olive oil in small nonstick skillet over high flame. Add beaten eggs—they will immediately begin to set on bottom of pan. With a spatula or nonstick egg lifter, pull the cooked egg from outer edges of pan toward center. The uncooked egg will spread and cook. Use spatula to help spread the liquid egg off top of cooked egg and onto exposed sections of pan bottom. Continue to do this until nearly all the liquid egg is set. Reduce heat to very low. The egg will continue to cook as you layer the following across the omelet: chard, currants, olives, and pine nuts. Sprinkle with a few drops of lemon juice. Season with salt and pepper. To serve, hold a plate close to the edge of skillet and, shaking skillet slightly, slip omelet onto the plate, either rolling it into a cigar shape or folding it over into a half-moon. Serve immediately. (Or, since this entire process takes only 2-3 minutes, you can keep the omelet warm in the oven while you make more of them.) Garnish with an herb sprig. Makes 1 serving.

*This is best if the chard has been cooked with garlic and onions.

Chinese Cabbage

Brassica rapa var. pekinensis

Chinese cabbage, commonly known as napa cabbage, is among the first transplants to be set out in early spring and is ready for harvest by early summer. Chinese cabbage will thrive again in the cool of fall, tolerating frost well. The cabbage heads must be harvested and stored properly before a heavy freeze, however.

The Chinese cabbage we are familiar with in this country is only one of many similar oriental varieties. Those with a compact head of leaves are grown extensively in northern China for their storage capabilities in winter. This vegetable has been cultivated throughout Asia since 500 A.D., but was not introduced in this country until the late 19th century. Though gaining in popularity in the U.S., most Asian vegetables are still considered a specialty crop.

Chinese cabbage is not known for its nutritional value. Small amounts of vitamins A, C, and minerals are present, along with plenty of fiber and very few calories. It is very versatile, both raw and cooked.

Cooking Tips

- Chop raw Chinese cabbage into green salads.

- Substitute Chinese cabbage in traditional coleslaw.

- For an Asian-style salad, toss chopped cabbage with grated carrot, chopped green onion, toasted sesame oil, rice vinegar, and soy sauce.

- Chinese cabbage cooks quickly. Steam for 3-5 minutes, or until leaves are wilted down but remain slightly crisp. All cabbages are at risk for overcooking!

- Substitute Chinese cabbage for common cabbage in recipes, but reduce cooking time by 2 minutes.

- Chinese cabbage is a classic and popular stir-fry vegetable and also a main ingredient in egg rolls.

- You can stir-fry it alone with a little onion, toasted sesame oil, and soy sauce, or add it chopped toward the end of your mixed vegetable stir-fry.

- Chinese cabbage is excellent in soups, fried rice, mashed with potatoes, etc. Be creative and experiment with both traditional and nontraditional uses for this versatile vegetable.

Storage Tips

- Do not remove all of the outer tough leaves before storage. They will help retain moisture, keeping the inside crisp and fresh.

- Keep Chinese cabbage in the hydrator drawer of the refrigerator for up to 2 weeks.

For additional recipes that feature (or substitute with) Chinese cabbage, see the Cabbage and Seasonal Combinations chapters.

Asian-Marinated Tofu Napa Cabbage Salad   MACSAC

1 pound firm tofu, drained, dried in paper
   towels and cubed
4 tablespoons soy sauce, divided
1 tablespoon plus 2 teaspoons sesame oil, divided
1/2 teaspoon crushed red pepper flakes
1-2 cups very thinly sliced napa cabbage
1 carrot, cut into matchstick-size pieces

1/2 red bell pepper, cut into matchstick-size pieces
3 green onions, finely chopped
1 tablespoon sesame seeds
2 teaspoons lime juice
1 clove minced garlic
1 teaspoon sugar

Steam tofu over simmering water 10 minutes. Mix 2 tablespoons soy sauce, 1 tablespoon sesame oil, and pepper flakes; toss with tofu and marinate, tossing occasionally, 1-3 hours. Combine cabbage, carrots, bell peppers, and onions. Mix remaining 2 tablespoons soy sauce, remaining 2 teaspoons sesame oil, sesame seeds, lime juice, garlic, sugar, and 2 teaspoons water in another bowl. Toss with vegetables and tofu (include the marinade, too). Makes 4 servings.

Napa Wasabi Slaw   MACSAC

1 tablespoon wasabi paste
1 tablespoon soy sauce
1 1/2 tablespoons sugar
1 1/2 tablespoons rice vinegar
1/4 cup sesame oil

1 cup orange juice
1 head napa cabbage, very thinly sliced
6 carrots, shredded
3 chopped scallions
2 tablespoons sesame seeds

Whisk wasabi, soy sauce, sugar, vinegar, sesame oil, and orange juice until thoroughly combined. Toss with vegetables and sesame seeds. Makes 6-8 servings.

Napa Noodle Egg Rolls   MACSAC

3 1/2 ounces (about 100 grams) bean
   thread noodles
1/2 pound lean ground pork
1 cup finely chopped onions
2 cups finely shredded napa cabbage
1 egg, beaten
1 tablespoon sesame oil

salt and pepper to taste
1 pound egg roll wrappers
2 egg whites, beaten
3-4 cups vegetable oil
Hmong Hot Dipping Sauce
   (see Cilantro chapter)

Soak noodles in hot water 15 minutes. Drain well; chop. Mix with pork, onions, cabbage, egg, sesame oil, salt, and pepper. Place egg roll wrapper on work surface with one corner pointing toward you. Place 2 heaping tablespoons filling near bottom corner, shaping mixture to look like a cigar. Roll wrapper (lower end) over meat to middle of wrapper. Brush edges with egg white and roll up completely. Repeat with remaining filling and wrappers. Heat oil to 375 degrees. Deep-fry egg rolls in small batches until light brown, about 5 minutes. Drain on paper towels. Serve with Hmong Hot Dipping Sauce. Makes 20-25 egg rolls.

Chinese Cabbage Salad   Dog Hollow Farm

5 cups chopped Chinese cabbage
3/4 cup sliced or shredded radish (daikon is best)
1 1/2 cups chow mein noodles (the crunchy ones)
1 cup crushed peanuts
1/4 cup sesame seeds (black, if available)

2 tablespoons rice vinegar
4 tablespoons sesame oil
3 tablespoons soy sauce
1 tablespoon honey
1/2-1 teaspoon dry mustard

Combine cabbage, radishes, chow mein noodles, peanuts, and sesame seeds. Mix remaining ingredients. Toss with cabbage, using just enough dressing to suit your taste. Makes 6-8 servings.

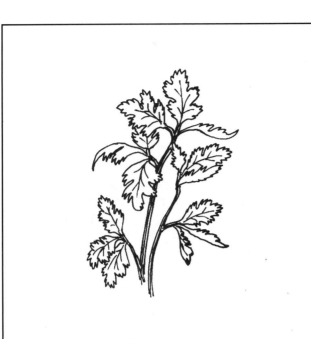

Cilantro

Coriandrum satirum

Cilantro, another of the ancient and old-world herbs, seems to have been native to a vast area ranging from southern Europe through the Near East all the way to India. Today cilantro is used in a variety of ethnic cookery, particularly Mexican, Chinese, Vietnamese, Thai, and Indian. Coriander, the seed of the cilantro plant, is a core ingredient in the Indian curry tradition.

Cilantro continues to gain popularity in this country. It is particularly well known for its role in delicious homemade salsa. Chips, anyone?

Cilantro is a pungent herb with a unique flavor. People respond to cilantro with either delight or disdain. Rarely does it elicit a wishy-washy response. If you are unfamiliar with cilantro, nibble a fresh leaf, then try using the herb in a variety of ways to discover your own attitudes about it. Don't give up too soon. You too may become one of cilantro's staunch supporters.

Cooking Tips

- Add fresh leaves to soups, stews, and stir-fries for an aromatic touch. Add cilantro toward the end of cooking time to retain fresh flavor and color.

- Toss fresh leaves into a green salad.

- Chop into pasta and potato salads.

- Use cilantro in ethnic cooking, such as Thai, Indian, Mexican, and Chinese.

- See Tomato and Tomatillo sections for salsa recipes.

Storage Tips

- For short-term storage, wrap cilantro in a damp towel or stand upright in a container with an inch of water, and refrigerate. Do not wash prior to refrigeration.

- Freeze fresh leaves in a plastic zip-lock bag. Remove air, seal, and freeze. Do not thaw before use.

- Cilantro is one of the few herbs that does not retain its flavor when dehydrated.

Cilantro Lime Vinaigrette   Madison Herb Society Cookbook, K. Milanich

2/3 cup (6 ounces) lime juice
3 tablespoons minced garlic
1/4 cup apple cider vinegar
pinch salt

2/3 cup packed cilantro leaves
2-4 dashes bottled hot pepper sauce
1 tablespoon cumin
1/4 cup canola oil

Place all ingredients except the oil in a blender. Turn on blender. Add oil very slowly through the "hole" in the middle. Use a little water if you lose the hole, but just enough to keep the little hole so the oil will get blended. Makes about 1 1/4 cups.

Hmong Hot Dipping Sauce   MACSAC

3-4 red or green Thai (or other)
   hot peppers, chopped
2 tablespoons chopped fresh cilantro

1 tablespoon bottled Thai fish sauce
juice of 1 lime or more to taste

Mash chopped hot peppers and cilantro with mortar and pestle (don't use a food processor) until they form a paste. Stir in fish sauce and lime juice. Use this as a dipping sauce for egg rolls, wontons, and spring rolls, or as a seasoning for fried rice, stir-fries, etc. Makes about 1/3 cup.

Poached Eggs in Cilantro Parsley Butter   MACSAC

4 eggs
3 tablespoons butter

1 1/2 tablespoons chopped fresh cilantro
1 tablespoon chopped fresh parsley

Fill a wide, shallow pot with enough water to come at least 4 inches up its sides. Bring water to a full boil. Turn off the heat and carefully crack eggs, one at a time, into the hot water, keeping eggs separate from each other as much as possible. Cover pot and set a timer for 3 minutes. Meanwhile, fill a shallow pan with a couple inches of cold water. After the 3 minutes are up, use a slotted spoon to carefully transfer each egg to the cold water. When eggs are cool, remove them with a spatula to a cutting surface. Trim off any ragged edges from the eggs with a paring knife. (Eggs may be held in the refrigerator at this point until a few minutes before you want to serve them.) To finish: Heat butter in a skillet over medium heat; add herbs and cook briefly. Adjust heat to low, add eggs, and heat through, basting them with the herb butter. Serve immediately with toast. Makes 2 servings.

Mango Cilantro Salsa   MACSAC

2 ripe mangoes
1 ripe avocado
juice of 1 lime
1 jalapeño, seeded and chopped

1/4 cup minced red or green onion
2 tablespoons chopped cilantro
1 teaspoon minced garlic, pressed to a paste

Peel and dice mangoes and avocado. Combine with remaining ingredients. Serve as a topping for grilled fish, tofu, or chicken, or as a dip for tortilla chips or rice crackers. Makes 1 1/2-2 cups.

Corn
Zea mays

All varieties of corn are grass, belonging to the gramineae family along with wheat, oats, and rye. Often referred to as maize, corn is an ancient staple food of the Americas, having gathered history and significance for many thousands of years. Maize pollen discovered near Mexico City dates back sixty to eighty thousand years. Five-thousand-year-old corn cobs have been found in Mexico and the southwest U.S. Ancient strains were small, brightly colored ears with compact, nutritious kernels. Interestingly, the earliest maize seems to have been a popcorn variety. Sweet corn is first referred to historically in 1779, after corn's introduction to European settlers. Strains were selected and adapted to emphasize their sugar content and sweetness, a process still going on today with our sweet corn hybrids.

Flavor and nutrition of the many diversified maize varieties has been sacrificed in the search for sweetness. Even so, a fresh, well-prepared ear of sweet corn still offers a significant amount of vitamin A, B-complex, phosphorous, and potassium, along with vegetable protein. As many traditional native dishes will illustrate, corn combined with most beans or dairy form a complete protein. Like other whole grains, corn is an excellent source of complex carbohydrates.

Nothing says summer like sweet corn. Enthusiasts know not to waste any time, as its season of availability is short. Get it while you can!

Cooking Tips

- Cook and eat sweet corn as soon as possible after harvest. The sugars quickly turn to starches once the ear is picked. Keep corn refrigerated or on ice to slow this process.

- It is not uncommon to find a worm or two enjoying your sweet corn. No need to discard the whole cob—simply cut out the damaged part.

- Corn on the cob is the most popular and flavorful way to enjoy fresh sweet corn. Steam corn in 1-2 inches of water for 6-10 minutes, or drop ears into boiling water for 3-6 minutes. Inner leaves may be left on if desired.

- For a real garden treat, try eating a freshly picked ear of sweet corn raw.

- Roast unhusked ears in the oven, an outdoor grill, or over a campfire for about 20 minutes.

- Older, less sweet corn or a mealy sweet corn can be added to chowders, stews, soups, baked dishes, stir-fries, omelets, corn bread, pancake batter, quiches, salads, bean dishes, fried rice, etc.

- Try a colorful vegetable salad: mix corn kernels, diced red or green bell pepper, and sweet onion rings with lemon juice, oil, and your choice of herbs or a favorite vinaigrette. Marinate 1 hour.

Storage Tips

- Refrigerate sweet corn immediately with husks on, and use as soon as possible to retain sweetness and flavor.

- Corn freezes well. Blanch on or off the cob for 3-5 minutes, rinse under cold water to stop the cooking process, and drain. Dry corn well, then pack it on or off the cob into airtight containers such as zip-lock freezer bags. See chapter on home food preservation for more information on freezing vegetables.

For additional recipes that feature corn, see the Seasonal Combinations chapter.

Harmony Valley Farm Sweet Corn Soup   L'Etoile Restaurant

3 tablespoons butter
2 large yellow onions, peeled and julienned
   (cut like matchsticks)
1 tablespoon salt
1/2 teaspoon black pepper
1 tablespoon sugar

1/4 teaspoon red pepper flakes
12 ears sweet corn, shucked and corn cut from cob
3 cups cream
3 cups whole milk
2 tablespoons snipped chives

Melt butter in 6- to 8-quart stockpot; add onions, salt, black pepper, sugar and pepper flakes. Sauté onions, stirring occasionally, until moisture has evaporated (thus concentrating their sweetness), about 20 minutes. Add corn, cream, and milk; bring to a boil and cook another 20 minutes. Cool to room temperature and puree in blender in small batches (blenders work better than food processors for this). Pass through a medium-fine sieve, season to taste, and reheat. Sprinkle each bowl with chives. Makes 8 servings.

Wave's Rave Sweet Corn Risotto   Chef Wave Kasprzak, The Dining Room at Monticello

4 ears sweet corn
2 tablespoons olive oil
1/4 cup diced onion
1/4 cup diced red bell pepper

2 teaspoons minced garlic
1/2 cup arborio rice
1/3 cup grated Parmesan cheese
salt and pepper

Cut kernels off corn cobs. Place cobs in a heavy saucepan with 6 cups water; bring to simmer and cook cobs 20-25 minutes. Strain; return water to pan. Add corn kernels; return to simmer. After 2 minutes, remove half the kernels and set them aside. Continue cooking remaining kernels until tender, about 10 minutes. Puree water-corn mixture in a blender, then strain it through a fine-meshed sieve. Heat oil in the same pan. Add onion, sweet pepper, garlic, and rice; sauté 1 minute. Reduce heat to low; add pureed mixture 1 cup at a time, stirring constantly, until absorbed. Continue to add pureed mixture only until rice is barely tender—you may or may not need to add all of it. Add reserved corn, Parmesan, and salt and pepper to taste, stirring until cheese melts. Serve immediately. Makes 4-6 small servings.

Sweet Corn Cheddar Pancakes   MACSAC

2/3 cup cornmeal
1/2 cup flour
1 teaspoon baking powder
1/2 teaspoon salt
1/4 teaspoon pepper
1 egg, beaten
1 1/4 cups buttermilk
1 tablespoon corn oil

1/2 cup shredded sharp cheddar cheese
4 tablespoons finely chopped green onions
1-2 tablespoons chopped cilantro
1/2-1 cup cooked corn kernels
additional corn oil, for cooking pancakes
spicy tomato salsa
sour cream

Combine cornmeal, flour, baking powder, salt, and pepper in bowl. Mix egg, buttermilk, and corn oil in another bowl; stir in cheese, green onions, cilantro, and corn kernels. Mixture can stand at room temperature up to an hour. Heat a griddle or large, heavy skillet over medium flame several minutes. Reduce heat to medium-low and brush cooking surface with corn oil. Cook pancakes in batches: Ladle batter onto hot griddle, 1/4 cup per pancake. Cook until first side is golden brown and pancakes have set well on the bottom. Flip pancakes and cook on other side until done. Serve hot with salsa and sour cream. Makes 10-12 pancakes.

Tequila Braised Corn Salsa   MACSAC

kernels cut from 2 ears of corn
3 tablespoons tequila
1-2 tablespoons finely minced jalapeño
2 tablespoons finely minced green onion

1 finely diced plum tomato
1 tablespoon minced cilantro
salt and pepper to taste

Heat a dry skillet over high heat, add corn kernels, and pan-roast them until they brown in spots, about 3-5 minutes. Stir in tequila, scrape up browned bits in bottom of pan, and boil until liquid evaporates. Remove from heat and stir in remaining ingredients. Serve as a snack with chips or as a topping for grilled meats or fish. Makes 2-4 servings.

Corn Chowder with Smoked Fish Sausage or Kielbasa   MACSAC

1 tablespoon butter
2 large shallots, minced
2 cups milk
3 medium Yukon Gold potatoes, scrubbed and
   diced (about 2 cups total)

1/4 pound smoked fish sausage or kielbasa, diced
1 1/2 cups corn kernels cut fresh from the cob
1 cup half-and-half
salt and pepper

Melt butter in saucepan over medium flame. Add shallots and cook, stirring occasionally, until tender, about 5 minutes. Add milk and potatoes; bring to low simmer, partially cover, and cook until potatoes are tender. Add sausage, corn, and half-and-half; bring to low simmer, and cook gently until corn is tender, about 3 minutes. Add salt and pepper to taste. Serve immediately. Makes 4 servings.

Rosemary Corn Bread with Cranberry Beans, Tomatoes, and Sweet Onions
MACSAC

Corn bread:
1 tablespoon vegetable oil
1 cup yellow cornmeal
1 cup flour
1 tablespoon sugar
2 teaspoons baking powder
1/2 teaspoon baking soda
1/2 teaspoon salt
2 large eggs
1 cup buttermilk
3 tablespoons melted butter
1 cup corn kernels cut from the cob
1 tablespoon minced fresh rosemary

Other:
3 cups shelled fresh cranberry beans
1 tablespoon minced garlic
3 sprigs fresh rosemary
1 cup finely chopped carrot
salt and pepper
thick-sliced tomatoes
thin-sliced sweet onions

To make corn bread: Measure vegetable oil into an 8- to 9-inch cast-iron skillet; place skillet in oven and heat to 425 degrees for 20-30 minutes. Whisk cornmeal, flour, sugar, baking powder, baking soda, and salt in bowl. Whisk eggs and buttermilk in separate bowl; stir into cornmeal mixture until nearly combined. Stir in melted butter, corn, and rosemary. Spread in hot skillet. Bake until toothpick inserted near center comes out clean, 20-25 minutes. To make beans: Combine beans, garlic, rosemary, and carrots in pot; barely cover with water, bring to simmer, and cook until tender, 20-30 minutes. There should be enough liquid left for a slightly soupy texture. Add salt and pepper to taste. To serve, scoop beans into soup plates, crumble warm corn bread over them, and top with tomato and onion slices and some of the bean liquid. Makes 6-8 servings.

Corn and Wild Rice Fritters   MACSAC

1 cup cooked wild rice
kernels from 2 ears cooked corn
1 cup flour
1 cup milk
1 egg
1/4 cup finely chopped green onion

1/4 cup finely chopped red bell pepper
2 tablespoons minced fresh parsley
1/4 teaspoon salt
canola oil
tomatillo salsa

Mix all ingredients except oil and salsa. Add oil to a heavy skillet to a depth of 1/4 inch. Heat over medium flame until oil looks shimmery and bubbles immediately when you drop a tiny amount of batter into it. Drop small amounts (as little as 2 tablespoons or up to 1/3 cup) of the batter into the oil, cooking a few fritters at a time to avoid crowding them. Cook each batch until brown and cooked through. Drain on paper towels and serve with salsa. Makes 8 larger pancakes or up to 24 small fritters.

Grilled Corn on the Cob with Compound Butters   MACSAC

There are two basic methods for grilling corn on the cob—one in the husk, one with flavored butter in foil:

Husk method: Pull husk back on corn without removing it. Remove the silk, then pull husks back up over corn. Twist top of husks to help close them. Soak corn in a bowl of water for about 10 minutes, then put onto a hot grill. Grill for about 20-25 minutes, turning the corn so that each side cooks evenly. Be careful when opening the husks—they're hot! Serve with plain or flavored compound butters.

Foil method: Remove husks and silk from the corn and soak the cobs in water for about 5 minutes. Smear about 1/2 tablespoon of butter on a square of aluminum foil, then place cob onto the foil and wrap tightly. Put foil packets onto hot grill and cook for about 20 minutes, turning the corn so that each side cooks evenly. Pass the compound butter and dig in!

Compound butters: The method is the same for the following butters. Put all ingredients into a mini food processor and pulse until all ingredients have combined (alternatively you can beat them with a wooden spoon until smooth). The butters can then be rolled into logs in plastic wrap and refrigerated or frozen for future use.

Jalapeño Lime Cilantro Butter
4 tablespoons unsalted butter, at room temperature
1 teaspoon finely minced jalapeño
1 teaspoon fresh lime juice
1 tablespoon minced cilantro
1/4 teaspoon salt

Lemon Thyme Butter
4 tablespoons unsalted butter, at room temperature
1 teaspoon grated lemon zest
1 teaspoon fresh-squeezed lemon juice
2 teaspoons chopped fresh thyme
1/4 teaspoon salt

Ancho Scallion Butter
4 tablespoons unsalted butter, at room temperature
1/2 teaspoon ancho chili powder
1 tablespoon finely chopped scallions
1/2 teaspoon salt

Roasted Pepper Butter
4 tablespoons unsalted butter, at room temperature
1 tablespoon minced roasted red pepper
1/4 teaspoon minced garlic
dash fresh lemon juice
1/4 teaspoon salt

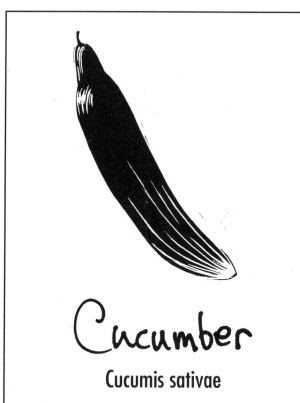

Cucumber

Cucumis sativae

The cucumber, first cultivated in India more than 3,000 years ago, is now a global food. Many cultures use cucumbers, raw and in pickled form, in their cuisine. Even Iceland grows cucumbers as a major crop, using natural steam for their hothouses!

Fresh, crisp summer-crop cucumbers are available from midsummer until cool weather sets in. A cucumber patch is short-lived but produces great quantities. Successive plantings late spring through early summer will insure a steady supply.

Cucumbers are 95 percent water and contain small amounts of vitamins A, C, and a few minerals. Although not the most nutritious of the garden vegetables, cucumbers are surprisingly rich in vitamin E. Like many vegetables, their gift comes with their seasonality. The summer heat usually coincides with a prolific cucumber patch. A light and cooling vegetable, the cucumber helps us replenish the fluids and minerals lost in our perspiration, leaving us "cool as a cucumber."

The cucumber is also an effective skin conditioner, perhaps due to its vitamin E content. Try rubbing an end slice or inside peel on your face and experience its refreshing benefits.

Cooking Tips

- No need to peel a cucumber unless it's waxed or not organic. Wash to remove any garden grit.

- Dice or slice into green salads or chilled vinaigrette-style salads.

- For a sliced decorative effect, peel alternating stripes down the length or score with fork tines.

- Use sliced cucumber in your sandwich or on top of your snack cracker for extra crunch.

- Kids enjoy munching on cucumbers in slices or whole.

- Make refrigerator pickles—simple and delicious!

- Try creamy cucumber salad: toss cucumber rounds with plain yogurt, a little mayonnaise, fresh or dried dill weed or seed, and a little salt and pepper.

- How about chilled cucumber soup? Blend cucumbers with plain yogurt, a pinch of fresh mint, basil, and salt and pepper.

- Add pureed or grated cucumber to a chilled vegetable soup stock.

Storage Tips

- Cucumbers are most stable at 45-50 degrees. However, refrigeration is necessary to retain moisture.

- Store cucumbers in the hydrator drawer of the refrigerator. They will keep up to 1 week.

- A cucumber refrigerated after being cut or peeled will deteriorate quickly. Use up leftovers as soon as possible.

For additional recipes that feature cucumbers, see the Seasonal Combinations and Kids' Recipes chapters.

Marinated Cucumber Tomato Salad   MACSAC

2 cucumbers, peeled and sliced into rounds
4 large tomatoes, sliced into rounds
1/2 cup thinly sliced red onion
1/2 cup extra-virgin olive oil
1/4 cup red wine vinegar

1 tablespoon sugar
salt and pepper
1 tablespoon slivered fresh basil strips
1 tablespoon chopped parsley

Arrange cucumbers, tomatoes, and onions in a shallow serving dish. Mix oil, vinegar, and sugar in a small bowl and pour over vegetables. Season well with salt and pepper. Cover and let marinate for at least 1 hour and up to 4 hours. Sprinkle with herbs just before serving. (The leftover marinade makes a good dressing for salad greens.) Makes 6-8 servings.

Honey Lemon Refrigerator Pickles   Karen Shepard, Blackberry Community Farm

6 cups thinly sliced cucumbers
2 cups thinly sliced onions
3/4 cup honey
1 cup lemon juice
1/2 teaspoon kelp powder

1/2 teaspoon mustard seed
1/2 teaspoon celery seed
1/2 teaspoon ground turmeric
1/2 teaspoon ground cloves

Place cucumbers and onions in large glass bowl. Combine remaining ingredients in a saucepan and bring to a boil. Cook and stir until honey is dissolved. Pour hot liquid over cucumbers and onions, toss well, and let cool. The cucumbers will give off some of their juices; keep them submerged in the liquid while they cool. Transfer pickles to 3 pint jars, cover tightly, and refrigerate for at least 24 hours before serving. They will keep for a week or so. Makes 3 pints.

Spicy Cucumber Salad   Twinhawks/Clearview Family Farms

2 cucumbers
1 tablespoon white vinegar or rice wine vinegar
2 tablespoons sesame oil
1/2 teaspoon salt

1 teaspoon soy sauce
1 tablespoon sugar
1 Thai Dragon hot pepper

Peel the cucumbers, cut lengthwise in two, and scrape out the seeds. Cut cucumbers crosswise into half moons. Whisk the remaining ingredients together and toss with the cucumbers to coat them. You can control how hot the dish becomes by removing the seeds and pulp of the pepper, or you can use just a slice or two of the hot pepper. If you don't have a Thai Dragon hot pepper, substitute hot red pepper flakes or hot pepper sauce. Makes 4 servings.

Cucumber Moons Sautéed with Fresh Dill   MACSAC

2 large or 3 medium cucumbers
3 tablespoons butter
3 tablespoons minced shallots or chopped
   green onions

2 tablespoons chopped fresh dill
salt and pepper

Peel cucumbers with potato peeler and slice in half lengthwise. Scoop out all the seeds with a spoon. Slice about 1/4- to 1/3-inch thick. Heat butter in large, heavy skillet over medium flame. Take care not to let the butter brown, but get it good and hot. Add the cucumbers and shallots and cook, tossing often, until cucumbers begin to get tender, about 4 minutes. Stir in dill plus salt and pepper to taste. Continue to toss and cook until crisp-tender, 1-2 minutes longer. Serve immediately. (Note: The cucumbers in this recipe could also be cut into "hoops": use a long spoon to scoop the seeds out of a peeled cucumber, then slice it into rounds.) Makes 4-6 servings.

Dill

Anetham graveoleus

Although the place of origin for this herb is unknown, it is believed to have grown wild all over the European continent. Today, while dill is highly regarded in some European cuisine, it is greatly disliked by others. Its name is derived from the old Norse word *dilla,* meaning "to lull." Indeed, the herb has carminative qualities as well as other medicinal uses.

Dill is a wonderful herb, fresh, dried or as seed. It has a unique yet mild flavor that enhances a wide variety of dishes. Dill is probably best known for its role in the popular flavor of the dill pickle.

Experiment to your heart's content—it would be very hard to wreck a dish with dill!

Cooking Tips

- For the most part dill is used alone to capture its unique flavor. It is rarely blended with other herbs such as basil and oregano.

- Chop fresh dill (or dried) into a variety of chilled summer salads, such as pasta, potato, tuna, and cucumber.

- Dill is excellent in many stews and soups.

- Make your own dill garlic butter: Melt butter over a low flame. Sauté garlic, being careful not to burn. Add finely chopped dill, fresh or dried, and continue to sauté for another couple minutes. Pour over potatoes or other cooked vegetables. With a splash of lemon it makes an excellent sauce for broiled or baked fish.

- Create your own salad dressing with dill. A yogurt/mayonnaise base is complementary, as is an oil and lemon base.

- Mix chopped dill into a soft, spreadable cheese.

- Knead some dill—weed or seed—into a batch of homemade bread.

- Sprinkle chopped dill on cooked potatoes, other vegetables, or fish.

- Dill seed is excellent for pickles. See Cucumber section for additional recipes that use dill.

Storage Tips

- Fresh dill is best used as soon as possible.

- For short-term storage, wrap dill in a damp towel or place upright in a container with an inch of water and refrigerate.

- For long-term storage, dill can be dried. See chapter on home food preservation for information on drying herbs.

Dill-Dipped Skillet Panfish   MACSAC

1 cup whole wheat pastry flour (or white flour)
1 tablespoon salt
1 teaspoon cracked black pepper
3 eggs
2-3 tablespoons chopped fresh dill

1 tablespoon clarified butter (may substitute whole butter)
2 tablespoons olive or corn oil
1 pound fresh perch, bluegill, crappie, or other panfish fillets

Combine flour, salt, and pepper in a pie pan. Beat eggs with dill in another pan. Heat half the butter and oil in heavy skillet over medium-high flame. Cook fish in batches without crowding the pan: Dredge in flour on both sides, shaking off excess. Dip floured fillets into egg mixture. Let excess drip off, then add to the hot pan (the fat should sizzle immediately) and cook 2-3 minutes. Brown on second side 2-3 minutes. Serve hot. These are good "plain" but you can also serve them with plain yogurt. Makes 4 servings.

Carrot Dill Soup   MACSAC

3 tablespoons butter
1 1/2 pounds carrots, peeled and sliced
1/2 cup chopped onion
6 cups chicken or vegetable stock
1 bay leaf

1 teaspoon sugar
1/2 teaspoon freshly grated or ground nutmeg
1 tablespoon chopped dill, or more to taste
salt and pepper to taste

Sauté carrots and onions in butter over medium flame. Add chicken broth, bay leaf, sugar, and nutmeg. Cover; cook until carrots are soft, about 20 minutes. Remove bay leaf. Add dill and puree mixture. Season with salt and pepper. Makes 6 servings.

Armenian Grape Leaves Stuffed with Dill, Parsley, and Rice   MACSAC

2 cups corn oil
7 cups finely chopped onions
2 bunches parsley, stems removed, chopped
2 cups long-grain white rice
2 bunches green onions, finely chopped

2-3 tablespoons chopped fresh dill or 1 tablespoon dried dill
1 tablespoon salt
2 16-ounce jars of grape leaves, stems snipped off
juice of 1 large lemon

Heat oil in large, heavy pot. Add onions and parsley; cook, stirring often, until onions are translucent, 10-15 minutes. Stir in rice, green onions, dill, salt, and 1 cup water. Cover and simmer over low heat, stirring often, until rice is nearly tender, 20-25 minutes. Uncover, stir, and cool completely. Line a large, heavy pot with several (unstuffed) grape leaves (use the ripped ones, if there are any). Place several grape leaves smooth side down on work surface. Wrap 1 to 2 tablespoons rice mixture in each grape leaf—that is, fold sides of grape leaf over rice and roll up tightly from stem end to tip into short cigar shape. Repeat until rice is used up. Layer stuffed leaves seam side down in leaf-lined pot. Add enough water (3 or more cups) to cover stuffed leaves. Weight with a plate to hold stuffed leaves under water. Cover and simmer 1 hour. Drain and cool. Sprinkle with lemon juice. Chill the stuffed grape leaves before serving. This recipe came from a friend, Araxy Arganian. Makes 50-75 stuffed grape leaves.

Dill and Horseradish Biscuits   MACSAC

1 cup all-purpose flour
1 cup cake flour
2-3 tablespoons chopped fresh dill
2 teaspoons baking powder
1/2 teaspoon baking soda

1/2 teaspoon salt
6 tablespoons cold butter, cut into bits
1 scant cup buttermilk
1 tablespoon prepared horseradish
additional buttermilk

Heat oven to 425 degrees. Mix dry ingredients. Cut in butter until pieces are size of sunflower seeds. Combine buttermilk and horseradish; briefly stir into flour mixture until sticky ball forms. Using floured hands, lightly roll dough into 10 balls and place on ungreased baking sheet. Brush with additional buttermilk; bake 14 minutes. Makes 10 biscuits.

Edible Flower

Edible flowers are a joyous celebration of the garden's offerings. Not only do they add beauty and character to the presentation of a dish, but they also introduce new and unusual flavors.

If it is hard to imagine eating a flower, think of it this way (and then give it a try): The fruits and vegetables we eat are often the same part of the plant, prior to or post flowering. A head of broccoli is made up of hundreds of premature flower buds. Left alone it will soon burst forth into as many bright yellow flowers. A tomato, pepper, or zucchini is the result of a pollinated flower maturing to a fruit.

Although edible flowers are appealing, some caution is warranted. Only certain flowers are safe to ingest; others can be toxic. Sometimes only certain parts of the flower are safe, such as the petals of roses, chrysanthemums, lavender, and calendula. The stems, blossoms, and leaves of others are known to be safe, such as violets, nasturtiums, and Johnny-jump-ups.

Enjoy the beauty and flavor of edible flowers, a delicate fresh food.

Cooking Tips

- Edible flowers are rarely cooked, with the exception of lightly sautéed male squash blossoms.

- Try a salad of only flowers, tossed with a light vinaigrette, or toss a few with salad greens for color contrast.

- Garnish creatively with edible flowers. Substitute for parsley.

- Decorate a birthday cake (or any cake)—no need to make flowers out of frosting.

- Freeze blossoms in ice cubes and add to herbal ice teas or punches.

- Mix petals into soft cheeses or butters, or press on top with a mold.

- Decorate hors d'oeuvres or a dessert plate.

Storage Tips

- Use edible flowers as soon as possible. To store, wrap lightly in plastic and refrigerate briefly. (Not all flowers will tolerate the temperature of the refrigerator.)

- Flowers can also be floated in water to help retain moisture, but will still deteriorate quickly. If you do not plan on using them to eat, enjoy them this way as a colorful centerpiece.

Bee Balm Tea MACSAC

3-4 tablespoons chopped bee balm petals   honey
4 cups boiling water

Steep bee balm petals in 4 cups boiling water. Serve hot or chilled over ice, with honey to taste. Makes 3-4 servings.

Sweet Butter Gems MACSAC

1/2 cup signet marigold petals (bitter   1/2 pound (2 sticks) butter, softened
   white ends removed)

Mix marigold petals with softened butter. Place in pastry bag and pipe into small, decorative shapes. Cover with plastic wrap; chill several hours or days to bring out flavor. Makes 25-50 butter pats.

Chive Blossom Vinegar MACSAC

1/3 cup chive petals   2 cups white wine vinegar

Place 1/3 cup chive petals in clean bottle. Pour in boiling white wine vinegar. Let cool. Cover and store at room temperature several weeks. Strain. Makes 2 cups.

Raspberry Rose Sauce MACSAC

1 pint raspberries   3-4 tablespoons chopped rose petals
4 tablespoons powdered sugar

Puree raspberries; strain out seeds. Whisk in powdered sugar until dissolved. Stir in chopped rose petals. Serve over frozen vanilla custard, on cake pieces, etc. Makes 1/2-3/4 cup.

Flower Gilded Ice Cream Angel Cake Twinhawks/Clearview Family Farm

1 large angel food cake   2 teaspoons light corn syrup
about 1 gallon high-quality ice cream, softened   2-3 dozen edible flowers (violas are beautiful)
1 pint heavy or whipping cream

Tear the angel food cake into bite-size pieces. Layer the cake pieces and ice cream into an angel food cake pan, bundt pan, or other large mold in the following manner: Alternating several hunks of cake and several large spoonfuls of ice cream, layer them into the mold, pushing down with a spoon to remove air pockets and to have the mixture conform to the mold. (Make sure the ice cream is on top of the cake in the first round.) Continue making these layers until the mold is tightly filled. Cover with plastic wrap to keep it airtight. Freeze at least 24 hours. You need to make sure that the cake is solidly frozen. Once it is, remove the cake from the mold in the following manner: Being careful not to get the cake wet, place the outside of the mold under or in warm water to loosen it, then invert it onto a large plate. Freeze it again for 2 hours, then remove from freezer and wrap well in plastic wrap. Return cake to freezer. It will keep this way for up to a week. Just before serving, whip the cream to soft peaks; add the corn syrup, and continue whipping a moment or two longer. Unwrap the cake and place it on a serving platter. Frost it with the whipped cream and decorate it with flowers. Any edible flower petals can be used—let your imagination go! This is a beautiful summer dessert. Makes 12 or more servings.

Eggplant

Solanum melongena

Eggplant is a curious but beautiful vegetable. It is related to several other garden vegetables, like the potato, tomato, and pepper. Many, many varieties exist, including varied shapes, sizes, and even colors. The most commonly cultivated and marketed are the oblong smooth deep purple-skinned eggplants. Also increasing in popularity is the longer, thinner Asian-style eggplant. Fortunately, eggplant varieties are interchangeable in recipes.

Eggplant is believed to have originated in India or Burma. Introduced through trade routes, it became popular in many Arab countries and Northern Africa around 900 A.D. Eggplant appeared in Europe in the 15th century, but believed poisonous, it was cultivated only as an ornamental curiosity. Eggplant reached the U.S. during the 17th century.

Eggplant is a seasonal treat, particularly in northern climes. Like tomatoes and peppers, it is very sensitive to cold. With adequate heat during the day and temperatures not dipping frequently below about 50 degrees at night, eggplant will be ready for harvest mid- to late summer in northern areas. Barring severe pest or disease problems, plants will continue to bear for several weeks or until temperatures become too cool and plants cease flowering. The first frost will usually kill the plant.

Eggplant is low in calories and high in fiber, and offers very small amounts of vitamins and minerals. It is traditionally eaten with other, more nutritious foods.

Cooking Tips

- Eggplant can be peeled, but peeling is not essential. It depends on personal preference and the intended dish.

- To remove any acrid flavors and excess moisture, lightly salt slices of eggplant and allow them to sit in a colander for 10-15 minutes. Gently squeeze out any liquid. Eggplant will now soak up less oil and need less salt in preparation.

- Eggplant is always cooked, eliminating a toxic substance called solanine.

- Eggplant is surprisingly versatile! Here are some very basic ideas. Don't hesitate to elaborate:

  To bake: Prick eggplant all over with a fork and bake at 400 degrees until flesh is tender, about 30-40 minutes. Flesh can be pureed.

  To stuff: Bake 20 minutes, scoop out seeds, replace with stuffing, and return to oven for 15 minutes.

  To sauté: Try dipping slices or chunks in flour or eggs and bread crumbs before sautéing. Sauté in hot oil until light brown. Season with herbs, garlic, grated cheese, etc.

  To steam: Whole eggplant will steam over an inch of water in 15-30 minutes. Use the flesh for pulp or season with olive oil, lemon, salt, and pepper, or cover in a tomato sauce.

- Blend cooked eggplant with lemon juice and seasonings of choice for a dip or spread.

- Grill slices along with other vegetables, such as peppers, or skewer and grill along with other shish kabob ingredients.

- Dip in a favorite batter and lightly fry in vegetable oil.

Storage Tips

- Eggplant is best when it's fresh. Store unrefrigerated at a cool room temperature, or in hydrator drawer of the refrigerator for up to 1 week.

- For long-term storage, dishes like baba ghanouj and ratatouille freeze well in airtight containers.

For additional recipes that feature eggplant, see the Seasonal Combinations chapter.

Chinese Steamed Eggplant   Dog Hollow Farm

1 large eggplant, cut into 6 wedges
2 tablespoons vegetable oil
1 large green onion, cut into 2-inch pieces
2 cloves garlic, minced

3 tablespoons soy sauce
1/4 teaspoon sugar
pinch of black pepper

Steam eggplant until tender, about 30 minutes. Heat oil in wok or large skillet. Stir-fry green onion 1 minute. Add remaining ingredients. Stir-fry 3 more minutes. Makes 3-4 servings.

Grilled Eggplant Red Pepper "Caviar"   MACSAC

2 sweet red peppers
1 1/2 pounds oriental eggplant (the long,
   slender lavender-colored variety)
1 sweet onion, thickly sliced, brushed lightly
   with a little olive oil
1 large tomato, finely chopped

2 cloves garlic
salt and pepper
3-4 tablespoons olive oil
oil-cured black olives
Italian bread

Prepare charcoal in an outdoor grill. When the coals begin to flame, roast the red peppers, turning often, to blacken the skins all around. Remove to a cutting board, scrape off the skin with a sharp knife, and finely chop the flesh. When coals have burned down to medium-high heat, grill the whole eggplants and sliced onions, turning often, until tender. Peel the eggplants; drain them a few minutes in a colander. Mash or finely chop the eggplant flesh and finely chop the onions. Combine eggplant, onions, red peppers, and tomatoes in a bowl. Mince the garlic, sprinkle it with a little salt, and mash it to paste with a fork or the back of a knife. Stir garlic and olive oil into eggplant mixture. Serve with olives and hunks of Italian bread. Makes 4-6 appetizer-size servings or serve this as a main-course for two. Recipe adapted from *Essentially Eggplant,* by Nina Kehayan.

Thai Eggplant Dip   M. Snyder and S. Breckenridge, Isthmus, November 26, 1993

2 medium eggplants
3-4 cloves garlic
1 tablespoon minced fresh ginger
2 tablespoons soy sauce
2 tablespoons rice vinegar

1 tablespoon sesame oil
1 tablespoon minced fresh cilantro
1/2 teaspoon crushed red pepper flakes
salt to taste
pita bread

Cut off eggplant stems. Pierce eggplant several times with a fork. Place on a baking sheet and cook in a 350-degree oven until very soft, about 1 hour. When cool enough to handle, remove skin. With the motor running on a food processor, add garlic and ginger and mince. Add eggplant and whirl until smooth. Add remaining ingredients except bread. Refrigerate up to 4 days or freeze. Serve with warm pita bread triangles. Makes about 2 1/2 cups.

Savory Eggplant with Seasoned Yogurt   MACSAC

1 quart plain yogurt
2-3 cups mashed or finely chopped cooked
   eggplant (roasted, baked, grilled, sautéed, etc.)

2-3 teaspoons finely minced garlic,
   mashed to a paste
2-3 finely chopped fresh mint or cilantro

Stir 3/4 cup water into the yogurt. Stir in eggplant, garlic, and mint or cilantro. Serve immediately or chill first. Serve as a side dish, or use as a topping for grilled foods, as a dip with bread, or a dressing for cooked vegetables, rice, etc. Makes 6-8 servings.

Pete's Grilled Eggplant Tomato Soup   Peter Lundberg

3 large eggplants, sliced lengthwise
1 cup olive oil
2 large yellow onions, diced
6 cloves garlic, minced
6 cups diced tomatoes (fresh or canned)
6 cups chicken stock or vegetable stock
juice of 1 lemon

1 teaspoon ground cumin
2 teaspoons dried oregano
1 teaspoon gray or sea salt
1 teaspoon black pepper
thin, round lemon slices
sour cream

Slice eggplant lengthwise into 1/2-inch-thick planks. Grill or broil them until moderately charred. Meanwhile, place olive oil, onions, and garlic in large soup pot; cook on high heat, stirring frequently, until translucent. Dice the charred eggplant, add it to the pot, reduce heat to medium, and cook 10 minutes, stirring frequently. Add tomatoes and cook 5 minutes. Add stock, lemon juice, and spices; simmer 30 minutes. Let it cool a little, then puree in small batches. The color will be a rich brick hue. You may add salt and additional spices to taste. Reheat the soup when you're ready to serve it, garnishing each bowl with a lemon slice topped with a dollop of sour cream. The soup may also be served chilled in the summer. This is the type of soup you may improvise with, adding other vegetables if you have them. Makes 12 servings.

Eggplant Caponata   Christine Mulvey

1 1/2 pounds eggplant, cut into 3/4-inch cubes
2/3 cup olive oil, divided
salt and pepper
3 cups diced red onions
1 1/2 pounds plum tomatoes, seeded and chopped

1 cup green olives, pitted and chopped
3 tablespoons capers
1 cup thinly sliced celery
1/3 cup red wine vinegar
2 teaspoons sugar

Heat oven to 500 degrees. Toss eggplant cubes with 1/3 cup olive oil and season with salt and pepper. Spread in a single layer on large baking tray and roast 10 minutes. Continue roasting until eggplant browns, another 10-15 minutes, stirring every few minutes. Heat remaining oil in large skillet and sauté onions 10 minutes. Add tomatoes, olives, and capers. Reduce heat to simmer, cover, and cook about 15 minutes. Add eggplant and celery to pan and continue cooking, covered, for about 8 minutes. Remove cover, turn heat up to high, and stir in vinegar and sugar. Cook until vinegar evaporates and all flavors meld, about 3 more minutes. Season to taste with salt and pepper. Serve hot or cold, with bread, pasta, etc. Makes 8 servings.

Eggplant Basil Sandwiches   Abby Mandel

1 firm, slim medium eggplant, peeled and cut
   crosswise into 1/4-inch-thick slices
   (about 4 cups or 20-24 slices)
kosher salt
1 package (8 ounces) light cream cheese, softened
1/2 cup minced fresh basil

3/4 cup soft bread crumbs
3/4 teaspoon salt
1/4 teaspoon cayenne pepper
2 large eggs
vegetable oil (for cooking eggplant)

Lightly salt eggplant slices with kosher salt; place in colander and weight the slices with a heavy pot. Let stand in sink at least 30 minutes. Rinse with cold water and pat dry with paper towels. Mix cream cheese and basil in small bowl until smooth. Combine bread crumbs, 3/4 teaspoon salt, and cayenne pepper on sheet of waxed paper. Crack eggs into a pie plate or shallow dish; froth with a fork. Spread eggplant slices with herbed cheese, using about 2 teaspoons on smaller slices and slightly more on larger ones. Make sandwiches with the slices. Dip sandwiches first in beaten eggs, then in crumbs until well coated. Heat oil to 1/8-inch depth in large, nonstick skillet over medium heat. When very hot, fry sandwiches, in batches without crowding, until crisp and golden on both sides, about 3 minutes per side. Serve warm (not hot). Sandwiches can be kept warm in preheated 225-degree oven while remaining sandwiches are cooked. These are nice with a thick tomato sauce. This recipe is contributed by Abby Mandel and is from her book, *Celebrating the Midwestern Table*. Makes 8-10 small sandwiches.

Moroccan Couscous-Stuffed Eggplant MACSAC

2 eggplants (each about 1/2 pound)
olive oil (some for brushing eggplant plus
   1 tablespoon for cooking vegetables)
salt and pepper
1/3 cup couscous
1 cup chopped onion
4 teaspoons minced garlic
1 tablespoon ground coriander
1 tablespoon ground cumin
1 1/2 teaspoons ground cinnamon
1/4 cup toasted pine nuts
1/4 cup toasted almonds
2 tablespoons each fresh mint and cilantro, minced
3 tablespoons currants
3 tablespoons finely chopped dried apricots
3 tablespoons finely chopped pitted black Moroccan olives

Raita:
2 tablespoons minced scallions
2 tablespoons orange juice
1 tablespoon minced orange zest
1 tablespoon chopped fresh mint
1 tablespoon chopped cilantro
2/3 cup plain yogurt

Heat oven to 350 degrees. Cut off top and bottom of eggplants, then cut them in half lengthwise. To ease removal of flesh after roasting, run a knife along the perimeter of eggplant, being careful to cut only the flesh, not the skin. Score the center of the flesh. Brush with olive oil, sprinkle with salt and pepper, and place on a foil-lined baking sheet. Bake until flesh is soft, 20-40 minutes. Meanwhile, bring 2/3 cup water to boil in small saucepan. Stir in couscous, cover, and remove from heat. Let stand 5 minutes. Remove cover, fluff couscous with a fork, and let it cool.

When eggplant is baked, scoop the flesh from each half, taking care to keep skin intact. Return the "shells" to the baking pan. Roughly chop the eggplant flesh. Heat 1 tablespoon olive oil in a skillet, add onions, and cook, stirring occasionally, 3-4 minutes. Stir in garlic and cook 30 seconds. Add chopped eggplant and cook, stirring often, until vegetables are tender and turn golden brown, about 6 minutes. Stir in coriander, cumin, and cinnamon. Season generously with salt and pepper. Mix in all the remaining filling ingredients. Heap mixture into eggplant shells. Return to the oven and roast another 15 minutes. Meanwhile, mix the raita ingredients. Serve as a sauce for the eggplant. Makes 4 servings.

Imam Bayildi (Classic Turkish Stuffed Eggplant) Elisabeth Howard, Vermont Valley Farm member

2 medium eggplants
salt
6 or more tablespoons olive oil, divided
2 large onions, thinly sliced
1 green bell pepper, thinly sliced
2 garlic cloves, chopped

1 pound coarsely chopped fresh tomatoes or
   1 can (14 ounces) chopped tomatoes
3 tablespoons sugar
1 teaspoon ground coriander
black pepper
4 tablespoons chopped fresh cilantro or parsley, divided

Cut stems off eggplants and slice them in half lengthwise. Make a few slashes in the cut sides, sprinkle them very generously with salt, and set them on paper towels, cut side down, for at least 30 minutes. Heat oven to 375 degrees. Rinse salt off eggplants and dry them well with towels. Heat 3-4 tablespoons olive oil in large skillet over medium flame. Add eggplants, cut side down, and cook them 5-7 minutes. Arrange partially cooked eggplants, cut side up, in baking dish. Heat another 2 tablespoons olive oil, add onions, bell peppers, and garlic, and fry over medium flame until vegetables are soft, 10-15 minutes. Stir in tomatoes, sugar, coriander, and pepper to taste; bring to simmer and cook another 5 minutes. Stir in half the cilantro or parsley. Pour sauce onto eggplants and bake until eggplant is very tender, 30-45 minutes. Spoon any juices that have collected in the pan over the eggplants when they come out of the oven. You can serve this hot, but it is more traditionally chilled before serving. Top with remaining cilantro and drizzle on a bit more olive oil, if desired. It's great eaten with bread and yogurt. This recipe was adapted from one in *The Complete Encyclopedia of Vegetables and Vegetarian Cooking*, by Roz Denny and Christine Ingram. Makes 4 main-course or 8-12 appetizer-size servings.

Fennel
Foeniculum vulgaris

Fennel's history is as rich as its flavor! For centuries fennel has been utilized as a food, medicine, herb, and even insect repellent. In ancient Greece, fennel played a significant role in celebrations of the gods and goddesses. It was planted in the temple gardens in their honor and worshippers wore crowns of the feathery leaves. In Greek mythology knowledge sometimes came to humans from Mt. Olympus in the form of a fiery coal contained in a fennel stalk.

The ancient Egyptians, Greeks, and Romans believed fennel an excellent aid for digestion, bronchial troubles, poor eyesight, and nervous conditions. Today, in India, fennel seed is used for seasoning as well as chewed after the meal as a breath freshener and digestive aid. Nutritionally, fennel is very low in calories, but offers significant vitamin A and calcium, potassium, and iron.

Fennel grows wild around much of the world, but two varieties are cultivated: the bulbous Florence fennel and the common fennel grown for its seed and leaves. Belonging to the Umbel family, it is related to carrots, celery, parsley, dill (which it resembles in looks), and anise (which it resembles in flavor).

Fennel thrives in warm, moist climates, hence its success in Mediterranean cuisine. In northern states cultivating fennel is a tenuous thing. Seedlings are planted in the garden after danger of frost, and if all goes well, they're ready for harvest by midsummer and may continue to be available through early fall.

Cooking Tips

- Wash fennel bulb, trimming off any damaged areas or woody parts of the stalk.

- Try crunching a fennel stem or a slice of the bulb to familiarize yourself with the flavor. You might find it grows on you quickly.

- Try substituting for celery in most any recipe.

- Fennel can be baked, steamed, or sautéed with excellent results.

- Try cutting fennel into quarters, drizzle with olive oil, and bake until tender, about 35 minutes.

- Try a sauté of fennel, artichoke hearts, zucchini, tomatoes, sweet bell pepper, thyme, and a dash of salt and pepper.

- Steam fennel and chill it along with the other vegetables; dress with a spoonful of lemon juice, olive oil, chopped chives or green onion, and salt and pepper.

- Cut raw fennel into slices and use for dipping. To enjoy natural flavor, try dipping slices into a small bowl of extra-virgin olive oil seasoned with salt and pepper.

- Use feathery leaves as a fresh herb for seasoning. Try using it in place of dill. Fennel is excellent on baked or broiled fish with butter and lemon.

- Italians use fennel as part of an antipasto platter or for dessert along with a soft goat cheese.

- Add to soups, pureed or chopped. Slices can be sautéed first to lock in flavors.

Storage Tips

- Store fennel in a plastic bag in the refrigerator for up to 2 weeks.

- The delicate leaves will go limp. Wrap them in a moist towel and refrigerate.

Braised Fennel   Cathie Imes, Arbor House - An Environmental Inn

3 tablespoons butter
1/4 cup chopped shallots
seeds from 2 cardamom pods, crushed
1/8 teaspoon ground mace

2 medium fennel bulbs, cut lengthwise into
   6 pieces each
1 1/4 cups chicken stock
salt and pepper to taste

Heat oven to 350 degrees. Melt butter in heavy, ovenproof skillet over low heat. Add shallots, cardamom, and mace; sauté 8 minutes. Add fennel and toss to coat. Stir in stock, bring to boil, cover, and braise in oven 30 minutes, basting occasionally. Place skillet over high heat and boil until liquid thickens slightly, about 15 minutes. Season with salt and pepper. Makes 4 servings.

Carrot Fennel Orange Soup   Edith Thayer, Vermont Valley Farm member

2 tablespoons butter or butter-flavored cooking spray
1 medium fennel bulb, thinly sliced
   (reserve a few of the fronds)
4 cups sliced carrots (approximately 1 1/2 pounds)
1 garlic clove, sliced thin (you can add a couple of
   garlic scapes, if available)

4 cups water, vegetable broth, or chicken broth
   (or more for a thinner soup)
1/2 teaspoon salt, or more to taste
1/3 cup orange juice
1/4 cup sour cream

Heat butter in a large saucepan over medium heat. Add sliced fennel and cook, stirring often, until soft and beginning to turn golden. Add carrots and garlic; cook and stir for a minute or two. Add water or broth and salt; bring to simmer, cover, and cook until carrots and fennel are tender, about 20 minutes. Puree mixture in a food processor or blender, or with an immersion blender. Stir in orange juice and sour cream until smooth and creamy. Reheat on low heat, but do not boil. Serve each bowl garnished with fennel fronds. Makes 4 servings.

Tim's Layered Antipasto   MACSAC

2 large or 4-6 small fennel bulbs,
   quartered and sliced thinly
1 jar (16 ounces) mild cherry peppers
1 cup pitted, chopped imported black olives
8 ounces thin-sliced aged provolone cheese,
   cut into strips

8 ounces thin-sliced Italian salami, cut into strips
2 tablespoons balsamic vinegar
4 tablespoons olive oil
2 tablespoons chopped fresh fennel leaves
1/2 teaspoon freshly ground black pepper
Italian bread

Spread fennel in large, shallow serving dish. Drain off liquid from the jar of cherry peppers, reserving 1 tablespoon of it for the dressing. Quarter the peppers and rinse under running water to remove seeds. Spread pepper quarters over fennel. Arrange olives over peppers. Scatter cheese and salami over olives. Whisk remaining ingredients; drizzle evenly over salad. Serve at room temperature with plenty of fresh Italian bread to soak up the dressing. This is adapted from a recipe by a friend, Tim Mahoney of St. Paul. Makes 8-12 appetizer servings.

Fennel, Bean, and Pasta Salad   Sharon Redinger, member of Dog Hollow Farm

fennel bulbs, leafy tops removed and reserved
1 small onion
olive oil

1 can (28 ounces) kidney beans, drained
2-3 cups cooked pasta
1 teaspoon lemon pepper

Thinly slice fennel bulbs and onion; sauté in olive oil. Chop reserved fennel tops and add to cooked mixture with remaining ingredients. Serve chilled. Makes 4-6 servings.

Fennel Orange Muffins   Angele Theriault, Harmony Valley Farm member

1 medium seedless orange, peeled
2 eggs
1/2 cup vegetable oil
3/4 cup brown sugar
1 teaspoon vanilla

2 cups grated fennel bulbs
2 1/4 cups flour
1 1/2 teaspoons baking powder
1/2 teaspoon salt

Heat oven to 350 degrees. Oil muffin cups. Puree orange in blender, then combine with eggs, oil, sugar, vanilla, and fennel in a bowl. Sift flour, baking powder, and salt, then gently fold into wet ingredients. Do not overmix. Spoon into muffin cups; bake 20-25 minutes until golden brown. Makes 8-12 muffins.

Fresh Fennel Bulb Salad   Jenny Bonde and Rink DaVee, Shooting Star Farm

1 large or 2 small fennel bulbs
2 tablespoons white wine or red wine vinegar
1 teaspoon Dijon mustard
salt and pepper

2 tablespoons frozen orange juice concentrate,
  partially thawed
2 tablespoons extra-virgin olive oil

Remove fronds from the fennel bulb(s). Cut away the root and slice fennel into very thin pieces (it can also be grated). Make dressing by combining vinegar, mustard, 1/4 teaspoon salt, and orange juice concentrate in a bowl. Gradually whisk in olive oil. Pour over fennel and allow to marinate at room temperature 20 minutes or longer. Season to taste with pepper and additional salt. Makes 3-4 side-dish servings.

Grilled (or Griddled) Fennel and Onions with Parmesan   MACSAC

1/2 large sweet onion (do not cut off root end)
2 tablespoons olive oil
salt and freshly ground black pepper

2 fennel bulbs (stalks removed), about
  1 pound total
1/4 cup freshly grated Parmesan

Heat large cast-iron griddle (flat side down, ridged side up) on stove top over medium flame, or prepare outdoor grill for medium heat. Place flat surface of onion half on cutting board and cut into slices that are 1/3-inch thick, leaving some of the root end intact on each slice. Brush both sides of onions lightly with olive oil and sprinkle generously with salt and pepper. Grill onions on both sides until tender and lightly charred, 3-5 minutes per side. Meanwhile, slice whole fennel bulbs lengthwise in the same manner as onions. Steam them over boiling water 8-10 minutes; drain well. Brush lightly with olive oil and season with salt and pepper. Grill on both sides until tender and lightly charred, 6-8 minutes per side. Arrange onions and fennel on a colorful platter; scatter Parmesan over the top. This is delicious with grilled fish or lamb, or as a side dish with Italian tomato-based pasta dishes. Makes 6 servings.

Fennel Egg Salad   MACSAC

6 large eggs (not too fresh! they will be
  difficult to peel if very fresh)
1/3 cup finely chopped fennel stalk
2-3 tablespoons chopped fennel leaves
2-4 tablespoons finely chopped sweet red onion

4 tablespoons mayonnaise
1 1/2 tablespoons white wine vinegar
2 teaspoons Dijon mustard
salt and pepper to taste

Place eggs in saucepan and cover with cold water. Bring to boil. Turn off heat. Cover pan tightly and set timer for 9 minutes. When timer goes off, drain eggs and immerse them in ice water 10-15 minutes. Peel and quarter eggs; place in food processor and, using the pulse button, pulse until finely chopped, 8-12 times. Add remaining ingredients; pulse until ingredients are well blended, 3-6 more times. Use as a sandwich filling, a spread for crackers, a cold sauce for chilled asparagus, or a garnish for tossed green salads. Makes 2 cups.

Zucchini, Fennel, and Andouille Pie   MACSAC

1/2 tablespoon butter, softened
3 tablespoons bread crumbs
1 tablespoon olive oil
3/4 cup diced onion
3/4 cup diced fennel bulb
1 teaspoon minced garlic
2 cups diced zucchini
1 link (4 ounces) andouille sausage

1/2 teaspoon crushed fennel seed
salt and pepper
3-4 ounces Swiss cheese
3 large eggs
1/2 cup milk
for garnish: diced roasted red pepper, chopped
    black olives, or chopped fennel leaves

Heat oven to 350 degrees. Generously grease a pie plate with the butter. Sprinkle bread crumbs over buttered areas. Heat olive oil in skillet over medium flame. Add onion, fennel, and garlic; sauté until vegetables are partially tender, about 5 minutes. Raise heat to medium-high; stir in zucchini, andouille, fennel seed, and salt and pepper to taste. Sauté until zucchini is tender, 3-5 minutes. Spread mixture on platter; cool 10 minutes. Meanwhile, grate cheese; sprinkle two-thirds of it into pie pan. Beat eggs with milk in bowl. Stir cooled vegetable mixture into egg mixture; pour into pan. Sprinkle remaining cheese on top. Rim outer edge of pie filling with garnish choice. Bake until set, about 30 minutes. Cool 10 minutes before serving. Makes 6-8 servings.

Tomato, Fennel, and Italian Sausage Sauce for Pasta or Polenta   MACSAC

2 tablespoons olive oil, divided
1-1 1/2 pounds Italian sausage links (hot or mild)
1 cup finely chopped onion
2 tablespoons minced garlic
1 cup finely chopped fennel stalk
1 teaspoon fennel seed
2 cans (each 28 ounces) whole peeled tomatoes,
    pureed, or 7-8 cups peeled, chopped fresh tomatoes

2 tablespoons tomato paste
1/2 cup red wine
pinch sugar
red pepper flakes
salt and pepper
1-2 tablespoons minced fennel leaves (optional)
freshly grated Parmesan cheese

Heat 1 tablespoon olive oil in large skillet over medium flame. Add Italian sausage links and brown on all sides. Drain on paper towels. Heat remaining 1 tablespoon olive oil in a large saucepan. Add onion, garlic, chopped fennel stalk, and fennel seed. Cook, stirring often, until vegetables are tender. Stir in tomatoes, tomato paste, wine, sugar, and a pinch or two of red pepper flakes. Bring to simmer and cook, stirring occasionally, 20-30 minutes. Slice sausages into rounds and add to sauce. Continue to simmer 30 or more minutes. Season to taste with salt and pepper. Stir in minced fennel leaves just before serving, if desired. Toss with hot, cooked pasta (use a short, thick type like penne or corkscrew) or serve over hot polenta, with Parmesan cheese. Makes 8-10 servings.

Tangerine and Fennel Salad with Mixed Greens   MACSAC

6-7 small tangerines
1/4 cup olive oil
1/4 cup dry sherry or flat champagne
1/2 cup thinly sliced fennel bulb

2 tablespoons minced fresh fennel "leaves"
    (the feathery part of the plant)
salt and freshly ground black pepper to taste
4-5 cups mixed salad greens

Cut 1 of the tangerines in half and squeeze the juice into a medium bowl. Mix in olive oil, sherry, both kinds of fennel, salt, and pepper. Peel remaining tangerines; divide into segments. Pierce each segment with a sharp fork a couple of times (to absorb dressing). Add tangerines to dressing; toss well. Chill thoroughly. Divide greens onto 4 salad plates. Arrange tangerine mixture over greens, drizzling some dressing directly onto greens. Sprinkle with additional salt and pepper. Makes 4 servings.

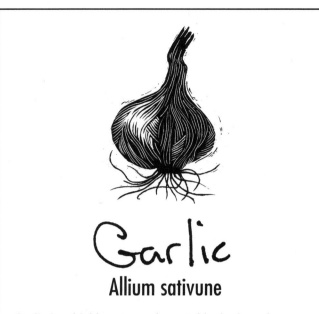

Garlic

Allium sativune

Garlic is a highly esteemed vegetable, herb, and medicine in many cultures around the world. Its rich history speaks to its culinary and medicinal importance, beginning with the first recorded writings on garlic in Sanskrit in 5000 B.C. Garlic glorification continues right up to the 125 medical articles in the National Library of Medicine in Bethesda, Maryland, all written since 1983.

Garlic lore is fascinating. Slaves forced to build the great Egyptian pyramids refused to work without a daily garlic ration. Garlic's protective powers extended beyond its medicinal properties. Wreaths of garlic were believed to ward off witches and vampires. Jockeys may rub their horses' bits with garlic or tie a clove to the bridle to prevent other horses from passing. Bullfighters may wear garlic around their necks to protect them from the bulls' horns.

Truthfully, garlic does offer more than great-tasting dishes. It's gaining recognition for its health and healing benefits as more and more medical studies reveal excellent results. Some of garlic's believed therapeutic benefits include fighting infections, cancer prevention, stimulating the immune system, prevention and relief of chronic bronchitis, use as an expectorant and decongestant, and reduction of blood pressure, cholesterol, and triglycerides. Note: If the medicinal benefits are what you're after, use your garlic raw!

The 100 sulfur-containing compounds that instill garlic's medicinal properties also contribute to "garlic breath." Chew a little raw parsley to remedy any odors that might annoy you, and continue to enjoy garlic's many gifts.

Cooking Tips

- Garlic greens in the spring may be chopped or diced raw into green or pasta salads, sautéed in place of bulb garlic, sprinkled onto pizza, eaten raw, or used anywhere garlic flavor is desired.

- Press, mince, or slice garlic cloves. A sharp knife yields best results when chopping. One medium clove of garlic equals 1 teaspoon minced.

- To mellow garlic's strong flavor, opt for longer cooking. To enjoy its more pungent flavors and increased medicinal benefit, use it raw or with minimal cooking.

- Sauté garlic only until translucent, as it will burn quickly, producing a bitter unpleasant flavor.

- Add to soups at beginning of cooking and again at the end or just before serving.

- For garlic aroma try rubbing a cut clove around the rim of a serving bowl.

- Make garlic butter: Use 1/2 cup of softened butter mashed with 4 minced cloves of garlic.

- Try roasted garlic. Cut tops off garlic bulbs to expose cloves, brush or dab with olive oil, and bake for 1 hour at 350 degrees. Squeeze garlic out of its skins and spread on a good crusty bread. A gourmet treat!

Storage Tips

- Garlic stores well in a cool, dark, dry, and well-ventilated place for several months. Warm temperatures will encourage garlic to sprout.

- Do not refrigerate, unless storing peeled cloves for a short time. Keep in airtight container to avoid garlic odor spreading to other foods.

- For very long-term storage, garlic can be minced and covered or blended with olive oil and placed in small airtight containers and frozen. After removing from the freezer, keep it in refrigerator.

Braised Garlic with Creamed Chevre   Lucy Ito, Harmony Valley Farm member

4 bulbs garlic, separated into cloves
1/4 cup butter (1/2 stick), cubed or sliced
1/4 cup extra-virgin olive oil
salt and freshly ground pepper
a few sprigs of fresh thyme or 1/2 teaspoon dried

1/2 cup dry white wine
8 ounces soft goat cheese, at room temperature
1/4 cup heavy cream
baguette or peasant bread

Heat oven to 275 degrees. Place cloves in casserole dish. Dot with butter and drizzle with olive oil. Season with salt and pepper. Stick thyme sprigs here and there throughout garlic. Bake uncovered for a half hour, basting occasionally. Add wine, cover, and bake another hour or until cloves are soft. Mix goat cheese and heavy cream. Serve braised garlic and creamed goat cheese with slices of good bread. Makes 6-8 appetizer servings.

Roasted Garlic Dip   Amy Simonson

1 head garlic
1/2 tablespoon plus 1/4 cup olive oil, divided
freshly ground black pepper

1/4 cup freshly grated Parmesan cheese
baguette or other crusty bread

Heat oven to 275 or 300 degrees. Cut 1/4-1/2 inch off top of garlic head to expose tips of cloves. Lay garlic head cut-side up in small baking dish. Drizzle 1/2 tablespoon olive oil over top; sprinkle on some pepper. Roast until soft, fragrant, and lightly browned, about 45 minutes. Cool completely. Squeeze cloves from the base and use a fork to dislodge flesh from skin. Mash garlic with a fork on small plate. Stir in Parmesan, additional 1/4 cup olive oil, and pepper to taste. Serve with baguette or crusty bread. Makes 2-4 appetizer servings.

Sopa de Ajo (Spanish Garlic Soup)   MACSAC

5 tablespoons olive oil, divided
4 cloves garlic, peeled and sliced
1 1/2 teaspoons sweet paprika, divided
4 cups chicken broth (homemade preferred)
salt and pepper

1 tablespoon minced garlic
4 cups stale French bread, in 3/4-inch cubes
6 eggs
1 cup diced ham

Heat 1 tablespoon olive oil in pot over medium-low flame. Add sliced garlic and cook briefly, without browning. Stir in half the paprika, chicken broth, and 3 cups water; cover and simmer 45 minutes. Season lightly with salt and pepper. Combine remaining olive oil and minced garlic in skillet; heat briefly over low flame. Add bread and cook, stirring often, until crisp, 10-15 minutes. Toss in remaining paprika. Heat oven to 450 degrees. Place 6 ovenproof bowls on baking sheet. Pour a little simmering broth into each bowl. Break an egg into each bowl, then scatter ham over eggs. Fill bowls with remaining broth. Bake until eggs are set, 3-5 minutes. Scatter in "croutons"; serve immediately. Makes 6 servings.

Buttermilk Garlic Dressing   MACSAC

1-2 medium garlic cloves
4 tablespoons minced green onion
3 tablespoons white wine vinegar
1/2 cup buttermilk

1/3 cup sour cream
large pinch sugar
1/2 cup olive oil

Mince garlic; mash to a paste with fork or back of knife. Whisk garlic, green onion, vinegar, buttermilk, sour cream, and sugar in bowl. Gradually whisk in the olive oil. Season generously with salt and pepper to taste. Makes almost 1 1/2 cups.

Greens-Cooked

Experience the vitality of fresh garden greens! The more common cooking greens—arugula, collards, kale, mustard greens, turnip greens, beet greens, Swiss chard, dandelion greens, spinach, and radish tops—may be used interchangeably. Experiment with the different greens available to you and get to know their unique and mild to pungent flavors. See the section on salad greens for information on the variety of tender greens generally eaten raw. Also, see the sections on kale, Swiss chard, and spinach for more ideas and recipes appropriate for greens.

Most garden greens love cool weather. They grow quickly and will be among the first vegetables of the season in spring and the final leafy ones in the fall.

Their vibrancy and freshness are a gift of flavor and health. Greens are packed with nutrition. Properly prepared, greens offer generous amounts of vitamins A and C, some B vitamins, and folic acid, as well as minerals such as calcium and iron. Greens are very high in dietary fiber and low in calories. In the health world, dark leafy greens also receive attention for their roles in disease prevention. So don't forget to eat your greens!

Cooking Tips

- Wash greens thoroughly before cooking to remove hidden garden grit.
- Be careful not to overcook. Overcooked greens will be mushy, tasteless, and significantly reduced in nutrition.
- Greens will generally cook down to 1/4 or 1/8 of their original volume.
- Boil greens for 2-4 minutes, or steam for 5-8 minutes, depending on maturity and toughness of greens. Watch for the color to brighten; this signals cooking is complete or nearly complete. Colors will darken and fade in vibrancy when overcooked.
- Baby greens are excellent for sautéing, and larger mature greens are best for stir-frying—add them toward the end of the cooking time…anywhere from 2-5 minutes is usually adequate for both.
- Most greens are interchangeable, but pungency does vary. The milder greens include spinach, Swiss chard, collards, beet greens, and kale. The spicier greens include turnip, mustard, arugula, and radish.
- Try raw tender greens like spinach, Swiss chard, or beet greens in your sandwich or burrito.
- Greens add color, texture, and flavor to soups and stews.
- Serve cooked greens simply. Here are a few suggestions: Toss with red wine vinegar, olive oil, salt and pepper. Toss with sesame oil, rice vinegar, and soy sauce. Toss with a lemon vinaigrette. Top with a pat of butter or eat totally plain!
- Mix greens into omelets, quiches, lasagna, and casseroles.
- Sauté precooked greens in garlic butter and onion.
- Baby greens make an excellent raw salad.

Storage Tips

- Store preferably unwashed, wrapped in a damp towel or plastic bag in the hydrator drawer of the refrigerator. Best used very fresh, but may last for up to 1 week if properly stored. Keep moist.
- For long-term storage, greens freeze well. Blanch washed greens for 2-3 minutes. Rinse in cold water to stop the cooking process, drain, and pack into airtight containers such as zip-lock freezer bags. See chapter on home food preservation for more information on freezing vegetables.

For additional recipes that feature cooked greens, see the Chard, Spinach, Kale, Seasonal Combinations, and Kids' Recipes chapters.

Fresh Greens Pasta Pie   Crystal Lake Gardens

6 ounces vermicelli
2 tablespoons butter or margarine, softened
1/3 cup grated Parmesan cheese
5 eggs
2 teaspoons cooking oil
1 small onion, chopped
2 cups chopped fresh spinach or other greens

1 cup (4 ounces) shredded mozzarella cheese
1/3 cup milk
1/2 teaspoon salt
1/4 teaspoon freshly ground pepper
1/8 teaspoon ground nutmeg
several shakes hot pepper sauce (optional)

Heat oven to 350 degrees. Lightly grease a large pie plate. Cook vermicelli according to package directions; drain. Stir butter and Parmesan cheese into hot vermicelli. Beat 2 of the eggs and stir well into pasta. Spoon mixture into pie plate, and use a spoon to shape vermicelli into a pie shell. Cover with aluminum foil and bake 10 minutes. Set aside. Heat oil in small skillet, add onion and sauté until tender. Beat the remaining 3 eggs and combine with spinach, mozzarella, milk, seasonings, and sautéed onions. Spoon spinach mixture into pasta shell. Cover pie with aluminum foil. Bake 35 minutes; uncover and bake an additional 5 minutes. Let stand 10 minutes before slicing. Makes 6 servings.

A Simple Greens Soup   Matt Overdevest, Harmony Valley Farm (summer 2002)

2 tablespoons butter or oil
1 small yellow onion, medium-diced
1 pound peeled Jerusalem artichokes or other
   root vegetable, medium-diced
4 cups water or low-sodium chicken broth

1 bunch watercress, sorrel, Red Russian kale,
   or nettles, washed and chopped
salt and pepper
1/2 cup heavy cream (optional)

Heat butter or oil in saucepan over medium heat. Add onions; cook slowly, stirring occasionally, until they are translucent (don't let them brown). Add the Jerusalem artichokes and water or broth. Bring to a boil, then reduce to a simmer and cook until the artichokes are soft when pierced with a fork, approximately 15 minutes. Add the greens and cook them until they wilt, about 3 minutes. (If you're using kale, let it cook about 5 minutes.) Puree the soup with an immersion blender (or in batches in a blender or food processor) until smooth. Season to taste with salt and pepper. Optional: You may pass soup through a strainer to take out the little bits and make it smoother. If you plan to do this step, you may also skip peeling the artichokes as the skins will strain out. For a creamy version, add heavy cream at the end and heat through. Makes 4 servings.

Will's Collard Greens   Will Allen, Growing Power

1 bunch colllard greens, stems cut
   out and discarded
1/4 cup olive oil
1/2 teaspoon salt

1/4 teaspoon pepper
1 teaspoon sugar
1 teaspoon minced garlic (optional)

Wash the collard leaves and stack them (5-10 leaves at a time). Roll them up tightly, then slice thinly so you have a chiffonade of greens. Heat the olive oil in a large pan over medium heat with salt, pepper, sugar, and garlic. When the oil is hot, add collards and stir often for 15-20 minutes, until collards are tender, taking care not to burn the greens. Add more oil if necessary. Makes 4 servings.

Shelled Cranberry Beans and Arugula   MACSAC

1 1/2 cups shelled fresh cranberry beans
1 teaspoon minced garlic

3/4 cup chopped fresh arugula
salt and pepper

Bring a medium potful of salted water to boil. Add cranberry beans and garlic; simmer until beans are tender, 12-15 minutes. Drain off nearly all the liquid. Stir in arugula. Season to taste with salt and pepper. Serve immediately. Makes 2-4 servings.

Summer Greens and Potato Fry-Up   Mara Rosenbloom

1 tablespoon butter
1 teaspoon chili oil (or substitute vegetable oil with
  a little crushed red pepper)
1 baking potato, or 3-4 small red potatoes, thin-sliced
1 leek or small onion, finely chopped
salt and pepper
1/2 pound fresh spinach, chard or other mild-flavored
  greens, washed and stemmed

1/2 teaspoon dried ground thyme
3/4 cup cooked sweet corn
3 sprigs fresh oregano, torn up (or other fresh
  herbs except mint)
1/2 teaspoon paprika
grated Parmesan (optional)

Heat butter and chili oil in large nonstick skillet over medium flame. Add potatoes and leeks or onions, and season
well with salt and pepper. (You may also partially cook the potatoes first in salted water until nearly tender before
frying them.) Let the potatoes brown lightly in the pan on one side for several minutes. Toss potatoes, season with
more salt and pepper, and let them brown lightly again. When potatoes are almost tender, toss in greens and thyme,
then add a little less than a 1/4 cup water, cover the pan, and raise heat to high. Let steam until greens are nearly
done, 1-2 minutes. Uncover, add corn, oregano, and paprika, and allow potatoes to finish cooking and browning.
Season to taste and top with Parmesan, if desired. Serve with fried eggs if you like. Makes 2-4 servings.

Asian-Style Sauté   Harmony Valley Farm

2 tablespoons sesame oil
3-4 cloves garlic, chopped
1/2 pound mixed greens, coarsely chopped

1 tablespoon vinegar
2 tablespoons tamari
freshly ground black pepper

Heat oil in wok or large skillet to moderate heat. Add garlic and sauté 2 minutes. Remove garlic and set aside. Sauté
the greens until just wilted. Remove from heat, and stir in vinegar, tamari, pepper, and garlic. Serve immediately.
Great as a side dish or with rice. Makes 2-4 servings.

Spicy Potato Sausage and Greens Soup   JoAnn Hoffman, Vermont Valley Farm member

1 pound bulk hot Italian sausage
1/2 cup chopped onion, or more to taste
4 cups chicken broth
4 cups thinly sliced potatoes (slice them with
  skins on)

4 cups water
2 packed cups torn or chopped fresh kale,
  spinach, chard, or other greens
1/3 cup whipping cream
salt and pepper

Heat soup pot over medium flame. Add sausage and onions and cook until meat is no longer pink. Add broth,
potatoes, and 4 cups water. Bring to boil, reduce heat, and simmer until potatoes are tender, 10-15 minutes. Stir in
greens; cook 1-2 minutes. Stir in whipping cream and season to taste with salt and pepper. Serve right away, or, for
more developed flavor, let cool, then chill and reheat later or the next day. This recipe was inspired by a soup at Olive
Garden restaurant. Add some buttered biscuits and it's a perfect winter meal. Makes 8-12 servings.

Spanish Greens   MACSAC

2 tablespoons olive oil
3 cloves garlic, flattened or smashed with
  the flat of a knife
1 pound spinach, chard, collards, or other
  greens, stemmed and well washed

salt and pepper to taste
1/4 cup golden raisins
3 tablespoons toasted pine nuts

Heat oil over high flame in very large skillet. Add garlic cloves and stir-fry until golden, about 30 seconds. Discard
garlic. Toss in greens. Season with salt and pepper. Cover; wilt greens 2-3 minutes. Add raisins and pine nuts. Check
for seasoning and serve. Makes 2-4 servings.

Oven Polenta with Glazed Baby Onions, Mustard Greens, and Blue Cheese
MACSAC

20-24 small ("boiling") onions (about 1 pound)
1 cup yellow cornmeal (medium grain)
4 1/2 cups chicken or vegetable stock, divided
salt and pepper
2 tablespoons butter
2 teaspoons sugar
2 teaspoons cider vinegar

2 tablespoons olive oil
2 teaspoons minced garlic
1/4 teaspoon crushed red chile flakes
1 pound mustard greens, thick stems discarded, leaves
   chopped (or substitute turnip or other spicy-
   flavored greens)
4 ounces blue cheese, crumbled

Bring a pot of water to boiling. Cut a tiny "X" in root end of onions, drop them in the boiling water, and cook 1-2 minutes. Drain, cool, and slice off ends, leaving a little root end intact so onions won't fall apart when cooked further. Remove skins. Heat oven to 350 degrees. Oil a large ovenproof skillet (preferably nonstick). Add cornmeal, 4 cups stock, and 1 teaspoon salt; stir well (it won't get smooth until it's cooked). Bake uncovered, *without stirring*, until liquid is absorbed, 40-50 minutes. Meanwhile, melt butter over medium heat in skillet. Add onions, sprinkle with salt, and cook until nearly tender, 8-10 minutes, shaking pan frequently to prevent sticking. Add sugar and continue to cook, shaking pan, 2 to 3 minutes. Add remaining 1/4 cup stock and vinegar. Raise heat; cook until liquid becomes a glaze, again shaking pan. Remove onions to a bowl. Wipe out skillet; add olive oil. Add garlic, chile flakes, and greens; cook, stirring often, until tender, 4-5 minutes. Stir in onions; add salt and pepper to taste. When polenta is done, serve it in wide shallow bowls topped with greens and blue cheese. Makes 4-6 servings.

Spinach Feta Brown Rice Bowl   Bridget Zinn, Vermont Valley Farm member

2 tablespoons olive oil, divided
1 cup plain brown rice
1 onion or 1 bunch spring onions
large bunch of spinach (or other greens),
   stems removed, leaves chopped

1 bunch or large handful fresh dill
salt
a 2-4 ounce chunk of feta cheese, diced

Heat 1 tablespoon olive oil in saucepan over medium flame. Stir in rice and heat gently, stirring often, about 1 minute. Add 2 1/8 cups water to the pan. Bring to a boil, reduce heat to low, cover pan, and cook 45 minutes. Remove from heat. Remove lid, stir rice, cover it again, and let stand about 10 minutes. While rice cooks, heat remaining olive oil in a large skillet over medium flame. Add onions and cook, stirring occasionally, until translucent. Stir in chopped spinach and cook, stirring occasionally, until spinach is wilted. Stir in dill and a little salt. Let cook for a minute or so, then remove from heat. Stir spinach and feta into the cooked rice. Makes 4 servings.

Baked Eggs with Collards and Cheddar Garlic Grits   MACSAC

1 large bunch (3/4-1 pound) collards
   (or other greens)
1 tablespoon balsamic vinegar
salt and pepper

1 garlic clove, cut into slivers
1 cup quick-cooking grits
1-1 1/2 cups grated sharp cheddar cheese
4-6 eggs

Oil individual baking dishes. Heat oven to 400 degrees. Wash collards; cut out the stems. Chop greens. Steam or sauté greens until just wilted. Sprinkle with vinegar and season with salt and pepper. Set greens aside. Place 3 1/4 cups water and garlic in saucepan and bring to boil. Stir in quick grits; lower heat, cover, and cook gently, stirring occasionally, 5 minutes. Stir in cheese and half the cooked greens. Portion grits into baking dishes. Make a well in the center, nestle the remaining greens into the indentations, and crack an egg over the top of each. Sprinkle with salt and pepper. Bake until eggs are set, 10-15 minutes. Makes 4-6 servings.

Greens-Salad

A wonderful new trend in green salads continues to grow in popularity. There is a burgeoning enthusiasm for the old phrase "Eat your greens!" All the excitement is over daring combinations of baby greens, tossed alone or with other seasonal vegetables, lightly dressed, and slowly but steadily replacing salads of only lettuce. Often referred to as salad mixes or mesclun, this trend is a fantastic improvement in flavor, decorative appearance, and, perhaps most importantly, nutritional value.

There are almost endless possibilities in combining tender young edible greens. There are many variations in shades of greens and reds, and different shapes and textures. The greens also vary in pungency—some are mild, while others are distinctive, imparting unique bitter or mustardy flavors. Blends of the mild and pungent greens are the most popular. Examples of the greens you might discover while creating your mix: a variety of baby lettuces—usually loose-leaf—arugula, corn salad or mache, chicory, escarole, dandelion greens, radicchio, watercress, oriental greens (such as mizuna, tat soi, purple mustard), sorrel, baby kale, baby beet greens, baby spinach, baby Swiss chard, baby turnip greens, and so on.

Cooking Tips

- Wash well in cool water bath to remove fine grit from underside of leaves.

- Try a salad mix of varied baby greens with no lettuce at all, or dilute down a very pungent blend by tearing in extra lettuce.

- Many salad greens taste excellent lightly braised, sautéed, or stir-fried. Watch out! They cook very quickly.

- Use salad greens to decorate a platter.

- Toss green salad with dressing at the last minute to avoid sogginess.

- Toss salad with your choice of fresh herb leaves, such as basil, cilantro, dill, or parsley.

- Pile your favorite salad greens into sandwiches, tacos, burritos, or omelets.

- Cook and add greens to quiches, lasagna, or other baked dishes.

Storage Tips

- Salad greens are best if used within a few days. Wrap in damp towel or place in plastic bag in the hydrator drawer of the refrigerator.

- Add paper towel to plastic bag to keep greens fresh longer.

For additional recipes that feature salad greens, see the Spinach and Seasonal Combinations chapters.

Salad Greens with Chinese Salad Dressing   Oak Ridge Farm

1/3 cup sesame or olive oil
1 teaspoon minced garlic, pressed to a paste
1-2 teaspoons grated fresh gingerroot
   or 1/4 teaspoon powdered ginger
dash of cayenne

2 tablespoons fresh lemon juice
1 teaspoon sesame seeds
1 tablespoon chopped green onion
salad greens

Mix all ingredients (except greens); toss with greens. This is also good with bok choy, snow peas, or cucumbers. Makes about 1/2 cup dressing.

Salad Greens with John's Oil and Vinegar Dressing   Zephyr Community Farm

1 cup red wine vinegar
1 cup olive or canola oil
1 tablespoon horseradish mustard
5 tablespoons tahini (sesame seed paste)

1 tablespoon honey
1 pinch salt
1 pinch pepper
salad greens

Mix all ingredients (except greens). Toss with greens. This recipe was inspired by Rob Summerbell. Makes about 3 cups dressing.

Charlemagne Salad with Hot Brie Dressing   Matthew and Susan Smith, Blue Valley Gardens

2-3 medium heads romaine, leaf lettuce,
   or fresh spinach (or a combination)
garlic croutons
1/2 cup olive oil
4 teaspoons minced shallots or green onions
2 teaspoons minced garlic

1/2 cup white wine vinegar
2 tablespoons lemon juice
4 teaspoons Dijon mustard
8-10 ounces ripe brie, rind removed, cheese cut
   into small pieces and brought to room temperature
freshly ground pepper

Clean the greens; dry them in a salad spinner or kitchen towels. Tear greens into bite-size pieces and toss with garlic croutons in a large bowl. Warm oil in a heavy skillet. Add shallots or onions and garlic and cook until golden, 3-5 minutes. Blend in vinegar, lemon juice, and mustard. Add the cheese a little at a time, stirring constantly. Toss the hot dressing with the greens and croutons. Serve immediately with freshly ground pepper. Makes 6 servings.

Raspberry Breakfast Salad   MACSAC

2 tablespoons raspberry preserves
1 tablespoon honey
2 tablespoons raspberry vinegar
   (or raspberry balsamic vinegar)
1/2 teaspoon Dijon mustard

5 tablespoons olive oil
salt and pepper
8-10 cups assorted salad greens
1 red apple, thinly sliced
1 cup fresh raspberries

Make dressing: Combine raspberry preserves, honey, vinegar, and mustard. Gradually whisk in olive oil. Season to taste with salt and pepper. To serve, toss greens with just enough dressing to lightly coat them. Portion onto plates and garnish with sliced apples and berries. Makes 6 servings.

Jerusalem Artichoke

Helianthus tuberosus

The Jerusalem artichoke is related to neither Jerusalem nor the artichoke. Alternately and more aptly named sunchoke, this vegetable is the root tuber of a wild sunflower native to the U.S. Native Americans introduced these to the colonists, who found them to be a staple food in staving off famines during the "six weeks' want," the period between the last of the winter food stores and the beginning of the first harvest.

Sunchokes most likely came by their misleading double name when introduced in Europe in the 17th century. "Jerusalem" seems to have been a confusion of the Spanish word *girasole,* meaning "sunflower," and *artichoke,* a familiar name given in the hope that it would make them acceptable to the peasants. Jerusalem artichokes have been considered a delicacy and have been totally rejected in various European countries over the centuries. They remain particularly popular in France.

The six- to 10-foot-tall perennial sunflower produces lovely yellow flowers in the fall, after which the tubers enlarge. Harvest begins in late fall. Light frosts increase the sweetness of the tuber, but once the ground is solidly frozen, they become difficult to dig.

The sunchoke is worth a creative effort in the kitchen. Its mild, sweet, nutlike flavor is very adaptable. Nutritionally it is a good source of iron and niacin. Surprisingly, sunchokes are free of any starch, and have instead a polysaccharide called inulin that's digested slowly and lowers blood sugar, making it a highly recommended food choice for diabetics. In fact, a sweetener for diabetics is manufactured from the sunchoke.

Cooking Tips

- Rinse sunchoke tubers under cold water, scrubbing well to remove any soil. A stiff bristled brush may be helpful.

- Sunchokes can be eaten raw or cooked. They can be peeled or not. The flesh will darken if peeled. To prevent this darkening, soak the tubers in a mixture of 2 tablespoons lemon juice and 1 quart of water.

- Try them sautéed, stir-fried, steamed, or simmered, alone or with other vegetables.

- Bake whole sunchokes, as a change from potatoes, at 350 degrees for 30-40 minutes depending on size and age of chokes. Rub with oil or place around roasting meats for added flavor.

- Steam 10-15 minutes whole, less if cubed or sliced. To avoid mushy texture, do not overcook them. Serve with butter, a squeeze of lemon and parsley, or a dusting of nutmeg.

- Try them sliced or julienned in salads, or along with other raw veggie sticks and dip.

- Thicken soups and stews with mashed artichokes.

- Try choke chips; slice chokes very thin and drop into hot oil. Fry just to brown, drain in a paper bag, salt lightly, and serve.

- Sunchokes are an excellent addition to baked root veggies.

Storage Tips

- Store in plastic bag in refrigerator for up to 2 weeks. They will shrivel as they dry out.

- To restore crispness, soak in ice water.

- For long-term storage, bury sunchokes in damp sand in a cold but not freezing environment like a root cellar, garage, or basement.

Glazed Sunchokes   Harmony Valley Farm

1 pound sunchokes
1 teaspoon lemon juice
1 large onion, chopped

3 tablespoons butter
1/2 cup pecans
1 tablespoon honey

Cut sunchokes into 1/2-inch pieces and place into bowl of water mixed with lemon juice. Bring a saucepan of water to boil; add sunchokes and onions; cook 7 minutes, drain, then stir-fry them in butter, stirring in pecans and honey. Cook until onions begin to brown. Makes 3-4 servings.

Roasted Carrot and Sunchoke Soup   Odessa Piper, L'Etoile Restaurant

4 pounds carrots, peeled and chopped
2 pounds sunchokes, peeled and chopped
2 tablespoons chopped fresh thyme

3 cups vegetable stock or half-and-half
nutmeg, salt, and pepper

Place vegetables in shallow pan with thyme and 1/2 cup water. Cover; roast at 275 degrees until tender, 1-1 1/2 hours. Place in blender with stock or half-and-half; blend until creamy. Pass through fine-meshed strainer. Season to taste with nutmeg, salt, and pepper. Makes 10 servings.

Roast Chicken with Jerusalem Artichokes, Parsley Root, and Tarragon White Wine Sauce   MACSAC

a 4-pound organic chicken
sea salt and freshly ground black pepper
several sprigs fresh tarragon
4-6 cloves garlic, peeled
2-3 tablespoons butter, well softened
1/2-2/3 pound Jerusalem artichokes,
   scrubbed and cut into chunks

1/2 pound parsley root, peeled and cut into chunks
1/2-2/3 cup dry white wine
1 tablespoon chopped fresh tarragon
1/2 cup half-and-half or 1/4 cup water mixed
   with 1 tablespoon flour (optional)

Rinse bird inside and out with cold water; pat dry with paper towels inside and out, then let stand until it comes to room temperature, about 1 hour. Heat oven to 450 degrees. Sprinkle chicken inside and outside with salt and pepper (don't be shy here!). Tuck the tarragon sprigs and garlic inside the body cavity. Spread butter all over outside of chicken (if you can get some under the skin, do that, too). Place chicken in a roasting pan that is just big enough to hold it and the vegetables (but don't add the vegetables yet). Place it in the hot oven with the legs toward the back of the oven. Roast the chicken 20-30 minutes, then baste it and scatter the vegetables around it, coating them with fat from the bottom of the pan. Continue to roast the chicken with the legs toward the back, basting it every 20-30 minutes. After each basting you may also, if desired, turn the chicken in the pan a quarter-turn to brown all the sides. It will take a total of about 1 1/2 hours to get it nice and brown and fully cooked. Remove chicken from pan and let it rest on a cutting board. Let the vegetables and pan drippings stand for 5-10 minutes, then skim off excess fat. Add wine and chopped tarragon and simmer 10 minutes. You may serve the sauce as is, enrich it with the cream, or thicken it with the water/flour mixture. Carve the chicken and serve it with the vegetables and sauce. With a bottle of cold white wine and a crisp green salad, this is living. Makes 4-6 servings with leftovers.

Sunchokes au Gratin   Harmony Valley Farm

2 pounds sunchokes
salt and pepper to taste

1/2 cup grated Parmesan cheese
2 tablespoons butter, in pieces

Scrub or peel Jerusalem artichokes. Steam or boil until just tender. Slice thinly and lay out in a casserole dish. Add salt and pepper. Cover with cheese and dot with butter. Bake at 375 degrees 7-10 minutes, or until cheese has melted and browned. Makes 6-8 servings.

Righteous Roasted Jerusalem Artichoke Puree Soup   Monique Jamet Hooker

2 pounds Jerusalem artichokes
3 tablespoons olive oil, divided
1/2 cup finely chopped shallots
4 cups chicken or vegetable stock
2 cups heavy cream

1/2 teaspoon salt
1/4 teaspoon pepper
1/8 teaspoon nutmeg
1-2 tablespoons freshly chopped parsley

Soak Jerusalem artichokes in cold water and scrub to remove gritty dirt and blemishes. Dry well in kitchen towels. Heat oven to 400 degrees. Place artichokes in a roasting pan, drizzle with 2 tablespoons olive oil, and roll them around to coat. Roast until tender, 20-30 minutes (the time will depend on the size of the chokes). Heat remaining 1 tablespoon olive oil in a soup pot, add the shallots, and sauté until tender but not brown. Add roasted chokes and stock, bring to simmer, and cook until chokes are really soft and falling apart, about 10 minutes. Puree the soup with an immersion blender or in a food processor, then pass it through a fine strainer back into the pot. (You may also skip the final straining for a less elegant but heartier soup.) Add the cream, salt, pepper, and nutmeg and cook very gently—without boiling—for 10 minutes. Adjust the seasonings to your taste. Serve garnished with a little chopped parsley. Makes 6 servings.

Wild Rice with Jerusalem Artichokes, Mushrooms, and Walnuts   MACSAC

1 1/2 tablespoons walnut or peanut oil
6 ounces crimini mushrooms, sliced
1/4 cup finely chopped shallots
6-8 Jerusalem artichokes, scrubbed and chopped
1 cup wild rice, well rinsed and drained

1 1/2 teaspoons salt
2 1/2 cups boiling water
freshly grated black pepper
1/2 cup walnut halves, roasted at 350 degrees
   6-10 minutes

Heat oil in saucepan over medium-high flame. Add mushrooms and shallots; cook, stirring often, 3-4 minutes. Stir in sunchokes, wild rice, salt, and water. Reduce heat, cover, and cook until water is nearly absorbed and rice is tender. (If rice gets tender before water is absorbed, remove some water.) Season to taste with pepper. Sprinkle with walnuts just before serving. Makes 4-6 servings.

Smoked Trout and Sunchoke Salad on a Bed of Arugula   MACSAC

2 cups smoked trout chunks (make sure all
   the bones are removed)
4 tablespoons mayonnaise
2-3 tablespoons sour cream
4 slender green onions, finely chopped
3-4 small Jerusalem artichokes, scrubbed
   and finely diced
4-5 tablespoons or more fresh lemon juice, divided
2-3 tablespoons chopped fresh dill

salt and freshly ground black pepper
4-6 cups arugula leaves, cleaned and dried in
   salad spinner or kitchen towels
garnishes (choose 2): grapes, kalamata olives,
   halved cherry tomatoes, quartered radishes or
   other ingredients of your choice
whole wheat crackers
1-1 1/2 tablespoons olive oil

Place smoked trout, mayonnaise, and 2 tablespoons sour cream in food processor. Using the pulse button, pulse the mixture until fish is finely chopped, 5-10 times. Add green onions, Jerusalem artichokes, 3 tablespoons lemon juice, and the dill to processor. Pulse 2-4 times to blend. Stir in additional sour cream, if desired. Stir in salt and pepper to taste. Divide arugula onto 4 to 6 large plates. Use a small ice cream scoop to portion smoked fish salad onto the plates (2 small scoops per plate). Garnish as desired. Add a few crackers to each plate. Sprinkle greens with remaining lemon juice. Sprinkle with olive oil. Makes 4 large or 6 smaller servings.

Sunflower Sunchoke Salad MACSAC

2 pounds Jerusalem artichokes, scrubbed
2 tablespoons apple cider vinegar
1 1/2-2 tablespoons olive oil
salt and pepper

1/2 cup coarsely chopped sunflower (or other) sprouts
1/4 cup toasted sunflower seeds
4 tablespoons minced garlic chives

Chop Jerusalem artichokes into bite-size chunks and boil in salted water until barely tender. Drain well and toss with vinegar, olive oil, and salt and pepper to taste. Toss the mixture occasionally while it cools. Stir in remaining ingredients just before serving. Serve at room temperature. Makes 6-8 servings.

Jerusalem Artichoke Salad   M. Drake, *Madison Herb Society Cookbook*

2 1/2-3 cups thinly sliced Jerusalem artichokes
1/2 cup chopped onion
2-3 teaspoons minced garlic
1/4 cup olive oil
1/3 cup cider vinegar

3 tablespoons chopped fresh dill weed
  or 1 tablespoon dried
1 1/2 teaspoons chopped fresh tarragon
  or 1 teaspoon dried
salt and pepper to taste

Toss all ingredients in a bowl. Marinate in refrigerator, stirring occasionally, 12-24 hours. Radish and mushroom slices may also be added. Makes 4-6 servings.

Jerusalem Artichokes with Garlic and Tamari   Ken and Judith Keppers, Keppers' Produce

peanut oil
chopped or sliced Jerusalem artichokes

minced garlic
tamari sauce

Heat a wok or heavy skillet over high flame. When pan is very hot, add a little peanut oil and swirl the pan to coat its surface. Add Jerusalem artichokes and stir-fry until nearly tender. Add minced garlic a minute or two before they're done. Add tamari and toss well just before serving. Makes any number of servings.

Kale

Brassica oleracea var. acephola

Kale is the oldest member of the cabbage family and among the earliest cultivated. It was a favorite vegetable in ancient Rome, and has remained popular in Scotland and Ireland for many centuries. Although cultivated in North America, kale has not achieved the kind of widespread use here as it has in many European countries. The largest consumer of kale in this country is Pizza Hut, but not for eating—it is used only to decorate the salad bar, frustrating those familiar with kale's many virtues who wish it was *in* the salad bar. Have you ever been caught forking a salad bar garnish onto your plate?

Nutritionally, kale is vastly superior to most vegetables. It is very rich in vitamins A, C, and the mineral calcium. B vitamins and other minerals are also in excellent supply. Kale is also the highest in protein content of all the cultivated vegetables.

If this isn't enough reason to become friendly with kale in your kitchen, its flavor and versatility will surely win you. Kale has a distinct but not overpowering flavor, and is interchangeable with broccoli and other hearty greens in recipes. Kale is a very cold-tolerant plant and is often harvested from the garden long after snow cover. In fact, a few good freezes render kale sweeter and more tender, a truly delectable treat.

Cooking Tips

- Wash kale leaves well, checking the underside of each leaf for soil and garden pests.

- Remove stems from mature kale leaves by folding the leaf in half lengthwise and stripping or slicing away thick stems. Baby or very tender young leaves may be cooked stem and all.

- Steam mature kale leaves approximately 4-5 minutes, depending on age, size, and amount in steamer. It is ready when limp but still retaining some texture.

- Toss steamed kale with olive oil, lemon juice, and a dash of salt and pepper. Try adding diced raw garlic.

- Sauté tender young kale leaves. Try a light sauté in butter with garlic and onions.

- Add sautéed kale (chopped) to omelets, quiches, scrambled eggs, casseroles, or mashed potatoes.

- Add chopped or sliced raw kale to hearty soups and stews toward the end of cooking time.

- Refer to sections on Greens and Chard for more recipes and suggestions appropriate for leafy greens.

Storage Tips

- Wrap kale in a damp towel or in a plastic bag and refrigerate, preferably in hydrator drawer, for up to 1 week. Leaves will wilt if allowed to dry out.

- For long-term storage, kale can be frozen. Wash, de-stem, and blanch leaves for 2 minutes. Rinse in cold water to stop the cooking, drain, and pack into airtight containers such as zip-lock freezer bags. Refer to chapter on home food preservation for more information on freezing.

For additional recipes that feature kale, see the Chard, Greens (Cooked), Spinach, and Seasonal Combinations chapters.

Nancy Jane Pierce's Spicy Kale   Crystal Lake Gardens

kale leaves from 2 bunches (or other strong
   greens—turnip, mustard, or collards)
1 tablespoon olive oil

1-5 garlic cloves, minced
crushed red pepper flakes
1/3-1/2 cup chicken or vegetable broth

Bring 2 quarts of salted water to boil. Add kale or other greens, reduce heat to simmer, cover, and cook 7 minutes. Drain and immediately rinse in cold water to stop the cooking. Squeeze water out of greens. Heat olive oil in same pot. Add garlic and red pepper flakes to taste. Sauté 1 minute, then stir in kale and chicken or vegetable broth. Simmer 4-5 minutes. Makes 4-6 servings.

Kale and Potato Tarragon Salad   Jenny Bonde and Rink DaVee, Shooting Star Farm

2 pounds small yellow potatoes, scrubbed
7 tablespoons olive oil, divided
1 medium onion (yellow, sweet, or white), diced
1 bunch lacinato kale, large stems removed,
   leaves chopped into 1-inch pieces

1 clove garlic, minced
2 tablespoons white vinegar
2 tablespoons lemon juice
1/4-1/2 teaspoon tarragon, divided
salt and pepper to taste

Steam or boil potatoes until fork-tender. Drain, cut into large bite-size pieces, place in large bowl, and cover to keep warm. Meanwhile, heat 1 tablespoon olive oil in a wide skillet over medium heat. Add onions; sauté until translucent. Add kale and garlic; cook until kale is tender, about 5 minutes more (you can cover pan to help wilt kale). Combine vinegar, lemon juice, 1/4 teaspoon dried tarragon, remaining 6 tablespoons olive oil, and salt and pepper. Add kale mixture to potatoes and pour dressing over everything. (It's important to toss the dressing while the mixture is hot, to soak in the flavors.) Add more salt, pepper, or tarragon if necessary. Serve warm or at room temperature. Makes 6 servings.

Kale and Blue Cheese Roll-Ups   MACSAC

1 package (8 ounces) cream cheese, softened
6 ounces blue cheese, softened
3-4 tablespoons minced green garlic shoots
   or fresh garlic chives

1 pound kale leaves, blanched until wilted,
   drained, squeezed dry, and finely chopped
freshly ground black pepper
1 loaf soft sandwich bread, crusts removed
extra-virgin olive oil

Heat oven to 375 degrees. Beat cream cheese, blue cheese, and chives until smooth. Mix in kale. Season with pepper to taste. Flatten bread slices with a rolling pin. Spread a layer of kale/cheese mixture over slices and roll up. Brush each roll with olive oil and place seam side down on baking sheest. Bake until lightly browned, about 15 minutes. Serve immediately. Makes 20-24 roll-ups.

Easy Kale and Tomatoes   Karen Shepard, Blackberry Community Farm

1 large bunch kale, stems removed
   and leaves coarsely chopped
1 large tomato, chopped
1 large onion, chopped

water or tomato juice
olive oil
salt and pepper

Place kale, tomatoes, and onions in pot with just enough water or tomato juice to keep them from burning while it cooks. Cook over medium heat until kale is tender, about 20 minutes. Add a little olive oil, plus salt and pepper to taste, before serving. This is also great with chopped dried tomatoes or home-canned tomatoes instead of fresh. Makes 2 servings.

Kale, Mushroom, and Dill Triangles   MACSAC

2 tablespoons butter
4-6 ounces fresh mushrooms, finely chopped
1 1/2 pounds kale, cleaned, blanched, drained
6 eggs, beaten
1 cup heavy cream or half-and-half

3 tablespoons chopped fresh dill
1/3 cup minced green onion
1/3 cup freshly grated Parmesan cheese
1 teaspoon salt
1/4 teaspoon pepper

Heat oven to 350 degrees. Butter an 8 1/2-by-12 1/2-inch baking dish (or one that is similarly sized). Heat butter in skillet over medium-high flame. Add mushrooms and cook, stirring often, until tender and liquid has evaporated. Cool 10-15 minutes. Squeeze excess liquid from kale; chop it and combine with remaining ingredients, including cooled mushrooms. Spread evenly in prepared pan. Bake until set, 25-30 minutes. Cool 10 minutes. Cut into 18 squares, then cut each square into 2 triangles. Serve warm or at room temperature. Makes 36 triangles.

Sesame Kale Salad   Doug Wubben, Drumlin Community Farm

1 pound fresh kale (or chard, spinach, or
   other greens)
2 tablespoons soy sauce
2 tablespoons toasted sesame oil
1 tablespoon toasted sesame seeds
   (crush these into a powder, if desired)

1 clove garlic, minced
2 teaspoons honey (or other sweetener)
1 tablespoon apple cider vinegar
dash of black or ground red pepper, or more to taste

Separate kale leaves from stems. Chop stems and greens. Steam stems a couple of minutes, then add the greens and steam until just tender. Drain; let kale cool enough to handle it. Squeeze out as much water as possible. Place in serving bowl. Mix the remaining ingredients in another bowl; add to greens. Mix, chill, and serve. Makes 4-6 servings. Adapted from *Extending the Table: A World Community Cookbook*, by Joetta Hendrich Schlabach.

Kale Soufflé   MACSAC

softened butter to grease dish
2 tablespoons freshly grated Parmesan cheese
4 tablespoons butter
4 tablespoons flour
1 2/3 cups milk, warmed
salt and pepper
pinch cayenne

5 egg yolks
1 cup cooked and finely chopped kale,
   at room temperature
1 cup grated Gruyere or aged Swiss cheese
2 tablespoons chopped fresh dill or
   2 teaspoons dried dill weed
7 egg whites, at room temperature

Heat oven to 400 degrees. Butter bottom and sides of an 8-cup soufflé dish or deep, round baking dish; sprinkle buttered areas with Parmesan. Melt 4 tablespoons butter in saucepan; stir in flour and cook over low heat several minutes, stirring often. Whisk in milk until thickened; season with salt, pepper, and cayenne. Cool 10-15 minutes. Beat in egg yolks 1 at a time. Stir in kale, Gruyere, and dill. (You may chill the mixture at this point, but return it to room temperature before finishing the soufflé.) To finish: Beat egg whites and a pinch of salt in a clean bowl with electric beaters (or a whisk and a strong arm!) until firm peaks form. Fold a quarter of the whipped egg whites into kale mixture, then gently fold in the rest (don't overmix). Gently spread mixture into prepared pan. Place in oven, reduce heat to 375 degrees, and bake until high, golden, and barely set in the center, 35-40 minutes. Serve *immediately*. Makes 6 servings.

Skillet Eggs with Kale and Chorizo   MACSAC

1/4 pound Spanish-style chorizo (or other spicy, hard sausage like Italian salami or garlic summer sausage), diced
1 bunch kale, stems removed, leaves chopped coarsely
lemon juice
pepper
4-6 eggs
grated Parmesan or asiago cheese (optional)

Heat large, nonstick skillet over medium-high flame. Add diced chorizo and cook, stirring often, about 3 minutes. Add all the kale and cook, tossing often, until wilted, about 3 minutes. Sprinkle a little lemon juice and pepper over the mixture and toss well, then push kale/chorizo mixture to outer edges of pan. Reduce heat to medium and crack eggs 1 at a time into center of pan. Cook briefly uncovered, then sprinkle 3 tablespoons water over kale and eggs, cover, and cook until eggs are set, about 3 minutes. Sprinkle a little grated Parmesan or asiago cheese over the dish and serve immediately, right from the pan. Makes 4-6 servings.

Wonderfully Easy Pasta with Kale   Ann Romanczuk, Common Harvest Farm

1/3 pound penne or farfalle pasta
2-3 tablespoons olive oil
1 small onion, diced
2 or 3 garlic cloves, minced
1/2 pound chopped kale leaves
salt and pepper

Bring 6-8 cups salted water to a boil; add pasta and cook until tender. Meanwhile, heat olive oil in a large skillet over medium heat, add the onions and garlic, and cook until tender. Add the kale and sauté until wilted. Drain the pasta and combine it with the onions, garlic, and kale. Season with salt and pepper and serve immediately. Makes 2 servings.

Potato Kale Soup   Jim Harvey, MACSAC member

4 tablespoons olive oil
2 medium onions, chopped
10 cloves garlic, chopped
1/2 tablespoon red chile flakes or to taste
1 1/4 teaspoons salt
6 medium potatoes, peeled and diced into 3/4-inch cubes
3 cups coarsely chopped kale
black pepper

Heat oil in soup pot; add onions, garlic, chile flakes, and salt, and sauté until onions are translucent. Add potatoes and enough water to cover by 4 inches. Bring to boil and cook, covered, until potatoes are about half done. Add kale and cook, uncovered, until potatoes are tender, 10-15 minutes. Puree soup in blender or food processor. Season with pepper to taste. Makes 6-8 servings.

Classic Colcannon   Tony and Dela Ends, Scotch Hill Farm

4-6 large potatoes (about 3 pounds)
2 tablespoons butter
3 cups, packed, chopped kale leaves
1 cup chopped onion
1/2-2/3 cup milk, warmed
1-2 tablespoons chopped parsley
salt and pepper

Peel and cut up potatoes. Boil in salted water until tender. Meanwhile, melt butter in skillet over medium flame. Add kale and onion; cook, stirring occasionally, until onions are barely soft. Drain potatoes and mash them with the milk; mix in kale/onion mixture and parsley. Season with salt and pepper to taste. Spread in buttered baking dish; bake at 375 degrees for 20 minutes. This is from a fall 2000 Scotch Hill Farm newsletter written by former intern Ben McCann. It's excellent with corned beef and cabbage. Makes 4-6 servings.

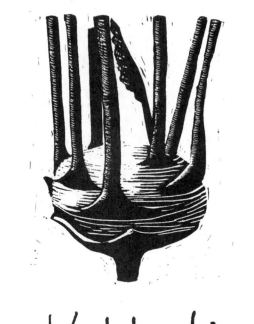

Kohlrabi
Brassica oleracea var. gongylodes

Kohlrabi shares its botanical name, brassica oleracea, with its close relative, broccoli. But *kohl*, meaning "cabbage," and *rabi*, meaning "turnip," better describes this delicate but unusual vegetable. Many botanists believe kohlrabi is actually a hybridization of these two vegetables. Kohlrabi resembles a root vegetable, but actually the edible globe is the modified swollen stem. The edible leaves jut from the globe portion of the kohlrabi like sparse hairs on a head, giving this vegetable its distinctive look.

Kohlrabi, like other brassicas, thrives in cool weather. It is very fast growing and will usually be available locally by late spring. Depending on the growing season, kohlrabi may be available all summer and well into the fall. Purple and green varieties are often grown.

Kohlrabi also mimics its brassica relatives nutritionally. It offers generous amounts of vitamins A and C, and emphasizes the minerals potassium and calcium. It's high in fiber and contains only 40 calories per cup.

Cooking Tips

- After washing, trim away any woody or tough portions of skin. Kohlrabi does not have to be peeled after cooking.

- Kohlrabi is excellent cooked or raw. Try it both ways to familiarize yourself with its flavors.

- Grate kohlrabi raw into salads, or make a non-traditional coleslaw with grated kohlrabi and radish, chopped parsley, green onion, and dressing of your choice.

- Try raw kohlrabi, thinly sliced, alone or with a dip. Peel kohlrabi and eat it raw like an apple.

- Steam kohlrabi whole 25-30 minutes or thinly sliced 5-10 minutes. Dress slices simply with oil, lemon juice, and fresh dill weed, or dip in flour and briefly fry.

- Sauté grated kohlrabi in butter; add herbs or curry for enhanced flavor.

- Add sliced or cubed kohlrabi to hearty soups, stews, or a mixed vegetable stir-fry.

- Chill and marinate cooked kohlrabi for a summer salad. Add fresh herbs.

- Mash cooked kohlrabi, mix with cooked potato, form into patties, and fry in butter.

- Larger, older kohlrabi are good stuffed. Scoop out center, fill with chosen stuffing mixture, and simmer, covered, for 20 minutes.

- Kohlrabi leaves can be used like other greens. You may want to remove center rib. See section on greens for suggestions and recipes.

Storage Tips

- Store kohlrabi globe and leaves separately. The globe will last for 1 month refrigerated in a plastic bag. Wrap leaves in a damp towel or place in a plastic bag and keep in hydrator drawer of refrigerator. Use greens as soon as possible.

For additional recipes that feature kohlrabi, see the Seasonal Combinations chapter.

Sautéed Kohlrabi   Oak Ridge Farm, adapted from the *Cook's Garden Cookbook*

2 kohlrabi (3 if small)   1 tablespoon fresh herbs (thyme, chives, sage, etc.)
4 tablespoons butter or light oil   1 teaspoon salt
1 medium onion, diced

Grate kohlrabi, place in colander, and sprinkle with salt. Let stand 30 minutes to drain. Heat butter over medium heat, add onions, and sauté a few minutes. Stir in kohlrabi, reduce heat to low, cover, and cook 10 minutes. Increase heat to medium and cook 2 more minutes. Remove from heat and stir in fresh herbs. Makes 2-4 servings.

Low-Fat Kohlrabi Cakes with Yogurt Mint Sauce   Barb Bishop, Harmony Valley Farm member

Sauce: Kohlrabi cakes:
1/3 cup plain yogurt   4 kohlrabi bulbs
3 tablespoons chopped fresh mint leaves   1/4 cup chopped green garlic
1 teaspoon lemon juice   Egg Beaters equivalent to 2 eggs (or 2 eggs, beaten)
pinch of salt or more to taste   2 tablespoons dried bread crumbs
                                                1 teaspoon salt
                                                1/4 teaspoon crushed red pepper flakes
                                                black pepper to taste
                                                oil cooking spray

Mix sauce ingredients in bowl and chill at least 30 minutes before serving. Meanwhile, peel and shred kohlrabi. Transfer to a mixing bowl by fistfuls, squeezing out excess moisture as you go. (This is essential.) Combine kohlrabi with green garlic, egg substitute or eggs, bread crumbs, salt, red pepper flakes, and black pepper; stir until blended. Heat large skillet and spray it generously with cooking spray. Drop mixture by large spoonfuls into hot pan and fry the cakes in batches until golden brown, 3-4 minutes per side. Drain on paper towels. Serve hot with yogurt mint sauce. This recipe is adapted from *The New Basics Cookbook* by Julee Rosso and Sheila Lukins. If you don't have green garlic, use green onions and add a small clove of finely minced garlic. Makes 4-6 servings.

Kohlrabi and Pea Vine Patties with Cilantro Yogurt Sauce
Linda Halley and Jordan Lichman, Harmony Valley Farm

Sauce: Patties:
1 bunch cilantro, stemmed, finely chopped   1 tablespoon Dijon mustard
juice of 1 lime   1 tablespoon minced ginger
1/2 teaspoon salt   1 tablespoon minced garlic or green garlic shoots
1 teaspoon honey   1 tablespoon curry powder
5 ounces plain yogurt   salt and pepper to taste
                                                1/2 cup packed chopped pea vines or Asian greens
                                                3 medium kohlrabi, peeled
                                                2 tablespoons flour
                                                1 egg
                                                1/4 cup vegetable oil
                                                1 cup bread crumbs

Combine sauce ingredients and let stand 30 minutes. Meanwhile, mix all ingredients for the patties except breadcrumbs and vegetable oil. Heat oil in a large nonstick skillet over medium heat. Form kohlrabi mixture into small patties, squeezing hard to extract excess moisture. Roll patties in the bread crumbs. Fry patties on both sides until golden brown, about 4 minutes per side. Drain on paper towels. Serve with cilantro dipping sauce. Makes 6 patties.

Cool Kohlrabi Ideas   Summer chef Jordan Lichman, Harmony Valley Farm

- Medallions of blanched kohlrabi bulb topped with a smoked fish salad (Erna's Elderberry House, Oakhurst, California)

- Blanched sections of kohlrabi served with wild Copper River salmon on a bed of seasonal vegetables (Opera House restaurant, Madison)

- Kohlrabi stems and leaves: Remove the stems and roughly chop the greens. Sauté the greens with some shallots and butter (or any flavorings you want), add a cup of water, and cook, covered, over medium heat until tender but still toothsome, about 20 minutes.

Couscous with Kohlrabi and Chermoula Dressing   MACSAC

1-2 teaspoons minced garlic	3 tablespoons olive oil
2 tablespoons minced cilantro	2-3 cups cooked couscous, cooled to warm temperature
2 tablespoons minced fresh parsley	2 cups peeled, diced kohlrabi
1 teaspoon paprika	1/2 cup diced radishes
1/2 teaspoon ground cumin	16 kalamata or oil-cured imported black olives,
salt	chopped (optional)
3 tablespoons fresh lemon juice	1/2 cup crumbled feta cheese (optional)

Mix garlic, cilantro, parsley, paprika, cumin, and salt to taste. Stir in lemon juice and olive oil. Toss this mixture with couscous. Bring to room temperature. Gently toss with kohlrabi, radishes, and olives (if desired). Serve as is, or sprinkle with feta cheese. Makes 6 servings.

South-of-the-Border Kohlrabi Snacks   MACSAC

peeled kohlrabi	chili powder
fresh lime juice	

Slice the kohlrabi into rounds (not too thick). Dip the lower third of each round into lime juice, then into chili powder. Makes any number of servings.

Chilled Curried Kohlrabi and Chick-Pea Soup   MACSAC

1 quart buttermilk	1 teaspoon curry powder
1 large or 2 medium kohlrabi, peeled and diced	1/2 teaspoon each ground cumin, coriander, and ginger
1 can (15 ounces) chick-peas, rinsed and drained	dash cayenne pepper (or more to taste)
3 tablespoons chopped fresh parsley	salt to taste
3 tablespoons extra-virgin olive oil	grated zest and juice of 1 lemon
2 teaspoons minced garlic, mashed to a paste	thin slices of lemon

Mix all ingredients except lemon slices in glass bowl; cover and chill well. Ladle into bowls. Serve each bowl garnished with a lemon slice. This unusual, cooling concoction was inspired by a recipe from Deborah Madison's *Vegetarian Cooking for Everyone*. Makes 4-6 servings.

Three Ways to Handle Kohlrabi   Catherine Murray

- Braise diced or sliced kohlrabi in just enough chicken or beef stock to cover it. Add a little butter and some caraway seeds to the stock and simmer until tender, about 12 minutes. Sprinkle with parsley. (From *The New Foods* by Camille Cusumano)

- Serve kohlrabi either raw or steamed with bagna cauda sauce: Cook 1/2 cup butter, 1/4 cup olive oil, and 6 thinly sliced garlic cloves very gently for about 15 minutes. Add 4 ounces (2 cans) of anchovy filets, minced, and stir until they dissolve into the sauce. Keep the sauce hot for dunking the kohlrabi. (From *The Green Grocer* by Joe Carcione and Bob Lucas)

- Sauté kohlrabi Chinese-style in a little peanut oil with shiitake mushrooms, sweet red peppers, shallots, minced gingerroot, and cashew or pine nuts. Season with rice wine, soy sauce, sesame oil, and a pinch of sugar. You can also thicken this with a little cornstarch mixed with water. (From *Farmacopeia* by Pete Napolitano, aka Produce Pete)

Spinach, Cabbage, and Kohlrabi Salad with Horseradish Vinaigrette   MACSAC

1 large bunch tender spinach	2 teaspoons prepared horseradish
2 cups thin-sliced purple cabbage	1/2 teaspoon brown mustard
1 kohlrabi, cut into small, narrow strips	1/2 teaspoon sugar
3 tablespoons olive oil	salt and pepper
2 tablespoons red wine vinegar	4 tablespoons sunflower seeds

Wash and stem spinach; tear into bite-size pieces; dry in salad spinner or towels. Place in large bowl with cabbage and kohlrabi. Combine olive oil, vinegar, horseradish, mustard, and sugar in small jar with lid. Season with salt and pepper; shake vigorously. Toss dressing with salad; divide onto plates and garnish with sunflower seeds. Makes 4-6 servings.

Bratwurst Kohlrabi Vegetable Soup with Pumpernickel Dill Croutons   MACSAC

1 tablespoon butter, divided	1/3 cup thin-sliced dill pickles
2 cooked bratwursts, thin-sliced	1/2 teaspoon dill weed
1 cup chopped onions	salt and pepper
2 medium kohlrabis, peeled, thin-sliced, and chopped	
1/2 cup thin-sliced celery	Croutons:
2 teaspoons fennel seeds	1 1/2 tablespoons butter, melted
3 cans (each 14 1/2 ounces) beef broth	1/2 teaspoon dill weed
1 cup thin-sliced potatoes	1 1/2 cups cubed pumpernickel bread

Brown bratwurst in pot with 1/2 tablespoon butter. Remove and reserve meat. Add remaining 1/2 tablespoon butter, onions, kohlrabi, celery, and fennel seeds; sauté 5 minutes. Stir in beef broth, potatoes, pickles, dill weed, bratwurst, and 2/3 cup water; simmer 40 minutes. Season to taste with salt and pepper. Let stand 1 or more hours to develop flavor. To make croutons, combine ingredients; bake 10-15 minutes in 400-degree oven, tossing occasionally. Serve with reheated soup. Makes 6 servings.

Kohlrabi Sandwiches   Leslie France

unsalted butter, softened	thick-sliced kohlrabi
pumpernickel bread	sea salt and freshly ground black pepper

Generously butter 2 slices of bread and make a sandwich with the kohlrabi as the "meat." Add salt and pepper to taste. Makes 1 serving.

Leek

Allium porrum

Leeks belong to the lily family, along with their close relatives onions, garlic, scallions, shallots, and chives. The leek is a striking and graceful vegetable. Broad, flat, dark green leaves cascade like a fountain around the contrasted white of its base. Milder and more refined in flavor than onions, leeks produce a pleasing aroma and sweeten as they cook. And there are no tears while cutting a leek.

Native to the Mediterranean area, leeks may have originated in Egypt, where they were cultivated and worshipped, or, as it has been written, "where onions are adored, and leeks are gods." Leeks have been a cooking staple in Europe and the British Isles for centuries. France and Wales particularly have glorified the leek in both their lore and cooking.

In North American markets, leeks are still a specialty item, available at inflated cost. For those who have come to appreciate the leek's subtle, unique flavor and great versatility, a steady seasonal supply at a reasonable price is a must. In northern climes, leeks are available midsummer through late fall and often into the winter. It's no surprise to see waves of deep green leaves emerging from a snow-covered garden.

Cooking Tips

- To clean: remove green tops to within 2 inches of the white section. Peel off outside layer. Cut leek in half lengthwise and wash thoroughly under water to remove grit and soil between the layers.

- Leeks may be eaten raw, chopped into a variety of salads.

- Leeks may be cooked whole; try braising or baking.

- Steam or boil leeks for 10-12 minutes. Top with butter, a dash of salt, pepper, and Parmesan cheese.

- Layer thin slices of leek in a favorite sandwich. Leek, tomato, and melted cheese is a winner.

- Lightly sauté chopped leeks alone or with other vegetables.

- Chop or slice leeks into quiches, egg dishes, casseroles, stews, stocks, soups, and stir-fries.

- Substitute leeks for onions in recipes and notice the subtle flavor changes.

- Puree cooked leeks for a soup base.

- Add leek leaves to long-cooking dishes, such as grains, beans, or stews, for added flavor.

- Add cooked leeks to mashed potatoes.

Storage Tips

- Refrigerate leeks unwashed and dry with roots attached for up to 2 weeks. Wrap lightly in plastic to avoid aromas spreading to other foods.

- For longer-term storage, leeks can be buried in moist sand and kept in a cool but not freezing location.

For additional recipes that feature leeks, see the Seasonal Combinations chapter.

Cock-a-Leekie Soup   MACSAC

3-pound whole chicken, rinsed and quartered
2 quarts chicken stock
1 bay leaf
10 peppercorns
4 whole cloves
5 cups chopped leeks

1 cup chopped carrots
1/2 cup pearl barley
3 tablespoons chopped parsley
1/2 cup chopped prunes (optional)
salt and pepper

Place chicken in large pot with 1 quart water; add stock, bay leaf, peppercorns, and cloves. Bring to low boil, skimming as needed. Reduce to low simmer and cook about 1 1/2 hours, skimming as needed. Remove chicken; let cool. Remove any fat floating on stock, then strain through a very fine mesh colander lined with cheesecloth. Clean out soup pot and return stock to it. Add leeks and carrots, bring to boil, and add barley. Simmer until barley is cooked, about 35 minutes. Meanwhile, remove skin and bones from chicken; shred the meat. When barley is cooked, stir in chicken, parsley, and prunes, if using. Heat through. Season to taste. Makes 6-8 servings.

Pork Tenderloin with Leek Apple Cream and Frizzled Leeks   MACSAC

2 cups chicken stock
2 tablespoons salt
2 sprigs thyme
1 bay leaf
2 1/2 pounds pork tenderloin
3 large leeks, divided
2 cups peanut or vegetable oil
2 tablespoons canola oil, divided

2 tablespoons butter, divided
2 leeks, well cleaned and slivered
2 apples, cored and diced
1/3 cup brandy or Calvados (apple brandy)
1 tablespoon Dijon mustard
1 cup whipping cream
additional salt
pepper

Bring stock, salt, thyme, and bay leaf to boil; stir to dissolve salt. Allow to cool completely, then add pork and let it marinate in the refrigerator at least 2-14 hours. For frizzled leeks: (this may be done 2-3 hours before serving): Cut off the deep green upper sections of 3 leeks. Slice leeks in half lengthwise, then into 2-inch sections. Sliver these sections lengthwise. Clean them well and set aside about 2/3 of them. Thoroughly dry remaining third of the leeks in paper or cotton towels. Heat oil in a saucepan until it reaches 350 degrees on a candy thermometer. Deep-fry the leeks about 1 minute at a time in small batches, removing each batch from oil with a slotted spoon and draining them well on paper towels. Sprinkle with salt while hot. Set aside. To finish the dish: Heat oven to 400 degrees. Remove meat from marinade and pat dry. Melt 1 tablespoon each oil and butter in large skillet over medium-high flame. Brown meat on all sides, transfer to a baking pan, and roast until internal temperature is 145 degrees (or desired doneness), 10-15 minutes. Allow meat to rest, but keep it warm. Meanwhile, in same skillet, melt remaining oil and butter over medium-high flame and sauté 2 slivered leeks about 5 minutes. Add apples and sauté another 8 minutes. Stir in brandy and boil until almost dry, then add mustard and cream. Boil to a sauce consistency, about 8 minutes. Season with salt and pepper. Slice the pork. Spoon sauce onto a platter, arrange pork over sauce, and top with fried leeks. Makes 6-8 servings.

Creamy Leek, Potato, and Sour Cream Chive Soup   MACSAC

3 tablespoons butter
2-3 leeks, thinly sliced (white and pale green parts
    only; about 4 cups total)
1 teaspoon dried tarragon
1 pound Yukon Gold potatoes, peeled, thinly sliced

4 cups chicken stock
1/2-1 cup sour cream
4 tablespoons chopped fresh chives, divided
salt and pepper

Melt butter in pot over medium-low flame. Add leeks and tarragon; cover and cook slowly, 15-20 minutes. Add potatoes and stock; bring to simmer, cover, and cook until tender, 10-15 minutes. Puree mixture. Return puree to pot; stir in sour cream and 2 tablespoons chives. Add salt and pepper to taste. Sprinkle each serving with additional chives. Makes 6 servings.

Mentha sp.

Mint is well known for its aromatic, medicinal, and culinary uses. It is a familiar remedy for ailments ranging from indigestion to bee stings, as well as a popular ingredient in recipes for jellies, juleps, and teas.

Their square stems and serrated or jagged edged leaves most easily identify mints. Two main mint varieties are spearmint and peppermint.

All mints contain the compound menthol, giving mint its fresh, cool quality. Menthol is used in medicines for upper respiratory ailments (Vicks®) and in rubs for sore muscles (BENGAY®). Insects and other pests find it offensive. One of the largest commercial uses for Wisconsin-grown spearmint is (of course) toothpaste.

The history of mint can be traced back to Greek myth. Persephone's jealousy over Pluto's love for a nymph named Minthe caused her to transform the poor nymph into a plant. Because Pluto did not have the power to reverse the spell, he did his best to soften it. He enhanced the sweet smell of the "Minthe plant" to smell sweeter when tread upon.

Mints, native to five of the seven continents (Europe, Asia, Africa, America, and Australia), grow easily in full or partial sun. They flower in warm months and crossbreed easily. They can be rampant spreaders if not contained. Plant mints with tomatoes and cabbages to repel cabbage butterflies.

Cooking Tips

- There are more than 25 different species of culinary mints. Different flavored mints go with different dishes.

- Remove mint leaves from their stem before using. Wash gently to remove soil.

- Mints go well with veal, chicken, pork, eggplant, cabbage, cucumbers, new potatoes, carrots, white beans, black beans, lentils, yogurt, vegetable soups, and fruit salads. And more!

- In the heat of summer, utilize mint's cooling properties by adding a few sprigs to drinking water.

- Keep leaves attached to stems and stir into fruit beverages, teas, liqueurs, and cordials.

- Use fresh mint leaves for pesto.

Storage Tips

- Pick mint in the coolness of the morning, before the sun evaporates its essential oils.

- Keep freshly picked mint in a glass of water in the refrigerator. Be sure to change the water periodically.

- For short-term storage, wrap mint in a slightly dampened towel and refrigerate. Do not wash before refrigerating.

- Freeze fresh leaves whole in plastic zipper bags or minced in water in ice cube trays.

Minted Lemonade   Madison Herb Society

juice of 1 lemon
1 cup apple juice
juice of 2 large juice-type oranges

2/3 cup Mint Syrup (see recipe below)
mint sprigs for garnish

Combine the fruit juices and mint syrup; shake or stir well and chill. Pour over ice cubes and garnish with mint sprigs.

Mint Syrup

1/2 cup mint leaves
1/2 cup water

1 cup sugar or 1/2 cup honey

Combine ingredients in a saucepan and bring to a boil. Reduce heat to low and cook until thickened (about 5 minutes). Strain if desired. Makes 2/3 cup.

Fresh Mint Salsa for Grilled Lamb Chops   MACSAC

3 plum tomatoes, seeded and finely diced
1/2 cup finely diced red onion
2 tablespoons olive oil
2 teaspoons lemon juice

3-4 tablespoons chopped fresh mint
salt and pepper to taste
8 lamb loin chops

Combine all ingredients except lamb; chill 1 hour. Prepare charcoal or heat outdoor grill. Cook lamb chops to medium-rare, 4-6 minutes per side. Top each serving (2 chops) with salsa; serve immediately. This recipe came from Jim Cardiff when he was chef at The Creamery Restaurant in Downsville, Wisconsin. It's also delicious with pork tenderloin. Makes 4 servings.

Minted Pears   Madison Herb Society

1 pound pear halves
juice of 1 lemon

1/2 cup sugar or 1/4 cup honey
2 tablespoons chopped fresh spearmint

Peel pears and poach in water with lemon juice. Drain pears into a bowl, reserving 1 cup of the liquid. Combine the liquid with sugar or honey and heat until sugar dissolves. Add fresh mint and simmer 10 minutes. Pour hot liquid (strained, if desired) over pears. Cool and chill thoroughly. Serve with lamb. Makes 4 servings.

Tan (Armenian Mint Yogurt Beverage)   MACSAC

2 cups plain nonfat yogurt
2 cups cold water

sprigs of fresh mint

Stir yogurt until smooth; gradually add water. Chill thoroughly; serve over ice with fresh mint. The recipe came from a friend, Araxy Arganian. Makes 4 servings.

Double Mint Iced Sun Tea   MACSAC

fistfuls of fresh mint sprigs

Gently but thoroughly rinse freshly picked mint sprigs. Lightly pack a large, clear jar with most of the sprigs. Fill jar with cool water. Set in direct, hot sun to brew for an afternoon. Meanwhile, carefully remove the best leaves from some of the remaining sprigs. Fill ice cube trays with water and place one or two perfect leaves beneath the surface of the water in each compartment. Freeze until solid. When water in jug is well flavored with mint, transfer jug to refrigerator. Chill thoroughly. To serve, place mint ice cubes in tall, narrow glasses. Strain the mint tea (it will still look like plain water) over the ice. Use the remaining mint sprigs to garnish the glasses. Makes any number of servings.

Onion

Allium cepa

There are 300 species of onion within the allium genus, 70 of which are native to North America. They vary in size, shape, taste, and smell, and include our familiar kitchen varieties, scallions, shallots, leeks, onions, and garlic.

The bulb onion is the most universal seasoning used by humans. The onion probably originated in the Middle East and southwest Asia. References date back to 3200 B.C. The ancient Egyptians saw the concentric circles of the onion as a symbol of the universe and treated it as an object of worship. In North America, native peoples used wild onion long before European settlers arrived with cultivated varieties.

The compact leaves of the onion form the edible bulb. This is the plant's nutrient storage for the following years growth. Most onions are biennials and will go to seed in the spring if not harvested the preceding fall. Our common bulb onions are reddish purple, white, or yellow with a tan skin. The purple and white tend to be sweeter and milder, while the tan-skinned storage onion is the most pungent.

Bulb onions are available summer through fall, and throughout the winter with proper storage. In spring and early summer we rely on chives, scallions, and bunching onions to satisfy our onion needs. Baby bulb onions and the first of the leeks follow soon thereafter.

The pungency of an onion reflects the amount of sulfur in the soil in which it was grown. A compound within the onion turns into sulfuric acid when it comes into contact with the water in eyes, causing a cook painful tears. The many gifts of the onion are worth it. Besides flavor, the onion is touted for its various health and healing benefits. Join the global community and chop an onion.

Cooking Tips

- Chill onions thoroughly in fridge or cut under running water to subdue fumes that cause tears during chopping.

- The longer an onion is cooked the milder it becomes. For strongest flavors and medicinal benefits use onion raw or lightly cooked.

- Onion is very versatile. Almost any cooking method is appropriate: steam, boil, sauté, stir-fry, braise, bake, grill, roast, etc.

- Boil onions until tender (15 minutes for small ones, 30 for large). Try them topped with butter, a sprinkling of herbs, and Parmesan cheese.

- Long baking or oven roasting brings out sweetness and caramelizes the natural sugars. Try surrounding a roasting meat with small to medium yellow onions.

- Add chopped onions to a hearty homemade bread dough or corn bread batter.

- Add chopped or diced raw sweet onion, chives or scallions to a variety of salads, such as green, pasta, potato, or any marinated-style salads.

- Onions are a flavor enhancer; use them generously in soups, stews, casseroles, etc.

- Try topping a pizza—homemade or not—liberally with diced onion.

Storage Tips

- Bulb onions will store for several months in a cool, dry ventilated place. Warmth and moisture will cause sprouting.

- Store cut onion in the refrigerator in an airtight container to avoid transference of flavors to other foods. Use as soon as possible.

- Store chives or scallions wrapped in a damp towel or plastic bag in hydrator drawer of refrigerator for 2-3 days.

Balsamic Braised Onions   Jenny Bonde and Rink DaVee, Shooting Star Farm

2 pounds small cippolini onions, peeled,
  ends trimmed off
1/4 cup extra virgin olive oil
1 cup good-quality balsamic vinegar

1/3-1/2 cup water
1 teaspoon salt
freshly ground black pepper

Pack the onions tightly in a single layer in a large skillet or saucepan. Combine remaining ingredients and pour over onions. Bring to low simmer and cook, uncovered, until onions are tender, turning them over about halfway through the cooking. This will take about 15 minutes. Raise heat to high and boil, carefully turning the onions occasionally to prevent sticking, until liquid is reduced to a glaze, 15-20 minutes. Add additional salt and pepper to taste. Serve warm or cold. This recipe is adapted from one that came with a purchase of balsamic vinegar. It's important to use a high-quality balsamic vinegar or the flavor will be harsh. Makes 6-8 servings.

Savory Green Onion Noodle Cake   MACSAC

4 eggs
1/2 cup chopped green onions
2 tablespoons chopped cilantro
1/2 teaspoon grated ginger
8 ounces spaghettini (thin spaghetti), cooked,
  rinsed, drained well and tossed with
  2-3 teaspoons sesame oil

salt and freshly ground black pepper
3 tablespoons peanut oil, divided
sprigs of cilantro

Beat eggs; stir in green onions, cilantro, and ginger. Add spaghetti and salt and pepper to taste; mix very well with your hands. Heat half the peanut oil in an 8- to 10-inch nonstick skillet over medium-high flame. Spread pasta mixture into pan, press it down, and even the edges with a spatula. Cook until bottom is golden and cake is "set," 6-10 minutes. Wearing oven mitts, place a platter over skillet and flip noodle cake onto platter. Heat remaining oil in skillet, slide cake back in, and cook until second side is golden. Slide noodle cake back onto the platter and garnish with cilantro sprigs. Makes 4-6 servings.

Beer Batter Onion Rings   MACSAC

1 1/2 cups flour
1 1/2 cups beer
4-5 large onions

4 cups vegetable or corn oil
popcorn salt

Whisk flour and beer in bowl until smooth. Cover and let stand at room temperature 3 hours. Slice onions into 1/4-inch rounds and separate into rings. Heat oil to 375 degrees. Dip onion rings in batter, a few at a time, then immerse in hot oil and fry until golden brown, turning once. Drain each batch on paper towels and salt lightly. Serve hot. Makes 4-6 servings.

Red Onion Marmalade for Grilled Fish, Meat, or Tofu   MACSAC

3 tablespoons butter
2 large red onions, sliced

2 tablespoons sugar
3 tablespoons balsamic vinegar

Heat butter in large skillet over medium flame. Stir in onions and sugar and cook, stirring frequently, until onions are caramelized (thoroughly wilted and deepened in color), about 20 minutes. Deglaze the pan, i.e., stir vinegar into pan to release any bits from bottom of pan and then cook until all the vinegar has been absorbed into the onion mix and the flavors come together, about another 7 minutes. This makes a delicious topping for grilled fish, meats, chicken, or tofu. Makes 4 servings.

Oregano

Origanum vulgare

Oregano is a low-growing perennial herb that has a spicy taste with a "bite." It is stronger in flavor than marjoram, which is very similar in appearance.

Oregano became enormously popular after World War II, when soldiers returning from Italy shared its uses for pizza and many other tomato-based dishes and sauces.

The word *oregano* comes from the Greek for "joy of the mountain." Legends say that Greek and Roman wedding couples were crowned with oregano to banish sadness.

The flavor of oregano plants varies markedly. To find a plant with good flavor, rub the leaves and smell them, or pinch off a small piece of the leaf and taste it. It should have a strong, hot taste with a "bite" to it.

Oregano is believed to be antispasmodic, antiseptic, bactericidal, stomachic, an expectorant, and a sedative. It alleviates colic, stimulates the appetite, facilitates digestion, and is thought to have a beneficial effect on the respiratory system.

Cooking Tips

- Use with other herbs to make Italian seasoning.

- Use to make herb butter or add to melted butter for frying veggies.

- Oregano is a perfect complement to tomato dishes.

- Add oregano to vinegar for herbal vinegar.

- The flower heads of oregano are edible.

- It goes well with basil.

- Tuck sprigs of oregano under the skin of chickens for roasting or in the cavity of any fish to be baked.

- Flavor is best just before flowering.

Storage Tips

- Can be wrapped in slightly dampened cloth and stored in the refrigerator.

- Leaves can be left on the stem and dried.

- It dries well and should be stored, like most herbs, in a cool, dry place out of the light.

Herbed Greek Salad   Cathy Peterson, Madison Herb Society

1/2 cup crumbled feta cheese
1/2 cup sliced black Greek olives
1 cup sliced radishes
1/4 cup chopped green onions
2 small cucumbers, thinly sliced
1/2 cup extra virgin olive oil
2 tablespoons lemon juice

2 tablespoons chopped fresh parsley
2 tablespoons chopped fresh oregano
1 teaspoon chopped fresh basil
1/2 teaspoon chopped fresh thyme
1-2 teaspoons minced garlic
salt and pepper to taste

Combine cheese, olives, radishes, green onions, and cucumbers in a large bowl. Combine remaining ingredients in a small bowl. Toss dressing with vegetable mixture. Chill 1-2 hours. Makes 6-8 servings.

Greek-Style Grill Sauce for Lamb, Chicken, Fish, or Vegetables   MACSAC

1/4 cup extra-virgin olive oil
2-3 tablespoons chopped fresh oregano
2 teaspoons minced garlic

juice of 1 lemon
1/2 teaspoon freshly ground black pepper

Combine all ingredients. Use this sauce to drizzle over grilled shoulder-cut lamb chops, chicken breasts, fish steaks, or "grillable" vegetables like eggplant or zucchini (cut into planks). Apply the sauce right after the food comes off the grill. Serve immediately. Inspired by a recipe from *How To Cook Meat* by Chris Schlesinger and John Willoughby. Makes enough for 4 servings.

Pizzeria Scalloped Tomatoes   MACSAC

2 tablespoons olive oil
2 cups cubed stale Italian bread
4 large tomatoes, seeded and diced
2 teaspoons minced garlic

2-3 tablespoons chopped fresh oregano leaves
salt and freshly ground black pepper
1/3 cup freshly grated Parmesan cheese
1/2 cup canned pizza sauce

Heat oven to 350 degrees. Heat oil in medium skillet over medium-high flame. Add bread cubes and cook, stirring frequently, until bread is lightly browned, 5-8 minutes. Add tomatoes and garlic; cook, stirring often, until tomatoes produce a little juice, about 3 minutes. Stir oregano into the mixture and season to taste with salt and pepper. Spread mixture into an attractive baking dish. Sprinkle with some of the Parmesan, drizzle with the pizza sauce, and then add the rest of the Parmesan. Bake 25-30 minutes. Makes 4-6 servings.

Zucchini with Oregano and Sun-Dried Tomatoes   MACSAC

1 teaspoon olive oil
1 pound young zucchini, cut into 1/2-inch-thick
   rounds, cubes, or wedges
salt and pepper

1/3 cup oil-packed sun-dried tomatoes, cut into strips
1-2 teaspoons minced garlic
1 tablespoon chopped fresh oregano
fresh lemon juice to taste

Heat oil in cast-iron pan over medium-high flame. Add zucchini, season well with salt and pepper, and sauté, tossing often, 2-3 minutes. Stir in sun-dried tomatoes, garlic, and oregano. Continue to sauté, stirring often, until just tender, about 2-3 minutes longer. Toss with lemon juice to taste and serve immediately. Makes 3-4 servings.

Parsley

Petroselinum crispum

Parsley's reputation in this country does not inspire confidence. Indeed, that limp, yellowing garnish on the side of your plate in a restaurant is probably parsley. No wonder people don't eat this herb! That attitude can be changed as soon as a vibrant fresh bunch enters your kitchen. Forget your old thoughts of parsley and begin to think of it as a new and wonderful vegetable.

Parsley offers not only wonderful flavor and rich color but also outstanding nutrition. Did you know that parsley has more vitamin A than carrots and more vitamin C than oranges? It's also very high in minerals, particularly iron. It's time we started eating our parsley!

The two varieties of culinary parsley are the Italian flat-leafed and the more common curly-leafed. Both are native to the Mediterranean countries. Ancient Greco-Romans used the smooth flat-leafed in their cooking, and the curly-leafed primarily for ornamental purposes, like garlands to crown athletes and poets. Today, in this country, the curly-leafed is more widely recognized, while in European cooking the flat-leafed still predominates. Both are flavorful, decorative, and nutritious. Try them both and discover your favorite.

Cooking Tips

- Think of parsley as a green and toss it into a salad with the other greens.

- Use it as a green in stir-fries. Add it toward the very end of cooking to retain color, flavor, and nutrition.

- Chop it into just about any chilled pasta or vegetable salad.

- Excellent in soups and stews. If using parsley fresh, add it toward the end or after cooking is completed.

- Use your fresh or dried parsley in a homemade tomato sauce.

- If using parsley as a garnish, don't forget to eat it! Parsley is famous for freshening the breath at the end of a meal.

Storage Tips

- For short term storage, wrap parsley in a damp towel or place upright in a container with an inch of water and refrigerate.

- For longer term storage, parsley can be dried. See chapter on home food preservation for information on dehydrating herbs.

Kim's Excellent Parsley Salad   MACSAC

fresh parsley
very thinly sliced red onion or finely
  chopped green onion
chopped hard-cooked eggs
cooked chick-peas or other beans

garlic chives (optional)
olive oil
fresh lemon juice
salt and freshly ground black pepper

Clean and cut up lots of parsley, as much as you would clean for lettuce in a salad. Combine with red onion, eggs, chick-peas, and garlic chives, if available. Shake oil and lemon juice together (2 parts oil to 1 part lemon juice). Toss salad with dressing, salt, and lots of pepper. Adapted from a friend's recipe. Makes any number of servings.

Chimichurri Sauce for Grilled Steak, Chicken, Fish, or Vegetables   MACSAC

1/3 cup olive oil
3 tablespoons white wine vinegar
1/2 teaspoon red pepper flakes
1 cup chopped parsley

3 tablespoons chopped cilantro
2 teaspoons minced garlic
1 teaspoon chopped fresh oregano

Combine all ingredients with 1/3 cup water and let stand at least 1 hour. The flavors really bloom as they sit. Serve over grilled steak, chicken, fish, or vegetables. Makes about 1 cup.

Garlic Parsley Pesto with Pasta   K. Blakeslee, *Madison Herb Society Cookbook*

1 cup low-fat cottage cheese or part-skim ricotta
5 tablespoons grated Parmesan cheese
1/2 cup boiling water
1/2 cup loosely packed fresh parsley

1/2 cup fresh basil
2 large cloves garlic
salt and coarse pepper to taste
3 cups tender-cooked pasta

Have cheeses at room temperature. Blend with remaining ingredients (except pasta) until smooth in blender or food processor. Toss with pasta. This is also good on baked potatoes, cooked rice, or steamed vegetables. Makes 3 servings.

Parsley Pasta Sauce   J. Jacobson, *Madison Herb Society Cookbook*

cooked pasta
1 cup packed fresh parsley leaves
1/4 cup olive oil
2 teaspoons dried basil
1 1/2 teaspoons dried marjoram
1 teaspoon finely dried oregano

1/2 teaspoon salt
2 cloves garlic
scant 1/2 teaspoon fresh ground black pepper
1 cup sour cream
1/4 cup grated Parmesan cheese
sunflower kernels

While pasta cooks, prepare sauce: Combine parsley, olive oil, basil, marjoram, oregano, salt, garlic, and pepper in food processor. Chop finely. Add sour cream and Parmesan; puree. Place mixture in saucepan; heat to almost boiling. Serve sauce over pasta and sprinkle with sunflower kernels. Makes 4 servings.

Parsnip
Pastinaca sativa

Parsnips are among the most underrated garden vegetables in the United States. In other parts of the world, however, parsnips have enjoyed great popularity since ancient times.

Parsnips once grew wild over much of the European continent, and were heavily cultivated during medieval times. They were more popular than carrots and as staple a starch as the potato later became. Sugary varieties were commonly fermented into wine. Introduced in North America in the 17th century, parsnips have never been more than a minor crop here.

But parsnips may win the "most sweet and delicious" award of all the root vegetables. Due to a very long growing season, parsnips are not available until late fall. They improve in taste and sweetness after exposure to frost, as the starch is transformed into sugar. For this reason many gardeners prefer to harvest their parsnips in early spring, after the ground has thawed. Parsnips store well in appropriate root cellar conditions and are a hearty and warming addition to a seasonal winter diet.

Nutritionally speaking, parsnips are noted most for mineral content and are particularly high in potassium. They top their nutritious cousin the carrot for vitamin C content, and rival the ever-popular potato for carbohydrate and vegetable protein.

Cooking Tips

- Scrub parsnips with a stiff vegetable brush under running water to remove garden soil.

- To cook evenly, cut parsnips into uniform-size pieces, or add narrower sections halfway through cooking.

- Boil 1-inch parsnip chunks for 8-10 minutes, or until tender but not mushy.

- Steam 1-inch chunks for 5 minutes longer if intended for puree. Enjoy parsnips plain or topped with butter.

- Sauté thin parsnip slices in butter, with a dash of salt and pepper.

- Grate parsnips raw into a variety of salads, or cut into thin sticks for a dipping vegetable.

- Try parsnips cooked and mashed; top with butter and chopped parsley. Leftover mashed parsnips may be added to sauces, gravies, or soups as a thickener, or shaped into thin patties and fried.

- Oven-roast parsnip chunks, or grill them outdoors.

- Coarsely grate parsnips and substitute in a potato pancake recipe.

- Puree parsnips with onion and curry spices into a creamy soup.

- Try a great snack for kids: Slice parsnips lengthwise into sticks. Bake at 350 degrees until soft, yet firm. Brush on a little melted butter with cinnamon. Serve warm.

- Bake or roast with other root vegetables.

Storage Tips

- Trim off parsnip tops and refrigerate unwashed in a plastic bag for up to 2 weeks.

- For long-term storage, bury parsnips in moist sand and keep in a very cool but not freezing location.

- Parsnips may be frozen. Blanch 1-inch chunks for 2-3 minutes, run under cold water to stop the cooking process, drain, and pack into airtight containers, such as zip-lock freezer bags. Parsnip puree freezes well, also. See chapter on home food preservation for more information on freezing vegetables.

Parsnip Patties   Brantmeier Family Farm

4 medium parsnips
1 egg yolk
salt and pepper
1 egg white, slightly beaten

1 cup soft whole wheat bread crumbs
    (mixed with cornmeal or wheat germ, if desired)
butter and/or oil for frying

Chop parsnips; steam until tender. Mash thoroughly. Mix in egg yolk and salt and pepper to taste. Form into patties, dip into egg white, then roll in crumbs. Sauté in oil and/or butter until golden brown. These can also be cooked in an ungreased skillet or in the oven. Make 4 servings.

Parsnip Gratin   MACSAC

1 pound parsnips
1 tablespoon butter
1 cup unsalted chicken stock

salt and pepper
4 tablespoons heavy cream
1/2 cup freshly grated Parmesan

Peel parsnips; slice into thin rounds or cut into matchsticks. Heat butter in skillet over medium flame. Add parsnips and cook, tossing often, until partially tender, about 3 minutes. Add stock and bring to strong simmer. Lower heat, cover skillet, and gently simmer parsnips until almost tender, 5-6 minutes. Uncover, raise heat to high, and cook until liquid reduces to a syrupy glaze. Season to taste with salt and pepper. Heat oven to 400 degrees. Butter a baking dish. Place half the parsnips in dish. Drizzle with half the cream and sprinkle with half the Parmesan. Repeat layers with remaining ingredients. Bake until golden brown, about 20 minutes. Makes 4 servings.

Oven-Fried Parsnips   MACSAC

2 pounds parsnips
2 tablespoons olive oil

coarse sea salt

Heat oven to 400 degrees. Line 2 baking sheets with parchment paper. Peel parsnips. Cut them crosswise into 2 1/2-inch chunks, slice the chunks lengthwise into 1/4-inch-thick planks, and cut planks into sticks. Toss with olive oil and a little sea salt. Spread in single layer on baking sheets. Bake 15 minutes; toss well and add additional salt. Continue to bake, tossing occasionally, until golden brown and crisp, about 30 minutes total. Makes 4-6 servings.

Grated Parsnip Apple Salad with Meyer Lemon Dressing   MACSAC

juice of 1 Meyer lemon*
2 teaspoons Dijon mustard
4-5 tablespoons olive oil
3 cups peeled, shredded parsnips

1 1/2 cups peeled, shredded apples
1 cup loosely packed Italian parsley leaves
salt and pepper

Mix lemon juice and mustard; whisk in the olive oil in a thin stream. Combine parsnips, apples, and parsley in a bowl; toss with dressing and season to taste with salt and pepper. Serve immediately or chill 1/2 hour. Makes 6 servings.

*Meyer lemons have a wonderful, sweet flavor, and are sometimes available from California. You may substitute juice from half a small regular lemon and juice from half of an orange.

Parsnip Cake with Lemon Cream Cheese Icing   Punky Egan, Madison Area Technical College

1 2/3 cups whole wheat pastry flour or
   unbleached white flour
1 cup sugar
1 1/2 teaspoon cinnamon
1 teaspoon baking powder
1 teaspoon baking soda
1/2 teaspoon salt
3 eggs, beaten
1/2 cup canola oil
2 cups grated parsnips (or use half parsnips
   and half carrots)

1 cup peeled, grated apple
1/2 cup hickory nuts or black walnuts, chopped
1 package (8 ounces) cream cheese, softened
1 package (3 ounces) cream cheese, softened
11 tablespoons unsalted butter, softened
5 cups powdered sugar, sifted
1 1/2 teaspoons lemon extract (or vanilla extract)
finely chopped hickory nuts or black
   walnuts and dried cherries (optional)

Heat oven to 350 degrees. Grease and flour two 8-inch round cake pans (or substitute a greased 9-by-13-inch cake pan). Whisk flour, sugar, cinnamon, baking powder, baking soda, and salt in large bowl. Combine eggs, oil, parsnips, and apples in a second bowl; stir well. Stir wet mixture into dry until barely combined. Stir in nuts. Divide batter evenly into pans. Bake until cake springs back when lightly touched in the center, 25-35 minutes. Cool 10 minutes, then turn cakes out of pans to cool thoroughly. To make icing, cream the cream cheese and butter. Beat in powdered sugar and lemon extract until smooth. Cut the cooled cakes in half horizontally with a long, thin, sharp knife. Frost layers to make a four-layer cake (or make a two-layer cake instead). Decorate with finely chopped nuts and/or dried cherries, if desired. Makes 12-16 servings.

Parsnip Puree in Zucchini Boats   Elisabeth Atwell, Dog Hollow Farm member

parsnips
nutmeg

salt and pepper
small zucchini

Roast or grill parsnips, then puree with a dash of nutmeg to bring out the sweetness and the hint of chestnut in their flavor. Season with salt and pepper to taste. Serve in hollowed-out zucchini boats that have been steamed slightly but retain their crispness. Makes any number of servings.

Parsnips with Dark Beer Glaze   MACSAC

1 pound parsnips, cut into small chunks
1 cup sweet-flavored stout or brown ale
1/4 teaspoon cinnamon
1/8 teaspoon cloves

2 teaspoons butter
salt and pepper
1-2 tablespoons maple syrup (optional)

Combine parsnips, stout, cinnamon, and cloves in heavy saucepan. Cover and simmer until barely tender, 8-10 minutes. Remove cover and simmer hard until liquid reduces to a glaze. Stir in butter. Season to taste with salt and pepper. Stir in optional maple syrup. Make 3-4 servings.

Cream of Parsnip-Leek Soup   Harmony Valley Farm

1 pound parsnips, scrubbed and diced
2 leeks, washed and sliced
5 cups chicken or turkey stock, seasoned
   with salt and pepper to taste

1/4 cup skim milk powder
tamari or soy sauce
chopped parsley

Cook parsnips and leeks in stock (just enough to cover) until tender. Puree in a blender. Add remaining stock and heat in double boiler. Whisk skim milk powder into 1 cup water; add to soup about 10 minutes before serving. Add tamari or soy sauce, correct the seasoning, and garnish with chopped parsley. Makes 4-6 servings.

Curried Lamb and Parsnip Stew MACSAC

2 pounds boneless lamb shoulder meat,
  cut into large cubes
salt and freshly cracked black pepper
3-4 tablespoons olive oil, divided
1 large onion, thinly sliced
2 tablespoons minced garlic
3 tablespoons minced fresh ginger
1 tablespoon curry powder
1 teaspoon cumin
1 teaspoon garam masala

1/2-1 teaspoon cayenne pepper
1/2 cup ketchup or 1 cup tomato sauce
about 3 cups lamb or chicken stock
1 pound parsnips, peeled and cut into chunks
2 tablespoons flour
1 1/2 cups peas, fresh or thawed
juice of two limes (about 1/4 cup)
1/3-1/2 cup chopped cilantro
1-2 cups plain yogurt

Dry lamb with paper towels and season generously with salt and pepper. Heat 1-2 tablespoons olive oil in deep, heavy pot over medium-high flame until very hot but not smoking. Brown lamb on all sides in batches (do not crowd the pot), transferring the browned pieces to a plate and adding additional oil to the pot as needed. When all the meat is browned, pour off or add fat/oil to the pot to get 2 tablespoons. Reduce heat to medium, add onions, and sauté until golden, about 10 minutes. Stir in garlic, ginger, curry, cumin, garam masala, and cayenne; cook, stirring, about 1 minute. Return lamb to pot. Stir in ketchup or tomato sauce and enough stock to barely cover the ingredients. (If you don't have enough stock, you can add beer to get the right amount.) Bring to simmer, skimming surface. Cover pot, reduce heat to low, and slowly simmer, stirring occasionally, until meat is tender, 1 1/2-2 hours. Stir in parsnips and simmer until tender, about 10 minutes. Mix flour with 2 tablespoons water; stir into stew to thicken it. Cook a few more minutes, then add salt and pepper to taste. The stew is most delicious if you let it come to room temperature at this point and reheat it later, but you can also serve it right away. To serve, add peas to stew and heat through. Stir in lime juice and most of the cilantro. Serve immediately over rice, garnishing each portion with some yogurt and some of the remaining chopped cilantro. Inspired by a recipe in *How to Cook Meat* by Chris Schlesinger and John Willoughby. Makes 6 or more servings.

Northern Comfort Roast Parsnip Soup MACSAC

1 medium head garlic
2 pounds parsnips, peeled, seeded, and
  cut into 1-inch chunks
1/4 pound shallots, peeled
2 tablespoons olive oil
8-10 sprigs fresh thyme or 1 1/2 teaspoons
  dried thyme, divided

1 cup dry white wine, divided
salt and pepper
3-4 cups chicken stock (preferably homemade),
  divided
4 tablespoons half-and-half or soy milk (optional)

Heat oven to 375 degrees. Remove papery outer layers from garlic head; slice off and discard top quarter of the head. Toss garlic head, parsnips, and shallots with olive oil in large baking dish. Scatter half the thyme sprigs around vegetables; drizzle with 1/2 cup wine. Season with salt and pepper to taste and cover tightly with foil. Roast 20 minutes; uncover and continue to cook until vegetables are soft, 20-30 minutes longer. Discard the cooked thyme sprigs. When garlic is cool enough to handle, squeeze "meat" out of cloves; combine with parsnips, shallots, and pan drippings in food processor or blender. Add 1 cup stock; puree until smooth. Place mixture in large saucepan; stir in 2 cups stock plus remaining 1/2 cup wine. Chop remaining sprigs of thyme and stir into soup. Bring to low simmer and cook gently 15 minutes, stirring often. Stir in half-and-half, if desired. Thin the soup as desired with additional stock. Cook gently 5 minutes. Season to taste with salt and pepper. Makes 6 servings.

Pea

Pisum sativum

Peas are most certainly a seasonal treat. Savor them fresh while they last! They are available beginning late spring or early summer and are usually finished by the onset of the summer heat. Like sweet corn they are at their absolute best immediately after harvest, as their sugars rapidly convert to starch, reducing flavor and sweetness.

Peas are as ancient a cultivated food as wheat, barley, and garlic. They have been found in famous excavations and date back to 7000 and 10,000 B.C. Perhaps originating in northern India, peas moved to the Near East, the Mediterranean, northern Europe, and the British Isles. Peas remain staples in many of these regions—particularly in their dried form—as an important protein and carbohydrate source.

Nutritionally, fresh peas have much to offer as well. They are an excellent source of vitamins A, C, K, and the Bs. They are also high in the minerals iron, potassium, and phosphorous. All of this in a high-protein, high-carbohydrate, high-fiber package.

Three basic types of peas are available seasonally and locally. The most common is the shell pea. At the right moment these peas are succulent and sweet, but they lose these qualities as they age, and their pod is inedible. The sugar snap pea features sweet, juicy peas encased in a crunchy but very edible pod, and the snow pea is a flat edible pod with undeveloped peas inside. Each one has its special place in the pea lover's kitchen.

Cooking Tips

Shell Peas

- Kids love peas. Teach them how to shell peas and then give them a big supply. Great for snacks, picnics, or the main veggie of their meal.

- Add shelled peas to stews, soups, mixed veggie sautés, or stir-fries.

- Blanch or steam shelled peas 2-4 minutes. Watch for color to heighten, and be careful not to overcook. Add them to fresh vegetable salads, rice salads, pasta salads, or fried rice.

- To enjoy young, sweet peas, lightly cook them and serve totally plain or topped with butter.

Snap Peas

- Snap peas need stringing: Snap off stem tip toward the flat side of pod and pull downward.

- Eat young, fresh snap peas raw. Put out a heaping bowl for snack or mealtime, arrange decoratively with other vegetables on a platter, or cut into a variety of salads.

- Cook quickly, no more than 2 minutes. Add to a chilled, marinated vinaigrette-style salad.

- Deep-fry in a tempura batter along with other vegetables.

Snow Peas

- Snow peas are a classic stir-fry vegetable, particularly popular in Chinese cooking.

- Sauté alone or with other veggies and/or meats, adding pea pods in the last few minutes of cooking.

- Add raw or lightly cooked pea pods to a variety of salads.

Storage Tips

- Use as soon as possible. Refrigerate in a plastic bag for 4-5 days maximum. Storing peas sacrifices some of their sweet flavor and crisp texture.

- Peas freeze well, but will lose their crunchy texture. Blanch all kinds of peas for 2 minutes (shell peas must be shelled), rinse under cold water to stop cooking process, drain well, and pack into airtight containers such as zip-lock freezer bags. See chapter on home food preservation for more information on freezing vegetables.

Fresh Pea Pod, Broccoli, and Rice Salad   Crystal Lake Gardens

1 package (6 ounces) long-grain and wild rice mix
1 1/2 cups chopped broccoli
1/3 cup sliced red or green onions
1/4 cup bottled clear Italian salad dressing
1 tablespoon lemon juice
1/2 teaspoon lemon pepper
1-1 1/2 cups edible pea pods
1/3 cup slivered almonds

Prepare rice mix according to package directions. Cool slightly. Steam broccoli until crunchy-tender. (For a variation, substitute uncooked sweet peppers for the broccoli.) Toss with remaining ingredients and refrigerate 2-24 hours. Makes 4 servings.

Garlic Stir-Fried Snap Peas   Oak Ridge Farm

3 cups sugar snap peas
1 tablespoon oil (any mild one)
2 large garlic cloves, minced
2 teaspoons fresh lemon juice
salt and pepper to taste
cooked rice (optional)

Heat oil in skillet. Stir in garlic. Add peas; cook and stir 2-4 minutes on medium heat. Remove and sprinkle on lemon juice, and salt and pepper. Serve over rice, if desired. Makes 3-4 servings.

Sesame Snow Peas   MACSAC

1 pound snow peas
1/4 red bell pepper, cut into thin matchsticks
1 1/2 teaspoons sesame seeds
2 teaspoons toasted sesame oil

Steam peas over simmering water until bright and crisp-tender, 1-2 minutes. Cool under running cold water. Drain well and let stand to dry. Toss with remaining ingredients. Makes 4 servings.

Snow Pea Red Pepper Slaw   MACSAC

2 cups slivered snow peas
1 red bell pepper, cut into fine matchsticks
1/2 cup fresh-squeezed orange juice
3 tablespoons fresh-squeezed lime juice
2 teaspoons sugar
1 tablespoon rice wine vinegar
1 teaspoon ground cumin
1 tablespoon chopped cilantro
1 teaspoon minced garlic
1/2-1 jalapeño, minced
salt and pepper to taste

Toss all ingredients in a bowl. Makes 4-6 servings.

Herbed New Potatoes, Onions, and Peas   MACSAC

1/2 pound spring onions
1 pound small new potatoes
2/3 pound sugar snap peas
1-3 tablespoons chopped fresh mint, dill, or cilantro
butter
salt and freshly ground black pepper

Trim stems from onions; leave a little of root end on. Combine with potatoes in pot with water to cover. Bring to low boil; cook until nearly tender, 10-12 minutes. Add peas; boil until just tender. Drain and toss with herbs, butter, and salt and pepper to taste. Makes 4-6 servings.

Pepper
Capsicum annuum

Peppers are members of the Solanaceae family, along with their garden relatives, the tomato, potato, eggplant, and tomatillo. Native to South and Central America, pepper seeds found in Mexico have been dated to before 5000 B.C. Dried peppers have been found in Incan tombs. Following Columbus's voyage, peppers spread quickly through Europe and all the way to India, where they were rapidly assimilated into the native diet.

Hot peppers have played a predominant role in Central and South American and Asian cooking, while sweet bell peppers are most widely used in this country. Sweet peppers come in a dazzling array of colors, shapes, and sizes. Most of the popular colored peppers, like the expensive sweet red pepper, are simply green peppers allowed to mature and ripen on the plant. Pepper plants are very cold sensitive, and die off with the first frosts.

Capsaicin produces the pungency of hot peppers. This substance is soluble in alcohol and milk but not water, which may explain why hot Indian dishes are frequently accompanied by yogurt and perhaps a beer. Most of the intensity of a hot pepper resides in its seeds and inner ribs. Remove these to reduce heat, but retain them in cooking for the full blast. Always take precautions when preparing hot peppers, however (see Cooking Tips).

Peppers are nutritionally significant. High levels of vitamins A, C, and E and the minerals iron and potassium characterize most varieties. Hot chile peppers and red sweet bell peppers are exceedingly high in vitamins A and C. Anyone who has enjoyed hot pepper in their food can attest to the medicinal effects of clearing nasal passages and lung congestion, and cleansing through perspiration!

Cooking Tips

- Be careful when preparing hot peppers of any kind. For greatest safety wear rubber gloves while chopping and handling them. DO NOT touch eyes, nose, mouth or other places. Wash hands thoroughly when finished.

- For greatest nutrient retention eat bell peppers raw: Thinly slice lengthwise for a crunchy snack or for dipping, layer slices into a favorite sandwich, or dice into a variety of salads.

- Add peppers to soups, stews, omelets, quiches, casseroles, and stir-fries.

- Try the famous roasted pepper: Place bell pepper under broiler, above hot coals, or over open flame. Toast it, turning often, until the skin is blackened evenly. Place pepper in a brown bag, close, and allow to steam 10-15 minutes. Skin will peel off easily with the aid of a paring knife.

Storage Tips

- Refrigerate peppers unwashed in hydrator drawer for 1-2 weeks.

- Peppers may be frozen: Wash and dry peppers. Cut into bite-size pieces and place in an airtight container or zip-lock freezer bag. Peppers will soften when thawed, so take out only the amount you need and replace the rest in the freezer.

- Peppers also dry well. See chapter on home food preservation for more information about drying or freezing vegetables.

For additional recipes that feature peppers, see the Seasonal Combinations and Kids' Recipes chapters.

Stuffed Peppers   Lizzie Breuer, Zephyr Community Farm member

a little oil
2 cloves garlic, minced
2 onions, chopped
3 cups raw brown rice
6 cups water, chicken or vegetable stock,
    or tomato juice

1/2 teaspoon allspice
1/2 cup almonds, chopped
1 cup chopped tomatoes
3/4 pound cheddar cheese, grated
salt and pepper
9 large peppers, tops cut off, seeds removed

Heat oil in large skillet; add and sauté garlic and onions. Add rice and brown about 5 minutes. Add desired liquid and allspice. Cover and cook until rice is done, about 40 minutes. Toast almonds in dry skillet or hot oven several minutes, tossing often. Stir in tomatoes, cheese, almonds, and salt and pepper to taste. Cook peppers in boiling water 2 minutes. Drain and stuff peppers with rice mixture. Bake at 350 degrees 30 minutes. Makes 9 servings.

Chiles Rellenos José   Nancy Crabb, Zephyr Community Farm member

whole or halved hot or semi-hot chiles
    (Hungarian wax, Anaheim, jalapeños, etc.),
    enough to cover bottom of a 7-by-13-inch pan
1 pound Monterey Jack cheese, cut into thin strips
5 large eggs

1/4 cup flour
1 1/4 cups milk
1/2 teaspoon salt
1/2 pound grated cheddar cheese
1/2 teaspoon paprika

Seed the chiles. Slip strips of Monterey Jack cheese inside chiles. Beat eggs and gradually add flour, milk, and salt. Arrange chiles in well-greased pan. Sprinkle on the cheddar. Pour on egg mixture. Sprinkle on the paprika. Bake uncovered at 350 degrees 45 minutes. Makes 6-8 servings.

Roasted Cheese-Stuffed Green Peppers   Peggy's Biodynamic Garden

bell peppers

low-fat cheese

Using tongs or long-handled fork, hold whole pepper over open flame, turning occasionally, until skin blisters all around. Cool and peel off skin. Open pepper from top carefully; remove seeds and core. Fill with low-fat cheese, and pop in low oven until cheese melts and conforms to shape of pepper. Chill overnight. Slice pepper; serve with other vegetables or use in a sandwich. Makes any number of servings.

Red Pepper Salsa for Grilled Fish   Springdale Farm Cookbook

1 cup chopped red peppers
    (use roasted peppers, if desired)
1/3 cup chopped pitted black olives
    (brine-cured is best)
1/3 cup coarsely grated Parmesan cheese
2 tablespoons olive oil

2 tablespoons chopped fresh basil
1 tablespoon chopped fresh parsley
1 teaspoon chopped fresh oregano
    or 1/4 teaspoon dried
salt and pepper to taste

Combine all ingredients; let stand 30 minutes. Serve with grilled fish. Makes 6-8 servings.

Roasted Red Peppers with Rosemary   MACSAC

2 large sweet red peppers
2-3 teaspoons sherry vinegar
1 tablespoon virgin olive oil

1/2-1 teaspoon minced fresh rosemary (optional)
salt and pepper to taste

Skewer peppers on long forks; roast over high open flame, turning often, until skin is uniformly blackened. Remove peppers to cutting board. Place a paper towel underneath right side of cutting board (left side if you are left-handed!). Using a sharp knife, lightly scrape off blackened skins, pushing charred pieces onto towel. Cut off stem ends and pull out cores. Slit each pepper open and scrape off seeds. Cut into 1/2-inch strips. Place on plate; sprinkle with remaining ingredients. Serve at room temperature with French bread. Makes 4 servings.

Roasted Red Pepper Corn Bread with Bacon or Blue Cheese   MACSAC

1 tablespoon bacon fat or vegetable oil
1 cup stone-ground yellow cornmeal
1 cup whole wheat pastry flour or white flour
2 teaspoons sugar
2 teaspoons baking powder
1/2 teaspoon baking soda
1/2 teaspoon salt

2 large eggs
1 1/4 cups buttermilk
2 tablespoons melted butter or melted bacon fat
4 slices thick-cut bacon (about 1/4 pound), cooked, drained, and diced, or 3-4 ounces blue cheese, coarsely crumbled
3 flame-roasted sweet red peppers, peeled, seeded, and diced

Place 1 tablespoon bacon fat or vegetable oil in a 7- or 8-inch cast-iron skillet; place in oven and heat oven to 400 degrees. Meanwhile, whisk cornmeal, flour, sugar, baking powder, baking soda, and salt in a bowl until well combined. Beat eggs and buttermilk in a separate bowl. Stir in melted butter or bacon fat, crumbled bacon or blue cheese, and sweet peppers. Stir wet mixture into dry mixture until barely combined. Spread in hot skillet. Bake until toothpick inserted near center comes out clean, about 20 minutes. You could also make muffins: line muffin tins with paper liners and fill 3/4 full. Serve corn bread or muffins warm. Makes 8-12 servings or muffins.

Roasted Red Pepper Risotto   Amy Simonson

2 large red bell peppers
1 medium onion, finely diced
3 tablespoons chopped fresh dill
juice of 2 small lemons

8-9 cups vegetable stock
3 tablespoons olive oil
about 2 1/2 cups Arborio rice
1/2 cup dry white wine

Heat oven to broiling temperature. Place peppers on baking sheet. Broil close to heating element, using tongs to turn peppers to char skin evenly on all sides. Remove from oven, place in paper bag, and close bag. Let peppers stand while you chop onion and dill and juice lemons. Remove peppers from bag; peel off charred skin, remove stem and seeds (don't rinse them, as this will weaken the flavor), and cut into small strips. Heat stock in saucepan over medium-low flame. Heat oil in large saucepan over medium flame. Add onions; cook until soft. Stir in rice with wooden spoon until all grains are evenly coated. Add dill, stir 1 minute, then add wine and stir until wine is absorbed. Add 1 cup stock; stir until stock is absorbed. Continue cooking, stirring, and adding 1 cup of stock at a time until the rice is al dente and suspended in a smooth sauce, 15-25 minutes. Remove from heat; stir in lemon juice and red peppers. Makes 6-8 servings.

Chile Cumin Butter   MACSAC

8 tablespoons (1 stick) butter, at room temperature
2-4 serrano or other hot chiles, seeded and minced
grated zest of 1 lime

2 green onions, minced
1/2 teaspoon ground cumin

Beat together all ingredients. Use this mixture to spread on hot baked squash, to dress cooked green beans, to stir into chili, etc. Makes 8 tablespoons.

Green Chile Red Pepper Corn Bread Cobbler   Tricia Bross, Luna Circle Farm

2 tablespoons olive oil
2 medium onions, diced
6 green Anaheim or 4 poblano chiles, thinly sliced
2 red bell peppers, thinly sliced (or substitute
   green bell peppers)
1-2 tablespoons minced garlic
2 teaspoons cumin
salt and pepper
1/2 pound cheddar cheese, sliced or grated, and
   divided
8 ounces cream cheese, cut into chunks

Biscuit topping:
1/4 cup honey
1 cup milk
1 egg
3 tablespoons melted butter
1 cup yellow cornmeal
1 cup flour
2 teaspoons baking powder
1/2 teaspoon baking soda
1/2 teaspoon salt
sliced tomatoes, fresh tomato salsa, or sour cream

Grease an 8-by-12-inch baking dish. Heat olive oil in large skillet over medium flame. Add onions and cook, stirring often, until they begin to soften. Add chiles, bell peppers, garlic, and cumin; continue to cook, stirring occasionally, until vegetables are just tender. Season with salt and pepper to taste. Spread half the mix into baking dish. Arrange half the cheddar over mixture. Spread remaining chile mixture over cheese. Scatter the cream cheese over mixture. Heat oven to 400 degrees. To make topping: Mix wet ingredients in a bowl. Mix dry ingredients in another bowl. Stir the two together until just combined. Spread topping evenly over chile/cheese layers. Bake at 400 degrees, 25 minutes. Arrange or scatter remaining cheddar over topping and bake another 5 minutes. Serve with sliced tomatoes, salsa, or sour cream. Makes 12 servings.

Three-Pepper Sauté   Springdale Farm Cookbook

3 bell peppers (red, yellow, and/or green)
1 tablespoon olive oil
1 clove garlic, finely minced

1 tablespoon balsamic or red wine vinegar
salt and fresh pepper to taste

Remove stems, seeds, and ribs from peppers. Cut lengthwise into 1/4-inch-wide strips. Heat oil in large skillet over medium-high heat. Add garlic; cook until golden. Add peppers; stir and cook until crisp-tender, 3-4 minutes. Sprinkle with vinegar, salt, and pepper. Makes 4 servings.

Italian Stuffed Peppers   MACSAC

1 tablespoon oil
3 tablespoons chopped onion
2 teaspoons minced garlic
1/2 pound bulk Italian sausage
1 tablespoon tomato paste
1 cup tomato sauce
2 tablespoons chopped fresh parsley

1 teaspoon dried basil
1 teaspoon dried oregano
salt and pepper to taste
3 cups cooked white or brown rice
1 egg
8 short, squat sweet peppers
1/3 cup grated Parmesan cheese

Heat olive oil in skillet; add onions and sauté until opaque. Add garlic; sauté 30 seconds. Add and brown sausage. Stir in tomato paste, tomato sauce, parsley, basil, oregano, and salt and pepper. Cook about 8 minutes. Stir in rice. Beat egg and stir into rice mix. Slice off tops of peppers; remove seeds and cut away membranes. Fill with sausage and rice stuffing. Heat oven to 350 degrees. Place peppers in baking dish and add enough hot water to come 1/2 inch up the peppers. Cover with foil and bake 20 minutes. Uncover, sprinkle with grated cheese, and bake another 15 minutes. Makes 8 servings.

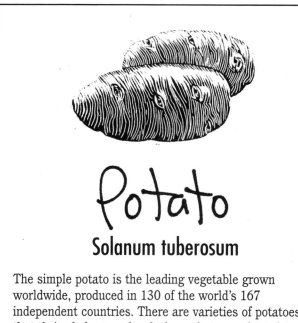

Potato

Solanum tuberosum

The simple potato is the leading vegetable grown worldwide, produced in 130 of the world's 167 independent countries. There are varieties of potatoes that thrive below sea level, those that are adapted to 14,000 feet above, and everything in between.

Potatoes are native to the Andean mountain regions of South America, where they have been cultivated since 3000 B.C. Rediscovered there by the Spaniards, they were introduced in Europe, and then to North America in the early 1700s. Europeans were slow to trust the potato, a member of the potentially poisonous nightshade family. This useful food was slowly adopted, however, in order to protect against famine wrought by grain crop failures. In countries like Ireland, dependence on the potato grew until its own crop failure in 1845 was a catalyst for a severe famine and a massive emigration to the U.S.

A person in this country eats an average of 75 pounds of potatoes annually. Unfortunately, most potatoes are consumed in the high-fat, high-sodium form of French fries and potato chips. Alone, the potato is an excellent source of complex carbohydrates and minerals, particularly potassium—providing the skin is consumed—and a fairly good source of vegetable protein. They form a complete protein when eaten with meat, dairy, or grains.

Potatoes are an excellent storage crop and are often a staple in a seasonal winter diet. The season begins with lovely new baby potatoes in warm weather and lasts throughout the summer and fall. Potatoes must be harvested before the ground freezes and stored properly to be enjoyed all winter. Some varieties store better than others.

Cooking Tips

- Scrub potatoes with a vegetable brush under running water to remove garden soil.

- No need to peel an organic potato. Most nutrients are in or near the potato skin. Do trim off any green spots and eyes (where the toxic solanin concentrates), and any damaged areas.

- Boil average-size potatoes in water for 20-30 minutes, or until tender. Stop cooking process while potato is still firm if intended for a chilled salad. Save water for soup stock.

- Steam potato chunks over an inch of water for 10-20 minutes, or until tender throughout.

- Make hash browns: Fry shredded or thinly sliced potatoes in butter or vegetable oil over low heat, covered, for 10 minutes until tender. Increase heat, remove cover, and flip potatoes until brown and crispy. Sprinkle with salt.

- Add potato chunks to soups, stews, or chowders 20-30 minutes before cooking is finished.

- New potatoes are best enjoyed when boiled and topped with butter, salt, and pepper. Dill weed, Parmesan cheese, garlic, and chopped green onion are also good additions.

- Brush potato wedges with oil, sprinkle with spices, and grill 5 minutes per side until tender.

- Thicken soups with grated or pureed potatoes.

Storage Tips

- Refrigerate baby new potatoes if not used within 2-3 days. Use within 1-2 weeks.

- Most potatoes will keep at room temperature for up to 2 weeks. Store away from light.

- For longer storage, potatoes will keep best at 45-50 degrees, high humidity, and in darkness. If their environment is too warm they will sprout and shrivel; if too cold, the starch will turn to sugar.

For additional recipes that feature potatoes, see the Seasonal Combinations chapter.

Spanish Potato Tortilla Julie Kruenen

1/2 cup olive oil
1 large yellow or white onion, finely diced
3-4 cloves garlic, minced and pressed or
    mashed to a paste
salt
3-4 medium to large baking potatoes, peeled,
    quartered lengthwise, and sliced crosswise
    into 1/8-inch-thick slices

4-6 eggs, well beaten
cayenne
freshly ground, black pepper
paprika
additional olive oil

Heat 1/2 cup olive oil in a skillet large enough to accommodate and move around all the ingredients. Add onions and cook, stirring often, 3-4 minutes. Stir in garlic and some salt; cook another 1-2 minutes. Gently stir in potato slices, thoroughly mixing them with the oil, onions, and garlic. Cook the potatoes, gently moving them around occasionally, until fork-tender but not browned, 10-15 minutes. Watch the heat level, lowering it if necessary. You may want to add some water, but no more than 1/3-1/2 cup, mixing well and covering skillet for several minutes, though continuing to toss mixture occasionally. Meanwhile, beat eggs in large bowl until slightly foamy. Add cayenne, coarsely ground black pepper, and paprika to taste. When potatoes are cooked, remove them with a slotted spoon to the eggs; this mixture should be soupy but with a high ratio of potatoes to eggs.

Now heat 2-3 teaspoons olive oil in a 7- to 9-inch nonstick skillet. Pour in the potato mixture and flatten evenly over bottom of pan to thickness of at least 1 inch. Lower heat and cook, occasionally shaking pan and loosening tortilla without breaking it, until eggs begin to brown underneath. Using oven mitts, invert a plate over the skillet; gripping skillet and pan firmly, flip the half-cooked tortilla onto plate. Quickly wipe skillet clean and add a bit more oil, then slide tortilla, runny-side down, back into skillet. Cook until golden. The interior of an authentic Spanish tortilla is moist and ever so slightly runny in the very middle. Slide tortilla onto a handsome plate and surround it with sprigs of parsley, olives, and/or chunks of feta cheese. This is an everyday dish in Spain's bars and homes. Fix it for yourself and slap a chunk into a crusty baguette *(un bocadillo de tortilla)* or take an entire round to a party. You will be praised, thanked, and congratulated for this honest, unpretentious, and highly satisfying dish. Serve warm or at room temperature. Makes 4-6 servings.

Potato Crust Quiche Crystal Lake Gardens

3 medium potatoes (to make 1 1/2 cups mashed)
1/3 cup butter, softened
2 cups mixed, chopped, cooked vegetables
1/2 cup shredded cheddar cheese
2 eggs

1 can (5.3 ounces) evaporated milk
1/4 teaspoon salt
1/8 teaspoon pepper
1 cup bread cubes (optional)

Cook potatoes in boiling water until tender; drain. Heat oven to 375 degrees. Mash hot potatoes with butter. Line bottom and sides of 9-inch pie plate with potato mixture. Spread vegetables over potatoes; sprinkle cheese over vegetables. Beat eggs, milk, salt, and pepper in bowl. Pour over quiche; top with bread cubes, if desired. Bake 40-50 minutes. Makes 8 servings.

Herb-Roasted Red Potatoes Patricia Schindler

1 pound red potatoes, cut in 1/2-inch pieces
1-4 cloves garlic, chopped
3-4 tablespoons of your favorite fresh herb:
    chopped parsley, rosemary, thyme, fennel, dill, etc.

3-4 tablespoons olive oil
salt and pepper to taste

Heat oven to 350 degrees. Coat potatoes with other ingredients and spread out on a shallow baking dish. Roast until tender, 40-45 minutes. Makes 2-4 servings.

Smashed Yukon Gold Potatoes with Blue Cheese and Toasted Hickory Nuts
Chef Eric Rupert, Sub-Zero Freezer and Wolf Appliance Co.

2 pounds young Yukon Gold potatoes (unpeeled)
4 tablespoons butter, softened
1/2 cup milk or cream

salt and pepper
1/2 pound blue cheese, crumbled
1/4 pound (about 1 cup) hickory nuts

Toast nuts in a 325-degree oven until light brown and aromatic, about 15 minutes. Boil potatoes in salted water until tender. Drain and place in large bowl. Add butter, milk, and a pinch of salt and pepper (or to taste). Smash with fork, leaving some large pieces. Lightly toss in blue cheese. Sprinkle with hickory nuts. Makes 6 servings.

Papas a la Huancaina (Traditional Peruvian Potato Salad)   MACSAC

juice of 1 lemon
1/8 teaspoon cayenne`
salt and pepper to taste
1 medium onion, thinly sliced
3 pounds potatoes
10 ounces queso fresco (available in Latino
    grocery stores)

1 cup heavy cream
2-3 hot yellow or green peppers, seeded
6 tablespoons olive oil
3/4 teaspoon turmeric
1 cup imported black olives
3-4 hard-cooked eggs, quartered

Combine lemon juice, cayenne, salt, and pepper in bowl. Add onion, separated into rings, and marinate at room temperature, tossing often. Boil potatoes in salted water until barely tender. Drain and keep warm. Blend cheese, heavy cream, and hot peppers in blender or food processor until thick and smooth. Heat olive oil and turmeric over low heat in large pan, add cheese mixture, and cook, stirring constantly, until smooth. Drain onions. Arrange potatoes on platter and pour sauce over them. Garnish potatoes with onions, olives, and eggs. Serve warm or at room temperature. Makes 8-10 servings.

Basmati Rice with Potatoes   Huma Siddiqui

2 tablespoons cooking oil
1 teaspoon whole cumin seeds
1 large (black) cardamom pod
1 small (green) cardamom pod
2 cloves
1-inch piece of cinnamon stick
1 bay leaf
1 medium onion, chopped
2-3 medium potatoes, cubed
2 medium tomatoes, chopped
1 bunch green onions, chopped

1 teaspoon minced garlic
1/2 teaspoon minced ginger
1/2 cup chopped fresh cilantro
1 teaspoon salt
1 teaspoon coriander powder
1/2 teaspoon chili powder
1/2 teaspoon cumin powder
1/4 teaspoon turmeric powder
2 cups basmati rice
4 cups warm water, divided
yogurt

Heat oil in a large saucepan over medium flame and add all the whole spices, bay leaf, and chopped onions. Fry, stirring occasionally, until onions are golden brown. Stir in potatoes, tomatoes, green onions, garlic, ginger, cilantro, salt, and all the ground spices. Add 1 cup warm water, bring to simmer, cover, and let the mixture cook on medium heat for about 10 minutes. Thoroughly wash and rinse the rice. Add rice to potato mixture. Stir in remaining 3 cups warm water, bring to boil, cover, and simmer until all the water is absorbed, about 20 minutes. Serve with yogurt. Huma Siddiqui contributed this recipe from her book, *Jasmine in Her Hair.* Makes 10-12 servings.

Warm Bavarian-Style Potato Salad with Sausage MACSAC

2 pounds Yukon Gold or large fingerling
  potatoes, scrubbed
3/4 cup chopped onion
1/2 cup apple cider or chicken stock
3 tablespoons olive oil

2 tablespoons apple cider vinegar or white wine vinegar
1 tablespoon prepared hot mustard
salt and pepper to taste
3/4 pound pork sausage links
3 tablespoons coarsely chopped fresh parsley

Cook potatoes in salted water until barely tender. Drain, cool slightly, peel, and slice 1/3-inch thick. Meanwhile, make sauce: Combine remaining ingredients (except parsley) in saucepan, bring to simmer, and cook 5-7 minutes. Gently toss with potatoes. Heat oven to 450 degrees. Arrange sausages on baking sheet; bake 8-10 minutes. Cut each link into 4 pieces. Add sausages and parsley to potatoes; mix gently. Season with salt and pepper. Makes 6 servings.

Peruvian Potatoes with Chiles and Cheese MACSAC

2 pounds red potatoes
2 tablespoons vegetable oil
1 cup finely chopped red onion
2 minced jalapeños
1 tablespoon minced garlic

1 cup milk
6 ounces feta, crumbled
3 hard-cooked eggs, chopped
2 tablespoons chopped cilantro
salt and pepper to taste

Boil potatoes in salted water until nearly tender. Heat oil in large skillet over medium-low flame. Add onions; cook 5 minutes. Add jalapeños and garlic; cook until tender, about 2 minutes. Drain potatoes; cut into cubes. Add potatoes and milk to onions. Simmer until potatoes absorb some liquid. Stir in feta and eggs; heat briefly. Stir in cilantro, salt, and pepper. Makes 6 servings.

Potato Tofu Pancakes Edith Thayer, Vermont Valley Farm member

1/2 pound tofu
1 large onion
8 medium potatoes (1 1/2-2 pounds)
1/4 cup finely chopped fresh parsley

1 teaspoon salt or more to taste
1/4 teaspoon black pepper or more to taste
1/2 teaspoon garlic powder or more to taste
3 tablespoons unbleached white flour

Blend tofu in food processor until smooth; remove to a bowl. Grate onion using grater attachment, and add to tofu. Grate potatoes in batches; as each batch is done, squeeze potatoes in towels to remove excess liquid, then stir into tofu mixture. Stir in remaining ingredients. Cook pancakes in batches: Spray a large frying pan with nonfat cooking spray. Spoon potato mixture into hot pan by the half-cupful, flattening each one. Fry until cooked through and golden brown on each side. Serve with applesauce and/or sour cream. Makes 4-6 servings.

Smoked Whitefish and Potato Cakes MACSAC

2 cups flaked whitefish (about 1 pound before
  boning), or other smoked fish
1 1/2 cups leftover mashed potatoes
3 tablespoons minced onion
2-3 tablespoons prepared horseradish

1 egg, beaten
pepper
2 tablespoons butter
sour cream
chopped fresh chives

Mash whitefish with fork and remove stray bones. Combine with potatoes, onions, horseradish, egg, and pepper to taste. Form into 3-inch patties (8-10 total). Chill 1 hour. Heat butter over medium flame in large skillet. Add patties and cook until lightly browned on bottom, 3-4 minutes. Carefully turn and cook other side. Serve with sour cream and chives. Makes 4 servings.

Pumpkin

Cucurbita pepo

The pumpkin is an endearing vegetable, particularly because of its association in this country with Halloween, carving jack-o'-lanterns, and being a kid! As food, the pumpkin is most highly regarded in its traditional and festive form, the pumpkin pie. Beyond these uses, pumpkin is cultivated mainly to feed farm animals in the U.S. This easy-to-grow, highly nutritious, delicious, versatile, and storable vegetable deserves broader popularity.

Pumpkin is a member of the cucurbitaceae family, along with all other squashes, melons, cucumbers, and gourds. Cultivation of the pumpkin dates back 9,000 years to its native regions of South and Central America. Native American tribes in the New England area cultivated pumpkins and other squashes as staples of their diet long before the arrival of the Europeans.

The two most common types of pumpkins are the sweeter, thicker-walled, and smaller pie pumpkin, and the larger jack-o'-lantern varieties generally used for carving and display. The Hokkaido pumpkin from Japan is also gaining popularity in this country. This medium-size, dark green pumpkin resembles a buttercup squash. With curing and proper storage, pumpkins may last for months, and definitely through the holiday season, when they are in greatest demand.

Pumpkins are an important winter vegetable for the seasonal eater, providing the most vitamin A of all common fruits and vegetables. They are also high in iron, potassium, and phosphorous. Don't forget to prepare the seeds—they offer excellent nutrition as well.

Cooking Tips

- Steam 1- to 2-inch chunks for 15-20 minutes. Puree or top with butter.

- Boil 1- to 2-inch chunks in salted water until tender, 8-10 minutes.

- Cut in half and bake cut-side down with a little water in the pan at 350 degrees for 40-50 minutes. Whole pumpkins can be cleaned out, brushed inside with melted butter, and baked with lid on for 35-40 minutes, or until adequately softened.

- Try simmering peeled chunks of pumpkin, particularly Kabocha, in a broth of water, shoyu (soy sauce), and a pinch of salt until pumpkin is tender. Drain and serve.

- Sauté 1/2-inch slices of pumpkin until golden brown on both sides with onion rings, fresh grated ginger, and a pinch of salt, or sweeten slightly with drizzled honey or maple syrup.

- Pumpkin may be cleaned out, steamed whole, and used as an edible, decorative bowl for a variety of grain and vegetable mixtures or for soups. Use top and handle for lid.

- Pumpkin seeds are a great snack. Scoop out seeds and rinse in colander, removing the stringy stuff. Pat dry and put in bowl with 2 tablespoons soy sauce and a minced clove of garlic. Marinate for 30 minutes. Drain and pat dry again. Bake at 250 degrees for 50-60 minutes, stirring once or twice. Allow to cool and crisp up.

Storage Tips

- Store pumpkin in a cool, dry place. Pumpkin will last at room temperature for several weeks, and at 40-50 degrees for several months. Do not refrigerate unless cut open.

- Pumpkin may be cooked, pureed, packed into airtight containers, and frozen for later use in soups or baked goods. See chapter on home food preservation for more information.

For additional recipes that feature pumpkin, see the Winter Squash and Seasonal Combinations chapters.

Toasted Walnut Risotto in Jack-Be-Little Pumpkins   Chef Patrick O'Halloran, Lombardino's

Pumpkins:
6 Jack-Be-Little pumpkins (or 1 large pumpkin)
butter, softened
brown sugar
salt

Risotto:
5 tablespoons butter, divided
1/2 cup finely chopped onion
1 carrot, peeled and finely chopped
1 rib of celery, finely chopped
1 1/2 cups arborio rice
1 bay leaf
about 8 cups vegetable or chicken broth, simmering
1/2 cup toasted walnuts, coarsely ground
salt and pepper
1/2 cup grated Parmigiano-Reggiano

Heat oven to 375 degrees. Cut off tops of 6 Jack-Be-Little pumpkins (or a large pumpkin) and scoop seeds (save those to make toasted pumpkin seeds). Rub inside of each with butter, brown sugar, and a pinch of salt. Put the tops back on and wrap in aluminum foil. Roast until pumpkins soften but are still sturdy, about 1/2 hour depending on the size (be careful not to over-roast, as pumpkins will collapse). Meanwhile, prepare the risotto: Heat 1 tablespoon of the butter in a heavy 4-quart saucepan over medium heat. Add the vegetables and sauté until translucent. Add the rice and cook, stirring for 1 minute, which toasts the rice and prepares it to accept liquid. Add the bay leaf and stir in a ladle of hot broth. Simmer, stirring, until most of the liquid is absorbed. Stir in another 1/2-3/4 cup broth and repeat the process. Keep the mixture at a steady simmer and continue adding broth in small amounts and stirring until the rice is plump, offers only the slightest resistance to the bite, and there is just enough thickened, creamy sauce to moisten the rice. This process should take 20-30 minutes. Remove the bay leaf and season the rice by stirring in the remaining 4 tablespoons butter, walnuts, and salt and pepper to taste. When the pumpkins are done, pour the juices that have collected during roasting into the risotto for added flavor. Let pumpkins stand 5 minutes before filling with the finished rice. Garnish with Parmigiano-Reggiano cheese and serve at once. Makes 6 servings.

Maple Pumpkin Black Walnut Cookies   Jae Almond, Granny's "Old Fashion" Bakery

1/2 pound (2 sticks) butter, softened
3/4 cup brown sugar
1/4 cup honey
1 egg, beaten
1 cup pumpkin puree (see Note, below)
1 teaspoon vanilla extract
2 1/4 cups flour
2 teaspoons cinnamon
1 1/2 teaspoons baking powder
1 1/4 teaspoons baking soda
3/4 cup chopped black walnuts, hickory nuts, or walnuts

Frosting:
3 cups powdered sugar
3 tablespoons butter, softened
1 teaspoon vanilla extract
about 4 tablespoons maple syrup
1/4 cup finely ground black walnuts, hickory nuts,
   or walnuts

(Note: To make pumpkin puree, cut a small pie pumpkin into pieces, remove the skin, and boil the flesh in water until tender. Drain, cook, and puree in food processor. Canned pumpkin may be used instead.) Heat oven to 350 degrees. Grease 2 cookie sheets. Cream butter in large bowl; mix in sugar. Mix in honey. Mix in egg. Mix in pumpkin puree and vanilla. Combine flour, cinnamon, baking powder, and baking soda. Stir into wet mixture. Stir in nuts. Drop batter by heaping teaspoons (or more if you prefer larger cookies) onto cookie sheets. Bake until golden brown on the edges and firm in the middle, 12-15 minutes. Cool 10 minutes on cookie sheets, then remove cookies from sheets and cool completely on racks. For the frosting, combine powdered sugar, softened butter, vanilla, and enough maple syrup (start with 4 tablespoons) to make a fairly thick frosting. Sprinkle each cookie with ground nuts immediately after frosting it. Let frosting "dry" before storing cookies in an airtight container. This recipe was a prizewinner in the 2002 Food for Thought Festival in Madison, Wisconsin. Makes 30-36 cookies.

Radish

Raphanus sativis

The name radish is derived from the Latin word *radix*, meaning root. Radishes vary in size, shape, color, and pungency, from the classic cherry-size red (also popular in white and purple) to a variety of finger-size icicle radishes. There are large black winter radishes and a group of Asian varieties, the most popular of which is the long, thick Japanese daikon radish. The daikon radish accounts for 15 percent of the total vegetable production in Japan, where it's eaten fresh, cooked, and pickled. U.S. consumers purchase more than 400 million pounds of radishes annually, mostly the familiar small red bunched varieties.

Illustrations of radishes have been found on the inner walls of Egyptian pyramids dating from 2000 B.C. Egyptians grew them largely for radish seed oil, used before they acquired the olive. Radishes were widely eaten in Israel and Greece. They were popular throughout Europe during the Middle Ages, and the leaves were valued as much as the root.

The radish root is 94 percent water and claims modest nutritional value, offering a smattering of minerals like potassium, phosphorous, magnesium, and iron. The greens, however, rank way up there with other dark leafies as an excellent source of vitamins A, C, and the Bs. Radishes are beneficial as blood cleansers and digestive aids as well.

The first radishes of the season are a welcome accompaniment to early spring greens. And just when you're looking for a splash of color or variation in the fall salad season, the radish reappears in the form of winter radishes and the daikon.

Cooking Tips

- Radishes may need a good scrubbing to remove garden soil, but do not need to be peeled. Trim off any damaged areas.

- Radishes are generally interchangeable in recipes. Pungency varies.

- Enjoy radishes raw. Eat them as is, sliced, or grated into salads and slaws, or sliced into sticks for dipping.

- Cook to tone down the "bite" of a pungent radish.

- Steam radishes 8-12 minutes, depending on size, until tender but not mushy. Roll in butter and add a dash of salt and pepper.

- Use in soups and stews as you would a turnip.

- Add radishes whole (if small) or sliced to mixed vegetable stir-fries. Cook longer to soften or add toward end of cooking to retain more crunch.

- Toss radish greens into mixed vegetable soups or stir-fries. (They cook quickly.) If they are young and tender toss into a green salad.

- Slice or grate raw and toss with other veggies in a vinaigrette or yogurt dressing.

- Try a radish sandwich. Spread butter on French or sourdough bread and layer with thin slices of radish and a sprinkle of salt. On any bread try a radish, raw spinach, and cheese sandwich.

Storage Tips

- Store radishes for up to 2 weeks in a plastic bag or damp-wrapped in the refrigerator. Store green tops separately, wrapped in a damp towel in the hydrator drawer. Use as soon as possible.

- For longer-term storage, daikon and winter radish varieties may be packed in moist sand and kept in a cool but not freezing location.

For additional recipes that feature radishes, see the Seasonal Combinations chapter.

Jicama and Daikon au Gratin   Edith Thayer, Vermont Valley Farm member

1 1/2 pounds jicama, peeled and cut into
   1-inch cubes
1 1/2 pounds daikon radishes, peeled and cut into
   1-inch cubes
1 tablespoon oil, or pan spray as needed
1 cup chopped onion
1 tablespoon butter
2 tablespoons flour

1 cup milk (skim, 2 percent, or whole)
1 teaspoon freshly grated ginger
1 teaspoon salt
1/2 teaspoon black pepper
1/3 cup half-and-half (fat-free, if desired)
1 cup cottage cheese (low-fat, if desired), drained
4 tablespoons freshly grated Parmesan cheese

Heat oven to 350 degrees. Grease an 8-by-8-inch baking pan. Cook jicama and daikon in boiling water until tender, about 15 minutes. Heat oil in skillet; add onions and cook, stirring frequently, until tender. Stir in butter and flour and stir over low heat, 3-4 minutes. Slowly add milk, stirring, and cook until sauce is thickened. Stir in ginger, salt, pepper, and half-and-half. Add drained cottage cheese and stir until cheese is somewhat melted. (It will finish melting while it bakes with the vegetables.) Spread jicama and daikon mixture into prepared baking dish. Pour the sauce over the vegetables and sprinkle with the Parmesan. Bake until bubbly and slightly brown on top, 45-60 minutes. If jicama is unavailable, the recipe could be made using all daikon. Makes 6-8 servings.

Radish Bulbs and Greens Sautéed with Green Garlic and Chives   MACSAC

2 bunches radishes
1 1/2 tablespoons butter
1 1/2 tablespoons chopped green garlic

1 1/2 tablespoons chopped fresh chives
salt and pepper

Clean radishes well under running water to remove all traces of dirt. Cut off the upper leaves and coarsely chop them. Cut off the remaining greens and stalks and discard them. Trim and quarter the bulbs. Heat butter in a large skillet over medium-high flame. Add quartered radishes and cook, stirring often, 2 minutes. Stir in greens, green garlic, and chives and cook until wilted, another 1-2 minutes. Season with salt and pepper to taste. This is a great side dish with poached, steamed, or grilled fish. Makes 4-6 servings.

Red, White, and Spring Green Crunch Salad   MACSAC

1 small bunch red radishes, stems, leaves,
   and ends trimmed off
1 medium turnip, peeled, or 4-5 salad turnips,
   scrubbed (about 1/2 pound)
1 small cucumber, halved lengthwise and seeded

4 tablespoons rice wine vinegar
1 tablespoon sugar
4 tablespoons chopped fresh mint
salt and pepper to taste

Finely dice the radishes, turnip, and cucumber. Combine with remaining ingredients and 4-6 tablespoons water in a bowl. Chill 1/2 to 1 hour before serving. Makes 6 servings.

Beet and Daikon Slaw   Bill Maddex, member of Drumlin Community Farm

1 yellow beet, peeled and cut into 1/8-inch
   julienne (matchsticks)
1 red beet, peeled and cut into 1/8-inch julienne
1 6-inch daikon radish, peeled and cut into
   1/8-inch julienne

1 teaspoon toasted sesame oil
2 teaspoons canola oil
1 teaspoon unsalted rice vinegar
1 teaspoon sea salt

Combine all ingredients in a non-reactive bowl, cover, and let stand at least 1/2 hour. Season to taste and serve. Makes 2 servings.

Sautéed Trout with Radishes and Leeks   Leah Caplan, The Washington Hotel

4 tablespoons butter
1/4 cup minced shallots
2 leeks, cleaned and thinly sliced
2 bunches radishes, cleaned and sliced

2 tablespoons olive or vegetable oil
4 lake trout fillets (each about 6 ounces)
flour seasoned with salt and pepper
chopped fresh chives

Heat butter in skillet over medium flame; add shallots and leeks and cook, stirring occasionally, until tender. Raise heat, add radishes, and cook quickly until barely tender; set aside. Heat oil in a large skillet over medium-high flame. Dredge fish fillets in flour, shake off excess flour, and place in hot pan. Cook about 3 minutes per side. Remove to a serving dish or individual plates and top with radish mixture. Sprinkle with chives and serve immediately. Makes 4 servings.

Easy, Elegant Watercress and Radish-Top Soup   MACSAC

2 bunches watercress, thick stems cut off
green leaves from 2 bunches of radishes
2 tablespoons butter
1/3 cup minced shallots or chopped
   green onions

4 cups chicken or vegetable stock
1/2 cup heavy cream (optional)
salt and pepper to taste
3 radishes, very thinly sliced

Wash all the greens thoroughly under cold running water to remove all traces of soil. Reserve 6 nice sprigs of watercress. Heat butter in saucepan over medium-low flame. Stir in shallots, cover, and cook, stirring occasionally, until shallots are tender, about 6 minutes. Raise heat to medium-high, add stock, and bring to simmer. Stir in all the greens (except the reserved watercress sprigs) and return to simmer. Lower heat and simmer gently until greens are wilted and very tender, about 5 minutes. Puree the mixture with an immersion blender, or in a food processor or blender. Stir in heavy cream, if desired, and season to taste with salt and pepper. Heat through and serve in soup plates, garnishing each bowl with a watercress sprig and a few thinly sliced radishes. Makes 6 servings.

Hmong-Style Daikon and Beef   MACSAC

1 tablespoon vegetable oil
1/2 cup chopped onion
1/2 pound ground round steak
1 cup sliced daikon radish
3 tablespoons chopped cilantro, basil, or mint
   (or a combination)

soy sauce
pepper
hot cooked rice
Hmong Hot Dipping Sauce (see Cilantro chapter)

Heat a wok or heavy skillet over highest flame for several minutes. Add vegetable oil and swirl the pan to coat its surface. Add onions and stir-fry 2 minutes. Add ground round and stir-fry until most of the pink disappears, another 2-3 minutes. Add 1/2 cup water. When it comes to a boil, stir in the radishes. Simmer until radishes are tender, 3-5 minutes. Stir in herbs. Season to taste with soy sauce and pepper. Serve with rice and dipping sauce. Makes 2 servings.

Radical Radish Ideas   MACSAC

- Stir-fry sliced radishes of any kind with fresh pea shoots, garlic, and ginger.
- Trim fresh-from-the-garden Easter Egg radishes, leaving about 2 inches of the stem to use as "handles." Use the cleaned leaves as a bed for the radish bulbs. Serve them with a tiny bowl of coarse sea salt mixed with chopped fresh chives. Dip and eat.
- Add chopped radish greens to stir-fries.
- Sauté quartered radishes with orange zest and minced gingerroot.
- Use sliced daikon radishes as "crackers" and top them with herbed cream cheese and smoked fish.
- Add chopped radishes to potato salad for a peppery crunch.
- Add thin-sliced radishes to a ham sandwich.

Confetti of Beauty Heart Radishes and Carrots   Tami Lax, chef, formerly of L'Etoile Restaurant

3 medium Beauty Heart radishes, peeled
4-6 medium carrots, peeled
8 ounces feta cheese (or substitute fresh chevre)
1/4 cup extra-virgin olive oil
2-3 tablespoons rice wine vinegar

2 tablespoons chopped fresh mint
2 tablespoons chopped fresh dill
1 tablespoon chopped fresh parsley
salt and pepper to taste

Shred radishes and carrots using hand-held cheese grater. Toss with remaining ingredients. Chill and serve. Makes 8 servings.

Radish and Feta Salad   Dog Hollow Farm

4 cups thinly sliced radishes
1/2 pound crumbled feta cheese

sliced black olives
chopped scallions or fresh mint
lemon vinaigrette

Combine radishes, feta cheese, olives, and chopped scallions or fresh mint. Dress with a lemony vinaigrette, and marinate for at least 30 minutes. Makes 4 servings.

Radish Cucumber Salad on Watercress with Oranges   MACSAC

1 cucumber, peeled
10-14 red radishes, trimmed and sliced
1/2 cup slivered red onion
1 cup plain yogurt
1/4 cup sour cream

3 tablespoons chopped mint
salt and pepper to taste
1 bunch of watercress, cleaned, thick stems removed
2 oranges, peeled and sectioned

Cut the cucumber in half lengthwise, scoop out the seeds, and slice the cucumber halves. Combine cucumbers, radishes, and onion slivers in a bowl. Mix yogurt, sour cream, and mint. Toss with radish mixture; season with salt and pepper to taste. Make a bed of the watercress on a platter, mound the radish salad on top, and garnish with orange segments. Inspired by Sheila Lukins' recipe for Russian Garden Salad. Makes 8 servings.

Rhubarb

Rheum rhabarbarum

Rhubarb is one of the first spring offerings of the garden. It is a vegetable related to the dock plant, a common weed. We think of rhubarb as a fruit, however, due to its traditional uses in desserts and sauces. Rhubarb is believed to have originated in China 4000 years ago, where it was widely used as medicine. In western Europe rhubarb was cultivated as a decorative garden plant. Russia was the first to widely use rhubarb as a food. It was not until the middle of the 18th century that the English began their love affair with rhubarb in pies, tarts, sauces, etc.

Rhubarb's slow takeoff as a popular food may be due to the fact that only the stalks of the rhubarb plant are edible; the leaves are highly toxic due to their significant oxalic acid content. Even the stalks are extremely acidic and sour, and are usually sweetened during preparation to mitigate and complement the tart flavor.

Nutritionally, rhubarb brings great rejuvenating gifts to the end of the seasonal winter diet. It's high in vitamins A and C and a variety of minerals, particularly calcium. Rhubarb is also believed to be a beneficial blood purifier and digestive aid. If nothing else, rhubarb's refreshing taste is a great spring revitalizer.

Cooking Tips

- Tartness increases with age. Young tender stems may be eaten raw. Dice into spring salads, or hot or cold cereal for a tart flavor.

- Add small rhubarb slices into spring soups. Add toward the end of cooking time to retain texture and taste.

- For a side dish, snack, or dessert, chop rhubarb, sweeten with a little brown sugar or honey, and bake 30 minutes at 375 degrees.

- Make a simple sauce: Chop stems into 1-inch chunks, cook in small amount of water with sweetener of your choice to taste. When fibrous stalks become stringy and mushy, it is done. Use as a jam, pour over cake or ice cream, or chill and eat as a side dish or dessert.

- Make a pie, a crisp, or tarts. Rhubarb is famous in combination with strawberries.

Storage Tips

- Store wrapped in a damp towel or in a plastic bag in the refrigerator for up to a week. Stems will soften and shrivel as they dehydrate.

- For long-term storage, rhubarb may be frozen (either cooked or raw). It should be washed, chopped, and drained. (Frozen rhubarb will be soft when thawed.) Place in airtight containers and freeze. See chapter on home food preservation for more information on freezing vegetables.

Rhubarb Marmalade   Miriam Grunes, REAP Food Group

3 whole oranges (including rind)
1 whole lemon (including rind)

5 cups rhubarb
3 cups sugar

Very thinly slice the oranges and lemons; remove seeds from fruit slices and cut into strips. (Alternatively, you may juice the citrus fruits, strain out the seeds, and thinly slice the rinds.) Cut rhubarb into 2-inch-long pieces. Place all fruit in large, heavy saucepan. Stir in the sugar, bring to boil, and boil rapidly, stirring often, 15 minutes. Reduce heat and simmer gently until marmalade reaches desired consistency. This could be up to an hour depending on how juicy the fruit is. Cool completely and refrigerate. This also freezes beautifully. Makes 2 pints.

Rhubarbade   Susan and Lee Greenler, Stoughton, Wisconsin

chopped rhubarb

sugar

Puree rhubarb in food processor or electric juicer. Strain through cheesecloth-lined strainer, pressing solids. Let stand several minutes, then skim froth from surface. Strain again. For every 2 cups rhubarb liquid add 3/4-1 cup sugar and 6 cups water, stirring until sugar dissolves. Serve iced. For every 2 cups rhubarb liquid, the yield is 2 quarts.

Strawberry Rhubarb Cobbler   MACSAC

1 pound fresh or partially thawed
  chopped rhubarb
3-4 cups fresh or partially thawed strawberries
3/4-1 cup sugar
2-3 tablespoons flour (use the smaller
  amount if fruit is fresh)
1 tablespoon grated orange zest

Topping:
1 1/4 cups flour
2 tablespoons sugar
3/4 teaspoon baking powder
1/4 teaspoon baking soda
1/2 teaspoon salt
5 tablespoons cold butter, cut up
1/2 cup sour cream
3 tablespoons milk

Heat oven to 375 degrees. Place first 5 ingredients in bowl. Toss fruit occasionally while you make the topping: Whisk flour, sugar, baking powder, baking soda, and salt in another bowl. Cut in butter until bits are size of sunflower seeds. Whisk sour cream and milk in small bowl. Stir into flour mixture just until combined. Turn dough onto floured surface; knead gently 4-6 times. Roll into 1/2-inch thickness and cut into rounds with biscuit cutter. Gather scraps and cut again. Spread fruit in an 8-inch square or similarly sized baking dish. Top with biscuits. Bake until browned and bubbly, 40-50 minutes. Serve warm with ice cream. Makes 8-9 servings.

Ruby Rhubarb Ginger Crunch   MACSAC

4 cups rhubarb (fresh or frozen)
1 cup cranberries, pitted tart cherries, blueberries,
  or strawberries (fresh or partially thawed)
1/2 cup sugar
1/2 cup honey
1/4 cup white flour or whole wheat pastry flour
1 teaspoon vanilla extract
1/2-3/4 teaspoon freshly grated ginger

Topping:
1/2 cup white flour or whole wheat pastry flour
1/2 cup brown sugar
1/3-1/2 cup chopped hickory nuts, pecans, or walnuts
4 tablespoons cold butter, cut into pieces

Combine rhubarb and cranberries (or other fruit) with sugar. Let stand 15 minutes, tossing often. Heat oven to 350 degrees; butter a deep-dish pie pan. Add honey, flour, vanilla, and ginger to fruit; toss well. Spread in pan. Bake 20 minutes. Meanwhile, make topping: Combine flour, sugar, and nuts. Cut in cold butter with pastry cutter or your fingers. Refrigerate while rhubarb bakes. When fruit has baked 20 minutes, sprinkle topping over it and continue to bake until bubbly, 30-40 minutes longer. Serve warm with vanilla ice cream or vanilla yogurt. Makes 6-8 servings.

Rosemary

Rosmarinus officinalis

Rosemary, a Mediterranean native, is an evergreen perennial. There is an upright bush type and a trailing variety, both usable for cooking. After centuries of use, rosemary is still a popular herb throughout the world, providing its unique taste to numerous cuisines.

A common ingredient used with chicken and lamb dishes, rosemary is also often added to bread dough for extra pizzazz. The flowers are added to salads for both flavoring and color. Don't be afraid to explore its flavor, by itself or combined with other herbs.

Rosemary, the herb of remembrance, is one of the ingredients in the legendary "Queen of Hungary Water." Besides being a culinary herb, it is used in cosmetics, soaps, perfumes, shampoos, hair conditioners, and aromatherapy.

Rosemary grows well during the warmer months. You can keep it as a houseplant in the winter.

Cooking Tips

- Can be used fresh or dried.

- All parts can be used: sprigs, whole or crushed leaves, and flowers.

- Place a sprig in the cavity of a chicken before cooking or roasting.

- Powdered leaves can be rubbed into meat before cooking.

- Use fresh flowers in salad or eat them right off the plant. They taste sweet.

- Add leaves to a marinade for vegetables and meat, especially lamb.

- Use a sprig to enhance applesauce, hot cider, and butter.

Storage Tips

- Pick just before use.

- When purchasing fresh rosemary, keep leaves on the stem and place in the refrigerator.

- To dry, hang by bundles in paper bags.

- Store dried herb in amber bottles or out of the light.

White Bean and Roasted Garlic Puree   Susan Streich-Boldt, Madison Herb Society

1 cup dried cannelloni or other dried white beans
1 bay leaf
1 sprig fresh thyme
1 thick wedge of onion

6 large cloves garlic, crushed
1 large sprig rosemary
2 tablespoons extra-virgin olive oil
salt and pepper

Rinse beans. Soak in cold water several hours. Drain. Place in a saucepan with enough water to cover the beans by 2 inches. Add bay leaf, thyme, and onion. Bring to boil, skim surface, reduce to simmer, cover, and cook until beans are very tender. Drain beans, reserving 1/2 cup of the cooking liquid. Discard bay leaf and thyme. Heat oven to 325 degrees. Combine garlic, rosemary, and olive oil in a small baking dish. Cover and bake until golden and tender. Cool the garlic slightly, then puree in a food processor with the beans and enough reserved cooking liquid to make a smooth spread. Season to taste with salt and pepper. Serve with bread, roasted vegetables, or meats.

Rosemary Poached Pears   MACSAC

1 cup white wine
1/2 cup honey
4 tablespoons pear brandy (optional)
3 sprigs fresh rosemary (about 4 inches each)
1 bay leaf

2 strips (3 inches each) orange rind
1/2 teaspoon vanilla extract
20-30 black peppercorns
2 1/2 pounds pears
1/2 pound nectarines (optional)

Combine all ingredients (except fruits) with 2 cups water in saucepan; simmer several minutes. Peel, halve, and core fruits; cut halves into 2-3 pieces. Add to poaching liquid, turn off heat, cover, and cool to room temperature. (If fruit is underripe, simmer for several minutes in the liquid before turning off heat.) Chill. The idea of scenting a poaching liquid with fresh herbs comes from Christopher Kimball's *The Cook's Bible* (Little Brown, 1996). Makes 6 servings.

Rosemary Roasted Mixed Nuts   MACSAC

1/2 pound mixed nuts
1 1/2 tablespoons olive oil
1 1/2 teaspoons minced fresh rosemary

1/2 teaspoon minced garlic, pressed to a paste
salt and freshly ground black pepper to taste

Heat oven to 350 degrees. Mix all ingredients in bowl. Spread on parchment-lined baking sheet. Bake 30-40 minutes, tossing well every 10 minutes. Remove from oven and sprinkle with additional salt. Eat them while they're still a bit warm or at room temperature. Store in an airtight container. Makes 1/2 pound.

Fresh Rosemary Biscuits   MACSAC

1 3/4 cups flour
1 scant tablespoon baking powder
1/2 teaspoon salt

4 tablespoons cold butter, cut into small pieces
2 tablespoons minced fresh rosemary
3/4 cup milk

Heat oven to 425 degrees. Whisk flour, baking powder, and salt in a bowl. Cut in butter until size of sunflower seeds. (Alternatively, mix dry ingredients in food processor, cut in butter using machine, then dump mixture into separate bowl.) Sprinkle rosemary over flour mixture. Pour in milk and stir briefly, just until a sticky dough forms. Turn onto floured surface. Knead lightly and briefly, 4 to 6 turns. Roll or pat to a thickness of 1 inch. Cut into rounds with floured biscuit cutter. Gather dough scraps and cut again. Place on ungreased baking sheet. Bake until high and golden, 11-13 minutes. Makes 6 large biscuits.

Rutabaga

Brassica napus var. napobrassica

The rutabaga is an obvious close relative of the turnip, though larger, sweeter, and more tan in color. While its origin is uncertain, it is believed to be a hybrid of the turnip and the cabbage, as is the kohlrabi, though selected for different traits.

The rutabaga appeared suddenly in the middle of the 17th century and first became popular in Sweden. In fact, rutabaga comes from the Swedish word *rotabagge*, meaning "baggy root." Rutabagas are also commonly referred to as Swedes or Swedish turnips. They were among the first vegetables grown by colonists in America as they began farming the untilled land, because the large roots helped break up poor soils. Rutabagas have never enjoyed wide popularity in this country, and have even fallen out of favor in middle Europe, where it was one of few staples available after World War II and was eaten to the point of monotony.

The rutabaga has many virtues worthy of discovery by the seasonal eater, however. Available in late fall and winter (with proper storage), it offers versatility and excellent nutrition. Rutabaga is high in carbohydrates, vitamins A and C, and some minerals, particularly calcium. Rutabagas belong to a handful of cruciferous vegetables believed to be effective in cancer prevention as well.

Cooking Tips

- Scrub rutabagas vigorously with a vegetable brush to remove garden soil. For maximum nutrition do not peel (unless you are preparing a commercially waxed rutabaga).

- Rutabaga can be grated raw into salads. Try a winter slaw combining grated rutabaga, celeriac, carrot, diakon radish, and apple with chopped parsley and a lemon/oil dressing.

- Steam 1-inch chunks for 30-35 minutes, or until thoroughly tender. Mash and serve with butter and sprinkling of black pepper. Mash with other vegetables, such as carrots and potatoes. A kids' favorite.

- Boil 1-inch chunks for 20-25 minutes, or until thoroughly tender. Add to casseroles or stuffing mixtures.

- Bake 1-inch chunks brushed with butter or oil for 40-50 minutes, or nestle alongside roasting meats.

- Add to a root vegetable bake.

- Grate rutabaga into a fritter batter.

- For a fluffy pudding, whisk eggs into mashed rutabaga and bake.

- Make rutabaga chips: Deep-fry 1/8-inch-thick slices in very hot vegetable oil until golden brown. Do not crowd pan while frying. Drain on paper towel, sprinkle with salt and pepper or seasoning of choice, and serve. Good for dipping.

Storage Tips

- Rutabaga will store adequately at room temperature for up to 1 week, or refrigerated in plastic bag or hydrator drawer for up to 1 month.

- For longer-term storage, rutabagas may be packed in moist sand and kept in a cool but not freezing location.

For additional recipes that feature rutabaga, see the Seasonal Combinations chapter.

"You Won't Believe These" Brown-Roasted Rutabaga Wedges   MACSAC

4 medium rutabagas (about 3 pounds)
2 tablespoons olive oil

3 tablespoons high-quality balsamic vinegar
sea salt

Heat oven to 500 degrees. Cut ends off rutabagas and peel them. Use a heavy, sharp knife to cut each rutabaga in half lengthwise, then cut each half into 3-4 long wedges. Place wedges in very large baking pan and toss with olive oil to coat them well. Spread them out into a single layer and try to keep them from touching one another. Roast in hot oven 20 minutes. Use tongs to turn each wedge over. Roast another 15-20 minutes. Remove from oven and toss with balsamic vinegar and salt to taste. Serve hot. This "hot-oven" approach to roasting is credited to cookbook author Barbara Kafka. Makes 6-8 servings.

Well-Thymed Rutabaga   Linda Halley, Harmony Valley Farm

1 1/2-2 pounds rutabaga
chicken or vegetable stock
1 cup sour cream

1-2 tablespoons minced fresh thyme or lemon thyme
salt and pepper to taste

Peel rutabaga, dice the flesh, and place in a saucepan. Add just enough stock to cover rutabaga, bring to simmer, and cook until tender. You can serve this three ways: 1) Soup: Stir in the remaining ingredients; 2) Side dish: Drain off stock and stir in remaining ingredients; or 3) Puree: Drain off most of the stock and puree rutabaga with remaining ingredients, using immersion blender, food processor, or blender. Makes 4-6 servings.

Mashed Rutabaga with Orange   Linda Simon, Dine-In Personal Chef Service

2 pounds rutabaga, peeled and diced
2 tablespoons frozen orange juice
   concentrate, thawed

1 tablespoon butter
salt and pepper
1 orange (optional for garnish)

Put diced rutabaga in a medium saucepan and add water to about halfway up the rutabagas. Bring to boil and cook, stirring occasionally, until very tender. Drain off the water. For a chunky texture, mash with a potato masher. For a smoother texture, run rutabagas through a food mill or process in a food processor until smooth. Stir in orange juice concentrate and butter and season to taste with salt and pepper. Garnish with fresh orange zest or thin slices of orange. This can be made ahead and refrigerated or frozen, then warmed in the oven. It goes well with sage-rubbed pork and mushrooms or ham. Makes 6 servings.

Rutabaga Carrot Coleslaw with Buttermilk Garlic Dressing   MACSAC

1 large or 2 medium rutabagas (about 1 pound)
1 large carrot (about 1/4 pound)
6-8 tablespoons Buttermilk Garlic dressing
   (recipe in Garlic chapter)

4 tablespoons chopped fresh parsley
salt and pepper to taste

Peel rutabagas and carrot; cut into large chunks and shred in food processor or on very large grate holes of hand-held grater. Toss with remaining ingredients and chill 1 hour. Makes 4 servings.

Rutabaga Custard Pie   Susan Hollingsworth, member of Harmony Valley Farm

3/4 pound rutabaga
2 large pears or apples
1 tablespoon maple syrup
1/2 teaspoon coriander
1/4 teaspoon ginger
1/8 teaspoon nutmeg

pinch salt
2 eggs
2 tablespoons brown sugar
1 cup half-and-half
1 9-inch pie crust

Heat oven to 400 degrees. Peel rutabaga, cut into 1-inch chunks; steam or boil 20 minutes. Peel, core, and quarter pears; add to rutabaga and cook 10 minutes longer. Puree, then add maple syrup, spices, and salt. In separate large bowl, beat eggs with sugar until thick. Stir in the rutabaga mixture and half-and-half. Pour into crust. Bake 15 minutes, reduce heat to 350 degrees, and bake 25-30 minutes longer, until custard is set. Makes 8 servings.

Rutabaga, Cheese, and Spinach-Stuffed Triangles   MACSAC

1/4 pound young spinach
1 1/2 cups cooked, mashed rutabaga,
    at room temperature or chilled
1/4 teaspoon ground nutmeg
1 tablespoon sugar
1 cup grated asiago cheese (2-3 ounces)

salt and pepper to taste
6-8 tablespoons butter
9 sheets packaged phyllo dough, thawed
    according to package instructions and
    brought to room temperature

Place spinach and a few tablespoons water in a pot; bring to simmer and cook until wilted, about 3 minutes. Run spinach under cool water; squeeze it to remove excess liquid, and chop it. Combine chopped spinach, mashed rutabagas, nutmeg, sugar, asiago, and salt and pepper. Melt butter. Set up a work area with filling, melted butter, a pastry brush, a sharp knife, phyllo dough, and a large ungreased baking sheet. To assemble the pastries: Carefully unfold the packaged dough. Pull off a sheet and place on work surface with long edge facing you. Brush pastry surface lightly with a little butter, emphasizing the edges (you don't have to cover every inch of the surface). Place another pastry sheet over the first and brush with butter. Repeat with a third sheet. (To prevent remaining dough from drying out, you can place a towel over it at this point.) Cut brushed layers vertically into 6 strips. Place heaping tablespoon of filling at bottom of each strip. Fold up each strip like a flag; that is, start at the bottom near the filling and fold the dough over the filling to form a triangle, then continue to fold triangle back and forth up the strip. Place folded pastry on baking sheet. Continue this process with remaining filling and pastry sheets. Lightly brush stuffed pastries with remaining butter. (At this point, you may cover and refrigerate the pastries until you're ready to bake them.) To bake: Heat oven to 375 degrees. Bake until golden brown, 20-30 minutes. Serve as an appetizer, or for any meal of the day. Makes 18 pastries, or about 6 servings.

Savory Rutabaga Blue Cheese Custard   MACSAC

1 1/2-2 pounds rutabaga
2 tablespoons butter, softened
3 ounces blue cheese, crumbled

2 eggs
salt and pepper

Heat oven to 350 degrees. Peel rutabaga, chop the flesh, and steam over boiling water until tender, about 10 minutes. Mash the hot rutabaga with butter and blue cheese. Beat in the eggs. Add salt and pepper to taste. Spread in a buttered baking dish and bake until set, about 30 minutes. Serve hot. Makes 6 servings.

Spiced Pickled Rutabaga   MACSAC

2 pounds rutabagas
3/4 cup sugar
1/2 cup rice vinegar
1/4 cup cider vinegar

4 slices fresh gingerroot
1 stick cinnamon
6 whole cloves
1/8 teaspoon hot red pepper flakes (optional)

Peel rutabagas with thin-bladed knife; cut into bite-size chunks. Combine with remaining ingredients and 1/2 cup water in a non-reactive saucepan. Simmer until barely tender, 3-5 minutes. Let cool, then chill overnight. Pickles will keep in refrigerator 2-3 weeks. Makes about 3 cups.

Steak and Rutabaga Pasties   MACSAC

Crust:
3 cups flour
1 teaspoon salt
1 cup (8 ounces) chilled shortening or lard,
   cut into pieces
1 egg
ice water

Filling:
1 1/2 pounds cubed sirloin
4 cups diced rutabaga
1 cup chopped onion
3 tablespoons heavy cream
4-6 tablespoons chopped fresh parsley
1 tablespoon salt
1 teaspoon pepper
3 tablespoons cold butter, cut into small pieces

To make crust: Whisk flour and salt in a large bowl. Cut in shortening or lard with pastry cutter or two knives until the pieces are no larger than peas. Break the egg into a cup measure and add enough ice water to make 1 cup. Mix egg and water; add to flour, tossing lightly with a fork until a dough forms. Cover and chill the dough at least 1 hour. To make filling, combine all the ingredients except the butter. To assemble and bake pasties: Heat oven to 400 degrees. Line 2 large baking sheets with parchment paper (or oil them). Lightly flour a large work surface. Divide the dough into 6 portions. Shape each portion into a ball, then roll it out with a floured rolling pin into an 8-inch round. Divide the filling equally among the rounds, placing filling on bottom half of each round. Scatter the butter pieces over the filling. Fold dough over the filling, using extra flour on your fingers to prevent sticking. Press to seal the edges, then fold small sections of the dough to make a ropelike edge. Place pasties on pans; cut a small slit into the top of each. Bake 15 minutes. Reduce heat to 375 degrees and continue to bake until golden brown and fully cooked, 35-40 minutes. Serve pasties with salsa, catsup, or beef gravy. Makes 6 large pasties.

Chili Roasted Rutabaga   MACSAC

2 tablespoons vegetable oil
1 1/2 teaspoons chili powder
1 teaspoon onion powder
1 teaspoon garlic salt

1/2 teaspoon sugar
1/2 teaspoon paprika
1/4 teaspoon cayenne
1 1/2 pounds rutabaga

Heat oven to 400 degrees. Mix first 7 ingredients in a medium bowl. Peel rutabagas and cut them into chunks that are about 2 inches long and 1/2-1 inch wide. Toss with spice mix. Transfer to large baking sheet, spreading pieces out evenly. Bake until tender and somewhat browned, stirring occasionally, about 25 minutes. Makes 4-6 servings.

Sage

Salvia officinalis

There are more than 900 species of salvia with culinary, medicinal, and ornamental uses. *Salvia officinalis,* or garden sage, is best known for culinary uses. In the U.S., it's often used in Thanksgiving stuffing.

A native to the Mediterranean countries and North Africa, sage has gray-green leaves that are velvety to the touch. In the northern United States it is a hardy perennial that prefers full sun and well-drained soil. It will even survive one or two frosts.

The word *salvia* comes from the Latin "salvare," meaning to rescue or to heal. The English word *sage* means "wise one."

In the Middle Ages, sage was thought to impart wisdom and improve the memory. It was valued for restoring energy, lifting the spirit, and promoting longevity.

To use the antioxidants in sage, Native Americans mixed it with bear grease for a salve that would cure skin sores. The leaves were also used as a sort of disposable toothbrush.

Sage is companion-planted with cabbage, making the cabbage more succulent and tasty and not as attractive to cabbage butterflies. It also grows well with carrots, rosemary, strawberries, tomatoes, and marjoram. It doesn't grow well with onions or cucumbers.

Cooking Tips

- Sage aids in the digestion of fatty meats like beef, pork, veal, fish, lamb, poultry, duck, and goose.

- Steep sage leaves in honey for an excellent baste.

- Fresh young leaves can be eaten in salads, soups, omelets, marinades, sausages, meat pies, yeast breads and rolls, and stuffing.

- Fresh leaves are also delicious dipped in batter and fried.

- Dried sage makes a great tea. If you add honey, it helps ease sore throats and colds.

Storage Tips

- Sage leaves have a strong taste that increases as they are dried.

- Harvest sage in the morning before the heat of the sun evaporates its essential oils.

- To dry: Pinch leaves from the stem and place on cloth or paper in the shade, or hang leaves in a bunch on the stem.

- When leaves are dry, store them in an airtight colored glass or solid container.

Blueberry Sage Muffins   *Madison Herb Society Cookbook*

2 cups blueberries
2 tablespoons minced fresh sage leaves
1/2 cup sugar
2-3 teaspoons grated lemon zest
1 egg, beaten
1/2 cup plain nonfat yogurt or sour cream
1/4 cup milk

2 tablespoons canola oil
1 tablespoon lemon juice
1 1/2 cups flour
2 teaspoons baking powder
1/2 teaspoon each baking soda and salt
Topping: 1 tablespoon sugar and 1/2 teaspoon
   ground cinnamon

Combine blueberries, sage, sugar, and lemon zest; let stand 30 minutes. Heat oven to 375 degrees. Line standard-size muffin cups with paper liners. Stir egg, yogurt, milk, oil, and lemon juice into blueberries. Sift flour, baking powder, baking soda, and salt into large bowl. Stir the 2 mixtures together until barely combined. Fill each muffin to 1/2 inch from the top. For topping, combine sugar and cinnamon; sprinkle on muffins. Bake until muffin springs back when touched on top, 20-25 minutes. Remove from muffin tins and cool on wire rack. Makes 12 muffins.

Chili Cheddar Sage Corn Bread   MACSAC

1 cup oil
2 cups shredded cheddar cheese
6 eggs
1 can creamed corn
1/3 cup minced pickled jalapeños
1/2 cup milk

4 cups yellow cornmeal
2 cups flour
1 cup sugar
1 tablespoon baking powder
2 tablespoons chopped fresh sage
1 teaspoon salt

Heat oven to 350 degrees. Grease a very large, heavy baking pan. Combine first 6 ingredients in large bowl. Combine last 6 ingredients in another bowl. Stir dry ingredients into wet ingredients until just combined (don't overmix). Spread batter in pan. Bake until toothpick inserted near center comes out clean, 30-35 minutes. Makes 24 servings.

Ravioli in Butter Sage Sauce   Amy Simonson

1 large package (20 ounces)
   cheese- or meat-filled ravioli
1/2 cup (1 stick) butter

1/8-1/4 cup fresh chopped sage
1/4 cup toasted pine nuts
1/2 cup grated asiago cheese

Boil ravioli according to package instructions. Meanwhile, melt butter in small saucepan over low heat. Add chopped sage. Drain ravioli, return to pot, and stir in butter sage sauce. Top with toasted pine nuts and asiago. Makes 4 servings.

Baked Chicken Breasts with Sage Shallot Apple Dressing   MACSAC

4 boneless, skinless chicken breasts
   (6 ounces each)
1 tablespoon butter
1/3 cup finely chopped shallots
1 cup finely chopped tart apple

2 tablespoons each chopped fresh sage and parsley
2 heaping cups dried bread cubes or croutons
salt and pepper to taste
1/2-2/3 cup chicken broth

Oil a baking pan. Trim chicken of all fat; flatten meat by pounding it lightly with a flat, heavy utensil. Place in pan. Heat oven to 350 degrees. Cook shallots in butter on stove top until tender, 4-5 minutes. Stir in apples, herbs, bread cubes, salt, pepper, and just enough chicken broth to make a moist stuffing. Mound on chicken. Bake until stuffing has browned and chicken is tender, 20-25 minutes. Makes 4 servings.

Spinach

Spinacia oleracia

Spinach is the most widely used dark leafy green in this country, popular for cooking and raw salads. It's often the first vegetable directly seeded into the garden in early spring, as it prefers and thrives in the cool, moist soil. Spinach is generally available until a heavy freeze or snow cover in late fall. Both the flat-leafed and the savoy (crinkly-leafed) varieties are commonly produced.

Spinach is related to beets and Swiss chard, and originated as a wild vegetable in the Middle East. The first record of its cultivation dates back to Persia, 2000 years ago. Interestingly, spinach was unknown to the ancient Greeks and Romans, though today it serves as a staple in many traditional dishes in Greece. It wasn't solidly established in Europe until the late 16th century.

Spinach is a nutritious green despite its 80 to 90 percent water content. It is high in chlorophyll, vitamin A, and vitamin C, all best retained by no or minimal cooking. Spinach contains valuable minerals, but they are not readily assimilated by our bodies. It contains oxalic acid in an amount that is not dangerous but does tend to bind the naturally occurring calcium and prevent its absorption.

Spinach's tender quality and mild flavor make it a truly versatile green.

Cooking Tips

- Rinse spinach leaves thoroughly in a cool water bath as garden soil and grit tend to accumulate on the underside of the leaves. Pat dry with a towel or spin dry (as you would lettuce leaves).

- Spinach cooks quickly. Be careful not to overcook by watching for bright green color. Remove from heat and cool.

- Steam 2 pounds of fresh spinach for 8-10 minutes, 1 pound for 5 minutes.

- Two to three pounds of fresh spinach reduces to 2 cups cooked. Half a cup of cooked spinach approximates a serving.

- Toss fresh and tender leaves into green salad, or try a simple salad by tossing spinach with olive oil, lemon juice, minced garlic, and a pinch of salt and pepper. Fresh basil leaves and feta cheese are optional but nice additions.

- Stuff your sandwiches, tacos, and burritos with fresh raw spinach.

- Add spinach at the last minute to soups, stir fries, and sautés.

- Toss tender raw leaves or cooked pureed spinach into pasta.

- Sauté onions, garlic, and curry spices, then add spinach leaves. Cook until thoroughly blended and creamy in consistency.

- Add spinach to crepes, quiche, lasagna, and other baked dishes.

- Puree cooked spinach for soup.

- Make a spinach pesto, substituting raw spinach leaves for some of the basil and parsley.

Storage Tips

- Store spinach in a damp towel or plastic bag in the refrigerator for up to 1 week.

- For longer-term storage, spinach may be frozen. Blanch for 1-2 minutes, rinse in cold water, drain well, and pack into airtight containers. See chapter on home food preservation for more information on freezing vegetables.

For additional recipes that feature (or substitute with) spinach, see the Greens (Cooked), Chard, Kale, Seasonal Combinations, and Kids' Recipes chapters.

Nana Maniscalco's Spinach Lentil Soup   Cathleen Maniscalco

3/4 pound lentils
1 tablespoon salt
1 stalk celery, diced
1/2 pound spinach leaves, finely chopped
1/3 pound ditalini pasta

1/2 cup olive oil
4 teaspoons minced garlic
additional salt as needed
pepper
grated Parmesan cheese

Pick through lentils and remove any stones or other foreign objects. Rinse lentils well and soak in 3 quarts of water for 1 hour. Drain. Combine lentils, 3 quarts fresh water, salt, and celery in soup pot; bring to simmer and cook 45 minutes. Add spinach and simmer 10-15 minutes longer. Meanwhile, cook pasta according to package directions; drain and keep warm. When you're ready to serve the soup, warm the olive oil in a small skillet over medium heat, add the garlic, and sauté about 45 seconds. Stir into soup along with salt and pepper to taste. Put a little pasta in each soup bowl and ladle soup over the pasta. This is best served with crusty bread and a little grated Parmesan cheese. Makes 6-8 servings.

Spinach Salad with Orange Honey Vinaigrette   MACSAC

1 tablespoon honey
2 tablespoons frozen orange juice concentrate,
    softened
1 teaspoon minced shallot
1 tablespoon red wine vinegar
1 tablespoon balsamic vinegar

1/2 cup olive oil
salt and pepper
1 bunch spinach, large stems removed
1 small red onion, sliced as thinly as possible
2 oranges, sectioned
1/3 cup roasted almonds

Whisk honey, orange juice concentrate, shallots, and vinegars in a bowl. Gradually whisk in oil. Season to taste with salt and pepper. Thoroughly clean the spinach and dry it in a salad spinner or kitchen towels. Toss spinach with onions, oranges, almonds, and just enough dressing to lightly coat. Makes 4-6 servings.

Spinach and Cheese Phyllo Pie   Bridget Zinn, Vermont Valley Farm member

2 tablespoons butter
4 tablespoons olive oil, divided
1/2 pound firm tofu
1/2 pound feta cheese
1 carton (12 ounces) cottage cheese
1/4 pound mozzarella, grated

2 eggs
1 large onion or 1 bunch of spring onions
3/4-1 pound spinach, large stems removed
1 large handful fresh dill leaves, chopped
salt
frozen phyllo dough, thawed in refrigerator 24 hours

Heat oven to 350 degrees. Melt butter and combine with 3 tablespoons of the olive oil. Puree tofu, feta, cottage cheese, mozzarella, and eggs in food processor. Heat remaining olive oil in large skillet over medium flame; add onions and cook, stirring often, until translucent. Add spinach and wilt it, stirring often. Stir in dill and small pinch of salt. Let cook for a minute, remove from heat, and let cool for a few minutes. Chop the spinach and stir into cheese mixture. To assemble pies: Open phyllo package and carefully unroll the pastry. Layer a sheet of phyllo lengthwise over each of 2 pie pans. Brush lightly with the butter/oil mixture. Layer another sheet of phyllo crosswise over each of the 2 pans. Brush lightly with butter. Repeat with 2 more layers for each pie, laying the final 2 layers at a diagonal across the pie pans. Brush extra butter/oil on the phyllo that is sticking out of the pans. Press the phyllo to fit the shape of the pans and then fold the excess phyllo until it all fits in the pan in the shape of a pie crust. Divide the filling between the pies. Bake until golden on top and set, 50-60 minutes. Let pies stand 10-15 minutes before serving. Makes 2 pies, or 8-12 servings.

Summer Squash

Cucurbita pepo

Summer squash, though in the same family as winter squash, is not to be confused with its tougher-skinned relative, famous for excellent storability. Zucchini, patty pan, yellow crookneck, and straightneck squash are the most popular summer squash varieties. They are delicate and perishable and must be enjoyed in their warm weather glory as they are intolerant of cooler weather.

As any gardener can tell you, summer squash comes on fast and furiously once it begins to bloom. It demands frequent harvesting and a sustained creative effort in the kitchen to keep up with the prolific supply. As summer squash season winds down, seasonal eaters breathe a sigh of relief. We can finally let up on all those tomatoes and summer squash and turn our attention back to leafy greens. Phew! But by the time midsummer rolls around again, we are eager for our first tastes of these seasonal delights.

Summer squash is approximately 94 percent water, very low in calories, and a great source of vitamins A and C, potassium, and calcium. Like other seasonal foods, its benefits are aptly timed. Easily digested, nourishing, and cooling, it also replaces lost fluids. Summer squash is a welcome summer staple.

Cooking Tips

- Rinse or wipe down summer squash if needed; no need to peel.

- Try raw summer squash cut into sticks or rounds with a dip.

- Grate or thinly slice into green salads, or shred to make a squash slaw.

- Steam squash whole or halved to best retain texture. Cook squash cut into 1- to 2-inch pieces for 10-15 minutes, chunks for 5-10 minutes, or until tender when a fork is inserted. Be careful not to overcook. Top with butter alone or with a squeeze of lemon, sprinkle of herbs, grated Parmesan cheese, or a pinch of pepper.

- Cut into chunks or thick slices and add to summer soups and stews. Add toward the end of cooking to retain texture.

- Grill small summer squash halves about 3-4 minutes on hottest part of grill and then 8-10 minutes on the side. Baste with oil or marinade. They are great for shish kabobs, too.

- Blanched baby patty pan, sliced across the circumference, makes a decorative sauté or stir-fry addition.

- Make a simple casserole: Layer blanched squash slices alternately with chopped onion cooked with bread crumbs. Repeat 2 or 3 times and top with butter. Heat at 350 degrees in oven until hot and bubbly.

- Make a special appetizer or side dish: Stuff patty pan squash with buttered fresh bread crumbs sautéed with garlic and fresh herbs. Heat through and serve.

- Mash cooked summer squash, drain well, and blend with butter and salt and pepper to taste. Add finely grated cheese, if desired.

Storage Tips

- Summer squash dehydrates quickly. Store in plastic bag or hydrator drawer in refrigerator for up to 1 week.

- Damaged or bruised squash will deteriorate very quickly.

- Cooked, pureed summer squash may be frozen for an addition to or as a base for winter soups. Freeze in an airtight container.

For additional recipes that feature summer squash, see the Zucchini, Seasonal Combinations, and Kids' Recipes chapters.

Baked Summer Squash   Karen Shepard, Blackberry Community Farm

1-1 1/2 pounds summer squash
  (4-5 medium zucchini, yellow squash, etc.)
salt and pepper
1 cup whole wheat flour
1-2 teaspoons dried thyme

1/2 teaspoon curry powder
1/8 teaspoon dried oregano
1/2 teaspoon salt
1/2 cup safflower oil
scant 1 cup tomato juice

Heat oven to 400 degrees. Oil a large baking dish. Slice squash lengthwise or diagonally 1/8-inch thick. Season with salt and pepper to taste. Place in baking dish to make overlapping layers. Combine remaining ingredients and spread on top of summer squash. Bake until lightly browned, 20-25 minutes. Serve hot. This recipe works great for thin-sliced eggplant, green tomatoes, and onions, too. Makes 4 servings.

Sage-Roasted Squash   MACSAC

2 medium zucchini
2 medium yellow crookneck squash
2 tablespoons olive oil

2 tablespoons chopped fresh sage
1 tablespoon minced garlic
salt and pepper

Heat oven to 350 degrees. Cut squash and zucchini into 1-inch dice, toss with other ingredients, and roast until tender, 15-20 minutes. Season with salt and pepper to taste. Makes 4 servings.

Red Devil Squash Creole   Vermont Valley Community Farm

6 medium crookneck summer squash
3 tablespoons butter
2 medium onions, sliced into rounds
1 red bell pepper, cut in strips
1 large green bell pepper, cut in strips

3 tablespoons brown sugar (optional)
3 tablespoons flour
1 quart tomatoes, quartered
salt and pepper
1/4 pound sharp cheese, grated

Steam or blanch squash until barely tender; drain. Melt butter in large skillet, add onions and pepper strips, and sauté until wilted. Sprinkle brown sugar over mixture; add flour, stirring gently. Stir in tomatoes; simmer a few minutes. Heat oven to 350 degrees. Butter a baking dish. Layer half the squash in baking dish; top with half the tomato mixture. Repeat layers. Season with salt and pepper; top with cheese. Bake 30 minutes, until cheese is browned. Makes 6-8 servings.

Mark's Sweet and Spicy Squash   Drumlin Community Farm

2 tablespoons olive oil
3-4 cups summer squash, cut into
  3/4-inch pieces
1/2 cup diced sweet onion

1 leek, chopped
2 Hungarian Hot wax peppers, diced
3 tablespoons honey
salt and pepper

Heat oil in skillet; add squash, onions, leeks, and peppers, and sauté until tender. Drizzle honey over vegetables. Stir in salt and pepper to taste. Turn off heat, cover, and let stand 3-4 minutes. Makes 4 servings.

Sweet Potato

Ipomoea batates

The sweet potato is one of only a few cultivated vegetable crops that originated in the Americas. The wild sweet potato has been traced back to Peru as early as 8000 B.C. Early Native American tribes relied on both wild and, later, cultivated varieties of sweet potatoes. Christopher Columbus introduced this versatile and nutritious storage crop to Europe.

Sweet potatoes are often erroneously referred to as "yams," a family of starchy tuberous roots originating in West Africa. The sweet potato is neither a potato nor a yam but a rooted tuber and member of the morning glory family.

The sweet potato is a warm-season crop, and in northern climes must not be planted until all chance of frost is passed. It's produced or, more accurately, regenerated from plants or sprouts called "slips" that come from the previous season's crop, or from vine cuttings.

In this country we generally see only a few of the sweet potato varieties cultivated worldwide, and these tend to be the familiar very sweet, thin-skinned yellow and orange fleshed types like the Garnet and Jewel. Most sweet potatoes offer a moist, succulent, and smooth texture, and they are loaded with a host of important nutrients our children need.

Cooking Tips

- To bake: Scrub the skin and cut away any damaged areas. Place them whole or halved in a pan (or with a pan underneath to catch caramelizing drips) and bake at 350 degrees for 40 to 50 minutes or until the centers are soft when a knife is inserted. Larger potatoes will take longer to finish. Hint: To bring out maximum sweetness, place sweet potatoes into a cold oven and then turn on heat, thus maximizing the time for the starches to be transformed to sugar before the high temperature denatures the enzymes responsible for this process. Serve plain or with butter mashed into the soft inside, like any baked potato. Skins can be eaten if clean.

- To steam: Place scrubbed and quartered sweet potato chunks in a steamer over boiling water and cook until tender, about 20 minutes. Let them cool enough to remove peels. To serve round discs, cook sweet potatoes whole, then peel and slice into rounds. Serve plain or drizzled with a toppings: sweet (butter and a tad of maple syrup), tangy (lime) or spicy (a red pepper or ginger sauce).

- Warm or cold sweet baked potatoes make a great snack for young and old alike. Kids like nature's "push-up"—a sweet potato cut in half, grasped in the hand and gently squeezed. As that yummy part of the sweet potato emerges upward, one simply gnaws away at it. This can also be done with a spoon—and instead of pushing the potato insides up, one digs down with a spoon. Even little ones can master both of these techniques and will have fun trying.

- Try adding well-cooked sweet potato to your usual mashed potatoes; blend thoroughly.

Storage Tips

- Store sweet potatoes in a cool, dry, well-ventilated place for up to several weeks.

- Do not store in plastic or refrigerate. Temperatures below 50 degrees will result in off-flavors, and excess moisture will encourage sweet potatoes to rot or sprout prematurely.

- Do not scrub clean or wash until just before preparation. Excess dirt may be removed without water prior to storing.

Val's Secret Southern Sweet Potato Fries   Velery Baerwolf, Val's Southern Cuisine

sweet potatoes, peeled
vegetable oil
cinnamon

nutmeg
sugar

"Peel them and slice 'em up into fry-like pieces. I fry them in vegetable oil until golden brown, but not too brown. They're ready when they float to the surface. Then mix cinnamon and nutmeg and a little white sugar in a bag. Shake it all up and sprinkle it over the hot fries. There you go. Now you know. Now I gave away a secret."

Sweet Potato Walnut Bread   MACSAC

2 cups flour
2 cups sugar
2 teaspoons cinnamon
1 teaspoon baking soda
1/4 teaspoon baking powder
1/4 teaspoon salt

3/4 cups vegetable oil
3 large eggs
1 teaspoon vanilla extract
3 cups grated sweet potato
1 cup chopped walnuts

Heat oven to 350 degrees. Grease a 9-by-5-inch loaf pan. Sift flour, sugar, cinnamon, baking soda, baking powder, and salt into a bowl. Combine oil, eggs, and vanilla in another bowl; mix well. Stir in sweet potatoes. Stir wet ingredients into flour mixture. Stir in walnuts until barely combined. Spread in pan. Bake until toothpick inserted near center comes out dry, about 1 hour and 20 minutes. Cool on a rack 15 minutes. Run a knife along edges of pan to release the bread and invert it onto rack to finish cooling. Makes 8 servings.

Sweet Potato Buttermilk Biscuit Stacks with Ham or Roasted Red Peppers   MACSAC

2 cups flour
2 teaspoons baking soda
1 teaspoon baking powder
1 teaspoon salt
1 tablespoon minced fresh rosemary
6 tablespoons frozen unsalted butter

1 cup cold, mashed baked sweet potato
about 3/4 cup buttermilk, divided
softened butter (optional)
thin-sliced ham and/or 1 roasted sweet
   pepper, peeled and sliced

Heat oven to 400 degrees. Whisk flour, baking soda, baking powder, salt, and rosemary in a bowl. Cut frozen butter into small pieces with sharp knife. Cut butter into flour mixture with a pastry cutter until the butter pieces are no larger than small peas. Using a light touch, work in the mashed sweet potato with your fingers. Stir in 1/2 cup buttermilk. Add just enough additional buttermilk to make a slightly sticky dough. Dump mixture onto floured surface and knead lightly for a minute. Shape mixture into a round about 3/4 inch thick. Use a 2-inch biscuit cutter to cut rounds (do not twist the cutter, just cut straight down the dough). Place biscuits on ungreased baking sheet. Gather up any scraps and cut out more biscuits. Bake until risen and light brown, about 15 minutes. Let cool just a few minutes, then split them open horizontally and spread with softened butter (if desired). Insert a small folded slice of ham and/or roasted red pepper strip between the halves. Serve immediately. This recipe was developed from one in *One Potato, Two Potato,* by Roy Finamore with Molly Stevens (Houghton Mifflin, 2001). Makes 16-20 small stacks.

Cajun-Roasted Sweet Potatoes   MACSAC

1-1 1/4 pounds sweet potatoes, peeled
   and cut into 1-inch chunks

2 tablespoons canola oil
2 tablespoons bottled Cajun seasoning

Heat oven to 400 degrees. Toss sweet potatoes with oil and seasoning; spread in a single layer on a baking sheet. Roast until cooked through and browned in spots, about 25 minutes. Makes 2-4 servings.

Sweet Potato Dill Pancakes   MACSAC

2 eggs
1 tablespoon minced fresh dill
3/4 pound sweet potatoes (1 large or 2 medium)
1/2 pound Yukon Gold potatoes (3-4 medium)
1/4 cup finely chopped shallots

salt and pepper to taste
3-4 tablespoons flour
peanut oil
sour cream, cottage cheese, or maple syrup

Beat eggs and dill in mixing bowl. Peel sweet potatoes and grate on large holes of hand grater or food processor. Dump sweet potatoes onto clean kitchen towels, roll up, and squeeze out excess liquid. Place in bowl. Scrub Yukon Gold potatoes; grate and squeeze them in towels and add to bowl. Add shallots, salt and pepper, and 3 tablespoons flour. Mix well and, if necessary, add enough additional flour so that mixture holds together lightly when you squeeze a handful of it. Heat a cast-iron griddle or large heavy skillet for several minutes over medium flame. Add a small amount of oil—enough to generously oil the griddle or skillet—and tilt the pan to cover cooking surface. Cook pancakes in batches: Scoop batter—about 1/3 cup per pancake—onto hot surface and flatten batter into rough circles. Do not crowd the pan. Fry pancakes until golden brown on one side, carefully flip them, and cook on other side until golden brown and fully tender. Add additional oil to pan between batches as necessary. Transfer cooked pancakes to a wire rack suspended over a baking sheet and keep warm in oven while you cook remaining batter. Serve pancakes hot with sour cream, cottage cheese, or maple syrup. Makes 4 servings.

Roasted Sweet Potato Puree Soup   Monique Jamet Hooker

Follow recipe for Righteous Roasted Jerusalem Artichoke Puree Soup (see Jerusalem artichoke chapter), substituting sweet potatoes for the Jerusalem artichokes.

Apple-Roasted Sweet Potatoes and Winter Squash   MACSAC

1 1/2-2 pounds winter squash
  (butternut, buttercup, etc.)
2 medium sweet potatoes
2 tablespoons olive oil

2 teaspoons chopped fresh rosemary or
  1 teaspoon dried
about 1 1/2 cups apple cider
salt and pepper

Heat oven to 350 degrees. Peel squash, cut them open, and remove seeds. Peel sweet potatoes. Cut squash and sweet potatoes into even-size chunks. Place in a baking dish just large enough to hold all the vegetables in 1 layer. Toss with olive oil and rosemary to lightly coat. Pour in enough apple cider to reach about halfway up the vegetables. Season with salt and pepper. Bake until vegetables are tender and juice is reduced to a glaze, 40-50 minutes. Makes 4-6 servings.

Sweet Potato Rolls   Gertrude Fox

1/4 cup warm water (90-100 degrees)
1 tablespoon sugar
1 package (1/4 ounce) active dry yeast
1 cup cooked and mashed sweet potato
  (cooled to 90 degrees)
1/2 cup butter, melted

2 teaspoons salt
1/4 cup sugar or honey
3/4 cup scalded milk (cooled to 90 degrees)
1 egg, lightly beaten
5-6 cups flour
additional melted butter

Stir 1/4 cup warm water with 1 tablespoon sugar and the yeast; let stand about 15 minutes for it to activate. Meanwhile, mix mashed sweet potatoes, melted butter, salt, sugar, milk, and egg in a large bowl. Stir yeast mixture into sweet potato mixture. Stir in just enough flour to form a stiff dough. Turn mixture onto floured surface and knead until dough is elastic, about 10 minutes. Grease the large mixing bowl, place dough in it, cover with a towel, and let rise in a warm place until it has doubled in size, about 1 hour. Punch down and knead dough again briefly to knock out air bubbles. Cut dough into 2-inch wads and form each wad into a ball, pinching dough to seal it at the bottom of the ball. Brush each dough ball with a little melted butter and place dough on cookie sheets, sealed side down. Allow rolls to double again in size, about 1 hour. Heat oven to 375 degrees; bake rolls 10-12 minutes. Makes about 2 dozen rolls.

Twice-Baked Sweet Potatoes with Orange Zest and Ginger   MACSAC

4 sweet potatoes (6-8 ounces each)
4 teaspoons freshly grated ginger
2 teaspoons minced garlic

grated zest and juice of 1 large orange
salt and pepper to taste

Heat oven to 350 degrees. Poke sweet potatoes with a fork in 2 or 3 places. Bake until tender, about 1 hour. Let cool 10 minutes or so, then slice the top quarter off of each potato. Carefully scoop out most of the flesh from the larger sections, leaving a little of the flesh behind to make a sturdy "boat." Scoop flesh from top sections, too. Puree the flesh with remaining ingredients. Fill the boats with pureed potatoes. They may be refrigerated at this point for later use. To serve, bake at 400 degrees until heated through. Makes 4 servings.

Chipotle Sweet Potato Gratin   MACSAC

3 pounds sweet potatoes, sliced into
   very thin rounds
2 tablespoons butter
1 cup chopped onion
2 tablespoons flour
1 cup milk

1/3 cup half-and-half
1/2 teaspoon salt
1/2 teaspoon ground black pepper
2 teaspoons pureed chipotle in adobo sauce (canned)
1 1/3 cup grated queso blanco, divided

Boil sweet potatoes in a large pot of water until barely tender, about 5 minutes. Melt butter in a saucepan over medium flame, add onions, and cook, stirring often, until translucent, about 8 minutes. Stir in flour, then slowly whisk in milk and half-and-half; cook until thickened. Add salt, pepper, and chipotle. Remove from heat and stir in 1 cup grated cheese. Heat oven to 350 degrees. Grease an 8-by-8-inch baking pan. Layer 1/4 of the sweet potatoes in the dish, sprinkle lightly with some salt, and pour 1/4 of the sauce over this first layer. Continue layering this way until all potatoes and sauce are used. Top with remaining grated cheese and bake until browned and bubbly, 35-45 minutes. Makes 6-8 servings.

Will's Sweet Potato Pie   Will Allen, Growing Power

3 medium sweet potatoes
1 cup heavy cream
3 large eggs
1 teaspoon nutmeg

1 teaspoon vanilla extract
2 cups sugar
9-inch pie shell (unbaked)

Heat oven to 350 degrees. Boil the sweet potatoes (skin on) until a fork or butter knife causes them to easily break apart when inserted. Cool the sweet potatoes slightly, then place them in a bowl and run cold water over them to assist you with removing the skins (since the potatoes will still be pretty hot). Beat potatoes with a mixer on medium speed, then add the remaining ingredients (except pie shell). Adjust the nutmeg and sugar to taste. Place in a pie shell and bake until top is golden and crust looks done, about 30 minutes. Cool completely before serving. Makes 6-10 servings.

Thymus vulgaris

Thyme, a Mediterranean native, is one of the world's oldest horticultural crops, dating back to 3000 B.C. Thyme is derived from *thymon,* the Greek word for courage. History notes that warriors took thyme-infused baths before going off to battle, and ladies embroidered thyme sprigs on their soldiers' tunics.

A small perennial of the mint family, thyme will often survive the winter in northern climates, especially when protected with mulch. Its sweet-smelling gray-green leaves have a bright, sharp taste.

There are many varieties of this lovely, tiny-leaved herb. The most popular is garden thyme, which gives off a minty, light lemony scent. Other varieties include English, French, caraway-scented, and lemon thyme.

Cooking Tips

- Thyme blends well with and enhances other herbs. For example, thyme is one of the primary components in both bouquet garni and herbes de Provence.

- Thyme is widely used in cooking to enhance the flavor of vegetables, meat, poultry, and fish dishes.

- Strip thyme leaves from stem and sauté with mushrooms. Use 1-2 tablespoons per pound of mushrooms or to taste; the resulting mixture can be used in omelets, added to quiches, or used in stir-fries.

- Chop thyme and add to flour, 1 tablespoon per cup of flour; use for dredging chicken for frying.

- Thyme works as a digestive aid and helps break down fatty foods.

- Try thyme as a tea.

Storage Tips

- Fresh thyme may be refrigerated in a plastic bag. Don't wash sprigs until you're ready to use them.

- To dry thyme, bunch together sprigs, secure with a rubber band, and hang in a dark, cool spot. Thyme dries easily and well, and successfully holds its flavor and aroma when dried.

- Thyme can also be frozen in airtight bags or other containers.

- You can also preserve thyme in vinegar or oil.

Carrot Thyme Soup   Pat Cook, Neenah Creek Inn and Pottery and Madison Herb Society

2 tablespoons melted butter
1 medium onion, thinly sliced
8 large carrots, thinly sliced
1 small bunch fresh thyme, tied with a string

2 quarts chicken or vegetable stock
salt and pepper
chopped fresh parsley
softened butter

Melt butter in soup pot over medium flame. Add onions and sauté gently until wilted. Add carrots, tied thyme bunch, and stock. Simmer until carrots are soft, about 30 minutes. Remove thyme. Add stock. Puree the soup with an immersion blender or in a food processor or blender. Season with salt and pepper to taste. Garnish each bowl with parsley and a teaspoon of softened butter. Makes 8 servings.

Honey Thyme Vegetables   Jan Jacobson, Madison Herb Society

4-5 cups fresh vegetables (broccoli, cauliflower,
   green beans, Brussels sprouts, etc.),
   cut into 2-inch pieces
2 tablespoons melted butter

2 tablespoons honey
1-2 tablespoons minced fresh thyme
   or 1/2-1 teaspoon dried
salt and pepper

Cook vegetables in a small amount of water until crisp-tender. Drain very well. Combine melted butter, honey, and thyme; toss mixture with the vegetables. Season with salt and pepper to taste. Serve immediately. Makes 3-4 servings.

Potato Thyme Rolls   Madison Herb Society

1/4 cup lukewarm water
1 tablespoon active dry yeast
2 tablespoons honey
1/2 cup mashed potatoes
1/2 cup buttermilk
3 tablespoons butter

3 tablespoons minced fresh thyme or
   1 tablespoon dried thyme
1 teaspoon salt
1 egg
3-4 cups whole wheat flour (or use a combination
   of whole wheat and white), divided
for glaze: 1 egg beaten with 1 teaspoon milk

Combine lukewarm water, yeast, and honey in a cup. Set aside for 10 minutes. Combine potatoes, buttermilk, butter, thyme, and salt in a saucepan or bowl; heat or microwave to lukewarm temperature. Combine the potato mixture, yeast mixture, and egg in a large bowl. Stir in 1 cup of the flour and beat well. Stir in just enough flour, 1/2 cup at a time, to form a soft, kneadable dough (add as little flour as possible). Place dough on lightly floured surface and knead by hand until smooth and elastic, 5-7 minutes. Transfer dough to an oiled bowl and turn dough to coat it with oil. Cover bowl with towel and let rise in a warm place until doubled in bulk, about 1 hour. Punch down the dough, turn it onto a floured surface, and divide it into thirds. Roll each portion into a 10-inch rope. Cut each rope into 18 pieces. Shape each piece into a ball. Butter muffin tins (for a total of 18 rolls). Place 3 balls in each muffin cup. Let rise in a warm place until doubled in bulk, 30-45 minutes. Heat oven to 400 degrees. Brush each roll with glaze. Bake until lightly browned, 12-15 minutes. Serve warm. Makes 18 rolls.

Farmer Biscuits with Fresh Thyme   Ben Hunter, Catacombs Coffeehouse

1 1/2 cups organic whole wheat pastry flour
1/2 cup all-purpose white flour
1 tablespoon baking powder
1 tablespoon chopped fresh thyme leaves

1 teaspoon salt
8 tablespoons frozen butter
1/2-3/4 cup buttermilk, milk or cream

Heat oven to 400 degrees. Whisk flours, baking powder, thyme, and salt in bowl. Grate in the butter, occasionally sprinkling some of the flour mixture over butter bits. Stir in milk just until a little of the dry mixture remains on bottom of bowl. Turn mixture onto floured surface; knead 3-4 minutes. Shape dough into a square, cut into 6-8 portions, and place on baking sheet. Bake 16-20 minutes. Makes 6-8 biscuits.

Tomatillo

Physalis ixocarpa

The tomatillo, or husk tomato, is a little-known or -utilized vegetable in this country. It is, however, important in authentic Mexican cooking, and is best known for its central role in a delicious *salsa verde,* or green sauce. The perfect blend of tomatillos, garlic, onion, hot chile pepper, lime juice, and fresh cilantro will send most anyone running to find another bag of tortilla chips...or cold drink!

Tomatillos belong to the solanaceae family, along with close garden relatives the tomato, pepper, and eggplant. Like these vegetables, tomatillos thrive in hot, humid weather. If the heat of the summer is adequate, the tomatillo plant will expand rapidly, blossom, and produce prolific quantities of fruit. During much of its growth, the tomatillo looks like a small, firm green tomato covered by a loose-fitting papery husk. They are generally harvested as they fill out the husk completely.

As one might guess, tomatillos are native to Central and South America, where they have been cultivated for centuries, even before the tomato. *Salsa verde* came first!?

Cooking Tips

- Tomatillo's most popular dish is *salsa verde.* Use a recipe or experiment with proportions of tomatillo, garlic, onion, hot chile pepper, lime juice, fresh cilantro, and salt.

- Flat-leaf Italian parsley is a good substitute for cilantro in a *salsa verde* variation.

- Tomatillos may be lightly stir-fried with other delicate summer veggies.

- Some people enjoy eating a raw, green tomatillo whole. It is known this way as a "tomato-apple."

- Tomatillos can be chopped into salads and made into preserves or even pies.

- Experiment!

Storage Tips

- Store at room temperature, with husks on, for up to 2 weeks.

- For longer-term storage, refrigerate in husks, but not a plastic bag.

Salsa Verde   Jill Watson, Taqueria Gila Monster Restaurant

1 pound tomatillos, husked
1 pound poblano chiles
1 yellow onion
8 serrano chiles, stemmed
6 garlic cloves

1/3 cup chopped cilantro
1 1/2 tablespoons freshly squeezed lime juice
1 teaspoon sherry vinegar
1 teaspoon molasses

Heat a gas grill or prepare coals for a charcoal grill. Grill tomatillos until soft and skins are slightly blackened. Grill poblanos until skins are evenly charred. Place in plastic bag and seal. Set aside. Peel onion and slice into thick rounds. Grill until soft and slightly blackened. Peel grilled chiles. Place all ingredients in food processor; pulse until salsa is mostly smooth, but still a bit chunky. Serve with tortilla chips for dipping, or as part of a Mexican meal. Makes 4 cups.

Strawberry Tomatillo Crisp   Dana McFall, Deb and Lola's Restaurant

4 cups coarsely chopped, husked tomatillos
approximately 1 cup sugar
1/2 teaspoon salt
3 teaspoons cornstarch
15-20 nice ripe strawberries, cleaned and sliced
4 tablespoons unsalted butter

1/2 cup flour
3/4 cup brown sugar
1/2 cup chopped toasted pecans
1 teaspoon cinnamon
1/2 teaspoon grated nutmeg

Place tomatillos in saucepan and cook over low heat while stirring in sugar and salt, until it has the flavor of a nice tart apple. Cook 10-15 minutes. Combine cornstarch with 3 tablespoons water and stir into tomatillos until mixture thickens; remove from heat and cool. Heat oven to 375 degrees. Spread filling in individual baking dishes (or 1 larger one). Top with strawberries. To make topping, mix remaining ingredients until crumbly, using your fingertips. Sprinkle topping over fruit; bake 5-10 minutes. Serve with ice cream. Makes 6-8 servings.

Tropical Tomatillo Banana Salsa   MACSAC

1/2 pound tomatillos
2-3 serrano chiles, seeded and minced
3-4 tablespoons minced green onion
1-2 teaspoons minced garlic

3 tablespoons chopped cilantro
2 tablespoons lime juice, or more to taste
1 medium banana
salt and pepper

Husk the tomatillos, wash them, and cut out the cores. Finely chop the flesh and place it in a bowl. Stir in the chiles, green onion, garlic, cilantro, and lime juice. Mash or finely chop the banana, then stir it into the salsa. Season with salt and pepper to taste. Serve with plaintain chips or tortilla chips, or use as a sauce to top grilled fish. Makes about 2 cups.

Pork Chops with Tomatillo Chile Sauce   MACSAC

4 pork chops (about 2 pounds total)
salt and pepper
1 tablespoon vegetable oil
1 cup chopped white onion
1 tablespoon minced garlic
3-4 finely chopped jalapeños

12-14 tomatillos (about 1 1/4 pounds total),
    husked and coarsely chopped
1 1/2 teaspoons dried oregano
1 1/2 teaspoons chile powder
1-2 teaspoons sugar

Season pork chops generously with salt and pepper. Let stand while you prepare the other ingredients. Heat oil in large, heavy skillet over medium-high flame. Add chops and brown well on both sides. Reduce heat to medium, transfer chops to a plate, and add onions, garlic, and jalapeños to skillet. Cook, stirring often, until tender, about 7 minutes. Stir in tomatillos, oregano, and chile powder. Bring to simmer and cook, stirring occasionally, until mixture is saucy, about 20 minutes. If it is very tart, stir in sugar to taste. Season with salt and pepper. Return pork chops to the skillet, nestling them in the sauce. Cover and simmer until chops are cooked, about 10 minutes. Corn bread is a great accompaniment. Makes 4 servings.

Tomato

Lycopersicum esculentum

Seasonal eaters and gardeners alike wait impatiently for the first ripe tomato of the season. We love tomatoes in this country, although along with the English we were the last to accept the tomato as edible. We now produce more than 2 billion pounds of tomatoes annually and import another 700-800 million pounds from Mexico. Only potatoes are produced in higher quantities in the U.S.

Thousands of varieties of tomatoes are known, and hundreds actually cultivated. The commercial tomato industry tends to utilize newer hybrids genetically selected for traits like sphere shape (to pack into boxes efficiently), thick skin (to survive mechanical harvesting and shipping), and slow ripening (for picking green and gassing with ethylene when redness is desired). Smaller, local market growers choose varieties that emphasize flavor, disease resistance, and nutritional content. Popular types include the cherry tomato, known for its tangy sweetness; the paste or roma, a meatier tomato famous for its role in sauce; the versatile slicer; and the low-acid yellow and orange varieties.

The word *tomato* derives from the ancient Mayan word "xtomatl." (Pronunciation, anyone?) Native to Peru, the tomato was first cultivated by the Aztecs and Incas in the 8th century. It wasn't until the 16th century that the tomato was introduced in Europe, via Spanish explorers. The Italians were the first Europeans to begin eating the tomato, followed by the Spanish and French. It wasn't globally accepted as a food until about 1850.

Enjoy fresh, vine-ripened tomatoes while they last, as tomatoes are very cold sensitive. If it's been a good hot summer and you've been inundated with tomatoes (and taxed to your creative limit in the kitchen), you may be ready for the first frost to staunch the flow. But don't be surprised, come next season, when you catch yourself eyeing the vines and hankering for the taste of that first ripe tomato!

Cooking Tips

- Tomatoes are versatile. Sauté, bake, broil or grill them…and, best of all, eat them raw!

- To remove skins, dunk whole tomatoes in boiling water for 15-30 seconds, lift out with slotted spoon, and remove skins.

- For a decorative, quick, and delicious side dish, slice tomatoes and arrange on a plate. Drizzle with olive oil (or a vinaigrette), chopped fresh basil or parsley, and a little salt and pepper.

- Add tomato to your list of shish kabob vegetables.

- Try frying or broiling sliced tomatoes topped with thin slices of cheese. Remove from heat when cheese is melted and tomatoes have softened and begin to bubble. It's a kid favorite.

- Top slices with a tangy guacamole or pesto spread for a great snack, hors d'oeuvre, or side dish.

- Add tomato chunks to summer soups or hearty stews, or puree tomato for a soup base or stock.

Storage Tips

- Hold tomatoes at room temperature for up to 1 week, longer if still ripening. Do not refrigerate.

- Damaged tomatoes will deteriorate quickly, as will cut tomatoes.

- Underripe tomatoes will continue to ripen stored out of the sun at 60-75 degrees.

- Tomatoes can be frozen whole. Core tomatoes, place on a cookie sheet, and freeze. When solid, place in zip-lock freezer bag and replace in freezer. Remove only as many tomatoes as you need at a time. Thawed tomatoes are appropriate only for cooking or purees.

- Salsa, sauces, and purees also freeze well.

For additional recipes that feature tomatoes, see the Seasonal Combinations and Kids' Recipes chapters.

Tomato Soup   Clare Shufflebotham, Harmony Valley Farm member

1 tablespoon butter
2 cloves garlic, minced
2 carrots, chopped
2 stalks celery, chopped
2 quarts canned tomatoes
   (or equivalent in fresh tomatoes and water)

pinch of sugar
1/2 cup fresh basil
salt and pepper to taste
grated Parmesan cheese.

Heat butter in skillet; sauté garlic, carrots, and celery. Add tomatoes and simmer 20 minutes. Add sugar, basil, salt, and pepper; simmer 5-10 minutes longer. Top with Parmesan. Makes 8 servings.

Basic Blender Italian Tomato Sauce   Anne Tedeschi, Dog Hollow Farm

lots of tomatoes
small amount of basil and parsley,
   dried or fresh
a large amount of oregano

minced garlic cloves
1 or 2 carrots, finely chopped
salt and pepper
olive oil

In Italy, no one follows a recipe for tomato sauce, so use your imagination for quantities. A couple of guidelines: Do not underestimate the amount of garlic; when in doubt, put in lots. Also, carrots are often the sweetener in Italian tomato sauce. Blend or process the tomatoes to an almost pureed texture. Gradually add herbs, garlic, and carrots. Slowly cook the mixture in a deep skillet (cast-iron is best). When sauce has reduced about halfway to the texture you want, add salt and pepper. Add several tablespoons of olive oil before reheating for serving. Makes any quantity.

Tomato Salsa   Sharon Redinger, Dog Hollow Farm member

1 small onion
1/2 green pepper
small bunch cilantro
3 minced garlic cloves

chile pepper to taste
1 tablespoon honey
salt to taste
1 3/4 pounds peeled, fresh tomatoes

Process all ingredients except tomatoes in a food processor. Add peeled tomatoes. Process again, and it's ready to eat. Will keep in refrigerator 1 week. Does not freeze well. Makes about 2 cups.

Camp-Style Sunny-Side Up Eggs with Sun Gold Tomatoes and Tarragon   MACSAC

1 1/2 tablespoons butter
8 large brown eggs
12-16 Sun Gold tomatoes, quartered

2-3 teaspoons chopped fresh tarragon
2-3 tablespoons finely chopped green onions
sea salt and freshly ground black pepper

Melt butter in large nonstick pan over medium flame. Carefully crack and add eggs 1 at a time to cover bottom of pan. Cover and cook until nearly set, about 5 minutes. Scatter quartered tomatoes, tarragon, and green onions around the setting yolks. Sprinkle with salt and pepper to taste. Serve immediately, straight from the pan. Makes 4-6 servings.

Southern Tomato Pie   Belva Halley, Harmony Valley Farm

1 sheet refrigerated pie crust
6 plum tomatoes, cut 1/4 inch thick
coarse salt (optional)
2 cups shredded mozzarella or Swiss cheese

olive oil
1/3 cup minced fresh basil
1/2 teaspoon freshly ground pepper

Heat oven to 450 degrees. Prepare pie crust sheet, using a 9 1/2-inch tart pan. Do not prick crust. Partially bake 9-11 minutes. (If crust puffs up, gently press back with back of wooden spoon.) Remove and cool crust; reduce oven heat to 375 degrees. Sprinkle tomatoes with salt, if desired, and place in single layer on paper towels; let drain 30 minutes. Pat dry. Sprinkle cheese evenly in cooled pastry shell. Arrange tomatoes over cheese in an overlapping circular pattern, covering surface. Brush tomatoes with olive oil. Sprinkle with basil and pepper. Bake 30-35 minutes. Let stand 10 minutes before slicing. Serve hot or at room temperature. Makes 8 servings.

Easy Cherry Tomato and Cucumber Salad   Jenny Bonde and Rink DaVee, Shooting Star Farm

1 pint cherry tomatoes
1 small cucumber
1/4 cup rice wine vinegar

pinch of sugar
salt to taste
1 tablespoon minced cilantro

Stem the cherry tomatoes; slice in half. Cut cucumber in half crosswise, quarter the halves, and slice. Combine all ingredients in a bowl and let stand at room temperature, stirring occasionally, for 20 minutes or so. Serve at room temperature. Makes 4 servings.

Sun Gold Sauce with Bow Ties   Jenny Bonde, Shooting Star Farm

2 tablespoons extra-virgin olive oil
1 quart whole Sun Gold cherry tomatoes,
  stems removed
1 large clove garlic, minced

1/4 teaspoon sugar
salt to taste
10 ounces bow tie pasta
fresh basil leaves, cut into thin strips

Heat olive oil in large nonstick skillet until quite hot but not smoking. Add tomatoes and let them sizzle for a minute or two, shaking pan occasionally. Add garlic and salt, stir, and cover. Cook over medium-high heat until the Sun Golds can easily be flattened with a wooden spoon, about 5 minutes. Meanwhile, cook pasta in large pot of salted, boiling water; drain and keep warm until sauce is done. Uncover cherry tomatoes and flatten them with wooden spoon to release all the juices. Continue to cook uncovered over medium-high heat, stirring occasionally, until sauce is thickened and juices are reduced by half, about 15 minutes. Add the sugar and additional salt to taste. Place cooked pasta in individual pasta bowls and spoon some sauce over each bowl (a little goes a long way). Sprinkle some basil over each bowl and serve hot. This recipe was a winner in the 2001 Food for Thought Recipe Contest in Madison, Wisconsin. Makes 3-4 servings.

Pasta with Fresh Tomato-Basil-Olive Sauce   Irene Mauro

4 cloves garlic, crushed
10 large basil leaves
1/4 cup toasted pine nuts
1 pound seeded, chopped tomatoes
  (about 4 medium tomatoes)

3 tablespoons extra-virgin olive oil
2 tablespoons pitted green olives
4 tablespoons freshly grated Parmesan cheese
salt and pepper to taste
1/2 pound pasta

Puree all ingredients except pasta. Cook pasta in lots of salted, boiling water; drain and toss with sauce. Makes 4 servings.

Caprese Skewers   MACSAC

15 small fresh mozzarella balls
1 pint cherry or grape tomatoes
3 tablespoons basil-flavored olive oil

salt and pepper
1 bunch of basil
30 short bamboo skewers or toothpicks

Halve the mozzarella balls and the tomatoes. Toss with basil oil; add salt and pepper to taste. Tear the basil into bite-size leaves. Skewer a piece of mozzarella, a piece of basil, and a tomato half onto a skewer or toothpick; repeat with remaining ingredients and skewers. Arrange skewers in a concentric circles on a platter. Makes 6 appetizer servings.

Fresh Tomato and Feta Sauce for Pasta   Twinhawks/Clearview Family Farms

1/2 pound angel hair pasta
fresh, great-tasting tomatoes (like Matt's Wild,
    Green Zebra, Amish Paste, or Hog Heart Paste),
    enough to make 2 cups chopped tomatoes or
    2 cups halved cherry tomatoes

2 1/2 tablespoons lemon juice
1/4 cup olive oil
salt and pepper
feta cheese

Boil pasta in large quantity of salted water until just tender. Meanwhile, chop tomatoes and place in bowl. (If you're using paste, or Roma-type, tomatoes, you may first cut a shallow X in the bottom of each, dip the tomatoes in the boiling pasta water 10-20 seconds, and remove skins.) Place lemon juice in a large bowl; whisk in oil and add salt and pepper to taste. Rinse and drain pasta; toss with oil mixture. Transfer pasta to a large, shallow platter and top with chopped tomatoes. Crumble feta on top, as much or as little as you like. Serve at room temperature. This recipe came from a sister's friend. You can vary the amounts to serve any number of people. Makes 3-4 servings.

Panzanella   Patrick O'Halloran, Lombardino's Restaurant

Croutons:
1 loaf French bread, torn by hand into
    rustic bite-size chunks
1 cup extra-virgin olive oil
salt to taste

Salad:
3 pounds heirloom tomatoes, roughly chopped
1 small red onion, thinly sliced
1 cucumber, peeled, seeded, and roughly chopped
1 cup fresh basil leaves, torn by hand into pieces
salt and freshly ground black pepper
1/4 cup good-quality balsamic vinegar
1 cup extra-virgin olive oil

To make croutons: Heat oven to 350 degrees. Toss bread chunks with olive oil; season with salt. Spread on baking sheet; bake until golden, 10-15 minutes. Let cool. To make salad: Place tomatoes and their juices in large bowl. Toss with remaining vegetables and cooled croutons. In true Italian fashion, season salad with salt and pepper to taste, then add balsamic vinegar and your best olive oil. Serve immediately or let it sit 10-15 minutes to allow bread to absorb oil and tomato juices. This recipe is a twist on a traditional bread salad from central Italy. It is best when made with a colorful array of heirloom tomatoes. Makes 6 large or up to 12 side-salad servings.

Green Tomato and Egg Gratin   Lisa Kivirist and John Ivanko, Inn Serendipity

1 1/2 cups chopped green tomatoes
6 hard-cooked eggs, sliced
5 tablespoons butter, divided

3/4 cup soft bread crumbs (pull soft or
    fresh bread into tiny pieces)
3 tablespoons unbleached flour
1 1/2 cups low-fat milk

Heat oven to 350 degrees. Alternate layers of egg slices and tomatoes in shallow baking dish. Melt 2 tablespoons butter in small saucepan. Add bread crumbs; stir well. Melt remaining butter in medium saucepan over low flame. Stir in flour and cook, stirring often, 3-4 minutes. Whisk in milk and cook, stirring constantly, until thickened. Pour milk mixture over tomato/egg layers. Top with bread crumbs. Bake 35-40 minutes. This can be assembled the night before, refrigerated, and baked the following morning, for a stress-free brunch. Makes 4-6 servings.

turnip

Brassica rapa var. rapifera

Turnips are one of the most ancient and globally used vegetables. They've played an important role as a reliable storage crop in times and places where diets were seasonal by definition. Despite this, the turnip has often been ridiculed, falling in and out of favor in cultures and cuisines. In Europe, turnips were once the vegetable of choice to throw at someone as an insult, and an eligible English maiden would present her suitor with a turnip when rejecting him. Along these lines *un navet*, the term for turnip in French, can also mean "a play that flopped."

Despite the centuries of abuse, the turnip is making a comeback; its virtues of storability, nutrition, and versatility are overcoming its comic reputation. The turnip's simultaneous sharp and sweet flavor is loved by many. Turnips are a good source of vitamin C (particularly raw), potassium, and calcium. Turnip greens top the nutritional charts as an excellent source of vitamins A, C, and B complex, and the minerals potassium, magnesium, and calcium. Turnips are also one of the cruciferous vegetables believed to prevent cancer.

As many of us "return to our roots" and explore the importance of a local seasonal food supply, turnips and other root vegetables, commonly rejected in standard American fare, become important once again.

Cooking Tips

- Scrub turnips with a stiff-bristled vegetable brush. No need to peel—simply trim away damaged areas.

- Try turnips raw. Slice or create turnip sticks and add to a veggie platter with favorite dip.

- Grate raw into salads or slaws.

- Boil 1/2- to 1-inch-thick turnip slices or cubes 8-10 minutes; boil small whole turnips 15-20 minutes.

- Steam 1/2- to 1-inch slices or cubes 12-15 minutes; steam small whole turnips 20-25 minutes.

- Bake turnips alone for 30-45 minutes at 350 degrees, basted with butter or oil, or bake along with other seasonal roots.

- Place turnips alongside roasting meats.

- Dice or cube turnips into hearty soups or stews, and thinly slice into stir-fries.

- Mash or scallop turnips, just as you would potatoes.

Storage Tips

- Store turnips unwashed in a plastic bag in the refrigerator for 1-2 weeks.

- Store turnip greens separately, wrapped in a damp towel or plastic bag in the hydrator drawer of the refrigerator. Use as soon as possible.

- For longer-term storage, turnips may be packed in moist sand and kept in a cool but not freezing location.

For additional recipes that feature turnips, see the Seasonal Combinations chapter and other root vegetable chapters (turnips may be substituted in many cases). For more recipes in which turnip greens may be substituted, see Greens—Cooked, Chard, Kale, and other chapters.

Turnip and Pea Potage   Elisabeth Atwell, Dog Hollow Farm member

1 pound turnips, peeled and diced
1 cup chopped onion
3 cups stock
1 cup instant dried milk

2 tablespoons butter
2 cups frozen green peas, defrosted
salt and pepper to taste

Boil turnips in water until tender. Drain. Combine with onion and stock in a soup pot. Puree dried milk, butter, and peas in a blender or food processor. Add to soup pot. Season with salt and pepper to taste. Heat and serve. Makes 4 servings.

Spring Turnips with Greens and Raisins   Jenny Bonde and Rink DaVee, Shooting Star Farm

2 tablespoons butter, divided
2 teaspoons olive oil
1 medium yellow onion, diced
1 bunch spring turnips and greens
   (about 10 small or 5 large turnips)

about 1/2 cup raisins
salt
12 ounces orzo or bow tie pasta, cooked
   and cooled (optional)

Heat 1 tablespoon of the butter and all the oil in a large skillet over medium flame. Add onions and cook, stirring often, until they begin to soften, about 5 minutes. Meanwhile, wash turnips and trim the leaves from the root. Chop the roots into 1-inch dice. Discard any yellowed turnip leaves and roughly chop the nice ones. Once the onions are softened, add the turnip roots. Sprinkle with a bit of salt, stir, and cover. Cook until the turnips can be easily pierced with a knife, about 8 minutes. Uncover, turn the heat up to medium high, and cook, stirring now and then, until turnips turn light brown at the edges. Add the chopped greens and raisins and cook until the greens are wilted and tender, another 3-4 minutes. Add remaining 1 tablespoon butter and salt to taste. Eat this as a side dish or toss it with cooked pasta for a main dish. Makes 3-4 servings.

Mashed Turnips with Cream and Crispy Shallots   Molly Bartlett, Silver Creek Farm

1 1/2-2 pounds turnips, peeled and
   coarsely chopped
3 tablespoons butter, divided
1 cup thinly sliced shallots
   (or substitute sweet red onion)

1/2 cup heavy cream
1/8 teaspoon grated nutmeg
salt and pepper
1-3 teaspoons minced Italian (flat-leaf) parsley

Place chopped turnips in large pot of cold water. Bring to boil and cook until tender, about 15 minutes. Drain well and puree turnips in a food processor (or mash them with a hand-held masher). Heat 2 tablespoons of the butter in small skillet over medium flame, add shallots, and cook, stirring often, until shallots are tender and golden brown, about 15 minutes. Remove shallots from skillet and drain them on paper towels. Combine the cream and remaining 1 tablespoon butter; bring to a simmer and stir into the pureed turnips. Season with nutmeg; add salt and pepper to taste. Place in a serving dish, garnish with shallots and parsley, and serve immediately. This recipe is adapted from one by a chef at Union Square Café in Manhattan. Makes 6-8 servings.

Wild Things

Throughout time and the world over, wild plants have been used both for food and as medicine. Many wild foods have now been lost completely from our environment and from our day-to-day lives and diets. Gradually, however, the trend toward local and seasonal eating is helping to reintroduce these foods.

Many delectable wild foods were purposely left out of this section to discourage widespread harvesting and the resulting negative effects on precious natural areas. Instead, this section focuses on a smattering of wild foods that are available seasonally either in farmers' markets or through CSAs.

This section's wild foods are available and in their edible prime in early spring. The vivacious flavors common to these first-of-the-season foods carry a nutritional and purifying punch.

As a rule, wild foods are highly perishable. Use them as soon as possible for optimum flavor, texture, and nutrition. When you must store them, wrap greens in a damp paper or cloth towel and then in plastic and refrigerate.

Watercress (*Rorippa nasturtium-aquaticum* and *Nasturtium Officinale*)—This subtle-looking little plant will surprise you with its crunchy hit of spicy, mustardy flavor. Generally cultivated in a watery habitat, it loves cool weather. Before cooking, submerge in cool water to remove any grit and debris or slimy leaves. Favorite basic uses include cress sandwiches (try it with great cheese and hearty bread), as a spicy addition to a fresh green salad, as a garnish or last-minute addition to soups, and as a bed for hot grilled meats or fish.

Dandelion *(Taraxacum officinale)*—The dandelion, native to Europe and Asia, deserves a place of respect in any wild food lover's culinary repertoire. Sadly, more residential herbicides are used against the innocent dandelion than any other weed. Both wild and cultivated varieties impart a distinctive bitter and slightly earthy flavor and are often combined with milder greens. The youngest and most tender dandelion greens will add an exciting bite to any spring salad. The slightly older and more fibrous leaves are best braised or added to soups.

Nettles *(Urtica dioica)*— Considered a tiresome weed by home gardeners, the stinging nettle contains formic acid, an ammonia-like substance also delivered by stinging ants. But the nettle may be the most nutritious, mild, and delicious of all the wild greens. Use as you would spinach or chard. Rinse well in cold water to wash off any grit, and then remove the greens by grasping with tongs. Cook thoroughly, but do not overcook. The cooking process will neutralize the nettle's sting.

Ramps *(Allium tricoccum)*—The ramp, a member of the lily family, is also known as the wild leek. Its strong, garlicky aroma is unforgettable, and it cooks up to a very pleasing sweet and mild flavor. Use ramps to replace any spring bulb onion in a recipe, or simply parboil and serve like asparagus. If you must store ramps, beware! Their aroma will invade other items in your refrigerator. Wrap in a damp towel, then in several layers of plastic. Use as soon as possible.

Sorrel *(Rumex acetosa)*—The word *sorrel* is derived from the word "sour," which is a perfect description of this tender wild green and its cultivated cousin. Garden sorrel, considered a vegetable by some and an herb by others, is finally gaining in popularity in this county. The bright green, broad leaf is famous for its tangy, lemony taste. Raw or cooked, it will brighten any dish or salad.

Spanish Tortilla with Ramps and Rosemary   MACSAC

1-2 bunches ramps (12-14 ramps total)
7 large eggs
salt and pepper
4-6 tablespoons olive oil, divided

2 teaspoons minced fresh rosemary, divided
20 stuffed green olives
Garnish: 2 whole ramps or 2 large rosemary sprigs

Clean ramps; finely chop the stems and leaves into separate piles. Beat eggs in a bowl with salt and pepper to taste. Heat broiler. Heat 2 tablespoons oil in 9- or 10-inch nonstick skillet over medium flame. Add ramp stems and sauté 2-3 minutes. Add ramp leaves and half the rosemary; sauté until wilted, another 1-2 minutes. Season to taste with salt and pepper; remove mixture to a bowl. Wipe out skillet, add another 2-3 tablespoons oil, and heat over high flame. Add beaten eggs. As they begin to set on the bottom, pull the eggs with a spatula toward the center of the pan so that more liquid gets exposed to the pan bottom and cooks. Continue this for a minute or two, then scatter the ramp mixture into the egg mixture. When most of the egg has set, reduce heat to low and cook several minutes. Neatly shape the outer edge of the tortilla with a spatula, then arrange olives around the outer rim, pressing them lightly into the tortilla. Set under broiler to finish the cooking; this will take 2-4 minutes, so watch carefully. When tortilla is cooked and starting to brown, remove it from the oven and sprinkle with remaining rosemary. Let stand 10 minutes or bring to room temperature before serving. Garnish with whole ramps or rosemary sprigs. Makes 6 servings, or 10-12 appetizer servings.

Sesame Linguine with Ramps, Asparagus, and Mushrooms   MACSAC

1 package (9 ounces) RP's fresh sesame linguine
(or substitute similar fresh pasta)
sesame oil
olive oil
1/2 pound fresh morels, shiitake, or other
mushrooms, cut in half or sliced

1/2 pound fresh asparagus, cut into
2- or 3-inch pieces
1 bunch ramps (6-8 total), chopped
1/4-1/2 cup fresh orange juice
salt and pepper

Cook pasta according to package instructions. Meanwhile, heat a little sesame oil and olive oil in a heavy skillet. Sauté the morels, asparagus, and ramps separately, each until not quite tender (transfer to a bowl as you finish each batch). Then combine all the vegetables in the pan, add the orange juice, and cook over medium-high flame until liquid is reduced to almost nothing and vegetables are just tender. Toss with cooked pasta plus salt and pepper to taste. Makes 3 servings and may be doubled.

Watercress and Lovage Salad   Twinhawks/Clearview Family Farms

1 tablespoon red wine vinegar
1 teaspoon honey
2 tablespoons dried cranberries, currants, or raisins
2 tablespoons olive oil

2 cups watercress leaves
(remove stems before measuring)
1/4 cup chopped lovage
salt and pepper

Heat vinegar and honey slowly until hot; add the dried fruit. Cool. Whisk in the olive oil. Toss dressing with the greens; sprinkle with salt and pepper to taste. This recipe comes from the friend of an intern at Twinhawks. Makes 4 servings.

Stir-Fried Daylily Buds   MACSAC

2 tablespoons peanut oil
2-3 cups daylily buds
1-2 teaspoons minced garlic
1-2 teaspoons minced fresh ginger

1 tablespoon soy sauce
1 teaspoon dark sesame oil
1 teaspoon grated orange zest

Heat wok or deep skillet over high heat for several minutes. Add oil and swirl it around the pan. Add daylily buds and stir-fry 2-3 minutes. Add remaining ingredients; stir-fry until tender, a few minutes longer. Makes 4-6 servings.

Fiddlehead Fern and Tomato Salad   MACSAC

3 cups fiddlehead fern tops (cut to about
  4-inch length)
4 small tomatoes, cut into small chunks
8-10 imported Greek olives, pitted and
  coarsely chopped

2-3 teaspoons best-quality balsamic vinegar
1-2 tablespoons virgin olive oil
1/2-1 teaspoon sugar
salt and pepper to taste

Steam fiddleheads over boiling water 1-2 minutes. Check for doneness: They should droop a bit but still have a crisp-tender texture when you bite into them. Rinse with cool water to stop the cooking. Drain and dry on towels. Toss with remaining ingredients. Let stand 1/2 hour before serving. Serve at room temperature. Makes 4-5 servings.

Pasta with Asparagus and Wild Greens   Edith Thayer, Vermont Valley Farm member

10-12 ounces pasta (any short shape)
1 pound fresh asparagus
1-2 tablespoons olive oil
2-3 cloves garlic, minced

6-8 ounces dandelion, arugula, or watercress greens,
  thick stems removed, greens coarsely chopped
1/2 cup freshly grated Parmesan, feta, or
  crumbly goat cheese
salt and freshly ground pepper to taste

Cook pasta according to package directions and drain. Trim woody ends from the asparagus spears. Cut spears into 2-inch-long pieces. Heat oil in a medium skillet, add garlic, and cook over low heat for a minute or two. Add asparagus and a tablespoon or two of water. Cover and steam until the asparagus is done to your liking but still bright green. Add the greens, cover, and steam just until wilted slightly, about a minute. Toss this mixture with the hot pasta and cheese in a serving bowl. Season with salt and pepper and serve at once. Makes 4-5 servings.

Morel and Fiddlehead Risotto   MACSAC

1/2 pound fiddlehead ferns
  (tightly curled, unopened)
3 tablespoons butter, divided
1/2 pound fresh morels (soaked or
  well washed in water, cut in half if very
  large, drained, and dried on paper towels)
1 1/2 tablespoons olive oil

1/2 cup finely chopped onion or 1/4 cup
  finely chopped shallots
1 1/2 cups arborio rice
2/3 cup dry white wine
4-5 cups chicken stock, hot
1/3-1/2 cup freshly grated Parmesan, divided
salt and pepper to taste

Cut fiddleheads into 3-inch pieces, keeping stems in separate pile from the heads. Heat half the butter in a heavy skillet; add fiddlehead stems and sauté 1-2 minutes. Add the tops and continue to sauté until crisp-tender, another 2-3 minutes. Remove fiddleheads from pan and add a bit more butter. Sauté morels in batches (don't crowd the pan) until tender, adding a bit more butter as needed with each batch. Return fiddleheads to pan; turn off heat, but keep the pan warm. Heat olive oil in deep, medium saucepan over medium flame. Add onions or shallots; sauté until tender. Stir in rice, then add wine and stir until most of the liquid is absorbed. Add 1 to 1 1/2 cups chicken stock and cook, stirring very often, until most of the liquid is absorbed. Continue adding 1/2-3/4 cup of stock at a time and stirring until it is mostly absorbed. When rice is creamy and tender to the bite, stir in the mushroom/fiddlehead mixture and about half of the Parmesan. Season with salt and pepper. Serve immediately, sprinkling each serving with a little more Parmesan. Makes 6 servings.

Doug's Dandy Dandelions with Spring Garlic   Doug Wubben, Drumlin Community Farm

1 tablespoon olive oil
3 spring pencil-thin garlic shoots, chopped
  (separate the stem and leaves)

1 bunch dandelion greens, chopped
  (can substitute nettles or other greens)
salt to taste

Heat olive oil in skillet. Add chopped garlic stems and sauté 2 minutes. Add garlic leaves and dandelion greens; sauté until just wilted, another 2-3 minutes. Season with salt. Makes 2-4 servings.

Greek-Inspired Sorrel Rice Soup MACSAC

2 tablespoons butter
1/2 cup finely chopped onion
1/3 cup long-grain rice
3 1/2 cups rich pork or chicken stock

3-4 cups packed sorrel leaves
1/2-1 cup half-and-half or heavy cream
2 eggs, beaten
salt and pepper

Heat butter in soup pot over medium flame. Add onions; cook a few minutes. Add rice and stock. Cover, bring to simmer, and cook 5 minutes. Cut sorrel into strips. Add 2/3 of it to soup; simmer until rice is tender. Reduce heat to low and stir in cream and remaining sorrel. Temper the eggs by whisking 1/2 cup soup broth into the eggs, then stir egg mixture into soup (do not boil). Season with salt and pepper. Makes 4 servings.

Potato, Leek, and Watercress Soup Edith Thayer, Vermont Valley Community Farm member

1 1/2 tablespoons canola or vegetable oil
3 large leeks, chopped (white and pale green
 parts only) and rinsed well
1 large onion, finely chopped
2 pounds potatoes, peeled and diced
1 bay leaf

chicken stock, light vegetable stock, or water
2 cups packed chopped watercress
1-1 1/2 cups low-fat milk or soy milk
salt and freshly ground pepper to taste
2 tablespoons chopped fresh parsley

Heat oil in a soup pot. Add chopped leeks and onions, cover, and cook over moderate heat, stirring occasionally, until the onions begin to turn golden. Add potatoes, bay leaf, and just enough stock or water to cover the vegetables. Bring to a boil, cover, and simmer until the potatoes are tender, 15-20 minutes. Mash some of the potatoes against the sides of the pot with a spoon. Add the watercress and milk or soy milk; simmer over very low heat 10 minutes. Season to taste with salt and pepper. Allow to stand off the heat for an hour or two before serving, or let cool and refrigerate overnight. Heat through before serving. Stir in the parsley. Adjust the consistency with more milk or soy milk, then adjust the seasonings to your taste. Adapted from *Vegetarian Celebrations*, by Nava Atlas. If you can't find watercress in the store, use spinach instead. Makes 6 or more servings.

Sorrel and Ramp Dip for Spring Things Leah Caplan, The Washington Hotel

1 packed cup sorrel leaves
1 packed cup ramp leaves

1 cup real mayonnaise
salt and pepper

Cut the sorrel and ramp leaves into small, very slender strips. Stir them into the mayonnaise and season to taste with salt and pepper. This dip is especially good for raw spears of asparagus, but try it also with tapered radishes, slender green onions, blanched baby carrots, etc., or use it as a spread for sandwiches. Makes about 2 cups.

Asian-Style Healing Power Puree of Greens Soup MACSAC

2-3 teaspoons peanut oil
1/3 cup finely chopped shallots
1 teaspoon minced garlic
1 1/2-2 teaspoons minced ginger
3-3 1/2 cups unsalted chicken stock
1-1 1/2 cups cubed, peeled baking potato or
 1/4 cup long-grain rice (optional)

3-4 cups watercress, nettles, or sorrel
4 thinly sliced green onions
2 ounces sesame peanut Thai-style baked tofu
 or any extra-firm tofu, cut into 1/4-inch cubes
1 tablespoon each soy sauce and dry vermouth,
 or more to taste

Heat oil in pot over medium-low flame. Add shallots, garlic, and ginger; cook, stirring occasionally, until translucent, 5-10 minutes. Add stock and potatoes or rice, if using. Simmer 5 minutes (or until potatoes or rice are soft, 10-15 minutes). Add greens and simmer 5-8 minutes. Puree with immersion blender or in food processor. Stir in remaining ingredients. Serve piping hot. Makes 3-4 servings.

Winter Squash

Cucurbita maxima

Autumn colors are accented in the garden by the decorative array of winter squashes. A variety of colors, shapes, sizes, and textures are represented in the harvest. Despite the diversity in looks, most winter squash are similar on the edible inside. The flesh of the squash, except for the unique spaghetti squash, tends to be orange in color and mild and sweet in flavor. Most winter squash are interchangeable in recipes.

Unlike summer squash, winter squash was not grown in North or Central America before European colonization. Originating and flourishing first in South America, winter squash finally found its way north, and by the early to mid-1800s was a staple product. It was particularly cultivated in New England as necessary winter storage food.

Its excellent storability and nutritive value make winter squash an important fall and winter vegetable for the seasonal eater. Winter squash boasts 10 times the vitamin A content of its summer squash relations, and is also an excellent source of potassium. Winter squash is high in fiber and complex carbohydrates, and its versatility means that sweet, warming squash will find its way into your heart…and your tummy.

Cooking Tips

- 1 pound trimmed squash equals 2 cups cooked squash.

- Boil or steam 1 1/2- to 2-inch chunks for 15-20 minutes, or until tender. You may peel the squash before or after; it's easier to peel after cooking, but it must cool first.

- Mash cooked squash and top with butter. Serve hot.

- Puree cooked squash for a creamy soup, or add uncooked chunks to hearty soups and stews.

- Winter squash is easy to bake. Slice most squashes in half lengthwise, scoop out the seeds, and place facedown on a cookie sheet. Water may be added around squashes to avoid drying out and hasten cooking. Squash flesh may also be basted with oil or butter. Squash will need 40 minutes to 1 1/2 hours, depending on size. Cook until very tender but not charred.

- Butternut makes an excellent "pumpkin" pie.

- Try spaghetti squash served hot with butter and Parmesan cheese or your favorite tomato sauce. Bake as above. Flesh is done when it scoops out easily in spaghetti-like strings.

- Acorn squash is famous baked faceup with melted butter and brown sugar or maple syrup.

- Cook squash chunks alongside roasting meats.

- Add small amounts of squash to yeast breads, quick breads, muffins, cookies, or pancake batter to add color, moisture, and sweetness.

Storage Tips

- Winter squash will store at room temperature for at least a month. Store for several months in a dry and cool (50-55 degrees) but not cold location.

- Bruised or damaged squash will deteriorate more quickly.

For additional recipes that feature winter squash, see the Pumpkin, Seasonal Combinations, and Kids' Recipes chapters.

Butternut Squash Coconut Curry Soup   Deb Boehm, Deb and Lola's Restaurant

1 tablespoon peanut oil
1/2 large onion, chopped
2 cloves garlic, minced
3 1/2 cups chicken or vegetable stock
1 medium butternut squash, peeled,
  seeded and chopped
1 small jalapeño pepper, chopped

1 can coconut milk
1/2 cup chopped lemongrass
2 citrus/kaffir lime leaves
1/2 cup bottled fish sauce
sugar to taste (start with 1 tablespoon)
juice of 1/2 lime

Heat oil in saucepan; add onions and garlic. Sauté until lightly browned. Add stock, squash, and jalapeño; simmer until squash is tender, 10-15 minutes. Add coconut milk, lemongrass, lime leaves, fish sauce, and sugar. Simmer (do not boil) 10-12 minutes. Puree and strain through fine mesh strainer. Add lime juice and adjust to taste with sugar and lime juice. Makes 4 servings.

Dave's Thai Squash   Dave French, Madison CSA supporter

oil or butter
3 cups diced onions
1/4 cup grated gingerroot
6 cloves garlic, crushed
1-2 hot peppers (fresh or dried), minced

1 can (14 ounces) coconut milk
2-3 tablespoons minced fresh basil
1 tablespoon dried galanga
6 cups butternut squash, in 3/4-inch cubes

Heat oil in large skillet; add onions, gingerroot, garlic, and peppers. Cook over low heat until tender. Add coconut milk and basil; cook until thickened. Meanwhile, boil galanga in 4 cups water for 20 minutes. Add squash and boil another 12-15 minutes. Drain and remove galanga. Combine with other ingredients and serve. Makes 12 servings.

Cranberry Acorn Squash   Molly Bartlett, Silver Creek Farm

1/2 cup raw fresh cranberries
1 small apple, cored, chopped into small pieces
1/4 cup currants
1/2 cup orange juice or apple cider

1 1/2 tablespoons honey or maple syrup
1 tablespoon melted butter
pinch salt
2 acorn squash, cut in half, seeds removed

Heat oven to 350 degrees. Combine cranberries, apples, currants, orange juice, honey, butter, and salt in a saucepan. Heat until berries are just tender. Place squash in ovenproof dish. Fill cavities with fruit. Cover dish and bake until squash is tender, about 35-45 minutes. Makes 4 servings.

Kabocha (or Buttercup) Squash, Japanese Style   Drumlin Community Farm

1 squash, cut into 2-inch cubes
1/2 cup soy sauce

1/4 cup honey or brown sugar

Bring several inches water to boil in a saucepan; cube and add squash, leaving the skin on. Add more water to cover if needed. Bring to boil again, reduce heat, and add soy sauce and honey. Cook until squash is tender, 10-15 minutes. Drain. Makes 4-6 servings.

Easy Butternut Squash Soup   Linda Taylor, Good Earth Farm

2 tablespoons butter or olive oil
3-4 cloves garlic, mashed with side of thick knife
1/2-1 cup chopped onion
2 1/2-3 pounds butternut squash, halved,
    seeded, and baked until soft
4 cups chicken stock or 2 bouillon cubes
    dissolved in 4 cups hot water

1 bay leaf
pinch of sugar
1/2 teaspoon or more curry powder
pinch of nutmeg
salt and pepper to taste
2 cups milk (low-fat or skim)

Heat butter or olive oil in large saucepan over medium flame. Add garlic and onions; cook, stirring often, 7-10 minutes. Puree the cooked squash in a food processor and stir into onion mixture. Stir in stock, bay leaf, sugar, curry powder, nutmeg, salt, and pepper. Simmer 20-30 minutes. Remove bay leaf. Add the milk; heat but don't boil. This is adapted from *The Complete Book of Soups and Stews,* by Bernard Clayton. Makes 6 servings.

Winter Squash with Cranberries   Linda Taylor, Good Earth Farm

1 small winter squash
1-3 teaspoons butter or olive oil

1 cup cranberries (fresh or frozen)
2-3 tablespoons raspberry jam or puree

Peel winter squash, chop flesh into 1/2- to 1-inch cubes, and steam over boiling water until soft but not mushy. Heat butter or olive oil in heavy skillet over medium flame. Toss in cranberries and stir frequently until they soften. Mash in skillet with fork or potato masher. Stir in jam. When squash is done, toss it with the cranberry mixture. Makes 4-8 servings.

Chipotle Butternut Squash Puree   MACSAC

3 pounds butternut or other winter squash
1 tablespoon butter

1-2 tablespoons canned chipotle in
    adobo sauce, finely chopped
salt and pepper

Preheat oven to 350 degrees. Prick squash all over with a fork. Bake on a foil-lined baking tray for about 35 minutes; turn squash over and bake another 35 minutes or until very tender all the way through. Allow to cool a few minutes, until you can handle the squash. Cut squash in half, remove seeds, scoop out flesh, and puree through a food mill, in a food processor, or with a potato masher. Melt butter in microwave oven or in a small saucepan and stir in chopped chipotle to taste. Stir butter/chipotle mixture into squash and season with salt and pepper to taste. Makes 4 side-dish servings.

Butternut Squash Soup with Ham and Peas   Keith Kluender

2 1/2 pounds butternut or other winter squash
8 tablespoons (1 stick) butter
1/2 pound ham steak, cut into 1/4-inch cubes

1 can (14 ounces) beef broth
1 package (10 ounces) frozen peas
salt and pepper

Peel and seed squash and cut into 1-inch cubes. Submerge squash cubes in a bowl of ice water for at least 30 minutes and up to 3 hours. Drain squash. Melt butter in saucepan over medium heat; add ham and sauté about 5 minutes. Remove ham with a slotted spoon and reserve in a bowl. Toss squash with the butter that remains in the pot, pour in broth, bring to a boil, and simmer until squash is tender, about 15 minutes. Puree soup with immersion blender or in food processor or blender. Add ham and peas and cook about 5 more minutes. Season to taste with salt and pepper. Makes 4-6 servings.

Penne alla Zucca (Roman Pasta with Pumpkin Sauce)   Leah Caplan, The Washington Hotel

3 tablespoons extra-virgin olive oil
2 onions, finely chopped
4 cups peeled and chopped winter squash
   or pumpkin flesh
1 garlic clove
1/4 teaspoon crushed red chile pepper

1/2 teaspoon sea salt
1/4 teaspoon freshly ground nutmeg
2 tablespoons chopped fresh sage
1 pound penne pasta or gnocchi
1/3 cup grated Parmesan

Heat olive oil in a large skillet over medium flame; add onions and cook, stirring often, until very soft and translucent. Meanwhile, in a food processor fitted with a knife blade, pulse the squash and garlic together in 2 batches until very fine. Add to onions with chile, salt, nutmeg, and 1 cup water. Cover and simmer until squash is soft and of a saucelike consistency, 10-20 minutes. Stir in sage. Cook pasta in lots of boiling, salted water until just tender. Strain, reserving 1 cup of pasta cooking liquid. Add pasta to hot sauce in pan, stir, and cook over high heat, adding cooking liquid if necessary, until pasta is coated. Stir in Parmesan and serve. Makes 4-6 servings.

Vegan Pumpkin or Winter Squash Pie   Luna Circle Farm

3 cups pureed, cooked pumpkin
3/4 cup maple syrup or honey
2 tablespoons molasses
1/4 teaspoon powdered cloves
3 teaspoons cinnamon

1 1/2 teaspoons ground ginger
1 teaspoon salt
1 1/2-2 cups scalded soy milk
whole wheat pie shell

Heat oven to 450 degrees. Cut pumpkin into large chunks; remove seeds. Steam until soft, 20-30 minutes. Scoop out flesh; mash or puree to a thick paste (add a tiny amount of water if necessary). Mix all ingredients (except pie shell) and pour into pie shell. Bake 10 minutes; reduce heat to 350 degrees and bake until set, 45-50 minutes longer. Cool before serving. Makes 8 servings.

Andrea's Aromatic Pumpkin and Chick-Pea Hot Pot   Andrea Robles, Drumlin Community Farm member

3 tablespoons vegetable oil
1 1/2 cups finely chopped onion
1/4 teaspoon salt or to taste
2 or more teaspoons bottled Thai-style red
   curry paste
1 teaspoon ground cumin
1 teaspoon ground coriander
2 tablespoons grated fresh ginger
2 pounds peeled, seeded pumpkin or other winter
   squash, cut into 1 1/4-inch chunks

2 cans (each 15 ounces) light coconut milk
1 cup chicken or vegetable stock, or water
3 tablespoons soy sauce
2 cans (each 15 ounces) chick-peas, drained
1 cup cubed tofu (plain or herb-flavored)
black pepper to taste
1 cup loosely packed cilantro leaves, finely chopped
cooked basmati rice and plain yogurt (optional)

Place a large wide pan or pot over medium heat and add oil. When hot, add onions and salt and sauté until softened but not browned. Stir in 2 teaspoons curry paste and sauté 1 minute. Stir in cumin, coriander, and ginger. Raise heat to medium-high and add pumpkin; stir about 1 minute to mix ingredients well. Stir in coconut milk, stock, and soy sauce. Bring to simmer, partially cover, reduce heat to low, and simmer gently until pumpkin is almost tender, 10-20 minutes. Stir in chick-peas and tofu, partially cover pan, and simmer 5-10 minutes. Stir gently and adjust salt and pepper to taste. If more spiciness is desired, add additional curry paste. Ladle hot pot into bowls or serve over rice on a plate. Sprinkle each serving with cilantro. If you like, have plain yogurt on hand to cool the tastebuds. Makes 6-8 servings.

Zucchini

Cucurbita pepo

Anyone who's ever grown zucchini will agree: this vegetable grows so fast that if you take the time to watch you can see the vines creep, the large leaves expand, the blossoms open, and the fruit getting bigger! Pick those tender young zucchini today, because tomorrow they will be huge, destined for more zucchini bread, stuffed zucchini boats, or the compost. It takes diligent daily harvesting in the field and a creative cook in the kitchen to keep pace with the generally prolific nature of zucchini.

Zucchini is a summer squash and is available from approximately mid- to late summer. It does not tolerate cold and will end its season by the first frost or before if temperatures are frequently cool. Unlike their winter squash relations, zucchini and other summer squashes are not known for their storability, but instead are a seasonal treat associated with the bounty of summer.

Like all squashes, zucchini is descended from native species originating in South America, (though it's believed to have been developed in Italy). Zucchini has been popularized throughout North America, most likely by Italian immigrants, their descendants, and their famous cuisine.

See the sections on summer squash for nutritional and other information.

Cooking Tips

- Simply rinse off zucchini—no need to peel.

- Zucchini is very versatile. Try it raw, broiled, steamed, fried, grilled, sautéed, or stir-fried.

- Steam small zucchini whole, halved lengthwise, or in larger chunks to best preserve texture, 5-15 minutes. Check tenderness with a fork. Be careful not to overcook. Top with butter, olive oil, and a pinch of salt and pepper and serve hot, or drizzle with olive oil or a vinaigrette and serve at room temperature.

- Grate or thinly slice raw zucchini into salad, or add zucchini sticks or rounds to a veggie platter with dip.

- Add slices to your favorite tomato sauce, pizza, quiche, or other baked dishes.

- Add chunks to soups and stews toward end of cooking time to retain texture, or use zucchini puree as a soup base.

- Substitute zucchini in a potato pancake recipe.

- Try this superb, seasonal, and quick dish: Fill a large frying pan with chunks of green onion or leek, zucchini, any other summer squash, bell pepper, tomato, and eggplant (optional), and salt and pepper to taste. Garlic and fresh basil are optional as well. Toss with light coating of olive oil, cover, and allow to simmer in its own juices until everything is very tender…even approaching mushy! Serve as side dish or over spaghetti. It is excellent cold as well.

- Grill zucchini sliced in half lengthwise (facedown) or skewer chunks for shish kabob.

- If squash is oversized, make a zucchini boat—the kids can help. Cut large squash in half lengthwise and scoop out pulpy middle. Prebake or steam upright in large pot to tenderize but not fully cook. Stuff zucchini with favorite mixture, such as pizza fixings. Place on cookie sheet and bake until heated through and fully tender.

Storage Tips

- Refrigerate zucchini in hydrator drawer for up to 3-4 days.

- For longer-term storage, freeze zucchini puree in airtight containers for use in winter soups, and grated zucchini for use in breads and muffins.

For additional recipes that feature zucchini, see the Summer Squash and Seasonal Combinations chapters.

Oven-Fried Zucchini Spears   Zephyr Community Farm

2 medium-sized zucchini or yellow
   summer squash
3 tablespoons dried bread crumbs
1 tablespoon grated Parmesan cheese
1 teaspoon dried oregano
1/2 teaspoon dried basil

1 teaspoon dried summer savory
1/4 teaspoon garlic powder
1/8 teaspoon ground black pepper
2 teaspoons corn oil
prepared marinara sauce (Italian tomato
   and herb sauce) (optional)

Heat oven to 475 degrees. Lightly oil a baking sheet. Wash zucchini and pat dry. Do not peel. Cut into eighths lengthwise, then halves crosswise. On a sheet of wax paper, toss bread crumbs, cheese, herbs, garlic powder, and pepper. Whisk oil and 2 tablespoons water in small bowl. Moisten zucchini spears in this mixture, then roll them in crumb mixture, covering all sides. Arrange on baking sheet. Bake 7 minutes, or until spears are lightly browned. Turn spears over; bake 3 minutes more. Serve immediately with hot marinara sauce, if desired. Makes 4 servings.

Mannie's Cold Zucchini Salad   Drumlin Community Farm

zucchini
canola oil

minced garlic
red wine vinegar

Slice zucchini into thin strips lengthwise. Fry lightly in hot oil until soft throughout. Transfer zucchini to a bowl; salt lightly. Discard most of the oil in the pan. Add generous amounts of garlic and sauté lightly. Add 1/4 inch of red wine vinegar to the pan and bring to quick boil. Toss sauce with squash. Cover and refrigerate; serve in a few hours. Makes any number of servings.

Cinnamon Zucchini Cake   Lisa Kivirist, Inn Serendipity

2 1/2 cups flour
2 cups sugar
1 1/2 teaspoons cinnamon
1 teaspoon salt
1/2 teaspoon baking powder
1/2 teaspoon baking soda
1 cup vegetable oil
4 eggs
2 cups shredded zucchini
1/2 cup chopped walnuts (optional)

Frosting:
4 ounces (1/2 package) cream cheese, softened
1/4 cup (4 tablespoons) butter, softened
1 tablespoon milk
1 teaspoon vanilla extract
2 cups powdered sugar

Heat oven to 350 degrees. Grease a 9-by-13-inch baking pan. Mix flour, sugar, cinnamon, salt, baking powder, and baking soda in a bowl. Mix oil and eggs in another bowl until smooth; add to dry ingredients and mix well. Add zucchini; stir until thoroughly combined. Fold in walnuts, if desired. Spread mixture in prepared pan; bake until a toothpick inserted near the center comes out clean, 35-45 minutes. Cool thoroughly. To make frosting, beat cream cheese, butter, milk, and vanilla until smooth. Add powdered sugar and mix well. Frost cake. Makes 12 or more servings.

Greek Stewed Zucchini   MACSAC

1 pound zucchini, sliced into 1-inch-thick rounds
1 cup tomato sauce
1 teaspoon chopped fresh oregano

2 diced plum tomatoes
3 tablespoons feta cheese
salt and pepper

Simmer zucchini in tomato sauce along with oregano and diced tomatoes until softened, about 8 minutes. Sprinkle with feta. Season to taste with salt and pepper. Serve as is or place it under the broiler until cheese is browned, 2-3 minutes. Makes 4 servings.

Savory Zucchini Bake   Lisa Kivirist, Inn Serendipity

3 cups peeled and grated zucchini
1 cup packaged quick baking mix
  (like Bisquick)
1 cup chopped onion
1/2 teaspoon each salt and pepper
1 tablespoon minced garlic

1/2-1 1/2 cups grated Parmesan or Swiss cheese
2 tablespoons chopped fresh parsley
1/2 teaspoon seasoned salt
1/2 teaspoon dried oregano
1/2 cup oil
4 eggs

Heat oven to 350 degrees. Grease a 9-by-13-inch pan. Mix all ingredients and pour into pan. Bake 30 minutes. Makes 12 servings.

Mock Apple Cobbler   Lisa Kivirist, Inn Serendipity

Filling ingredients:
3 pounds peeled, seeded, and
  chopped zucchini (about 8 cups)
2/3 cup lemon juice
1 cup sugar
1 teaspoon ground cinnamon
1/2 teaspoon ground nutmeg

Crust ingredients:
4 cups flour
2 cups sugar
1 1/2 cups (3 sticks) cold butter, cut into small pieces
1 teaspoon ground cinnamon

Combine zucchini and lemon juice in large saucepan over medium-low heat. Bring to simmer and cook until tender, about 20 minutes. Stir in sugar, cinnamon, and nutmeg; simmer 1 minute longer. Remove from heat. Heat oven to 375 degrees. Oil a 9-by-13-inch baking pan. Combine flour and sugar in a bowl; cut in butter with pastry cutter until mixture resembles coarse crumbs. Stir 1/2 cup of the crust mixture into zucchini mixture. Press half the remaining crust mixture into pan. Spread zucchini mixture over it, then crumble remaining crust mixture over zucchini. Sprinkle with cinnamon. Bake until golden and bubbly, 35 to 40 minutes. Makes 12 or more servings.

Toasted Zucchini Rye Snack   Lisa Kivirist, Inn Serendipity

2 cups shredded zucchini
1 teaspoon salt
1/2 cup mayonnaise or salad dressing
1/2 cup plain yogurt
1/4 cup grated Parmesan

1/4 cup finely chopped green pepper
4 green onions, thinly sliced
1 garlic clove, minced
1 teaspoon Worcestershire sauce
approximately 36 slices snack-size rye bread or crackers

Toss zucchini and salt in a bowl; let stand 1 hour. Rinse, drain, and press out excess liquid. Add the next 7 ingredients; stir until combined. There are 2 ways to serve this: Spread a rounded teaspoonful on each slice of snack rye bread; place on a baking sheet. Bake at 375 degrees for 10 to 12 minutes or until bubbly. Serve hot. Alternatively, pour zucchini mixture in an 8-by-8-inch baking pan and bake at 375 degrees until bubbly, 15-20 minutes. Serve hot with crackers. Makes about 36 total.

Grilled Baby Zucchini with Tarragon Mustard Vinaigrette   MACSAC

2-3 teaspoons minced garlic, pressed to a paste
2 teaspoons tarragon mustard
2 tablespoons wine vinegar
salt and pepper to taste

3 tablespoons olive oil
1 1/2 pounds young zucchini or yellow squash,
   halved lengthwise

Heat coals on outdoor grill. Combine garlic, mustard, vinegar, salt, and pepper; whisk in oil. Brush squash halves with a little of the dressing and grill slowly until barely tender. Place on platter; drizzle on the dressing. Serve warm or at room temperature. Makes 4-6 servings.

Sweet Zucchini Biscuits   Angele Theriault, member of Harmony Valley Farm

1/2 cup margarine or butter, softened
1 cup packed light brown sugar
2 eggs
1 tablespoon orange or lemon juice
2 1/2 cups all-purpose flour
2 teaspoons baking powder
1/2 teaspoon ground cinnamon

1/2 teaspoon ground mace
1/4 teaspoon salt
1 1/2 cups shredded, drained zucchini
1/2 cup chopped pecans
1 tablespoon grated orange zest
   (orange part of rind only)
powdered sugar

Heat oven to 350 degrees; grease 2 baking sheets. Beat margarine until fluffy. Beat in sugar, eggs, and orange juice. Combine flour, baking powder, spices, and salt; stir into egg mixture. Stir in zucchini, pecans, and orange zest. Drop by teaspoonfuls onto cookie sheets. Bake about 10 minutes. Cool on racks. Sprinkle with powdered sugar before serving. Makes 5 dozen biscuits.

Zucchini Shallot Sauté   Leslie France

very young zucchini, scrubbed
salt
butter

minced shallots
freshly ground pepper

Grate zucchini, place in colander, and salt liberally. Let stand 20-30 minutes, then rinse and squeeze a handful at a time. Dry further in paper towels. Heat butter in large skillet over medium-low flame. Add shallots and cook, stirring often, until tender, 2-3 minutes. Raise heat to high, add zucchini, and cook, stirring, until heated through, 2-3 minutes. Makes any number of servings.

Double Chocolate Zucchini Cake   Scotch Hill Farm

3/4 cup oil
1 1/4 cups sugar
2 eggs
1 teaspoon vanilla
2 cups grated zucchini
1/2 cup sour milk or buttermilk

3 tablespoons cocoa or carob powder
1/2 teaspoon baking powder
1 teaspoon baking soda
1/2 teaspoon each cinnamon and cloves
2 1/2 cups flour
small bag of chocolate or carob chips

Heat oven to 350 degrees; grease a 9-by-13-inch pan. Mix all ingredients and bake 30-35 minutes. Makes 16 servings.

Seasonal Combinations

Welcome to your favorite seasons of the year—winter, spring, summer, and fall! These recipes combine vegetables that are in season at the same time.

In your kitchen, every season is the perfect combination of new opportunities and old favorites. Every season heralds unique gifts and a perfection of plenty. Whether you are just waking up with the spring and seeking that revitalizing tonic, or storing up for that long winter's nap, whatever you need, your seasonal kitchen can surely provide, in a stunning array of glorious manifestations.

For many cooks, both amateur and celebrated, returning joyfully to the wonders of cooking with the seasons (as our ancestors did) is the wellspring of true creativity in the kitchen. Flavors, colors, textures, aromas, and nutritive qualities seem magically to fall into their rightful places in our menu repertoire, gracing our tables and nourishing our families with a vitality and wisdom we surely could not have concocted without this divine intervention. Freshness is paramount. It is what we are all about, when we abide by the seasonal menu plan.

Gourmet is in reach for us all. No fancy fuss, however. At the heart of gourmet are quality, freshness, balance, simplicity, and artful preparation and presentation. Combine fruits and vegetables that are produced locally or regionally in the same season. They inherently go together. Don't think of seasonal cooking as a skill to be mastered and acquired. Let the qualities of the vegetables lead, and you will follow!

In the following section you will find recipes that sing together the song of the seasons, beginning with late spring and moving chronologically through a culinary year. Let yourself experiment, and substitute to your heart's content. There is no one recipe in the world that calls for exactly what is in your CSA box this week, or what you may find in peak condition at the farmer's market on Saturday. There is no one recipe that asks for what will be thriving in your garden after next week's weather. And there is certainly no one recipe that requires exactly what you are in the mood to cook tonight!

Spring Green Dip with Early Vegetables   MACSAC

1/4 cup each whole fresh dill, mint, and
  cilantro leaves
1 cup nonfat cottage cheese
1/3 cup plain yogurt
2 tablespoons fresh lemon juice
1 green onion, coarsely chopped
freshly ground black pepper

radishes
blanched asparagus spears
blanched baby carrots
raw or blanched sugar snap peas
baby zucchini, cut lengthwise into wedges
whole green onions

Blend herbs, cottage cheese, yogurt, and lemon juice in food processor or blender until smooth as possible. Add chopped green onion and pepper to taste; blend a few seconds longer. Arrange vegetables on a colorful platter. Cover dip and vegetables with plastic wrap and chill until ready to serve. Makes 1 1/4 cups dip.

Roast Pork or Tofu Stir-Fried with Green and White Vegetables   MACSAC

1 or more teaspoons bottled garlic chile paste
3 tablespoons soy sauce
3 tablespoons bottled oyster sauce
1 tablespoon sherry
1/2 pound lean roasted boneless pork or
  baked tofu, sliced

1-2 tablespoons peanut oil
1/2 pound asparagus or borccoli
1/2 pound baby bok choy
1/2 pound baby leeks or spring onions
cooked brown rice

Combine chile paste, soy sauce, oyster sauce, and sherry in bowl. Add roast pork or tofu and toss to coat. Let stand while you prepare the vegetables: Remove tough ends from the asparagus (or broccoli) and peel the stalks. Cut the asparagus diagonally into 3-inch pieces (or thinly and evenly slice the broccoli). Cut the bok choy and leeks thinly on the diagonal. Heat a wok or large heavy skillet over highest flame for several minutes. Add a little of the oil and swirl to coat inside of pan. Stir-fry each type of vegetable separately, about 3 minutes for each type. When 1 type is done, remove it to a bowl and reheat the pan with a little more oil before adding the next vegetable. When all 3 types are done, stir-fry the pork, to heat through. Return all the vegetables to the pan, stir-fry to heat through, and serve over brown rice. Makes 4 servings.

Asian-Style Vegetable Noodle Rainbow Platter   Phyllis Davis

1/2 pound thin or medium Chinese noodles
  (fresh or dried)
5 tablespoons sesame oil, divided
1/2 cup peanut butter
2 tablespoons sugar
4 tablespoons soy sauce
4 tablespoons red wine vinegar
8 tablespoons water
1 tablespoon hot bean sauce, or to taste

3-4 cups of a variety of fresh, crisp vegetables:
  thinly sliced radishes; chopped thin
  asparagus; chopped green onions; seeded and
  shredded cucumber, drained; bean sprouts
  (blanched for 30 seconds, immersed in ice
  water and drained), etc.
2 cups shredded or diced cooked chicken, turkey,
  or pork (any leftover roast meat)

Cook noodles according to package directions. Drain well and toss with 1 tablespoon of the sesame oil. Arrange on an attractive platter to cool. Whisk peanut butter, sugar, soy sauce, vinegar, water, hot bean sauce, and remaining sesame oil until sugar is dissolved and mixture is smooth. Arrange vegetables and meat over the noodles. Drizzle sauce evenly over all and serve. This recipe was a winner in the 2000 Food for Thought Recipe Contest in Madison, Wisconsin. Makes 6 servings.

Curried Coconut Noodles with Early Summer Vegetables   MACSAC

8 ounces extra-wide egg noodles or other pasta
1 1/2 tablespoons peanut oil, divided
1 cup chopped young (spring) onions
1/2 cup sliced carrots
1 cup cut-up green beans
1 tablespoon minced garlic
1 tablespoon minced fresh ginger
1 teaspoon ground cumin
1/2-1 teaspoon red pepper flakes
1 teaspoon turmeric
salt and pepper
1 cup peas
1 cup sliced zucchini
1 can (14 ounces) canned coconut milk
  (shake before opening)
juice of 1 1/2 limes
1/2 cup basil leaves, cut into strips
garnish: lime wedges and additional basil strips

Cook noodles in salted water until barely tender (do not overcook them); drain, rinse with cold water, and drain again. Heat wok over highest flame 1-2 minutes. Add the peanut oil, swirl to coat pan, and heat until very hot but not smoking. Add onions, carrots, and green beans; stir-fry until vegetables begin to soften, about 3 minutes. Add garlic, ginger, cumin, red pepper flakes, turmeric, and salt and pepper to taste. Continue stir-frying 1-2 minutes. Add peas, zucchini, coconut milk, and lime juice. Boil mixture until sauce thickens and vegetables are barely tender, 10-12 minutes. Add noodles and basil; stir until all the noodles are coated. Heat through, stirring gently. Serve immediately. Garnish with additional basil and lime wedges. Makes 4-6 servings. This recipe is inspired by one in *Noodle Fusion: Asian Noodle Dishes for Western Kitchens,* by Dorothy Rankin.

Ensalada de Marcelo   Dela Ends, Scotch Hill Farm

2 cups cooked rice, at room temperature
2 cups assorted diced early summer vegetables:
  carrots, kohlrabi, peas, slightly steamed
  green beans, etc.
1/4 cup raisins
1/4 cup chopped olives
1/2 cup cubed provolone or other cheese
3-4 hard-cooked eggs, chopped
1/2 pound summer sausage, diced (optional)
olive oil
salt and pepper
salad greens

Mix rice, vegetables, raisins, olives, cheese, eggs, and sausage (if using). Dress with olive oil and salt and pepper to taste. Serve at room temperature on a bed of salad greens. This recipe comes from an agronomy intern from Uruguay who worked at Scotch Hill in 2001. Any or all of the listed ingredients can be included, or add your favorites, like spring onions or garlic scapes. Makes 4-6 servings.

Spanish Skillet Eggs   MACSAC

4 tablespoons olive oil
3/4 cup diced onion
1 teaspoon minced garlic
1/2 cup diced Spanish chorizo (this is like a
  hard salami; do not use Mexican chorizo for this)
1-2 cups cubed new potatoes
1 pound early season tomatoes, diced
1 cup cooked chopped green beans, or
  1/2 cup cooked peas
salt and pepper to taste
4 large eggs

Heat oven to 350 degrees. Heat oil in ovenproof skillet over medium-low flame. Add onions and garlic; sauté gently until tender. Raise heat to medium, add chorizo, and cook 1-2 minutes. Stir in potatoes; cook until potatoes begin to get tender, stirring often, about 6-8 minutes. Add tomatoes; cook until juice is evaporated and potatoes are fully tender. Stir in beans or peas. Season with salt and pepper. Crack 4 eggs over mixture. (Alternatively, you can divide the mixture into 4 serving-size baking dishes and crack an egg over each one.) Bake until eggs are set. Makes 4 servings.

Karachi Chicken with Spiced Tomatoes, Green Peppers, and Onions   Huma Siddiqui

2 tablespoons cooking oil, divided
2 whole cloves
1 large (black) cardamom pod
1 small (green) cardamom pod
1 inch-long piece of cinnamon stick
1 pound boneless, skinless chicken, cubed
1 tablespoon minced garlic
1 tablespoon minced fresh ginger
1 large onion, chopped

1 large green pepper, chopped
3-4 medium tomatoes, chopped
1/2 teaspoon chili powder
1/2 teaspoon garam masala
1/4 teaspoon turmeric
1/2 teaspoon salt
1/2 cup chopped cilantro
hot, cooked basmati rice

Heat 1 tablespoon oil in a large, deep skillet over medium-high flame. Add cloves, cardamom pods, and cinnamon stick and let them sizzle in the hot oil a moment or two. Add chicken, garlic, and ginger; cook, stirring often, until chicken is no longer pink, about 5 minutes. Transfer chicken to a plate or bowl. Heat another tablespoon of oil in the skillet; add onions and fry them until barely tender. Add green peppers and tomatoes. Fry the mixture for about 5 minutes, then stir in chili powder, garam masala, turmeric, and salt. Return chicken mixture to the pan and gently mix everything together with a slotted spoon. Sprinkle cilantro and cover the pan to simmer for about 10 minutes, until the sauce thickens. Serve with basmati rice. Huma Siddiqui contributed this recipe from her book, *Jasmine in Her Hair.* Makes 4-6 servings.

Summer Bread Salad with Zucchini, Tomatoes, and Feta Cheese   MACSAC

1 1/2-2 cups chopped baby zucchini
1-1 1/2 cups chopped tomatoes
1/2 cup crumbled feta cheese
1/4 cup chopped sweet or green onion
1/4 cup chopped imported olives (black or green)
1/4-1/2 cup chopped fresh basil

1/4 cup extra-virgin olive oil
3 tablespoons wine vinegar
2 teaspoons minced garlic
salt and freshly ground black pepper to taste
5-6 cups firm-textured bread cubes
   (sourdough, pita, etc.), dried or toasted

Toss all ingredients except bread in large bowl; let stand at room temperature to develop flavor, tossing occasionally, 1/2 to 1 hour. Toss in bread just before serving. Makes 4-6 servings.

Hearty Eggplant-Zucchini Toss   Anne Tedeschi, Dog Hollow Farm

1 small eggplant
3 medium zucchini
1 large onion
4 cloves garlic
3 medium tomatoes

1-2 stalks celery (optional)
1 tablespoon olive oil
2 tablespoons tomato sauce (optional)
2 tablespoons oregano
salt and pepper

Peel eggplant and cut it into chunks. Cut zucchini into 3/4-inch rounds. Chop onion coarsely. Mince the garlic. Quarter or halve the tomatoes. Chop the celery, if using. Heat oil in large skillet over medium flame and add all the chopped vegetables, the tomato sauce, plus the oregano and salt and pepper to taste. Toss well, cover the pan, and cook, stirring the vegetables occasionally. You must keep watch over this dish—it will form a watery sauce at first, and the vegetables should be stirred in it until they are all somewhat cooked, about 10-15 minutes. Then remove the cover and cook a few more minutes until the sauce is reduced. Serve as a sauce for rice or pasta. Meat may be added but is not necessary for a hearty meal. Makes 4-6 servings.

Grilled Mosaic of Vegetables with Curry Sauce   Kurt Schneider

Vegetables (use any or all of these or
  others you enjoy):
3-4 medium, unpeeled potatoes, cut into
  1/2- to 3/4-inch cubes
3-4 carrots cut into 1/2-inch-thick slices
1 sweet bell pepper (any color), cut into
  1/2-inch squares
1 medium onion, cut into 1/2-inch squares
1 bunch radishes, halved or quartered
4-6 asparagus spears, cut into 1-inch pieces
1-2 beets, cut into 1/2-inch cubes
2 cups button mushrooms, halved or quartered
2 cups cherry tomatoes
enough olive oil to coat vegetables
1 teaspoon each dried thyme, oregano, and basil
salt and pepper to taste
olive oil-based cooking spray

Curry sauce:
1/3 cup olive oil
1 1/4 teaspoons curry powder
1/4 teaspoon garlic powder
2 dashes Worcestershire sauce
1/4 teaspoon Lawry's salt
1/8 teaspoon pepper
1 teaspoon Dijon mustard
1/4 cup orange juice
2 tablespoons mild-flavored molasses

Start charcoal for indirect cooking method in large kettle-style grill. Precook (steam or microwave) potatoes, carrots, and beets until about 3/4 done. Place all vegetables in large bowl. Add olive oil, herbs, salt, and pepper. Gently mix to coat. Completely cover a large cookie sheet with aluminum foil. Spray its inside surface with cooking spray. Spread vegetable mixture evenly over cookie sheet. Arrange charcoal along two sides of grill. Place pan in center of grill (try to avoid having coals directly below pan). Mix all ingredients for curry sauce in a bowl. When vegetables are slightly browned (about 1 hour), pour curry sauce over vegetables and cook another 10 minutes. Remove from grill and serve immediately. Makes 4-6 servings.

How Sweet It Is Corn and Pepper Salad   MACSAC

4 ears sweet corn
1 green bell pepper, diced
1 red bell pepper, diced
1/4 cup diced red onion
2 tablespoons slivered basil

3 tablespoons balsamic vinegar
1 teaspoon Dijon mustard
1/2 cup olive oil
salt and pepper

Husk corn and boil or grill until crisp-tender. Cool and slice off the kernels. Place corn in bowl with sweet peppers, onions, and basil. Whisk balsamic vinegar and mustard in a small bowl, then slowly whisk in olive oil a little at a time. Toss with the vegetables. Season with salt and pepper to taste. Makes 4 servings.

Greek Village Salad   MACSAC

1 medium pepper, cut into small chunks
1 medium cucumber, sliced
1 small sweet onion, thinly sliced
2 large tomatoes, cut into small chunks
1/2 cup kalamata olives
3 ounces feta cheese, crumbled

Dressing:
1/4 cup olive oil
1/4 cup red wine vinegar
1 garlic clove, crushed
1/2 teaspoon dried oregano or 2-3 teaspoons chopped
  fresh oregano
1/2 teaspoon dried dill weed or 2-3 teaspoons chopped
  fresh dill
salt and freshly ground black pepper to taste

Place first 6 ingredients in bowl. Combine dressing ingredients in glass jar with lid; shake well. Pour over salad; toss gently. Serve at room temperature. Makes 4 servings.

Composed Summer Salad for One   Mary Falk, LoveTree Farm

3 or more slices garden-ripened heirloom tomato
   or several cherry tomatoes
2 slices sweet red pepper
4-5 slices fresh cucumber or a few lightly steamed
   fresh green beans

2- or 3-ounce wedge of LoveTree's Trade Lake Cedar
   cheese, at room temperature
extra-virgin olive oil
freshly ground black pepper
sprig of lemon basil
thick-sliced whole grain bread

Artfully arrange vegetables and cheese on a plate. Drizzle on some extra-virgin olive oil, sprinkle with freshly ground black pepper, and garnish with lemon basil. Serve with whole-grain bread. Makes 1 very easy, very satisfying lunch or snack.

Mexican "Succotash"   Jill Watson, Taqueria Gila Monster Restaurant

4 chayote (substitute zucchini or summer squash)
5 tablespoons raw pumpkin seeds
1 bunch cilantro
1/4 cup garlic cloves, peeled
2 tablespoons vegetable oil

1 yellow onion, thinly sliced
3 cups fresh corn kernels
3 poblano chiles
1 1/2 tablespoons salt
1 1/2 tablespoons freshly squeezed lime juice

Cook chayote in boiling water until crisp-tender. Cut into small cubes. Toast pumpkin seeds over medium-low flame until they all pop. Stem the cilantro and place in food processor with pumpkin seeds and garlic; process to a coarse paste. Heat oil over medium-high heat, add sliced onions, and sauté until translucent. Add pumpkin seed mixture; sauté until fragrant. Add chayote and corn kernels; warm over low heat. Roast chiles over flame until skins blister and blacken somewhat. Place in sealed plastic bag to steam a few minutes. When chiles are cool, peel, seed and cut them into fine strips. Add to squash mixture; season with salt and lime juice. Serve with warm corn tortillas, beans, rice and salsa. Makes 6-8 servings.

Mexican Pickled Vegetables   MACSAC

Pickling ingredients:
3 cups vinegar (cider or fruit vinegar
   would be best)
1/2 cup vegetable oil
8 bay leaves
1 tablespoon dried thyme
2 tablespoons dried oregano
1 tablespoon pepper
2 teaspoons salt
2 heads fresh garlic, quartered
1/4 cup pickled jalapeños, sliced
1/2 cup pickled jalapeño juice

Vegetables:
4 pounds carrots, sliced thickly
2 large green peppers, in chunks
1-2 large onions, thick-sliced

Combine all pickling ingredients with 6 cups water in large, nonreactive pot (stainless steel works great). Bring to boil and add the vegetables. Bring to a boil; turn off heat and cover pot. Let stand 6-8 hours (stir occasionally, if possible). Chill and keep refrigerated.

French Ratatouille   Linda and Roger Petterson, Harmony Valley Farm members

sliced tomatoes
1-2 heads garlic, peeled and slivered
zucchini, eggplant, onions, and green pepper,
   all cut into 1 1/2-inch chunks

chopped fresh parsley
chopped fresh basil
olive oil

Heat oven to 300 degrees. Starting with tomatoes, layer vegetables and herbs in baking dish, filling it very full. Drizzle 1-2 tablespoons olive oil over each layer. Cover and bake 3 hours. If soupy, uncover during last hour. Baste with liquid if you like. Makes any number of servings.

Southwestern Strata   MACSAC

1 1/2-2 cups cooked dried beans
   (a red or black variety is best)
1/2 cup chopped sweet red pepper
1/2 cup corn kernels
1/4 cup minced green onion
5 eggs
1 2/3 cups milk

1 cup tomato salsa
1/2 cup sour cream
2 tablespoons chopped cilantro
1 teaspoon cumin
5 6-inch flour tortillas
1/2-1 cup shredded sharp cheddar

Combine beans, red pepper, corn, and green onions in bowl. Whisk eggs and milk in second bowl. Combine salsa, sour cream, cilantro, and cumin in third bowl. Oil a deep, round baking dish that's about the width of a tortilla. Place a tortilla in dish. Spread on a quarter of the bean mixture. Pour on a quarter of the milk mixture. Repeat layers 3 more times and end with a tortilla. Spread sour cream mixture over top. Refrigerate 3 or more hours. Heat oven to 350 degrees. Sprinkle cheese over strata. Bake until firm, 45-55 minutes. Makes 6 servings.

Grilled Summer Vegetable Pasta Salad   MACSAC

1 zucchini
1 yellow squash
1 eggplant
4 tomatoes
4 portobello mushrooms
1 red bell pepper
olive oil spray

3 tablespoons garlic powder
salt and pepper to taste
1 pound penne, cooked, rinsed, and cooled
4 ounces fresh mozzarella, sliced
3 tablespoons toasted pine nuts
3 tablespoons chopped fresh basil
approximately 1 cup vinaigrette made with
   balsamic vinegar

Heat/prepare an outdoor grill. Slice zucchini, squash, and eggplant into long 1/2-thick "planks." Cut tomatoes in half. Remove stems from mushrooms. Cut pepper into quarters; discard core and seeds. Spray veggies with light coating of oil. Sprinkle with garlic powder; season with salt and pepper. Grill until lightly charred and barely tender. Chop and place in large bowl with pasta, cheese, nuts, and basil. Toss with vinaigrette. Season with salt and pepper. Makes 6-8 servings.

Pasta Ramatuelle   Margaret Pennings, Common Harvest Farm

1 cup packed fresh basil
1 small onion
1/4-1/2 cup olive oil (or to taste)
3 large cloves garlic

5-6 tomatoes
salt and pepper to taste
1 pound rotini
freshly grated Parmesan

Blend all ingredients except rotini and Parmesan in a blender or food processor. Cook rotini, drain, and mix with basil/garlic mixture. Top with Parmesan. Makes 6-8 servings.

Late Summer Bruschetta   Bridget Zinn, Vermont Valley Farm member

2-3 large tomatoes
1 crunchy sweet pepper
1 medium sweet onion
2-3 cloves garlic, minced

olive oil
small handful fresh basil, chopped (optional)
crusty bread (like baguette)
shredded mozzarella or grated Parmesan (optional)

Chop the vegetables into a midsize dice. Combine with garlic, 1-2 tablespoons olive oil, and optional basil. Slice baguette down the middle and lay the 2 sides cut side up. Brush with additional 1-2 tablespoons oil and sprinkle on cheese, if using. Broil bread for several minutes until bread or cheese browns a bit. Top the sections (you may cut them smaller, if desired) with some of the vegetable mixture. This recipe is similar to one eaten at the Lawn Beach Inn in Lake Nebagamon, Wisconsin. Makes 4 servings.

Grand Gazpacho Salad   MACSAC

Dressing:
12 teaspoons minced garlic, mashed to a paste
2 tablespoons red wine vinegar
1 tablespoon Worcestershire sauce
1 teaspoon sugar
4 tablespoons olive oil
salt and pepper to taste

Salad:
5 large heirloom tomatoes, seeded and chopped
3 tablespoons chopped fresh parsley
salt and pepper
1/3 cup finely chopped sweet onion
1/2 cup each green pepper; peeled, seeded cucumber;
   hard-cooked eggs, all finely chopped
freshly grated Parmesan

Mix first 4 dressing ingredients; whisk in olive oil and season with salt and pepper. Layer ingredients in a clear glass bowl in the order above. Chill before serving. Makes 5-6 servings.

Easy Eggplant Cheese Casserole   Dela Ends, Scotch Hill Farm

olive oil
2 small eggplants (about 1 pound total),
   sliced into 1/3-inch-thick rounds
salt and pepper
1 onion, sliced into rounds

1 red or green pepper, cut into strips
2 cups tomato sauce or chopped fresh tomatoes
3-4 tablespoons chopped fresh basil
1 cup grated mozzarella and/or Parmesan

Heat 2 tablespoons oil in nonstick skillet; add eggplant and cook (in batches if necessary) on both sides until barely tender. Lay eggplant in a baking dish and season well with salt and pepper. Sauté onions and pepper strips until barely tender in a bit more oil. (Alternatively, you may brush vegetables with oil and grill them.) Layer onions and peppers over eggplant. Season with salt and pepper. Cover with tomato sauce (or tomatoes) and basil. Top with cheese. Bake at 375 degrees, 45 minutes. This can easily be increased to feed a crowd. Summer squash can be substituted or used with eggplant. Serve with a big salad, fresh bread, and goat cheese. Makes 4 servings.

Crostini with Leeks and Sweet Peppers   MACSAC

1 1/2 tablespoons olive oil
2 leeks (about 2/3 pound), sliced into
   1/4-inch-thick rounds
1 large sweet red pepper, cut into small diamonds

1/2 cup Greek olives, pitted and chopped
3-4 tablespoons vinaigrette
salt and pepper to taste
sourdough bread, thinly sliced and toasted

Heat olive oil in skillet over medium flame. Add leeks; cook 3-5 minutes. Add sweet peppers; cook, stirring, until mostly tender, 3-5 minutes. Add olives and vinaigrette; cool. Season with salt and pepper. Serve at room temperature on toasted bread. Makes 2-3 cups leek mixture.

Eggplant Italian Sausage Stew   MACSAC

3 tablespoons olive oil, divided
2 pounds hot or mild Italian sausage links
1 large onion, cut into chunks
2 tablespoons minced garlic
2 teaspoons oregano
2 pounds eggplant, peeled (if desired),
   cut into chunks

3 pounds plum tomatoes, peeled and quartered
1 1/2 cups dry red wine
1 1/2 teaspoons freshly ground fennel seeds
   (use a mortar and pestle or coffee grinder)
2 bay leaves
salt and pepper to taste
freshly grated Parmesan

Heat a little olive oil in skillet over high heat, add sausage, and brown well. Reduce heat to low; continue cooking sausages, turning occasionally, 15 minutes. Drain on paper towels. Heat remaining olive oil in large pot over medium heat. Add onions, garlic, and oregano; cook until translucent. Raise heat to medium, add eggplant, and cook until eggplant begins to color, 5-10 minutes. Stir in tomatoes, wine, fennel, and bay leaves. Simmer 30 minutes. Cut sausages into chunks; add to stew. Simmer 10-15 minutes longer. Season with salt and pepper. If possible, let stew come to room temperature, then reheat to serve. Serve with Parmesan. Makes 8-10 servings.

Eggplant Potato Moussaka   MACSAC

2 pounds eggplant
salt
1 1/2 pounds large potatoes
1 1/2 tablespoons olive oil
2 cups chopped onions
2 1/2 cups spaghetti (Italian tomato) sauce
1 teaspoon dried oregano
1/4 teaspoon cinnamon

5-6 tablespoons chopped fresh parsley, divided
pepper
4 tablespoons butter
scant 1/2 cup flour
2 1/4 cups milk
1/8 teaspoon nutmeg
3 eggs
1/2 cup freshly grated Parmesan

Cut eggplants lengthwise into 1/4-inch planks. Sprinkle both sides with 1-2 tablespoons salt; drain in colander 30 minutes. Rinse, squeeze out liquid, and place on oiled baking sheet. Bake in 400-degree oven, turning once, until tender (about 20 minutes). Meanwhile, peel potatoes and cut lengthwise into 1/8-inch slices. Boil in salted water until not quite tender. Drain. Heat olive oil in skillet, add onions, and sauté until tender. Stir in spaghetti sauce, oregano, cinnamon, half the parsley, and pepper to taste. Simmer low until very thick, about 30 minutes. Melt butter in saucepan, stir in flour, and cook over low heat a few minutes. Meanwhile, heat milk with nutmeg and salt and pepper to taste. Whisk hot milk into flour mixture; cook until thickened. Beat eggs in small bowl; whisk a few tablespoons of the white sauce into eggs, then whisk egg mixture into sauce. Stir and cook over low heat until thick; do not boil. Stir in Parmesan, a little at a time, until sauce is smooth. Taste and adjust seasonings. Layer half the eggplant, half the potatoes, and half the tomato sauce in a deep baking dish. Repeat these layers. Pour white sauce over all. Bake in 350-degree oven until topping is set and lightly browned, 45-60 minutes. Let stand at least 10 minutes before cutting. Garnish with remaining chopped parsley. Makes 12 servings.

Barbecued Vegetable Toss   MACSAC

1 teaspoon minced garlic
1 tablespoon minced fresh rosemary
   (or other herb)
1/2 teaspoon salt
4 tablespoons red wine vinegar

4 tablespoons olive oil
salt and pepper to taste
8 cups assorted vegetables, cut into equal-size
   chunks, such as: zucchini, onions, peppers,
   mushrooms, eggplant, parboiled potatoes

Mash garlic, rosemary, and salt to a paste. Stir in vinegar, olive oil, salt, and pepper. Toss in vegetables to coat. Heat coals for outdoor grill. Skewer vegetables (one-of-a-kind per skewer), then grill over medium-hot coals, turning often, until tender. Toss vegetables with marinade again to soak it all up; serve hot or at room temperature. Makes 4 servings.

Lusty Mediterranean Pasta   MACSAC

2 tablespoons olive oil
1 cup diced red onion
1-2 tablespoons minced fresh garlic
4 cups seeded, chopped plum tomatoes
1 jar (6 1/2 ounces) marinated artichoke hearts
1 roasted red pepper, chopped
1 tablespoon capers

3-4 anchovy fillets, minced
1-2 tablespoons balsamic vinegar
2 tablespoons chopped fresh parsley
salt and freshly ground black pepper
12 ounces pasta (penne, rotini, or other short
   or tubular shape)
freshly grated Parmesan

Heat olive oil in saucepan over medium flame; add onions and garlic; sauté until tender. Stir in tomatoes. Slice artichokes and add these with liquid from their jar. Bring to simmer; add roasted peppers, capers, anchovies, vinegar, and parsley. Simmer 15 minutes. Add salt and pepper to taste. Cook pasta in salted boiling water until tender. Drain well, toss with sauce, cover, and let stand 5 minutes in a warm place. Toss again with lots of fresh Parmesan. Makes 4-6 servings.

Creamy Broccoli Parsnip Soup with a Considerable Kick of Curry   MACSAC

2 tablespoons butter
3/4 cup chopped onions
4 cups vegetable stock
2 cups chopped parsnips
3 1/2-4 cups coarsely chopped broccoli florets

1 teaspoon bottled red curry paste
1/4 teaspoon ground cumin
1 cup milk
salt and pepper to taste

Melt butter in saucepan over medium flame. Add onions and cook, stirring occasionally, until tender, 6-8 minutes. Add stock and parsnips. Bring to simmer, cover, and cook gently until parsnips are nearly tender, 5-6 minutes. Stir in broccoli, curry paste, and cumin; cook until broccoli is tender, 5-6 minutes. Partially puree the mixture, so that some small chunks remain suspended in a smooth base. Stir in milk and season with salt and pepper. Makes 5 servings.

Parsley Potato Carrot "Hash"   MACSAC

2 tablespoons olive oil
1-2 tablespoons butter
1 1/2 pounds potatoes, scrubbed and cut into
   small cubes

1 large carrot (about 1/2 pound), scrubbed and
   cut into small cubes
salt and pepper
1/4-1/3 cup finely chopped shallots
1/3-1/2 cup coarsely chopped fresh parsley

Heat olive oil and butter in a cast-iron skillet over medium flame. Add potatoes and carrots, season generously with salt and pepper, and toss well. Cook undisturbed 4-5 minutes to brown on one side, then toss and brown again for 4-5 minutes. Lower heat, stir in shallots, and continue to cook, stirring occasionally, until tender. Stir in parsley. Note: You could add chopped ham, chicken, or hard-cooked eggs to the mixture along with the parsley. Makes 4-6 servings.

Orecchiette with Pumpkin, Pecans, and Shallot Sage Brown Butter   MACSAC

5-6 ounces orecchiette ("little ears") pasta
6-8 tablespoons butter
3 tablespoons finely chopped shallots
2 teaspoons minced garlic
2 tablespoons minced fresh sage

3 cups cubed, cooked pumpkin
salt and pepper to taste
1/2 cup chopped, toasted pecans
   (toast at 350 degrees, 6-10 minutes)
freshly grated Parmesan

Cook pasta in lots of boiling salted water until tender. Meanwhile, heat butter over medium flame in large skillet. Add shallots, garlic, and sage; cook until butter just begins to brown. Reduce heat to low and stir in pumpkin. Add salt and pepper. Drain pasta; toss with pumpkin and pecans. Serve immediately with freshly ground Parmesan. Makes 4-6 servings.

Spanish Potato Pepper Stew   MACSAC

1 1/2 tablespoons olive oil
1 cup chopped onion
3 pounds potatoes, peeled and thick-sliced
6 ounces andouille or other smoked spicy
   sausage, chopped
1 can (14 1/2 ounces) chicken broth

1 bell pepper, quartered and thick-sliced
3 tablespoons chopped flat-leaf parsley
2 tablespoons sweet paprika
1/2 ounce dried ancho or Anaheim chiles,
   soaked in hot water (optional)
salt

Heat olive oil in large, heavy pot over medium-high heat. Add onions; sauté until limp. Stir in potatoes and sausage; cook 10 minutes, stirring often. Add 1 cup chicken broth; cook, stirring often, 10 minutes. Add remaining broth, peppers, parsley, paprika, and 1/2 cup water. If you are using chiles, drain, remove seeds, mince, and add to potatoes. Simmer, stirring occasionally, until potatoes are tender and sauce is thickened, 15-20 minutes. Season to taste with salt. This recipe is adapted from one in *The Mediterranean Diet Cookbook,* by Nancy Harmon Jenkins. Serve it as main course or side dish, or even for brunch. Makes 6-8 servings.

Hearty Turnip Herb Dip   Lisa Kivirist and John Ivanko, Inn Serendipity

2 tablespoons lemon juice
2/3 cup vegetable oil
1 1/2 cups whole wheat flour
1 cup sunflower seeds
3-5 garlic cloves, minced or crushed through a
   garlic press
1 1/2 cups nutritional yeast
1/4 cup soy sauce
2 teaspoons dried basil

1 teaspoon dried thyme
1 teaspoon dried sage
1/2 teaspoon nutmeg
2 cups boiling water
3 cups shredded turnips
1 1/2 cups very thinly sliced or shredded onion
1 1/2 cups shredded carrot
6 bay leaves

Heat oven to 350 degrees. Grease a 9-by-13-inch baking dish. Combine 7 seven ingredients and stir well. Stir in spices and boiling water. Add vegetables; stir until well combined. Pour mixture into baking dish; arrange bay leaves on top and press them lightly into the mixture. Bake until firm and golden brown, about 1 hour. Serve warm or cold (but not hot out of the oven) with rye crackers. This recipe can be made with a variety of shredded root vegetables, depending on tastes. Combinations of turnips, beets, potatoes, carrots, and onions work well. Makes enough to serve 8-10 as an appetizer.

Braised Lamb with Red Peppers, Potatoes, and Zucchini   MACSAC

4 lamb shoulder steaks
1 teaspoon olive oil
1 small sliced onion
1 tablespoon minced garlic
2 sweet red peppers, thin-sliced

3 cups chicken stock
3-4 small russet potatoes, peeled
1/2-1 cup sliced zucchini
1/2 cup Greek olives
salt and pepper

Remove excess fat from lamb. Heat oil in braising pan over high flame. Brown meat. Remove meat from pan and reduce heat to medium. Add onions, garlic, and red peppers; sauté a few minutes. Add stock; bring to simmer, return meat to the pan, cover the pan, and cook over very low heat, 45 minutes. Cube potatoes. Add potatoes to stew; cover and simmer until everything is tender and potatoes have thickened the broth, 25-35 minutes (you can crush some of the potatoes against the side of the pan to thicken it more, if desired). Add the zucchini and olives during the final 10 minutes of cooking. Season to taste with salt and pepper. Serve with couscous or rice. Makes 4-6 servings.

Root Vegetable Gratin with Cheddar and Horseradish Rye Crumb Crust   MACSAC

1 pound rutabaga, peeled and cut into chunks
1 pound sweet potatoes, peeled and cut
   into chunks
1/2 pound parsley root or turnip, peeled and
   cut into chunks
1-2 tablespoons olive oil
1/3 cup apple cider or wine
1 tablespoon minced garlic

salt and pepper
3 tablespoons butter
3 tablespoons flour
2 cups whole milk, heated
1/8 teaspoon nutmeg
2 tablespoons horseradish
4 ounces grated aged cheddar cheese
1/2 cup rye bread crumbs

Heat oven to 375 degrees. Spread vegetables in large baking dish, drizzle with olive oil and cider or wine, scatter on the garlic, season to taste with salt and pepper, and toss well. Cover dish tightly with aluminum foil and bake 20 minutes, then remove foil and continue to roast until vegetables are brown-tipped and tender, 20-35 minutes longer. Meanwhile, make a white sauce by melting the butter in a saucepan; stir in flour and cook over low heat several minutes. Whisk in milk, bring to simmer, and cook gently 10 minutes, stirring often. Season well with salt and pepper. Stir in nutmeg. Gently fold the sauce into the roasted vegetables. Transfer to a buttered baking dish (or leave it in the same dish the vegetables were roasted in). Mix horseradish, cheddar, and bread crumbs with your fingers and scatter the mixture evenly over the vegetables. Continue to bake until bubbly, 20-30 minutes. Makes 6 servings.

Corn Bread and Pine Nut-Stuffed Acorn Squash   MACSAC

8 very small acorn squash or other very
   small winter squash
1 cup finely chopped red onion
6 tablespoons butter, divided
1 cup finely chopped sweet red or green pepper
4 cups stale corn bread in 1-inch cubes (equivalent
   to approximately 1 8-by-8-inch pan of corn bread)

6 tablespoons pine nuts
3 tablespoons chopped fresh oregano
salt and pepper
3-6 tablespoons apple cider

Heat oven to 350 degrees. Cut a thin slice off bottom of each squash, so it can stand up. Cut off a quarter of each squash from the top and discard. Scoop out seeds and membranes. Place squashes top side down in baking dish; add water to depth of 1/4 inch. Cover with foil; bake until tender, 45-60 minutes. Discard water. Melt 3 tablespoons butter in skillet over medium heat. Add onions and cook, stirring often, until nearly tender. Add sweet peppers and cook, stirring often, 3-4 minutes. Crumble the corn bread; combine with cooked vegetables, pine nuts, oregano, and salt and pepper to taste. Stir in just enough apple cider to moisten stuffing. Fill squash cavities with stuffing. Melt remaining 3 tablespoons butter; drizzle or brush on stuffing. Place in baking dish and bake at 350 degrees about 30 minutes. Makes 8 servings.

Winter Squash, Leek, and Saffron Risotto   MACSAC

5-6 cups chicken stock
1/2 teaspoon saffron threads, pulverized
3 tablespoons olive oil
1/2-1 cup finely chopped leeks
   (white and pale green sections only)

1 1/2 cups arborio rice
2/3 cup dry white wine
2-3 cups cooked, pureed winter squash
3/4-1 cup grated Parmesan, romano, or asiago cheese
salt and pepper

Bring stock and saffron to a simmer in saucepan. Heat olive oil in large, heavy saucepan. Add leeks; cook over medium-low heat until softened, several minutes. Raise heat to medium-high and stir in rice. Keep stirring rice 1-2 minutes, then add wine. Stir and cook until nearly all the wine has evaporated, about 2 minutes. Add two ladlefuls hot stock (enough to barely cover the rice); stir frequently until most is absorbed. Continue to add stock a ladleful at a time and stir very frequently until nearly absorbed. Risotto is done when rice is barely tender and mixture is creamy; this should take 25-35 minutes. (Adjust heat if rice is absorbing liquid too quickly.) Stir in squash during last 10 minutes. Fold in most of the grated cheese. Season with salt and pepper to taste. Serve immediately, with a little more cheese on top of each serving. Makes 6-8 servings.

Lauri's Favorite Winter Salad with Creamy Tahini Dressing

Lauri McKean, Zephyr Community Farm member

2 cups any combination of grated beets,
   carrots, and/or red cabbage
2 cups any combination of grated celeriac,
   turnips, kohlrabi, Jerusalem artichokes,
   green cabbage, and/or winter radish

1 1/2 cups chopped kale and/or parsley
1 medium red onion, finely chopped
1 cup sprouts (optional)
1/2 cup chopped fennel (optional)

Toss all ingredients and serve with Creamy Tahini Dressing, below, or your favorite dressing. Makes 4-6 servings.

Creamy Tahini Dressing

3 tablespoons sesame seeds
1/2 cup tahini
1/4 cup lemon juice
1/4 cup sesame oil

1/4 cup canola oil
1/4 cup soy sauce, tamari, or shoyu
dash of bottled hot pepper sauce or pinch of cayenne
1 teaspoon dried dill weed

Toast sesame seeds in dry skillet or hot oven several minutes, tossing often. Cool and mix with remaining ingredients and 1/4 cup water. Makes 1 1/2 cups.

Drawing by Sarah Thomas, age 12

Kids' Recipes

Barb and Rebecca Perkins

What if your kids don't eat vegetables? What if they say they don't like vegetables? That's the challenge and the fun. Community supported farms offer so many opportunities for involvement that kids can't help gaining an understanding, appreciation, and "friendship" with the vegetables and with the farm where their food is grown.

In our own experience, kids become involved by learning to cook and eat the vegetables and through visits to the farm. It starts when farm members pick up their vegetables from a drop-off site each week. Children look forward to this weekly ritual. As they approach the site, they may be asking: "I wonder if we'll be getting any more of those yummy peas?" "What was that round, purple one we had last week? I liked it. I hope we have another one this week." "I want more spinach."

Different farms distribute vegetables in different ways; they may be preboxed, prebagged, or in bulk waiting for you to pack them. You may also have some vegetable choices. Kids get excited by and involved in this process. They examine the newfound vegetables, feel the textures, look at the shapes and colors, and even find that vegetables have distinct smells. "What is it?" "I wonder what it tastes like?" These discoveries put food and eating in a new light for children.

What happens when these new and interesting vegetables find their way to your kitchen? Most vegetables can be eaten and enjoyed raw. Dipping vegetables into a favorite dip is a good, nutritious, and fun way for kids to get to know different vegetables and pass the time while someone is making dinner. Most kids like vegetables alone, not mixed up with other things. Steam a couple different vegetables and let the kids eat them that way. Get the kids involved in food preparation as well; let them scrub, scrape, grate, and chop.

A city child is likely to discover objects of interest and amusement at the farm: the animals, the stream, the dog, the dirt, the barn, the tractor, the insects, other kids, the open space, the vegetables, the tire swing, and the plants. A visit to the farm lets your child become aware of the origin of the vegetables that he or she eats, and understand that the vegetables they eat are grown on a real farm by real people, with whom they are connected.

Children also learn about the process of farming and how a CSA farm works by visiting the farm. According to Rebecca, age 11, there is much work to be done on a CSA farm. She lists the types of work she has been involved in or seen at the farm. First, the farmers order seeds from a vegetable catalog. Second, they plant the seeds in flats and care for them in the greenhouse until the seedlings are ready to be planted. Third, while the plants are growing the farmers weed, water, watch, and pick bugs off the plants. Fourth, the farmers harvest the vegetables by digging or picking them. Fifth, after all the vegetables are harvested, the farmers pack them in boxes or bags. Sixth, the farmers bring the vegetables to delivery sites where people come and pick them up. Seventh, members have vegetables at their houses that they eat for meals. Rebecca notes that belonging to a CSA may change the way you eat, but in a good way.

Children get more excited about eating vegetables when they see how they are grown and help prepare them. So have fun with the vegetables. Listen to what the kids have to say about them. Keep it simple and ENJOY!

Barb Perkins is a member of MACSAC and farmer at Vermont Valley Farm. She and her husband Dave have three children, and she has worked in family child care since 1985. Barb has a strong interest in integrating children into farms and food preparation. She has found that the more her children are in touch with where their vegetables come from, the more likely they are to try them.

Kid-Friendly Salad Dressing   Oak Ridge Farm

3 tablespoons mayonnaise
1/4 cup olive oil
2 tablespoons lemon juice

1 small garlic clove, pressed
salt to taste

Mix all ingredients. Makes 1/2 cup.

Cheesy Spinach   Max, the cook at Red Caboose Day Care Center

Mix:
3 eggs
1 1/2 teaspoons lemon juice
1 cup brown rice, cooked
1 1/2 teaspoons dried parsley
2 tablespoons grated Parmesan cheese (optional)
salt and pepper to taste

Mix separately:
1 large bunch of spinach, chopped and steamed
1 cup cottage cheese
1 cup grated cheddar cheese
4 eggs
salt and pepper to taste
a pinch of cayenne pepper

Spread the ingredients from the first mixture in the bottom of a greased casserole. Spread the spinach mixture over them. Bake at 350 degrees until firm, 45-60 minutes. Makes 10-12 servings.

Red Green Yellow Chicken Kebabs
Katie Koza, REAP Food for Thought Recipe Contest Winner, 2003 (Elementary school category)

1 teaspoon Chinese 5-spice powder
2 pounds boneless, skinless chicken, cut
   into 1-inch pieces
2 medium zucchini, cut in 1/2-inch slices
2 medium yellow summer squash, cut in
   1/2-inch slices
18 cherry tomatoes

For the marinade:
1/2 cup soy sauce
1/2 cup honey
1 walnut-size piece of ginger, grated
1/2 cup catsup
1/4 teaspoon pepper
1 clove garlic, minced
Also needed: skewers and cooking spray

Sprinkle 5-spice powder on chicken; toss well. Mix marinade ingredients; pour over chicken. Marinate at least 1 hour in the refrigerator. Put vegetables and chicken on skewers. Spray with cooking spray and grill on low for 20 minutes, turning once. Enjoy! Makes 6 servings.

Spinach Roll-Ups   Peggy's Biodynamic Gardens

fresh whole spinach leaves

food for stuffing: peanut butter, cheese, meats, etc.

Roll the stuffing(s) up in the spinach leaves.

Bean-Nut Pasta and Veggie Confetti   Kris Rasmussen, Dog Hollow Farm member

8 ounces pasta (break up if using long noodles)
1 cup Veggie Confetti (recipe on next page)

1 cup Bean-Nut Butter (recipe on next page)

Cook pasta and drain. Toss with Bean-Nut Butter and Veggie Confetti. Serve hot or cold. Makes 6-8 servings.

Bean-Nut Butter   Kris Rasmussen, Dog Hollow Farm member

2 cups cooked garbanzo beans   1/4 cup hot water
3/4 cup peanut butter

Combine beans and peanut butter in food processor or blender. Slowly add water while processor is running until mixture is light and smooth. Makes 2 or more cups.

Veggie Confetti   Kris Rasmussen, Dog Hollow Farm member

2 carrots   1 red bell pepper
2 small zucchini   corn from 2 ears of sweet corn

Dice carrots, zucchini and pepper to size of corn kernels. Steam corn and carrots 4 minutes. Add zucchini and steam 3 minutes longer. Add red pepper and steam 1 minute longer. Toss veggies and serve hot or chilled. (The confetti is also great in corn muffins.) Makes about 3 cups.

Zucchini Pie   Twinhawks Hollow Farm

1 big zucchini   1/2 cup sugar
apple pie spices to taste   pastry for double pie crust
2 tablespoons flour

Cut the zucchini into slices (as you would an apple) and mix with spices, flour, and sugar. Fill pie crust, cover with more pastry, and bake as you would an apple pie.

Wrap-Up-the-Harvest Veggie Sandwich   Wisconsin Homegrown Lunch

1 soft flour tortilla (kids like the naturally   1/4 cup grated carrot
  colored ones)   1/4 cup shredded purple cabbage
1 tablespoon cream cheese, plain yogurt, or   several fresh spinach leaves
  other favorite dressing   1 ounce sliced turkey, if desired

Spread cream cheese on tortilla (or a dressing can be drizzled on top of veggies). Add veggies and turkey (if using), roll up like a burrito, and enjoy! Or you can fold in all 4 sides to make an easy-to-hold wrap. This recipe was created as a main dish for a Wisconsin Homegrown Lunch event in 2003. It has lots of healthy ingredients and can be seasonally adapted with different vegetables—and kids and adults love it. Makes 1 serving.

Pumpkin Cookies   Scotch Hill Farm

1 cup butter or margarine   1 tablespoon cinnamon
1 1/4 cups brown sugar   2 teaspoons baking powder
2 eggs   2 teaspoons baking soda
1 teaspoon vanilla   2 teaspoons nutmeg
2 cups cooked pumpkin   1/2 cup raisins
4 3/4 cups flour

Heat oven to 350 degrees. Grease 2 cookie sheets. Cream butter or margarine and brown sugar. Mix in eggs, vanilla, and pumpkin. Mix dry ingredients separately, then stir into first mixture. Stir in raisins. Drop by spoonfuls onto cookie sheets. Bake 15 minutes.

Yam Kaopoon Taii (Bean Noodle Salad)

Crystal Khamphouy, REAP Food for Thought Recipe Contest Winner, 2003 (middle school category)

8-12 ounces boneless, skinless chicken breast
2 small packages Lungkow bean thread noodles
1/2 cup sugar
1 cup Mae Ploy brand bottled chili sauce
1/2 cup fresh lime juice

1/2 cup bottled fish sauce
1/2 cup each thinly sliced cabbage, purple
  cabbage, carrots, purple onion and yellow onion
1/2 cup sweet Thai basil leaves, cut into small pieces
1/2-1 cup chopped peanuts

Simmer chicken in water until tender; let cool, then cut into thin pieces. Soak bean thread noodles in water 10 minutes. Drain. Then soak them in boiling water briefly; drain right away. To make dressing: Bring 1/2 cup water to boil in saucepan, then add sugar; let it cool. Stir in Mae Ploy sauce, lime juice, and fish sauce until well combined. Toss with chicken, noodles, all the vegetables, the basil, and peanuts. Makes 4 servings.

Double-the-Fun Tacos MACSAC

large flour tortillas
hot refried beans
hard taco shells
cooked chicken, pork, or black beans
shredded lettuce
chopped green onions
chopped tomatoes

chopped green peppers
chopped zuchhini
shredded cheese
sliced black olives
sour cream
mild salsa

Heat a tortilla briefly in a hot skillet or on the grill. Spread refried beans over it (don't spread beans all the way to the edges). Place a taco shell in middle of tortilla and fold up tortilla around the shell (the beans are the "glue"). Fill the taco shell with your choice of any of the remaining ingredients. Dig in. Makes 1 serving.

Mint-ato   Emma Conover-Crockett, REAP Food for Thought Recipe Contest Winner, 2003 (elementary school category)

2 mint leaves   1 cherry tomato

Put mint leaves in your mouth. Spit them out. Then eat the tomato. Makes 1 bite.

Home Food Preservation

Lauri McKean

Preserving local foods in your home is a great way to continue eating locally throughout the winter months. Foods preserved at home are usually less expensive and much tastier than those purchased at the store. Home food preservation also provides an outlet for surplus farm and garden produce. In addition, foods preserved at home—applesauce, pickles, jams and jellies, pesto, strings of dried peppers—make wonderful gifts.

Preserving foods at home can be fairly simple. Many people already know the basics of freezing greens, dehydrating herbs, and storing potatoes and onions. Although canning is a bit more complicated, it can be learned from books, videos, or other people. In this section, I will focus on the food preservation techniques that are the easiest to learn: freezing, dehydrating, and cold storage. I will also briefly outline techniques for canning, pickling, and preserving jams and jellies. This brief introduction is not intended to be an instruction manual for any of these procedures, and I encourage everyone interested in home food preservation to consult the resources section at the end of this book.

Freezing

Freezing food is probably the most common and easiest method of food preservation in this country. Freezing maintains the vitamin content of food better than most other preserving methods. Many people feel that freezing food best sustains the original flavor and texture of food, too. Freezing small quantities of excess produce in your refrigerator-freezer is very economical, in that no special equipment is needed. But freezing can be more costly in terms of money and energy if you are using a separate upright or chest freezer. If you are planning on purchasing a freezer, consider choosing the more energy-efficient chest model.

Freezing preserves food by stopping the growth of microorganisms. To obtain the best quality, it is important to package food in containers that are designed for freezer storage, like rigid freezer containers (plastic or glass), plastic freezer bags (fasten them securely), or heavy weight aluminum foil, plastic films, or waxed freezer paper. These containers keep moisture in and air out. If you are using rigid containers, it is best to fill them almost full to reduce the amount of air in the package. When freezing foods that contain liquids, leave at least 1/2 inch of space at the top for expansion. When using bags, press the air out of the unused part before sealing.

Blanching: With the exception of peppers, tomatoes, cooked pumpkin or squash, onions, and herbs, all vegetables need to be blanched before freezing. Blanching stops enzymatic action in vegetables and prevents off-flavors, discoloration, destruction of nutrients, and toughness. Blanching involves heating the vegetable briefly in either boiling water or steam.

Blanching times vary with the size and kind of vegetable. For example, peas are blanched in boiling water for 1 1/2 minutes, whereas corn on the cob takes 6-8 minutes to blanch. Blanching with steam takes slightly longer. In general, a vegetable has been blanched long enough when it brightens in color. Consult a home food preservation book or pamphlet for recommended blanching times for each vegetable. After the vegetables have been blanched, they need to be cooled immediately in a large quantity of cold or ice water. Cool vegetables for the same amount of time that they were blanched.

Antioxidants: Some fruits—including peaches, apples, and pears—will darken in color after they are peeled or cut for freezing. Although this does not affect the safety or taste of the fruit, you can prevent discoloration by using an antioxidant. There are three readily available antioxidants:

(1) Ascorbic acid (vitamin C) can be obtained in crystalline or tablet form. Dip the fruit in a mixture of 1/2 teaspoon ascorbic acid and 1 quart water for one minute.

(2) Commercial ascorbic-citric acid and ascorbic acid-sucrose mixtures are available in most grocery stores and should be used according to the manufacturer's directions.

(3) Lemon juice can be used to help prevent darkening, although it may not be as effective as the other options and may cause a slight flavor change. Use 1 tablespoon of lemon juice per quart of water as a dip.

Serving portions: When freezing food, you should consider how you will use it later. For example, you may want to freeze only a serving-size portion in each container in order to avoid having to chip away at a large block of frozen food. Another strategy is to place the individual pieces of food on a cookie sheet and freeze. Once they are frozen, transfer the individual pieces, which can then later be separated easily, to a plastic bag or rigid container. Some foods can be frozen in individual portions in an ice cube tray. For example, I puree large quantities of basil and spread it in an ice cube tray. Once the basil is frozen, I pop the cubes out of the tray into a freezer bag for further freezing. I use my individual basil cubes all winter long for soups and casseroles. This method works well with any type of herb, pesto, or chiles.

Dehydration

Dehydration is one of the most time-, energy-, and cost-efficient methods of food preservation. It is estimated that dehydrating costs less than canning and is 1/4 the cost of freezing. Dehydrated foods are easy to store since they shrink in size and are lighter in weight. A negative impact of dehydration is that significant amounts of vitamins A and C can be lost in the drying process. Nevertheless, dehydrated foods are wonderful for some types of cooking. In addition, it only takes a little bit of experimentation to learn how to cook with them.

Dehydration lowers the amount of moisture in the food to a point where microbes cannot survive and enzymatic changes cease. The temperatures needed to dehydrate food depend on the type of food being processed, ranging from 120 to 150 degrees (with the exception of herbs). As a general rule, dehydrate herbs at 95 degrees, vegetables at 125, fruits and fruit leathers at 135, and jerkies at 145.

The easiest and surest way to dehydrate food is to use an electric food dehydrator. These can be bought commercially or made at home. Several plans for home-made food dehydrators have been published in home food

preservation books (check the Resources list in this book). Electric dehydrators include trays to put the food on, a heating element, and some sort of air circulation method. Foods can also be dried in an oven as long as the door is left ajar 2-3 inches to allow for air circulation. This method, however, takes two to three times longer than using a dehydrator, is less energy efficient, and will heat up your house.

Although you will find plans for outdoor dehydrators in many magazines and books, most of these are designed for much drier climates. There are a few tested models that work in the upper Midwest. Plans for one of these are available by sending your request, $1.00, and an SASE to Larisa Walk and Bob Dahse, RR3 Box 163-A, Winona, MN 55987. I do not recommend drying meat in a solar dehydrator.

Herbs and peppers can be air-dried—even in high-humidity states. Simply attach herbs or peppers to a string and hang them in a well-ventilated and dry area. Enclosing herbs or peppers in paper bags will keep them from getting bleached or dusty. Herbs with short stems or larger, broad leaves can be air-dried by placing them on a screen. Herbs and leafy vegetables can also be dehydrated in a microwave.

As with freezing, dehydrated foods need to be correctly prepared before drying. Most vegetables need to be blanched before dehydrating to enhance color and flavor (tomatoes, peppers, and herbs are exceptions). Many fruits need to be placed in an antioxidant before dehydrating to prevent brown coloring (see the freezing section for more information on blanching and antioxidants). It is also important to cut the foods somewhat uniformly so that drying times are consistent.

The time required for complete dehydration depends on the thickness of the vegetable or fruit pieces and on the drying method used. Foods dried in a food dehydrator will take 6 or more hours (herbs take less time). Drying time is increased to 8 or more hours in an oven and to 1 to 2 days for solar dehydrating. Generally speaking, fruit drying is complete when the pieces are pliable, springy, and spongy and do not stick together. (Some fruits, like cherries and figs, will stick together when dried.) Vegetables should be brittle. Fruit leathers should be dry to the touch and peel away easily from plastic wrap.

Once the food is dehydrated, it should be stored in clean, dry containers—preferably away from light. Plastic bags or tightly sealed glass jars are good containers. Press the air out of bags and fill jars up completely to remove as much air as possible from the container.

Dehydrated foods can be fun, tasty, and nutritious. They are also easy to reuse—most just need to be rehydrated. This can be done as the food is being cooked (with soups) or by adding 1 1/2 to 2 cups of boiling water to each cup of dried vegetables. Generally speaking, dehydrated foods are best when used in soups, casseroles, sauces, stuffings, and stews. There are, however, a variety of other uses. Try dehydrating potatoes, onions, garlic, parsley, and an assortment of other vegetables to be pulverized and used as a soup broth. Dehydrated tomatoes are delicious when rehydrated and used in salads and pasta dishes or pureed in pesto. Dehydrated mixed vegetables make great soups and are handy for pack food on camping trips. Try using dehydrated fruits for snacks and in baking as well.

Cold Storage

Cold storage of winter vegetables is a wonderful option in states that get colder weather. Storing root crops, onions, garlic, and squashes in a cool environment is the easiest and most time- and cost-effective storage method available. When stored properly, the food retains its original taste and nutritional value. Even under optimal conditions, though, a small percentage of cold storage produce will spoil at some point. It is important to periodically check cold storage produce and remove spoiled foods.

An ordinary basement provides the minimum conditions needed for storing certain vegetables and fruits, including apples, pumpkins, and winter squash for several months and garlic, onions, and potatoes for much of the winter. Indoor and outdoor root cellars and other types of storage places present more optimal conditions. There are several low-cost options for creating optimal storage facilities, such as construction of a simple basement storage room, outdoor cellar, or temporary pits. Consult specific books and pamphlets on root cellaring to find plans for these facilities.

Some storage crops thrive on cool temperatures and moist conditions. Others need slightly warmer, dryer conditions.

The following is a list of the optimal conditions for various crops and approximate storage times.

Cold and moist conditions (32-40 degrees with 90-95 percent humidity): Root vegetables need to have their tops (greens) cut off before storage. They should also be placed in containers of damp sand, peat moss, sawdust, or leaves.

- beet, 1-3 months
- Brussels sprout, 3-5 weeks
- carrot, 4-6 months
- celeriac, 3-4 months
- celery, 2-3 months
- Chinese cabbage, 1-2 months
- horseradish, 10-12 months
- Jerusalem artichoke, 2-5 months
- kohlrabi, 2-4 weeks
- leek, 1-3 months
- parsnip, 2-6 months
- rutabaga, 2-4 months
- salsify, 2-4 months
- turnip, 4-5 months
- winter radish, 2-4 months

Cool and moist conditions (38-40 degrees with 80-90 percent humidity): Note: Do not store apples with potatoes, as they may cause potatoes to sprout.

- apple, 2-3 months
- pear, 1-2 months
- cabbage, 3-4 months
- potato, 5-8 months (keep in dark environs)

Cool and dry conditions (32-50 degrees with 60-70 percent humidity):

- garlic, 6-7 months
- onion, 5-8 months

Moderately warm and dry conditions (50-60 degrees with 60-75 percent humidity):

- pumpkin, 2-3 months
- winter squash, 3-6 months
- green tomato, 4-6 weeks
- dry bean, 1 year
- strings of dried peppers, 6 months

Humidity conditions can be monitored with a hygrometer, which can be purchased at most hardware stores. Humidity can be adjusted by packing storage vegetables in damp materials or by placing pans of water in a cold storage room or root cellar.

Canning

When compared with other methods of home food preservation, canning falls somewhere in the middle in terms of cost and vitamin loss. In its favor, canning often produces food that is of good quality and familiar (like applesauce, jams, and salsa). It does, however, take some time for preparation, canning, and cleanup. In addition, products canned incorrectly can harbor dangerous microorganisms or disease-causing spores. This should not be a problem if you always follow current and reliable guidelines.

There are two different canning methods. One is used for food that has a high acidity (ph of 4.6 or lower), and the other is used for low-acid foods. Both methods are explained below.

Water-bath canning for high-acid foods: This is the method used for most fruits, high-acid tomato varieties, and tested salsa recipes. The water bath canning method involves submersing the canning jars in boiling water for specific amounts of time. This submersion kills microorganisms that would cause spoilage and also creates a vacuum in each jar so the lid seals tight. This seal prevents the food from being contaminated by any other microorganisms. The minimal equipment needed for water-bath canning includes:

(1) A large pot with a tight-fitting lid. The pot must be large enough so that the level of the boiling water can be 2 inches above the top of the canning jars, and must have some sort of rack on the bottom so the jars are not in direct contact with the bottom of the pot. These racks are available commercially. Alternatively, canning rings can be used to line the bottom of the pot.

(2) Canning jars, which can be bought new or used. Canning jars come in many different sizes, ranging from 1/4 pint to 1 quart, and should be free of cracks and nicks on the lip.

(3) Lids for the canning jars. These are small disks that fit on top of the jar and are available commercially. Lids are not reusable, as they can form a tight seal only once.

(4) Rings that screw on each jar and hold the lid in place. Available commerically.

(5) A jar lifter or tongs to remove the jars from the boiling water. Available commercially.

Please consult a recent edition of a home food preservation book or University of Wisconsin (UW)-

Extension pamphlets for complete directions on canning high-acid foods. These resources are listed in the Resources section of this book.

Pressure canning for low-acid foods: Pressure canning is necessary for low-acid vegetables (any other besides tomatoes) and for canning meat. In order to make low-acid foods safe, the clostridium botulinum bacteria, which is found in soil and the food grown in the soil, must be destroyed. Botulinum bacteria spores are not destroyed in boiling temperatures, and thrive in low-acid (ph of 4.6 or higher), moist, and anaerobic conditions. These are precisely the conditions found in a jar of low-acid food if canned using the water-bath method. In order to make these foods safe, the food must reach 240 degrees Fahrenheit. This temperature is achieved by using pressure in a pressure canner.

Pressure canning involves using much of the same equipment listed in the water-bath canning section, except that a pressure canner replaces the large pot. Pressure canners can be purchased commercially and are available with either a dial or weighted gauge, which indicates when the jars have reached the necessary pressure.

For directions on pressure canning, please consult a recent edition of a home food preservation book or the UW-Extension pamphlets listed in the Resources section of the book.

Pickling

Pickling is one of the oldest known forms of preserving food. There are many different types of products that can be pickled, including fermented items such as sauerkraut and "deli" dills; fresh pack dill pickles; whole fruits (pears, peaches, and watermelon rinds) simmered in a spicy, sweet-sour syrup; and chopped, seasoned fruits and vegetables made into relishes.

Sauerkraut and other fermented pickles are preserved by the bacterial formation of lactic acid, which is acidic. The presence of salt also interferes with the growth of other microorganisms. In other pickled products, produce is combined with vinegar, which contains acetic acid and creates a high-acid environment. Pickled products should be processed in a water bath, which ensures that jars are sealed and microorganisms destroyed. The ratio of water to vinegar is important for the preservation of pickled products. Pickling recipes will specify the appropriate ratio to use—it is important not to alter these ratios.

There are several secrets to ensure that your pickled cucumbers are crunchy. First, use cucumbers that were bred for pickling—not those meant for slicing. Second, do not use cucumbers that float. Third, use cucumbers that are as fresh as possible and not more than 2 inches in diameter. Fourth, slice off the blossom end of the cucumber as it contains enzymes that can cause softening. Canning or pickling salt should be used for pickling. Iodized and regular table salt contain anti-caking agents and iodine, which will make the pickling solution cloudy and may cause darkening of the pickles.

The pickling process is not just for cucumbers! Try making some delicious dilly beans, green tomato pickles, pickled mixed vegetables, pickled onions, beet pickles, or corn relish. Using the water bath processing method to pickle can be easy and fun, and you'll be tickled (as well as pickled) with the results.

Jams and Jellies

"If you want the best jam, you've got to make your own," sings Michelle Shocked on her *Arkansas Traveler* album. I could not agree more. Homemade jam is a wonderful treat and makes great gifts as well. There are a variety of "jamlike" products that are easy to make. Jelly is a product made from fruit juice and is clear and firm. Jam is made from crushed fruit and is less firm than jelly. Preserves are made from large pieces or whole fruits packed in syrup. Conserves are made from a mixture of fruits, nuts, and raisins. Marmalade is made from pulpy fruits and is a clear, jellied liquid. Fruit butters are made by cooking pulpy fruits with sugar so they are easy to spread.

The sugar in jams, jellies, and other related products binds with water, creating an environment in which microorganisms cannot grow. Four ingredients are necessary to make these products: the fruit or juice, pectin and acid (both are responsible for gel formation), and sugar. Sweeteners such as honey, corn syrup, and fruit juice can be used as a partial or complete substitute for cane sugar, depending on the type of pectin used. There are a number of different kinds and brands of pectin available commercially. Low-methoxy pectin, such as Pomona's, requires no sugar in order to set. Jams and jellies can be made to be stored in the freezer or can be canned using the water-bath method. Use of paraffin wax to seal these products is not recommended, as this will increase the likelihood of mold growth.

Jamming, pickling, canning, storing, drying, and freezing seasonal produce is a natural next step to eating seasonally and locally. You will be surprised at how satisfying the process and the results can be.

Lauri McKean is an avid preserver of local food and completed the Dane County Extension's Master Food Preservation Program.

Find additional information in the Resources section under Food Preservation.

Resources

Changing Our Food System...

For more information on MACSAC farms, visit www.macsac.org or call 608-226-0300.

To find a CSA farm near you, see the national listing of CSA farms at www.csacenter.org or call the Robyn Van En Center at 717-264-4141 ext 3352.

Community Supported Agriculture (CSA) farms all over the world—and the members who support them—are creating an appetite for change in our food system. By providing delicious and nutritious food fresh from the farm, CSA farms also satisfy this appetite.

Banding together as a coalition of farms to support and promote one another, the Madison Area Community Supported Agriculture Coalition (MACSAC) has grown from 8 farms serving 275 households in 1993 to 18 individually operated farms serving more than 2,000 households in 2004—a genuine tribute to the power of cooperation.

We praise all CSA farms that take on the noble, challenging, and rewarding work of growing food for their communities. We pay special tribute to the farms of MACSAC, past and present, and to all their members, who have been such a positive force in promoting a more community-based food system in our southern Wisconsin region.

...One Share at a Time

MACSAC Farms, Past and Present

Italic type connotes past MACSAC farms

Abundant Earth Community Farm, Jason Huberty, Stoughton
AHA Acres, Jim Harvey, Cottage Grove
Avalanche Community Farm, James Welch, Viola
Blue Moon Community Farm, Jake Hoeksema and Kristin
  Kordet, Madison
Brantmeier Family Farm, Tom and Maria Brantmeier, Monroe
Clearview Family Farms, Ruben Yoder, Hillsboro
Cress Spring Garden, Stuart Smith, Hopper Block, Blue Mounds
Crystal Lake Gardens, George Riggin, Cottage Grove
Dog Hollow Farm, Sara Tedeschi and David Bruce, Ferryville
Drumlin Community Farm, Doug Wubben, Mike Moon, Mark
  Voss, Madison
Garden To Be, April Yancer and Scott Williams, Mt. Horeb
*Gathering Places Community Garden, Barbara Westfall and Carl
  Johnson, Mt. Horeb*
Greenspirit Farm, Jennifer and Andrew Kerr, Dodgeville
Harmony Valley Farm, Richard de Wilde and Linda Halley,
  Viroqua
Hilltop Community Farm, Rob McClure, LaValle
JenEhr Family Farm, Kay Jensen and Paul Ehrhardt,
  Sun Prairie
Luna Circle Farm, Tricia Bross, Rio
Nature's Acres, Bill Warner, Dodgeville
Oak Ridge Farm, Jenny Pardee, Janesville
Peggy's Biodynamic Gardens, Carrie Driver and family, Whitewater
Pleasant Hill Market Garden, Rob Baratz, Stoughton
PlumHill Farm, Michael and Linda Ball, Cambridge
Prairie Dock Farm, Greg David, Watertown
Shooting Star Farm, Rink DaVee and Jenny Bonde, Mineral Point
Scotch Hill Farm, Tony and Dela Ends, Brodhead
Stone Gate Gardens, Cyndy Millikin and Patrick Brown, Hillpoint
Sunflower Fields CSA, Michael Nash and Solveig Hanson,
  Postville, IA
Sweet-Earth Farm, Bill Monroe, Mineral Point
Tipi Produce, Steve Pincus and Beth Kazmar, Evansville
Troy Community Farm, Claire Strader, Madison
Twinhawks Hollow Farm, Kathy Bowman and Sandy Eldredge,
  Hillsboro
Vermont Valley Community Farm, Barbara and David Perkins,
  Blue Mounds
Zephyr Group Garden, Robin and John Greenler and Susan
  Coffin, Stoughton

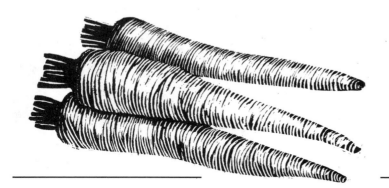

Farmers' Markets

Farmers' markets have increased dramatically in number in recent years, underscoring their importance as a venue for the exchange of farm-fresh produce between farmers and eaters. In 2002, there were more than 3,000 farmers' markets nationwide, up from about 1,700 in 1994. In Wisconsin alone, there are more than 165 markets, one of the most popular being the Dane County Farmers' Market (visit www.madfarmmkt.org).

Farmers' markets provide a wonderful source of locally grown, seasonal produce, and greatly benefit consumers, farmers, and communities:

- Consumers have access to locally grown, farm-fresh produce and the opportunity to personally interact with the farmer who grows the produce.

- Farmers have the opportunity to sell produce directly to and interact with their customers.

- The community gets opportunities to learn about nutrition and food preparation, a stronger local economy (since most money exchanged will stay local), and cleaner air since the produce travels many fewer miles.

In addition to fresh produce, farmers' markets are often a great source of other locally produced food products, education, and entertainment. Find one near you and check it out today!

Listed below are a number of market resources, including ways to find a market near you.

FarmersMarket.com—www.farmersmarket.com
Comprehensive state-by-state listing of farmers' markets in U.S.

The USDA Farmers' Markets Website—www.ams.usda.gov/farmersmarkets
Find a farmers' market in your area of the U.S. with the state-by-state listing, and get updated information and resources. You can also call 202-720-8317 to get the Farmers' Market contact person for your state.

Local Harvest—www.localharvest.org
A state-by-state guide to buying locally; includes a search for farmers' markets.

Openair-Market Net: The World Wide Guide to Farmers' Markets, Street Markets, Flea Markets and Street Vendors—www.openair.org
A growing listing of markets worldwide. Also, market organizations, action alerts to help save threatened markets, and links to other resources, including how to start a farmers' market and organizations working on sustainable development in their communities.

Organic Consumers Association—www.organicconsumers.org; 218-226-4164
A grass-roots, nonprofit organization concerned with food safety, organic farming, sustainable agriculture, fair trade, and genetic engineering. Has listing for local markets and other sources of local foods.

Restaurants and Grocers Supporting Local Farmers

Each day, every day, we face the basic question, "What shall we eat today?" Since our answer affects our personal health as well as the health of the land and our local economies, more and more of us are voting for a more sustainable and life-giving food system by choosing to eat locally. Although there's much we can get directly from farms through CSAs and farmers' markets, the reality of many of our lives dictates we also purchase food from grocery stores, and an ever-increasing number of us eat at restaurants multiple times a week. Why is this choice significant, and what options do we have as we place our vote with our food dollars? Below we list a few good reasons and a number of resources for finding establishments in your community .

Restaurateurs and grocers who purchase sustainable and locally grown foods are crucial assets because they:

1) keep smaller farms in business so we continue to have a wide variety of fresh foods available;

2) celebrate the sense of community created by connecting to those who produce the food we eat and educating their customers of the importance of this urban-rural interdependence;

3) teach us how to creatively use seasonally available foods and thereby create more demand for local products;

4) expand our knowledge of the diversity of foods and flavors available by weaving heirloom fruits and vegetables into seasonal menus.

Finding establishments near you that support local growers

- Visit local farmers' markets and talk with the vendors about which businesses purchase food from them.

- See *The Tofu Tollbooth,* by Elizabeth Zipern and Dar Williams (Ceres Press/Ardwork Press, 1988-2003; 888-804-8848, www.tofutollbooth.com). Guide to natural food stores and food co-ops around the U.S. Ask your local food co-op about farm-friendly restaurants.

- Local Harvest, at www.localharvest.org, offers web-based state-by-state listings for restaurants and food stores offering sustainably produced food.

- Organizations like Chefs Collaborative and Slow Food promote the buying of quality local products and defending vegetable, animal, and cultural diversity. There are regional contacts for each organization, and Chefs Collaborative has a printed and Web-based state-by-state listing of member restaurants. Slow Food USA National Office, 434 Broadway, 6th floor, New York, NY 10013, 212-965-5640, info@slowfoodusa.org, www.slowfoodusa.org. Chefs Collaborative, 262 Beacon St., Boston, MA 02116, 617-236-5200, www.chefscollaborative.org.

- Specialty directories and catalogues like the Green People and the National Green Pages have growing listings of grocers and restaurants with local, organic produce. Green People, 420 Raymond Ave., Ste. 12, Santa Monica, CA, 90405, 310-399-9355, www.greenpeople.org. Co-op America's Green Pages, 1612 K St. NW, Ste. 600, Washington D.C. 20006, 800-584-7336, www.coopamerica.org.

- Check the regional listing of organizations in the Recommended Resources section of this book for an organization near you that may have listings of farm-friendly businesses.

- Check with local chambers of commerce for restaurants. There is a limited state-by-state listing of farm-friendly restaurants at www.dietforasmallplanet.com/ideas/restaurants.php. Two examples of regional listings on the Web: www.sfgate.com/eguide/food for San Francisco and www.rawdc.org/dc/fruitDC.html for the Washington D.C. area.

Recommended Resources

The following listing of organizations, Web sites, and publications emphasize CSA and sustainable agriculture organizations but include a number of related topics and are regional, national, and international in scope. An emphasis is placed on the Midwest, though many national and some international resources are also listed. This resource list can also be found on MACSAC's website, www.macsac.org.

National Organizations

Alternative Farming Systems Information Center
National Agriculture Library Research Service, USDA, 10301 Baltimore Ave., Rm. 132, Beltsville, MD 20705-2351, 301-504-6559; fax: 301-504-6409, afsic@nal.usda.gov, www.nal.usda.gov/afsic

Bibliographies on CSA, organic farming, and related topics. Lots of links.

Appropriate Technology Transfer for Rural Areas (ATTRA)
P.O. Box 3657, Fayetteville, AR 72702, 800-346-9140, 800-411-3222 (Spanish only), www.attra.ncat.org

Packet of basic information on CSA. Also provides packets on topics like apprenticeships, organic farming, and marketing. Staff will either send you a preassembled packet or design a packet of information to answer your specific questions. Also has tapes and videos. Great service!

Beyond Pesticides
701 E. St. SE, Ste. 200, Washington, DC 20003, 202-543-5450, fax 202-543-4791, info@beyondpesticides.org, www.beyondpesticides.org

Wealth of information and resources for identifying and interpreting hazardous pesticides, assistance in designing safe pesticide management programs, and alternatives to pesticides; newsletter.

The Biodynamic Farming and Gardening Association
25844 Butler Rd., Junction City, OR 97448, 888-516-7797, fax 541-998-0106; biodynamics@aol.com, www.biodynamics.com

In addition to all the information and resources one would need about biodynamics, the Biodynamic Association lists publications on CSA, a database of CSA farms throughout U.S. and Canada, and intern and employment opportunities.

Community Food Security Coalition
P.O. Box 209, Venice, CA 90294, 310-822-5410, fax 310-822-1440, cfsc@foodsecurity.org, www.foodsecurity.org

Dedicated to building strong, sustainable, local and regional food systems that ensure access to affordable, nutritious, and culturally appropriate food for all people at all times.

E.F. Schumacher Society
140 Jug End Rd., Great Barrington, MA 01230, 413-528-1737, efssociety@smallisbeautiful.org, www.schumachersociety.org

Provides advice and information on all the ways small can be beautiful: land trusts, local currencies, sample leases, excellent de-centrist library. Many useful booklets on land trusts and local economics.

Equity Trust
539 Beach Pond Road, Voluntown, CT 06384, 860-376-1624, www.equitytrust.org

Information, a range of flexible solutions, and contacts with sources of funding for local land trusts. Fund for CSA, land tenure counseling, financing through revolving loan fund for CSAs, excellent source of information on land-related issues.

Family Farm Defenders
P.O. Box 1772, Madison, WI 53701, 608-260-0900, www.familyfarmdefenders.org

Works for rural justice, family farmers, consumer rights, and fair trade; newsletter.

Food First/Institute for Food and Development Policy,
398 60th Street, Oakland, CA 94618, 510-654-4400, fax 510-654-4551, foodfirst@foodfirst.org, www.foodfirst.org

Nonprofit "people's" think tank and education-for-action center; work highlights root causes and value-based solutions to hunger and poverty around the world with a commitment to establishing food as a fundamental human right.

Food Routes Network

P.O. Box 443, Millheim, PA 16854, 814-349-6000, fax 814-349-2280, www.FoodRoutes.org

Great resources on local food systems, toolkit for communicating about where our food comes from, and for building "Buy Local" campaigns. Their "Find Good Food Map" can help you connect with local farmers.

The GRACE Factory Farm Project

215 Lexington Ave, Ste. 1001, New York, NY 10016, 212-726-9161, www.factoryfarm.org

Works to end factory farms in favor of a sustainable food system. Organizing guides, resources, recent news clips.

National Campaign for Sustainable Agriculture

P.O. Box 396, Pine Bush, New York 12566, 845-361-5201, fax 845-361-5204, www.sustainableagriculture.net

Educates the public and influences public policy on the importance of a sustainable food and agriculture system that is economically viable, environmentally sound, socially just, and humane.

National Catholic Rural Life Conference (NCRLC)

4625 Beaver Ave., Des Moines, IA 50310, 515-270-2634, fax 515-270-9447, ncrlc@aol.com, www.ncrlc.com

Ethics of Eating and Green Ribbon campaigns for faith communities. Articles, resources, and initiatives on factory farms, biotechnology, animal welfare, food safety, and security.

National Family Farm Coalition

110 Maryland Ave., N.E., Ste. 307, Washington, D.C. 20002, 202-543-5675, fax 202-543-0978, nffc@nffc.net, www.nffc.net

National link for family farm organizations. Information and task groups on biotechnology, commodities, and trade; legislative updates; farm bill information; newsletter.

Natural Resource, Agricultural, and Engineering Service (NRAES)

Cooperative Extension, P.O. Box 4557, Ithaca, NY 14852-4557, 607-255-7654, fax 607-254-8770, nraes@cornell.edu, www.nraes.org

Great resource for producers, with excellent technical manuals on irrigation, produce handling for direct marketing, on-farm composting, refrigeration and controlled atmosphere for horticulture crops, greenhouse engineering, and more.

Organic Consumers Association (OCA)

6101 Cliff Estate Rd, Little Marais, MN 55614, 218-226-4164, fax 218-353-7652, www.organicconsumers.org

Genetic engineering, irradiation, toxic sludge fertilizer, mad cow disease, and rBGH are some of the issues it addresses. Publishes one print newsletter (Organic View) and two electronic newsletters (BioDemocracy News and Organic Bytes).

Robyn Van En Center for Community Supported Agriculture

Wilson College, Fulton Center for Sustainable Living, 1015 Philadelphia Ave., Chambersburg, PA 17201, 717-264-4141 ext. 3352, fax 717-264-1578, info@csacenter.org, www.csacenter.org

Offers a variety of services to existing and new CSA farmers and shareholders nationally, including a national, state-by-state listing of CSA farms and numerous resources, referrals, and links.

Rocky Mountain Institute

1739 Snowmass Creek Rd., Snowmass, CO 81654-9199, 970-927-3851, www.rmi.org

Provides research, training, and resource materials on sustainable energy, water, agriculture, transportation, and community economic development.

Sustainable Agriculture Network (SAN)
Andy Clark, Coordinator, 10300 Baltimore Ave., Bldg.
046 BARC-WEST, Beltsville, MD 20705-2350, 301-504-
6425, san@sare.org, www.sare.org

National outreach of the USDA Sustainable
Agriculture Research and Education (SARE)
Program. Provides publications on sustainable
agriculture, information on research projects
funded by SARE, videos, chat room, Web site.

Woods End Research Laboratory
Box 297, Mount Vernon, ME 04352, 207-293-2457, fax
207-293-2488, info@woodsend.org, www.woodsend.org

Compost information, supplies, testing and
consulting; source of Community Supported
Composting bags.

International Organizations

Canadian Organic Growers
323 Chapel St., Ottawa, Ontario, Canada K1N, 7Z2, 888-
375-7383, fax 613-757-1291, office@cog.ca, www.cog.ca

Canada's national information network for organic
farmers, gardeners, and consumers. Conferences,
policy work, magazine, publications for sale,
lending library, and links to finding organic food
throughout Canada.

Ecological Agriculture Projects
McGill University (Macdonald Campus), Ste-anne-de-
Bellevue, QC, Canada H9X 3V9, 514-398-7771, fax 514-
398-7621, eapinfo@macdonald.mcgill.ca,
www.eap.mcgill.ca

Technical information on organic agriculture
practices, pest control, and fertility management,
with many links.

Equiterre
2177, rue Masson, Bureau 317, Montreal (Quebec),
Canada H2H 1B1, 514-522-2000, fax 514-522-1227,
info@equiterre.qc.ca, www.equiterre.qc.ca

Listing of CSA farms, fair trade product
information, pesticide public education campaign,
and more.

Regional Organizations

California Certified Organic Farmers (CCOF)
1115 Mission St., Santa Cruz, CA 95060, 888-423-2263,
fax 831-423-4528, ccof@ccof.org, www.ccof.org

Organic certifier; directory of organic producers,
handler/processors; educational resources;
apprenticeships.

Carolina Farm Stewardship Association
P.O. Box 448, Pittsboro, NC 27312, 919-542-2402, fax
919-542-7401, cfsa@carolinafarmstewards.org,
www.carolinafarmstewards.org

Statewide networking organization, farm
directories, regional consumer guides, farmer
trainings, newsletter.

Center for Integrated Agriculture Systems (CIAS)
1450 Linden Dr., University of Wisconsin, Madison, WI
53706, 608-262-5200, fax 608-265-3020,
phaza@wisc.edu, www.wisc.edu/cias/

Research papers and resources available on
sustainable livestock and fresh produce production
and marketing systems, urban food systems,
institutional participation in regional food systems,
and pesticide use and risk reduction.

Center for Rural Affairs
145 Main St., P.O. Box 136, Lyons, NE 68038-0136, 402-
687-2100, fax 402-687-2200, info@cfra.org, www.cfra.org

Farm Bill implementation; agricultural, research,
and conservation policy; corporate farming and
market access; opportunities for beginning farmers;
newsletter.

CSA of North America at U of Mass Extension
Steve Moore, Director, Wilson College, 1015 Philadelphia
Ave., Chambersburg, PA 17201, 717-264-4141, ext. 3247,
fax 717-264-1578, info@csacenter.org,
www.umass.edu/umext/csa/

The Wilson College CSA Project can supply a
general informational brochure, a CSA information
packet, and other resources for starting up,
supporting, and eating from a CSA.

Community Alliance with Family Farms
36355 Russell Blvd., P.O. Box 363, Davis, CA 95617, 530-756-8518, fax 530-756-7857, www.caff.org

> CSA info and farm listings for California; programs affecting policy; variety of agriculture and community programs including information on various sustainable production techniques.

Illinois Stewardship Alliance
P.O. Box 648, Rochester, IL 62563, 217-498-9707, fax 217-498-9235, isa@illinoisstewardshipalliance.org, www.illinoisstewardshipalliance.org

> Citizens' organization promoting safe and nutritious food supply and healthy rural communities through socially just and ecologically sustainable production practices; newsletter.

Iowa Network for Community Agriculture (INCA)
Jan Libbey, Coordinator, 1465 120th St., Kanawha, IA 50447, 515-495-6367, libland@frontiernet.net, www.washingtoniowa.org/wedg/wlfp/INCA.html

> Links community agriculture projects across Iowa; farm internship program; support for new growers through field days, networking, and conferences; directory of farms and food projects.

Just Food
P.O. Box 20444, Greeley Square, New York, NY 10001-0008, 212-645-9880, fax 212-645-9881, info@justfood.org, www.justfood.org

> CSA support project in New York City; helps CSA farms get started and connects potential members to these farms; good materials on core groups and CSA budgeting and responsibilities; makes CSA accessible to low-income folks; newsletter.

Kansas Rural Center
P.O. Box 133, Whiting, KS 66552, 785-873-3431, ksrc@rainbowtel.net, www.kansasruralcenter.org

> Information on sustainable agriculture practices highlighting Kansas farmers; water quality and sustainable food system projects; newsletter with practical information on sustainable ag practices.

Land Stewardship Project
2200 4th St., White Bear Lake, MN 55110, 651-653-0618, fax 612-653-0589, gboody@landstewardshipproject.org, www.landstewardshipproject.org

> Newsletter, workshops, videos, on-farm training; listing of CSA farms and other sustainable growers serving Minnesota; projects linking farmers and consumers; grower resources, newsletter.

Land Trust Alliance
1331 H St. NW, Ste. 400, Washington, D.C. 20005-4734, 202-638-4725, fax 202-638-4730, lta@lta.org, www.lta.org

> A national network and service center; publications, conferences, and other services to keep land trusts abreast of legislation affecting their work; provides access to needed expertise and insurance; seeks to improve effectiveness of local and regional land trusts.

Leopold Center for Sustainable Agriculture
209 Curtiss Hall, Iowa State University, Ames, IA 50011-1050, 515-294-3711, fax 515-294-9696, leocenter@iastate.edu, www.leopold.iastate.edu

> Research and education center with statewide programs to research, provide support for implementing, and inform the public about sustainable agriculture practices; newsletter.

Maine Organic Farmers and Gardeners Association (MOFGA)
P.O. Box 170, Unity, ME 04988, 207-568-4142, mofga@mofga.org, www.mofga.org

> Helps farmers and gardeners grow food organically, conducts public outreach and education, and works on public policy.

Michael Fields Agricultural Institute
W2493 Cty Road ES, East Troy, WI 53102, 262-642-3303, fax 262-642-4028, mfai@michaelfieldsaginst.org, www.michaelfieldsaginst.org

> Nonprofit education and research organization; conducts research and outreach on sustainable farm practices; sponsors workshops and conferences; information on biodynamic agriculture; internship program on working farm; newsletter.

Michigan Agricultural Stewardship Association

Chuck Cornillie, 12974 New Lothrop Rd., Byron, MI 48418, 810-266-5475, www.sustainable-ag.org

Nonprofit educational organization with farmer-driven research focus; awards grants to farmers to explore innovative production and marketing techniques; conducts field days, tours, and educational opportunities throughout the state.

Michigan Farm and Food Alliance

P.O. Box 626, Gaylord MI 49734, 810-659-8414, info@moffa.org, www.moffa.org

Promotes local, organic agriculture in Michigan; publishes guide to organic producers and businesses, listing of CSA farms in MI, OH, and IN, bimonthly newsletter, and more.

Michigan Integrated Food and Farming Systems (MIFFS)

Tom Guthrie, 1405 S. Harrison Rd., 115 Manly Miles Bldg., East Lansing, MI 48823-5243, 517-432-0712, fax 517-353-1812, miffs@pilot.msu.edu, www.miffs.org

Supporting sustainable food and farming systems in Michigan; community- and farm-based projects; buy-local campaign; marketing ideas for growers.

Midwest Organic and Sustainable Education Services (MOSES)

P.O. Box 339 N7834 Cty Rd. B, Spring Valley, WI 54767, 715-772-3153, info@mosesorganic.org, www.mosesorganic.org

Sponsors of Upper Midwest Organic Farming Conference and Organic University; Upper Midwest Organic resource directory; resources for education professionals; bookstore; newspaper.

Minnesota Grown

Minnesota Dept. of Agriculture, 90 West Plato Blvd., St. Paul, MN 55107, Paul Hugunin at 651-297-5510, paul.hugunin@state.mn.us, www.mda.state.mn.us/mngrown/

Helps consumers locate fresh, high-quality, Minnesota-grown agricultural products; searchable and downloadable versions of the Minnesota Grown and Specialty Meats directories and tips for buying directly from farmers.

Minnesota Project

1885 University Ave, W. #315, St. Paul, MN 55104, 651-645-6159, fax 651-645-1262, mnproject@mnproject.org, www.mnproject.org

Programs on sustainable communities, agriculture, and energy; research and education papers on a number of related topics; newsletter on whole farm planning practice and policy; magazine subscriptions available.

Northeast Organic Farming Association (NOFA)

c/o Bill Duesing, Box 135, Stevenson, CT 06491, 203-888-5146, bduesing@cs.com, www.nofaic.org

Provides coordination and support for 7 state chapters; sponsors annual NOFA summer conference; publishes *The Natural Farmer* newspaper. Each state chapter provides educational conferences, workshops, farm tours, and printed materials for farmers, gardeners, consumers, and land care professionals.

Ohio Ecological Food and Farm Association (OEFFA)

P.O. Box 82234, Columbus, OH 43202, 614-421-2022, fax 614-421-2011, oeffa@oeffa.com, www.oeffa.com

Sponsors annual conference; consumer guide; organic certification service; apprenticeship program; newsletter. Great resource for consumers and growers.

Research, Education, Action and Policy on Food Group (REAP)

P.O. Box 5632, Madison, WI, 53705, info@reapfoodgroup.org, www.reapfoodgroup.org

Organizes annual Food for Thought Festival; Farm-Fresh Atlas consumer guide to local produce in southern Wisconsin; sponsors the Wisconsin Homegrown Lunch farm-to-school project.

Seattle Tilth Association

4649 Sunnyside Ave. North, Room 1, Seattle, WA 98103, 206-633-0451, tilth@seattletilth.org, www.seattletilth.org

Organic gardening resources, listing of CSA farms, workshops.

Seed Savers Exchange (SSE)

3094 North Winn Rd., Decorah, IA 52101, 563-382-5990, fax 563-382-5872, www.seedsavers.org; Madison store (retail only): 1919 Monroe St., Madison, WI 53711, 608-280-8149

> Nonprofit organization saving "heirloom" (handed-down) garden seeds from extinction. Makes rare heirloom varieties available to gardeners everywhere. Catalogs available. Retail garden store in Madison, WI.

Small Farms Program

WA State University Cooperative Extension, 11104 NE 149th St., Ste. C, Brush Prairie, WA 98606, 253-445-4597, muehleisen@puyallup.wsu.edu, www.smallfarms.wsu.edu

> Resources for farms on crop production, animals, soil and pest management, and marketing.

Sustainable Farming Association MN

29731 302 St., Starbuck, MN 56381, 320-760-8732, mforbord@sfa-mn.org, www.sfa-mn.org

Periodicals and Publications

Chelsea Green Publishing Co., P.O. Box 428, White River Junction, VT 05001, 802-295-6300, fax 802-295-6444, www.chelseagreen.com. Publishes a wide variety of books related to eco-agriculture and sustainable living.

Community Supported Agriculture

Alternative Farming Systems Information Center, 301-504-6559, www.nal.usda.gov/afsic/. Lots of CSA information.

The Community Farm: A Voice for CSA, Jim Sluyter and Jo Meller, 3480 Potter Rd., Bear Lake, MI 49614, 616-889-3216, csafarm@jackpine.com. Quarterly newsletter for the CSA community; $20/year subscription ($23 in Canada).

Farms of Tomorrow: Community Supported Farms, Farm Supported Communities. Trauger Groh and Steven McFadden, Biodynamic Farming and Gardening Association, 1990.

Farms of Tomorrow Revisited: Community Supported Farms, Farm Supported Communities. Trauger Groh and Steven McFadden, Biodynamic Farming and Gardening Association, 1997.

Robyn Van En Center for Community Supported Agriculture, 717-264-4141 ext. 3352, www.csacenter.org. The Robyn Van En Center offers a variety of services to existing and new CSA farmers and shareholders nationally, including a national, state-by-state listing of CSA farms, and numerous resources, referrals, and links.

Sharing the Harvest: A Guide to Community Supported Agriculture. Elizabeth Henderson with Robyn Van En, Chelsea Green, 1999. Step-by-step description of CSA, including history, philosophy, how to start and operate a CSA, management and production issues, and sample documents from working CSA farms. See Robyn Van En Center, above.

Composting

Composting: The Organic Natural Way. Dick Kitto. Thorsons, 1988.

Let It Rot. Stu Campbell.

The Rodale Book of Composting. Deborah Martin and Grace Gershuny, eds. Rodale Press, 1992.

The Urban/Suburban Composter: The Complete Guide to Backyard, Balcony, and Apartment Composting. Mark Cullen and Lorraine Johnson. St. Martin's Press, 1992.

Worms Eat My Garbage. Mary Appelhof. Flower Press, 1982.

"Food for Thought": The Politics of Food

Chicken Little, Tomato Sauce, and Agriculture: Who Will Grow Tomorrow's Food? Joan Gussow. Bootstrap Press, 1991.

Coming Home to Eat: The Pleasures and Politics of Local Foods. Gary Paul Nabhan. W. W. Norton, 2001.

Diet for a New America. John Robbins. Stillpoint, 1987.

Diet for a Small Planet. Frances Moore Lappe. Ballantine Books, 1991.

Hope's Edge: The Next Diet for a Small Planet. Anna Lappe and Frances Moore Lappe, J. P. Tarcher 2002. www.dietforasmallplanet.com. Innovations in sustainable food production, distribution, etc., from around the world.

Living at Nature's Pace: Farming and the American Dream. Gene Logsdon. Chelsea Green, 2000.

Nourishing Traditions: The Cookbook that Challenges Politically Correct Nutrition and the Diet Dictocrats. 2nd ed. Sally Fallon and Mary Enig. 1999. www.westonaprice.org, www.realmilk.com

Our Sustainable Table...Essays. Robert Clark, ed. North Point Press, 1990.

Rainforest in Your Kitchen: The Hidden Connection Between Extinction and Your Supermarket. Martin Teitel. Island Press, 1992. A look at the biodiversity crisis and how our food choices can protect the world's plant and animal species.

Slow Food: Collected Thoughts on Taste, Tradition, and the Honest Pleasures of Food. Carlo Petrini, ed. Chelsea Green Publishing, 2001. A volume for all those passionate about local foods.

This Organic Life: Confessions of a Suburban Homesteader. Joan Gussow. Chelsea Green Publishing. One woman's attempt to live responsibly in a world where thoughtless consumption is the norm.

To Till It and Keep It: New Models for Congregational Involvement with the Land. Dan Guenthner. Available from Job Ebenezer, Div. for Church in Society, ELCA, 8765 Higgins Road West, Chicago, IL 69631, 800-683-3522 ext. 2708.

Food Preservation

The Busy Person's Guide to Preserving Food. Janet Chadwick. Garden Way Publishing, 1995.

Canning and Preserving Without Sugar. Norma MacRae. Globe Pequot Press, 1993.

Garden Way's Guide to Food Drying. Phyllis Hobson. Garden Way Publishing, 1980.

Mary Bell's Complete Dehydrator Cookbook. Mary Bell. William Morrow and Co., 1994.

Putting Food By. Janet Greene, Ruth Hertzberg, and Beatrice Vaughan. Plume, 1991.

Root Cellaring. Mike and Nancy Bubel. Garden Way Publishing, 1991.

Stocking Up. Carol Hupping. Third edition of the classic preserving guide. Originally published by Rodale Press, 1984.

Organic Gardening and Farming

Acres USA, P.O. Box 91299, Austin TX 78709, 800-355-5313, fax 512-892-4448, www.acresusa.com. National monthly journal of sustainable agriculture with more than 30 years of continuous publication. Articles on fertility management, nonchemical weed and insect control, specialty crops and marketing, grazing, composting, natural care, and much more.

ATTRAnews: Quarterly Newsletter of Appropriate Technology Transfer for Rural Areas, 800-346-9140, askattra@ncatfyv.uark.edu, www.attra.ncat.org

Building Healthy Gardens: a Safe and Natural Approach. Catherine Osgood Foster. Storey Communications, 1989.

Bugs, Slugs, and Other Thugs: Controlling Garden Pests Naturally. Rhonda Massingham Hart. Storey Communications, 1991.

The City People's Book of Raising Food. Helga Olkowski. Rodale Press, 1975.

Ecolandtech, www.ibiblio.org/ecolandtech. Lots of information on gardening, permaculture, and herbs, with many links to other sites.

Four-Season Harvest. Eliot Coleman. Chelsea Green, 1992.

Growing for Market. Lynn Byczynski, Editor, P.O. Box 3747, Lawrence KS 66046, 785-748-0605, fax 785-748-0609, growing4market@earthlink.net, www.growingformarket.com. Newsletter for small growers who sell produce and flowers locally, written from organic perspective. Regular articles on CSA.

How to Grow More Vegetables and Fruits, Nuts, Berries, Grains, and Other Crops Than You Ever Thought Possible on Less Land Than You Can Imagine. The New Farm. www.newfarm.org. Excellent, practical, Web-based Farmer-to-Farmer know-how from the Rodale Institute.

The New Organic Grower, a Master's Manual of Tools and Techniques for the Home and Market Gardener. Eliot Coleman. Chelsea Green, 1989.

The New Seed-Starters Handbook. Nancy Bubel. Rodale Press, 1988.

Organic Gardening. Rodale Press, 800-666-2206, www.rodale.com. World's largest-circulation gardening magazine provides tools, ideas, sources, and information on how to grow without chemicals.

Permaculture. www.permaculture.net. The land of information and links on permaculture.

Pesticides and You, Newsletter of Beyond Pesticides. 202-543-5450, www.beyondpesticides.org

Practical Organic Gardening. Ben Easy. Faber and Faber, 1955.

Rodale's All-New Encyclopedia of Organic Gardening. Fern Marshall Bradley and Barbara Ellis. Rodale Press, 1984.

The Ruth Stout No-Work Garden Book. Ruth Stout and Richard Clemence. Rodale Press, 1971.

Small Farmers Journal. P.O. Box 1627, Sisters, OR 97759, 541-549-2064. Magazine about draft animal power, small-scale farming.

Start with the Soil: The Organic Gardener's Guide to Improving Soil for Higher Yields, More Beautiful Flowers, and a Healthy, Easy-Care Garden. Grace Gershuny. Rodale Press, 1993.

The Sustainable Vegetable Garden: Backyard Guide to Sustainable Agriculture. John Jeavons. Ten Speed Press, 1999.

Worm's Way. www.wormsway.com. Much information and supplies for gardening.

Seeds and Supplies

Beautiful Land Products, 360 Cookson Dr., P.O. Box 179, West Branch IA 52358, 800-227-2718, BLP@beautifullandproducts.com. Organic growing media and growing supplies.

Fedco Seeds, Box 520, Waterville ME 04903, 207-873-7333, fax 207-873-8317, www.fedcoseeds.com. Employee-owned cooperative. Bulk vegetable seeds and supplies, wholesale prices. Open seasonally.

High Mowing Seeds, 813 Brook Rd., Wolcott, VT 05680, 802-882-1800, www.highmowingseeds.com. 100 percent certified organic seed for home gardeners and commercial growers.

Johnny's Selected Seeds, 955 Benton Ave., Winslow, ME 04901, 207-861-3900, www.johnnyseeds.com. Mail-order seed company, vegetables, flowers, herbs, and supplies.

Peaceful Valley Farm Supply, Box 2209, Grass Valley, CA 95945, 888-784-1722, www.groworganic.com. Cost-effective, state-of-the-art organic growing supplies and tools and information to apply them.

Seeds of Change, 1364 Rufina Circle #5, Sante Fe, NM 87501, 888-762-7333, www.seedsofchange.com. Large variety of organic heirloom seeds, garden tools, and other information.

Seed Savers Exchange (see Regional Organizations, above).

Turtle Tree Seed, Camphill Village, Copake, NY 12516, 518-329-3038 turtle@taconic.net. All open-pollinated and untreated seed. Organic seed clearly indicated.

Sustainable Agriculture and Community Economics

Becoming Native to This Place, Wes Jackson. Counterpoint Press, 1996.

Wendell Berry. All books by Wendell Berry are recommended, including *Sex, Economy, Freedom and Community; The Unsettling of America: Culture and Agriculture; What Are People For?*

Dollars and Sense: What's Left in Economics? 1 Summer St., Somerville, MA 02143, 617-628-8411. Bimonthly. Analyses of current economic goings-on in the U.S. and around the world in language normal people can understand.

Family Farming: A New Economic Vision. Marty Strange. University of Nebraska Press, 1988.

From Columbus to Conagra: the Globalization of Agriculture and Food. Alessandro Bonanno. University Press of Kansas, 1994.

From Land to Mouth: Understanding the Food System. Brewster Kneen. NC Press, 1989.

GEO (Grassroot Economic Organizing Newsletter), 177 Kiles Rd., Stillwater, PA 17878, 800-240-9721, www.geonewsletter.org. Bimonthly; covers worker-owned enterprises, co-ops, community-based businesses, community-labor-environmental coalitions.

Hard Tomatoes, Hard Times: a Report of the Agribusiness Accountability Project on the Failure of America's Land Grant College Complex. Jim Hightower. Schenkman Publishing, 1973.

International Society for Ecology and Culture, P.O. Box 9475, Berkeley, CA 94709, 510-548-4915, isecca@igc.org, www.isec.org.uk. Numerous publications and resources geared toward "promoting locally based alternatives to the global consumer culture."

New Roots for Agriculture. Wes Jackson. University of Nebraska Press, 1980.

Sustainable Agriculture Organizations/Publications List, ATTRA, 800-346-9140, www.attra.ncat.org. Regional listings of organizations and publications about sustainable agriculture. Updated every 2 years.

Cookbooks and Other Food Resources

These cookbooks and other food literature are useful and/or inspiring for those who want to go seasonal and sustainable. We've included author and publication information as well as some comments to help you determine which ones might be most interesting to you. We've also labeled cookbooks as vegetarian or vegan when possible. Some of the listed resources are no longer in print, so look for them at a used bookstore or library.

An American Bounty, by the Culinary Institute of America. Rizzoli International Publishers. New York, NY, 1995.

A Well-Seasoned Appetite: Recipes from an American Kitchen, by Molly O'Neill. Viking Penguin, 1995. Recipes and smart, eloquent essays about cooking and eating with the seasons.

Broccoli and Company, by Audra and Jack Hendrickson. Garden Way Publishing, Storey Communications, Schoolhouse Road, Pownal, VT 05261, 1989. More than 100 healthy recipes for broccoli, Brussels sprouts, cabbage, etc.

The City Gardener's Cookbook: Totally Fresh, Mostly Vegetarian, Decidedly Delicious Recipes from Seattle's P-Patches, by the P-Patch Cookbook Committee. Sasquatch Books, 1994. Original seasonal recipes and growing tips from the Seattle Community Gardens folks.

Cooking with Flowers, by Jenny Leggatt. Fawcett Columbine, 1987. Tremendous number of fun and creative recipes using a variety of flowers.

Cooking with the Seasons: A Year in My Kitchen, by Monique Jamet Hooker and Tracie Richardson. Henry Holt and Co., 1997. A French-American chef/cooking instructor's charming journey through the seasons, with great French-inspired recipes based on heartland ingredients.

Cook's Garden Catalog, P.O. Box 535, Londonderry, VT 05148, 802-457-9703. Recipes are scattered throughout this garden catalog, well known for its beautiful woodcuts.

Earth Water Fire Air: A Vegetarian Cookbook for the 90s, by Barbara Friedlander. Meyer M. Evans and Co, Inc., 216 East 49th St., New York, NY 10017, 1992. Vegetarian and simple.

Eating Well Is the Best Revenge: Everyday Strategies for Delicious, Healthful Food in 30 Minutes or Less, by Marian Fox Burros. Simon and Schuster, 1995. Creative, easy meals that use a wide variety of vegetables.

Ecological Cooking, by Joanne Stepanik and Kathy Hecker. The Book Publishing Co., P.O. Box 99, Summerton, TN 38483, 1991. Vegan. Good resources: glossary, timetables for steaming and pressure-cooking veggies. Simple recipes.

Extending the Table: A World Community Cookbook, by Joetta Handrich Schlabach. Herald Press, 616 Walnut Ave., Scottdale, PA 15683, 1991. Learn about other cultures and how to eat better and consume less of the world's precious resources while enjoying delicious dishes from more than 80 countries.

The Enchanted Broccoli Forest, by Mollie Katzen. Ten Speed Press, 1982. Vegetarian, a "sequel" to the original *Moosewood Cookbook.*

Farmers Market Cookbook, by Susan F. Carlman. Chicago Review Press, 1988. Arranged seasonally from spring through winter. Gives tips on purchasing veggies, such as ripeness indicators. Excellent book, but out of print.

Fast and Healthy Ways to Cook Vegetables, by Penny Noepel. Storey Communications, 1990.

Fields of Greens: New Vegetarian Recipes from the Celebrated Greens Restaurant, by Annie Somerville. Bantam Books, 1993. Vegetarian. Beautiful recipes that are somewhat seasonal and of medium complexity.

Fresh Market Wisconsin, by Terese Allen. Amherst Press, P.O. Box 296, Amherst, WI, 1993. Contains many seasonal recipes contributed by people statewide, and information about vegetables and farmers' markets.

Fresh Ways with Vegetables, by the editors of Time-Life Books, 1986. Part of the Healthy Home Cooking series.

Friendly Foods, by Brother Ron Pickarski. Ten Speed Press, 1991. Vegan. Brother Ron Pickarski has been awarded many culinary honors for these creative and delicious gourmet recipes.

The Good Earth, by Jon Gregerson. White Cap Books, 1992. An alphabetical resource guide to whole foods including fruits, vegetables, herbs, spices, grains, and nuts.

The Good-for-You Garlic Cookbook: Over 125 Deliciously Healthful Garlic Recipes, by Linda Ferrari. Prima Publishing, P.O. Box 1260BK, Rocklin, CA 95677, 1994. Out of print.

The Goodness of Potatoes and Root Vegetables, by John Midgley, Pavilion Books Limited, 196 Shaftesbury Avenue, London WC2H 8JL, 1992. Good winter cookbook with simple recipes. Beginning has text on history and lists of varieties and other information.

Great Good Food: Luscious Lower-Fat Cooking, by Julee Rosso. Crown/Turtle Bay Books, 1993. Arranged seasonally. Many low-fat, delicious recipes. Sample menus also included.

The Green Kitchen Handbook, by Annie Berthold-Bons. HarperPerennial, 1997. Practical advice, references, and sources for transforming your kitchen into a healthful, livable place.

Greene on Greens, by Bert Greene, Workman Publishing Co., 1984. Out of print.

The Herbal Pantry, by Emelie Toley and Chris Mead. Clarkson Potter Publishers, 1992. The herbal recipes are coupled with stunning photos. Contains recipes for everything from herbal teas, oils, and vinegars to appetizers and main dishes.

Indian Vegetarian Curries, by Harvey Day. Thorsons Publishing Group, 1987. Vegetarian. A good resource for a variety of Indian recipes.

The Inspired Vegetarian, by Louise Pickford. Stewart, Tabori & Chang, Inc., 1992. Vegetarian. These recipes aren't the easiest around, but they are creative and tasty. The photography and writing will make your mouth water.

The Joy of Cooking, by Irma S. Rombauer and Marian Rombauer Becker. Bobbs Merrill, 1975. A classic of American cookery. Check out the latest edition for more updated recipes.

Keeping Food Fresh: Old World Techniques and Recipes, by the Gardeners and Farmers of Terre Vivante, foreword by Eliot Coleman. Chelsea Green, 1999. Little-known but traditional French techniques of storing and preserving fresh edibles.

The Kitchen Garden Cookbook, by Sylvia Thompson, Bantam Books, 1995. Includes gardening tips.

Kitchen Garden: The Art of Growing Fine Food (bimonthly magazine). Taunton Press, Inc., Newton, CT 06470-5506, (203) 426-8171. Combines gardening articles with recipes and other features.

Local Flavors: Cooking and Eating from America's Farmers' Markets, by Deborah Madison. Broadway Books, 2002. Exciting, enticing recipes and color photos from a cooking master.

Lorna Sass' Complete Vegetarian Kitchen: Where Good Flavors and Good Health Meet, by Lorna J. Sass. Hearst Books, 1992. Vegan. A truly wonderful cookbook with an amazing variety of veggie-centered recipes. Charts for regular and pressure cooking times for veggies, grains, and beans. Also includes sample menus, a large glossary, and a detailed reference section.

Louise's Leaves, by Louise Frazier. The Bio-Dynamic Farming and Gardening Association, Inc., P.O. Box 550, Kimberton, PA 19442, 1994.

Lynda's Low-Fat Kitchen: Meatless Meals for Every Day, by Lynda A. Pozel. Chariot Publishing, 1994. Vegetarian cookbook focusing on a variety of low-fat and low-cholesterol recipes. It also has food facts, techniques, and substitution tips throughout the book.

Madison Herb Society Cookbook: A Special Collection of Herbal Recipes from Our Members, Local Restaurants, Inns, Businesses, Organizations and Guests, by the Madison Herb Society. Contains a collection of members' favorite herb recipes, herb folklore, ideas, and hints.

May All Be Fed: Diet for a New World, by John Robbins. Avon Books, 1992. A great guide to responsible eating, with recipes.

The Meatless Gourmet, by Bobbie Hinman. Prima Publishing, 1995. Vegetarian. Good variety of ethnic recipes using many types of vegetables.

The Moosewood Cookbook, by Mollie Katzen. Ten Speed Press, 1977. Vegetarian. Mollie Katzen's first book became a standard for vegetarian cooking. The 1st edition of this book is heavy on dairy products. In 1992 she produced a revised edition that focused on less fat and added new recipes.

Moosewood Restaurant Cooks at Home: Fast and Easy Recipes for Any Day, by the Moosewood Collective. Simon and Schuster/Fireside, 1994. Mostly vegetarian (some fish). A wonderful and easy-to-use cookbook with delicious and creative yet fairly easy recipes.

The Moosewood Restaurant Kitchen Garden: Creative Gardening for the Adventurous Cook, by the Moosewood Collective. Simon and Schuster/Fireside, 1992. Vegetarian. Contains gardening information, culinary tips, and recipes for a large number of different herbs and vegetables.

The Natural Health Cookbook: More Than 150 Recipes to Sustain and Heal the Body, by Dana Jacobi and the editors of *Natural Health* magazine. Simon & Schuster, 1995.

The New Basics Cookbook, by Julee Rosso and Sheila Lukins. Workman Publishing, 1989.

The New Laurel's Kitchen, by Laurel Robertson. Ten Speed Press, 1986. Classic vegetarian cookbook with low-fat, tasty recipes. Large reference section in the back.

Ontario Rutabaga Producer's Marketing Board, P.O. Box 328, Lucan, Ontario, Canada, NOM 2J0. The Board prints a couple of pamphlets featuring rutabaga recipes titled "Ruby's Rutabaga Recipe Register" and "Grate, Bake, Boil, or Braise." No one is more enthusiastic about rutabagas.

Peppers: A Cookbook, by Robert Berkley. Simon and Schuster, 1992. Beautiful photos. Pictures for identifying peppers with Scoville units. Arranged from mild to hot peppers.

Pleasures of the Good Earth, by Edward Giobbi. Alfred A. Knopf, 1991. An instructive, inspiring book about raising your own food, with hundreds of seasonal recipes and lovely illustrations. James Beard Award winner.

Putting Food By, by Janet Greene, et. al. Plume, latest edition. A best-selling classic for freezing, canning, and preserving all types of food.

Recipes from a Kitchen Garden, by Renee Shepherd and Fran Raboff. Ten Speed Press, 1993. Out of print. Arranged by vegetable and includes many tasty and seasonal recipes. The authors have also recently published *More Recipes from a Kitchen Garden.*

Recipes from America's Small Farms: Fresh Ideas for the Season's Bounty, by JoAnn Hayes, Lori Stein, and Maura Webber. Random House, 2003. Another wonderful creation paying tribute to small farms featuring seasonal recipes, cooking techniques, and more.

Rodale's Basic Natural Foods Cookbook, Charles Gerras, ed. Rodale Press, 1984. More like a textbook than a cookbook, with lots of instructions, tables, charts, and recipes.

Roots: A Vegetarian Bounty, by Kathleen Mayes and Sandra Gottfried. Woodbridge Press Publishing Co., P.O. Box 209, Santa Barbara, CA 93102, 1995.

Roots: The Underground Cookbook, by Barbara Grunes and Anne Elise Hunt. Chicago Review Press, Inc., 814 North Franklin, Chicago, IL 60610, 1993. 100 recipes for 18 different root vegetables.

Rose Valley Farm's FoodBook for a Sustainable Harvest, by Elizabeth Henderson and David Stern. Rose Valley Farm, 4209 Covell Road, Rose, NY, 14542-0149, 1994. A wonderful book put out by Rose Valley Farm. It was the loose model and inspiration for this food book.

The Sage Cottage Herb Garden Cookbook: Celebrations, Recipes, and Herb Gardening Tips for Every Month of the Year, by Dorry Baird Norris. Globe Pequot Press, 1991. A good book for the herb gardener.

The Savory Way, by Deborah Madison. Bantam Books, 1990. Artfully delicious vegetarian recipes for everyday cooking.

Savoring the Seasons of the Northern Heartland, by Beth Dooley and Lucia Watson. Alfred A. Knopf, 1994. More than 200 recipes blending bold new flavors with the traditional foods of the upper Midwest.

Seed Savers: From the Preservation Garden (1996 Calendar), by Seed Savers Exchange, 3076 North Winn Road, Decorah, IA 52101. Recipes by Rue Judd. Published by Judd Publishing, Inc. Calendar features color photography of beautifully displayed heirloom vegetables, herbs, fruits, and flowers. Each month also features a recipe.

Seeds of Change Catalog, P.O. Box 15700, Santa Fe, NM 87506-5700. Catalog of the only national company that offers 100 percent organically grown seeds that are also all open-pollinated. The catalog reads more like a book with articles, recipes, and beautiful photography.

Shepherd's Garden Seeds Catalog, 30 Irene St., Torrington, CT 06790, (860) 482-3638. A good source of vegetables, herbs, and flowers as well as a few choice recipes. These are the folks who brought us *Recipes from a Kitchen Garden.*

Springdale Farm Cookbook, collected by and for subscribers of Springdale Farm, by Peter and Bernadette Seely, Springdale Farm, W7065 Silver Spring Lane, Plymouth, WI 53073, 414-892-4856.

Still Life with Menu Cookbook, by Mollie Katzen. Ten Speed Press, 1994. Vegetarian. Mollie Katzen's third cookbook, arranged differently than the others. Sections are arranged so recipes combine to make a comprehensive and coordinated meal.

Stocking Up, by Carol Hupping. Simon & Schuster/Fireside, 1990. All about food preservation.

Sundays at Moosewood Restaurant, by the Moosewood Collective. Simon and Schuster/Fireside, 1990. Mostly vegetarian (some fish). Arranged in sections by ethnic origin of recipes. Recipes are medium-high complexity but worth the effort.

The Tassajara Recipe Book: Favorites of the Guest Season, by Edward Espe Brown. Shambala/Random House, 1985. Vegetarian California cuisine.

The Tomato Cookbook: More Than Sixty Easy, Imaginative Recipes, Nicola Hill, ed. Courage Books, an imprint of Running Press Publishers, Philadelphia, PA, 1995. Out of print. Nice information on tomato varieties with their characteristics.

The Totally Corn Cookbook, by Helene Siegel and Karen Gullingham. Celestial Arts, Berkeley, CA, 1994.

Vegetables from Amaranth to Zucchini: The Essential Reference, by Elizabeth Schneider. Morrow Cookbooks, 2001. An encyclopedia, produce market manual, and treasure trove of chefs' recipes. This is a big, beautiful book, pricey but a fabulous reference for cooking with vegetables.

The Vegetarian Epicure, Book Two, by Anna Thomas. Knopf, 1978. See the revised edition, too.

The Vegetarian Table: France, by Georgeann Brennan. Chronicle Books, 1995. Recipes rely on fresh, seasonal ingredients, and the book includes beautiful photography.

The Vegetarian Times Complete Cookbook, by the editors of *Vegetarian Times* magazine. Simon & Schuster, 1985. Vegetarian. Great references: bibliography, cooking methods, food preservation, and mail-order sources.

The Victory Garden Cookbook, by Marian Morash. Alfred A. Knopf, Inc., 1982. A fabulous resource for information about cooking local, seasonal vegetables. Each vegetable has its own section containing gardening information, storage tips, and cooking tips. A number of excellent recipes ranging in complexity. If you want some meat with your veggies, this is the book for you.

Whole Food Facts, by Evelyn Roehl. Healing Arts Press, Rochester, VT, 1988. Includes information on use, nutrition, storage, and buying of fruits, vegetables, grains, legumes, dairy, and other foods.

Winter Harvest Cookbook: How to Select and Prepare Fresh Seasonal Produce All Winter Long, by Lane Morgan. Sasquatch Books, 1990. A great resource for some of the more obscure winter veggies.

The World in Your Kitchen: Vegetarian Recipes from Africa, Asia and Latin America for Western Kitchens with Country Information and Food Facts, by Troth Wells. The Crossing Press, 1993. The title says it all. Although the ingredients aren't exactly always seasonal or local, there are a number that can be adapted.

Recipe Index